Second Workshop on NLP for Positive Impact (NLP4PI 2022)

Abu Dhabi, United Arab Emirates
7 December 2022

ISBN: 978-1-7138-9144-4

Printed from e-media with permission by:

Curran Associates, Inc.
57 Morehouse Lane
Red Hook, NY 12571

Some format issues inherent in the e-media version may also appear in this print version.

Printed with permission by Curran Associates, Inc. (2024)

For permission requests, please contact the Association for Computational Linguistics at the address below.

Association for Computational Linguistics
209 N. Eighth Street
Stroudsburg, Pennsylvania 18360

Phone: 1-570-476-8006
Fax: 1-570-476-0860

acl@aclweb.org

Additional copies of this publication are available from:

Curran Associates, Inc.
57 Morehouse Lane
Red Hook, NY 12571 USA
Phone: 845-758-0400
Fax: 845-758-2633
Email: curran@proceedings.com
Web: www.proceedings.com

NLP4PI 2022

Second Workshop on NLP for Positive Impact

Proceedings of the Workshop

December 7, 2022

Introduction

The widespread and indispensable use of language-oriented AI systems presents new opportunities to have a positive social impact. Much existing work on NLP for social good focuses on detecting or preventing harm, such as classifying hate speech, mitigating bias, or identifying signs of depression. However, NLP research also offers the potential for positive proactive applications developed with responsible methods. Some top areas that we prioritize in this workshop correspond to the United Nations Sustainable Development Goals, such as applications of NLP to address poverty, healthcare, education, climate change, and so on.

This volume contains the proceedings of the Second Workshop on NLP for Positive Impact held in conjunction with the 2022 Conference on Empirical Methods in Natural Language Processing (EMNLP 2022). The workshop received 48 submissions of papers of which 22 were accepted (17 archival and 5 non-archival), for an acceptance rate of 46%. Additionally, 10 Findings of EMNLP papers will be presented at the workshop. We thank all Program Committee members for providing high quality reviews in assembling these proceedings. These papers cover diverse aspects of NLP for positive impact, including developing NLP technology to help applications like physical and mental health, climate change, crisis response, social mobility, education, employment, and culture preservation, as well discussing challenges and ethical implications of using NLP in these areas.

In addition to technical papers, this workshop also features invited keynote speakers and panelists to facilitate discussion and enhance knowledge of NLP for positive impact.

Keynote speakers:
Mike Bailey, Meta
Sam Bowman, New York University & Anthropic AI
Rada Mihalcea, University of Michigan
Preslav Nakov, MBZUAI
Milind Tambe, Harvard University

Panelists:
Luis Chiruzzo, Universidad de la República, Uruguay
Tara Chklovski, Technovation
Dora Demszky, Stanford University
Rada Mihalcea, University of Michigan

We are grateful to all the people who have contributed to this workshop, including speakers, authors, reviewers, and attendees, and we would additionally like to thank the EMNLP workshop chairs and program chairs for making the workshop happen.

We hope that our workshop can encourage future work on NLP for positive social impact and we look forward to welcoming you all to our hybrid workshop!

- Laura Biester, Dora Demszky, Zhijing Jin, Mrinmaya Sachan, Joel Tetreault, Steven Wilson, Lu Xiao, Jieyu Zhao

Organizing Committee

Organizers

Laura Biester, University of Michigan
Dorottya Demszky, Stanford University
Zhijing Jin, Max Planck Institute & ETH
Mrinmaya Sachan, ETH Zurich
Joel Tetreault, Dataminr
Steven Wilson, Oakland University
Lu Xiao, Syracuse University
Jieyu Zhao, University of Maryland

Program Committee

Reviewers

Agostina Calabrese, The University of Edinburgh
Mahdi Abavisani, Dataminr, Inc.
Ameeta Agrawal, Portland State University
Abeer Aldayel, King Saud University
Bashar Alhafni, New York University
Yejin Bang, Hong Kong University of Science and Technology
Delphine Bernhard, Lilpa, Université de Strasbourg
Eleftheria Briakou, University of Maryland
Chris Brockett, Microsoft Research
Agostina Calabrese, The University of Edinburgh
Sky CH-Wang, Columbia University
Serina Chang, Stanford University
Martin Chodorow, Hunter College and the Graduate Center of CUNY
Christos Christodoulopoulos, Amazon Research
Oana Cocarascu, King's College London
Mark Dredze, Johns Hopkins University
Yupei Du, Utrecht University
Pablo Duboue, Textualization Software Ltd.
Steffen Eger, Bielefeld University
Jennifer Foster, Dublin City University
Kathleen C. Fraser, National Research Council Canada
Andrea Galassi, University of Bologna
Mozhdeh Gheini, University of Southern California
Kartik Goyal, Toyota Technological Institute at Chicago
Aylin Gunal, University of Michigan
Ivan Habernal, Technische Universität Darmstadt
Lisa Anne Hendricks, DeepMind
Valentin Hofmann, University of Oxford
Oana Ignat, University of Michigan
Muhammad Imran, Qatar Computing Research Institute
Radu Tudor Ionescu, University of Bucharest
David Jurgens, University of Michigan
Ashkan Kazemi, University of Michigan
Ashiqur KhudaBukhsh, Rochester Institute of Technology
Hyunwoo Kim, Seoul National University
Svetlana Kiritchenko, National Research Council Canada
Ekaterina Kochmar, University of Bath
Hemank Lamba, Dataminr, Inc.
Mirella Lapata, University of Edinburgh
Anne Lauscher, University of Hamburg
Nayeon Lee, Hong Kong University of Science and Technology
Ji-Ung Lee, UKP Lab Technische Universität Darmstadt
Diane Litman, University of Pittsburgh
Robert L Logan IV, Dataminr, Inc.
Li Lucy, University of California, Berkeley
Jakub Macina, ETH Zurich

Julia Mendelsohn, University of Michigan
Sewon Min, University of Washington
Negar Mokhberian, University of Southern California
Roser Morante, UNED
Aurélie Névéol, Université Paris Saclay, CNRS, LISN
Eda Okur, Intel Labs
Ji Ho Park, Google
Chan Young Park, Carnegie Mellon University
Carla Parra Escartín, RWS Language Weaver
Thierry Poibeau, LATTICE (CNRS & ENS/PSL)
Hannah Rashkin, Google Research
Navid Rekabsaz, Johannes Kepler University
Laura Rimell, DeepMind
Björn Ross, University of Edinburgh
Mrinmaya Sachan, ETH Zurich
Danae Sánchez Villegas, University of Sheffield
Maarten Sap, Carnegie Mellon University
Sofia Serrano, University of Washington
Naomi Shapiro, University of Washington
Qinlan Shen, Oracle
Shubham Shukla, Independent Researcher
Kevin Stowe, Educational Testing Services
Sara Stymne, Uppsala University
Swabha Swayamdipta, University of Southern California
Paolo Torroni, Università di Bologna
Josep Valls-Vargas, Adobe
Lucy Vanderwende, University of Washington
Zijian Wang, AWS AI Labs
Ke Zhang, Dataminr, inc

Keynote Talk: Fighting the Global Social Media Infodemic: from Fake News to Harmful Content

Preslav Nakov
Mohamed bin Zayed University of Artificial Intelligence

Abstract: The COVID-19 pandemic has brought us the first global social media infodemic. While fighting this infodemic is typically thought of in terms of factuality, the problem is much broader as malicious content includes not only "fake news", rumors, and conspiracy theories, but also hate speech, racism, xenophobia, panic, and mistrust in authorities, among others. Thus, we argue for the need for a holistic approach combining the perspectives of journalists, fact-checkers, policymakers, social media platforms, and society as a whole.
We further argue for the need to analyze entire news outlets, which can be done in advance; then, we can fact-check the news before it was even written: by checking how trustworthy the outlet that has published it is (which is what journalists actually do). We will show how this can be automated by looking at variety of information sources.
The infodemic is often described using terms such as "fake news", which mislead people to focus exclusively on factuality, and to ignore the other half of the problem: the potential malicious intent. We aim to bridge this gap by focusing on the detection of specific propaganda techniques in text, e.g., appeal to emotions, fear, prejudices, logical fallacies, etc. This is the target of the ongoing SemEval-2023 task 3, which focuses on multilingual aspects of the problem, covering English, French, German, Italian, Polish, and Russian. We further present extensions of this work to the automatic analysis of various types of harmful memes: from propaganda to harmfulness and harm's target identification to role-labeling in terms of who is portrayed as hero/villain/victim, and generating natural text explanations.

Bio: Preslav Nakov is Professor at Mohamed bin Zayed University of Artificial Intelligence. Previously, he was Principal Scientist at the Qatar Computing Research Institute (QCRI), HBKU, where he led the Tanbih mega-project, developed in collaboration with MIT, which aims to limit the impact of fake news, propaganda and media bias by making users aware of what they are reading, thus promoting media literacy and critical thinking. He received his PhD degree in Computer Science from the University of California at Berkeley, supported by a Fulbright grant. He is Chair-Elect of the Association for Computational Linguistics (ACL), Secretary of ACL SIGSLAV, and Secretary of the Truth and Trust Online board of trustees. Formerly, he was PC chair of ACL 2022, and President of ACL SIGLEX. He is also member of the editorial board of several journals including Computational Linguistics, TACL, ACM TOIS, IEEE TASL, IEEE TAC, CS&L, NLE, AI Communications, and Frontiers in AI. He authored a Morgan & Claypool book on Semantic Relations between Nominals, two books on computer algorithms, and 250+ research papers. He received a Best Paper Award at ACM WebSci'2022, a Best Long Paper Award at CIKM'2020, a Best Demo Paper Award (Honorable Mention) at ACL'2020, a Best Task Paper Award (Honorable Mention) at SemEval'2020, a Best Poster Award at SocInfo'2019, and the Young Researcher Award at RANLP'2011. He was also the first to receive the Bulgarian President's John Atanasoff award, named after the inventor of the first automatic electronic digital computer. Dr. Nakov's research was featured by over 100 news outlets, including Forbes, Boston Globe, Aljazeera, DefenseOne, Business Insider, MIT Technology Review, Science Daily, Popular Science, Fast Company, The Register, WIRED, and Engadget, among others.

Keynote Talk: The Role of Social Networks in Economic Mobility

Mike Bailey
Meta

Abstract: Social capital—the strength of an individual's social network and community—has been identified as a potential determinant of outcomes ranging from education to health. We use data on 21 billion friendships in the US to measure and analyze different types of social capital including connectedness between different types of people, social cohesion, and civic engagement. We demonstrate the importance of distinguishing these forms of social capital by analyzing their associations with economic mobility across areas. The share of high-SES friends among individuals with low SES—which we term economic connectedness—is among the strongest predictors of upward income mobility identified to date. In a different paper we use social network data in India to show the importance of social networks to labor migrants and find that increasing social connectedness across space may have considerable economic gains, improving average wages by 3% (24% for the bottom wage-quartile) in a migration model.

Bio: Mike Bailey is a senior social scientist at Meta on the Computational Social Science team. His work focuses on the role of social networks on economic opportunity including migration, health, education, and social capital and his work has been published in top scientific journals such as Nature and the Journal of Political Economy and covered by outlets such as The Economist and The New York Times. He is a co-creator of the Social Capital Atlas dataset and the Social Connectedness Index which are publicly available datasets measuring social connectedness. Previously at Facebook Mike founded and led several research science teams including the Economics Research team, the Feed Science team, and the Society Research team. He holds a PhD in Economics from Stanford and a BS in Math and Economics from Utah State and is originally from Utah.

Keynote Talk: AI for social impact: Results from deployments for public health and conservation

Milind Tambe
Harvard University and Google Research

Abstract: With the maturing of AI and multiagent systems research, we have a tremendous opportunity to direct these advances towards addressing complex societal problems. I will focus on domains of public health and conservation, and address one key cross-cutting challenge: how to effectively deploy our limited intervention resources in these problem domains. I will present results from work around the globe in using AI for challenges in public health such as Maternal and Child care interventions, HIV prevention, and in conservation such as endangered wildlife protection. Achieving social impact in these domains often requires methodological advances. To that end, I will highlight key research advances in multiagent reasoning and learning, in particular in, restless multiarmed bandits, influence maximization in social networks, computational game theory and decision-focused learning. In pushing this research agenda, our ultimate goal is to facilitate local communities and non-profits to directly benefit from advances in AI tools and techniques.

Bio: Milind Tambe is Gordon McKay Professor of Computer Science and Director of Center for Research in Computation and Society at Harvard University; concurrently, he is also Principal Scientist and Director AI for Social Good at Google Research. Prof. Tambe's work focuses on advancing AI and multiagent systems for public health, conservation & public safety, with a track record of building pioneering AI systems for social impact. He is recipient of the IJCAI John McCarthy Award, AAMAS ACM Autonomous Agents Research Award, AAAI Robert S. Engelmore Memorial Lecture Award, and he is a fellow of AAAI and ACM. He is also a recipient of the INFORMS Wagner prize for excellence in Operations Research practice and Rist Prize from MORS (Military Operations Research Society). For his work on AI and public safety, he has received Columbus Fellowship Foundation Homeland security award and commendations and certificates of appreciation from the US Coast Guard, the Federal Air Marshals Service and airport police at the city of Los Angeles.

Keynote Talk: Recentering NLP Around ALL People

Rada Mihalcea
University of Michigan

Abstract: The field of NLP has come a long way, with many exciting achievements along several research directions, including language generation, large language models, machine translation, and more. However, while most of the NLP technologies built today are branded as one size fits all, the reality is that they are one size fits the majority, with many languages and many minorities left 'on the side'. In this talk, I will highlight some of the drawbacks associated with this strategy of building 'generic' NLP technologies, and make suggestions for ways to move towards NLP for ALL.

Bio: Rada Mihalcea is the Janice M. Jenkins Collegiate Professor of Computer Science and Engineering at the University of Michigan and the Director of the Michigan Artificial Intelligence Lab. Her research interests are in computational linguistics, with a focus on lexical semantics, computational social sciences, and multimodal language processing. She serves or has served on the editorial boards of the Journals of Computational Linguistics, Language Resources and Evaluations, Natural Language Engineering, Journal of Artificial Intelligence Research, IEEE Transactions on Affective Computing, and Transactions of the Association for Computational Linguistics. She was a program co-chair for Empirical Methods in Natural Language Processing 2009 and Association for Computational Linguistics (ACL) 2011, and a general chair for North American ACL 2015 and *SEM 2019. She directs multiple diversity and mentorship initiatives, including Girls Encoded and the ACL Year-Round Mentorship program. She currently serves as ACL Past President. She is the recipient of a Presidential Early Career Award for Scientists and Engineers awarded by President Obama (2009), and was named an ACM Fellow (2019) and an AAAI Fellow (2021). In 2013, she was made an honorary citizen of her hometown of Cluj-Napoca, Romania.

Keynote Talk: What's the deal with AI safety?

Sam Bowman
New York University

Abstract: Over the last few years, a research community has been forming to study questions about the potential negative impacts of future AI systems with broadly human-level capabilities. This community was initially largely separate from academic ML, with deeper roots in philosophy departments and industry labs. This has started to change, though, with AI safety researchers increasingly focusing on questions about progress in large language models, and with safety-related motivations increasingly steering investments in NLP at large labs like OpenAI and DeepMind. This talk presents the basic goals and projects of the AI safety research community, with a focus on large language models and connections to NLP and on connections to concerns about present-day deployed language technology.

Bio: Sam Bowman is a newly-tenured associate professor at NYU and, during a 2022–2023 sabbatical year, a member of technical staff at Anthropic. At NYU, he is a member of the Center for Data Science, the Department of Linguistics, and the Courant Institute's Department of Computer Science. His research focuses primarily on developing techniques and datasets for use in controlling and evaluating large language models, and additionally on applications of machine learning to scientific questions in linguistic syntax and semantics. He is the senior organizer behind the GLUE and SuperGLUE benchmark competitions and his work has been funded by the US NSF (including through a CAREER award), Google, Apple, Samsung, Schmidt Futures, and Open Philanthropy, among others.

Table of Contents

Program

Wednesday, December 7, 2022

13:15 - 14:00 *Opening Remarks and Introduction to NLP for Social Good*

14:00 - 14:30 *Invited Talk by Preslav Nakov*

14:30 - 14:45 *Preslav Nakov Live Q&A*

14:45 - 15:00 *Break 1*

15:00 - 16:00 *Physical Poster Session*

Securely Capturing People's Interactions with Voice Assistants at Home: A Bespoke Tool for Ethical Data Collection
Angus Addlesee

Towards Countering Essentialism through Social Bias Reasoning
Emily Allaway, Nina Taneja, Sarah-jane Leslie and Maarten Sap

Enhancing Crisis-Related Tweet Classification with Entity-Masked Language Modeling and Multi-Task Learning
Philipp Seeberger and Korbinian Riedhammer

Misinformation Detection in the Wild: News Source Classification as a Proxy for Non-article Texts
Matyas Bohacek

Breaking through Inequality of Information Acquisition among Social Classes: A Modest Effort on Measuring Fun
Chenghao Xiao, Baicheng Sun, Jindi Wang, Mingyue Liu and Jiayi Feng

Hate-CLIPper: Multimodal Hateful Meme Classification based on Cross-modal Interaction of CLIP Features
Gokul Karthik Kumar and Karthik Nandakumar

Participatory Translations of Oshiwambo: Towards Culture Preservation with Language Technology
Wilhelmina Nekoto, Julia Kreutzer, Jenalea Rajab, Millicent Ochieng and Jade Abbott

Challenges and Opportunities in Information Manipulation Detection: An Examination of Wartime Russian Media
Yulia Tsvetkov, Anjalie Field, Julia Mendelsohn and Chan Young Park

Wednesday, December 7, 2022 (continued)

Gender Bias in Meta-Embeddings
Naoaki Okazaki, Danushka Bollegala and Masahiro Kaneko

Fair NLP Models with Differentially Private Text Encoders
Aurélien Bellet, Mikaela Keller, Pascal Denis and Gaurav Maheshwari

Mitigating Covertly Unsafe Text within Natural Language Systems
William Yang Wang, Kathleen McKeown, Bruce Bimber, Desmond Patton, John Judge, Emily Allaway, Melanie Subbiah, Sharon Levy, Anisha Kabir and Alex Mei

Logical Fallacy Detection
Bernhard Schoelkopf, Rada Mihalcea, Mrinmaya Sachan, Zhiheng Lyu, Yiwen Ding, Xiaoyu Shen, Tejas Vaidhya, Abhinav Lalwani and Zhijing Jin

15:00 - 16:00 *Virtual Poster Session 1*

A Dataset of Sustainable Diet Arguments on Twitter
Marcus Hansen and Daniel Hershcovich

ClimaBench: A Benchmark Dataset For Climate Change Text Understanding in English
Tanmay Laud, Daniel Spokoyny, Tom Corringham and Taylor Berg-kirkpatrick

Modelling Persuasion through Misuse of Rhetorical Appeals
Amalie Pauli, Leon Derczynski and Ira Assent

Identifying Condescending Language: A Tale of Two Distinct Phenomena?
Carla Perez Almendros and Steven Schockaert

Beyond Model Interpretability: On the Faithfulness and Adversarial Robustness of Contrastive Textual Explanations
Mariette Awad and Julia El Zini

HARALD: Augmenting Hate Speech Data Sets with Real Data
Dan Vilenchik and Tal Ilan

Wednesday, December 7, 2022 (continued)

16:00 - 17:00	*Lightning Talk Session*
17:00 - 17:30	*Break 2*
17:30 - 18:00	*Invited Talk by Mike Bailey*
18:00 - 18:30	*Invited Talk by Milind Tambe*
18:30 - 18:45	*Mike Bailey & Milind Tambe Live Q&A*
18:45 - 19:15	*Invited Talk by Rada Mihalcea*
19:15 - 19:45	*Invited Talk by Sam Bowman*
19:45 - 20:00	*Rada Mihalcea and Sam Bowman Live Q&A*
20:00 - 20:15	*Break 3*
20:15 - 21:00	*Panel*
21:00 - 21:20	*Interactive Session*
21:20 - 21:30	*Closing Remarks and Best Paper Awards*
21:30 - 22:30	*Virtual Poster Session 2*
	A unified framework for cross-domain and cross-task learning of mental health conditions Huikai Chua, Andrew Caines and Helen Yannakoudakis
	Critical Perspectives: A Benchmark Revealing Pitfalls in PerspectiveAPI Lucas Rosenblatt, Lorena Piedras and Julia Wilkins

Wednesday, December 7, 2022 (continued)

Impacts of Low Socio-economic Status on Educational Outcomes: A Narrative Based Analysis
Motti Kelbessa, Ilyas Jamil and Labiba Jahan

Using NLP to Support English Teaching in Rural Schools
Luis Chiruzzo, Laura Musto, Santiago Gongora, Brian Carpenter, Juan Filevich and Aiala Rosa

Am I Answering My Job Interview Questions Right?": A NLP Approach to Predict Degree of Explanation in Job Interview Responses
Raghu Verrap, Ehsanul Nirjhar, Ani Nenkova and Theodora Chaspari

Generate Me a Bedtime Story: Leveraging Natural Language Processing for Early Vocabulary Enhancement
Trevor Hall, Maria Valentini, Eliana Colunga and Katharina Kann

BELA: Bot for English Language Acquisition
Muskan Mahajan

Transformers-Based Approach for a Sustainability Term-Based Sentiment Analysis (STBSA)
Blaise Sandwidi and Suneer Pallitharammal Mukkolakal

Understanding COVID-19 Vaccine Campaign on Facebook using Minimal Supervision
Tunazzina Islam and Dan Goldwasser

Conditional Supervised Contrastive Learning for Fair Text Classification
Yuan Tian, Han Zhao, Kai-Wei Chang, Yaodong Yu, William Shand and Jianfeng Chi

Handling and Presenting Harmful Text in NLP Research
Leon Derczynski, Bertie Vidgen, Abeba Birhane and Hannah Kirk

Don't Just Clean It, Proxy Clean It: Mitigating Bias by Proxy in Pre-Trained Models
Qinlan Shen, Michael Wick, Ari Kobren and Swetasudha Panda

A unified framework for cross-domain and cross-task learning of mental health conditions

Huikai Chua[♡*] **Andrew Caines**[♠] **Helen Yannakoudakis**[♣◇]

[♡]Amazon Alexa

[♠]Department of Computer Science & Technology, University of Cambridge, U.K.

[♣]Dept of Informatics, King's College London, U.K.

[◇]KinHub

huikaic@amazon.co.uk andrew.caines@cl.cam.ac.uk helen.yannakoudakis@kcl.ac.uk

Abstract

The detection of mental health conditions based on an individual's use of language has received considerable attention in the NLP community. However, most work has focused on single-task and single-domain models, limiting the semantic space that they are able to cover and risking significant cross-domain loss. In this paper, we present two approaches towards a unified framework for cross-domain and cross-task learning for the detection of depression, post-traumatic stress disorder and suicide risk across different platforms that further utilizes inductive biases across tasks. Firstly, we develop a lightweight model using a general set of features that sets a new state of the art on several tasks while matching the performance of more complex task- and domain-specific systems on others. We also propose a multi-task approach and further extend our framework to explicitly capture the affective characteristics of someone's language, further consolidating transfer of inductive biases and of shared linguistic characteristics. Finally, we present a novel dynamically adaptive loss weighting approach that allows for more stable learning across imbalanced datasets and better neural generalization performance. Our results demonstrate the effectiveness of our unified framework for mental ill-health detection across a number of diverse English datasets.

1 Introduction

Depression is a mental health condition characterized by low mood, energy and self-esteem (American Psychiatric Association, 2013). One of the most serious effects of depression is the loss of joy in life, which leads to an increased suicide risk among people with depression.[1] However, due to the social stigma surrounding depression, many people who suffer from it hesitate to seek help. Suicide is one of the leading causes of death globally, especially among young people: it is the second most common cause of death among people aged 15–24.[2] Post-traumatic stress disorder (PTSD), which is characterized, among others, by symptoms of emotional outburst and negative thought, may also co-occur with depression, and can be a common response to PTSD sufferers.

There has thus been interest in the development of natural language processing (NLP) models for detection and/or prevention intervention. For example, this has been the focus of multiple shared tasks at the Computational Linguistics and Clinical Psychology (CLPsych) workshops (Coppersmith et al., 2015; Milne et al., 2016; Zirikly et al., 2019) as well as the Audio/Visual Emotion Challenge (AVEC) (Valstar et al., 2016; Ringeval et al., 2017, 2019).

However, previous work has tended to focus primarily on a single domain and/or mental health condition at a time. Each of the shared tasks listed above were focused on a single dataset from one domain; for example, the CLPsych 19 shared task used only forum posts from Reddit. The top systems at these shared tasks also frequently made use of domain-specific meta features such as the number of Reddit posts per time period, which were found to be among the most informative in suicide risk detection (Ruiz et al., 2019). Meanwhile, research has shown a lack of generalizability across datasets in classification models for mental health NLP (Harrigian et al., 2020).

The goal of our research is to develop models that can capture domain-independent and interrelated characteristics of different mental ill-health detection tasks, and generalize better. The novelty of our work is in proposing an alternative way of formulating the modeling of mental health conditions, which is more robust and effective compared

*Work done while at the University of Cambridge

[1]https://www.who.int/en/news-room/fact-sheets/detail/suicide

[2]https://save.org/about-suicide/suicide-facts/

Proceedings of the Second Workshop on NLP for Positive Impact (NLP4PI), pages 1 - 14
December 7, 2022

to existing approaches, and we believe can benefit future research in this important task. We use English data from the CLPsych 2015 and 2019 shared tasks, which were obtained from Twitter and Reddit respectively, as well as the Distress Analysis Interview Corpus – Wizard of Oz (DAIC-WOZ) (Gratch et al., 2014), which consists of interview transcripts. Our open-domain setup precludes the use of domain-specific features such as the meta properties previously mentioned, as well as audiovisual cues from DAIC-WOZ interview recordings which may not always be available (e.g., due to user privacy concerns over voice and speech analysis).

To validate the general applicability of our approach, we experiment with two different types of approaches: 1) we develop novel multi-task learning architectures using a dynamically adaptive loss weighting scheduler that we show can lead to more effective learning across tasks/domains; and 2) we develop lightweight and interpretable models that, in contrast to the task-specific architecture and feature engineering used by many top shared task submissions (Mohammadi et al., 2019; Matero et al., 2019; Williamson et al., 2016), utilize a cross-task and cross-domain linguistic space that sets a new state of the art on several tasks while matching the performance of more complex task- and domain-specific systems on others.

To the best of our knowledge, this is the first approach towards a unified framework for open-domain (cross-domain) detection of different types of mental health conditions (cross-task).

2 Data & related work

We use data from two CLPsych shared tasks (Coppersmith et al., 2015; Zirikly et al., 2019), as well as the DAIC-WOZ corpus (Gratch et al., 2014) used in the AVEC challenges (Valstar et al., 2016; Ringeval et al., 2017, 2019), summarized below. While there has been little research in the development of cross-domain mental health models, there has been some effort to develop multi-task ones. These include models for different mental health conditions (anxiety, schizophrenia, panic, eating disorders) (Benton et al., 2017), or the use of auxiliary linguistic tasks such as figurative language detection (Yadav et al., 2020). However, all of the methods focus on a single domain (Twitter) and therefore capture a limited part of semantic space, whereas we focus on cross-domain methods that generalize across datasets.

2.1 CLPsych 15

The CLPsych 2015 shared task dataset (Coppersmith et al., 2015) was created by identifying Twitter users with depression or post-traumatic stress disorder (PTSD), based on whether they had publicly tweeted a diagnosis for either of these conditions. Each user is paired with an age- and gender-matched control, as estimated using the demographic classification tool from the World Well-Being Project (Sap et al., 2014). Up to the 3000 most recent tweets, excluding the original tweet of diagnosis, were collected for each user. The distribution is summarized in Table 4 in Appendix A.1.

The organizers set three binary classification tasks at the user level across each of three classes: **CD** (control vs depression), **CP** (control vs PTSD) and **DP** (depression vs PTSD). The best submission used supervised topic modelling and linear SVMs (Resnik et al., 2015).

2.2 CLPsych 19

The University of Maryland Reddit Suicidality Dataset (Version 2), used for CLPsych 19 (Zirikly et al., 2019; Shing et al., 2018), is made available with the assistance of the American Association of Suicidology. It contains the Reddit post history of $11,129$ control users and another $11,129$ users who have posted in r/SuicideWatch, a subreddit dedicated to supporting users who had or have suicidal thoughts. Of these users, 1097 were randomly sampled for annotation, with 993 annotated by crowdsourcing. These were then split into a training and test set as shown in Table 5 in Appendix A.1. Suicide risk has been annotated from 'None' to 'Severe' (given as character labels from 'a' to 'd').

The shared task organizers set three four-way classification tasks at the user level with different goals and restrictions on which posts may be used for classification: **Task A:** assessing a user's risk based on posts in the SuicideWatch reddit (typically a few posts per user); **Task B:** similar to Task A, but now all user posts, including those outside the SuicideWatch subreddit, may be used; **Task C:** this task is about screening users who may be at risk based on general posts (i.e., all posts *except* SuicideWatch posts may be used).

The best model on CLPsych 19 Tasks A and C used an SVM meta-classifier on top of eight sub-models based on CNN, RNN, bi-GRU and bi-

LSTM layers (Mohammadi et al., 2019). The sub-models utilized pretrained GloVe and ELMo word embeddings to produce user-level representations from user posts. An attention mechanism weighted each post based on their expected importance in predicting suicide risk. Finally, a fusion component weighted the user representations produced by each sub-model and then the SVM output the final predictions based on the weighted representations. The best model on CLPsych 19 Task B used various user-level post statistics (e.g., average unigram length, average unigrams per post) as well as information about the specific subreddits the users posted in, and processed posts separately based on that information. They also included a set of subreddit features, including one derived from popular subreddits, and one derived from subreddits distinctive of high-risk users.

2.3 DAIC-WOZ

The Distress Analysis Interview Corpus – Wizard of Oz (DAIC-WOZ) (Gratch et al., 2014) consists of transcribed interviews with veterans of the U.S. military and members of the general public from the Los Angeles area. The interviews were conducted using a virtual avatar controlled by a human interviewer, and then automatically transcribed with IBM Watson. The corpus includes Patient Health Questionnaire-8 (PHQ-8) scores for each participant as well as binary labels indicating depression. We utilize the binary labels and predict depression as a classification task. Although the corpus includes audio recordings and visual information such as facial and pose data, we opt not to make use of either audio or interviewer turns in DAIC-WOZ as we focus on modelling cross-domain user texts and task generalizability.

The best shared task classifier for DAIC-WOZ achieves 70% F1 (Williamson et al., 2016), in a submission to the AVEC 2016 challenge (Valstar et al., 2016). The approach used an ensemble model fusing predictions from audio, video, and semantic (text) features (e.g., task-specific audio features such as loudness variation and vocal tract physiology features). The authors also modeled the joint dynamical properties across facial action units using the video features, as well as included interviewer prompts in the text features, which they found to be more informative than user text alone.

2.4 GoEmotions

Previous work has found that fine-grained bag-of-emotions are useful features in depression detection in Reddit posts (Aragón et al., 2019). We extend the use of affective features across domains and different mental health conditions either in the form of lexicon-based emotion features (Section 3.1) or via the addition of an emotion detection auxiliary objective, **GoEmo** (Section 3.2), using the GoEmotions (Demszky et al., 2020) dataset. GoEmotions comprises around 58, 000 Reddit comments manually annotated using a fine-grained taxonomy of 27 emotions plus 'neutral', including a wide range of positive, negative and ambiguous emotions such as 'realization'. We use the released training, development and test splits,[3] consisting of 43410, 5426, and 5427 examples respectively. The number of examples per class ranges from over 5000 for the most frequent ('admiration'), to around 100 for the least frequent one ('grief').

2.5 Speaker characteristics

The datasets used are not necessarily balanced for representation. While the exact demographic labels are unavailable, CLPsych 15 is estimated to be roughly 80% white and nearly 90% female (Aguirre et al., 2021). Meanwhile, Reddit is estimated to be dominated by American users, which comprised nearly 50% of site traffic in 2020,[4] mostly male and under 25, according to a 2016 Reddit survey.[5] Therefore, it is likely that CLPsych 19 and GoEmotions, which are both collected from Reddit, follow similar demographic characteristics.

DAIC-WOZ features interviews with U.S. military veterans and residents of the Los Angeles area (Section 2) and thus was designed to specifically represent these social groups. However, in contrast to the CLPsych datasets, the gender distribution is approximately balanced between male and female (no other genders are declared in the dataset).

Overall, the corpora we use are dominated by young, male, North American users of social media. However, we note that annotator characteristics may differ. GoEmotions was annotated by native English speakers from India, while CLPsych 19 was annotated by crowdworkers from around the

[3]https://github.com/google-research/google-research/tree/master/goemotions/data

[4]https://www.statista.com/statistics/325144/reddit-global-active-user-distribution/

[5]https://www.reddit.com/r/dataisbeautiful/comments/5700sj/ octhe_results_of_the_reddit_demographics_survey/

world on CrowdFlower.

3 Models

3.1 Lightweight feature-based model

Feature-based models have been shown to achieve state of the art results on various mental ill-health detection tasks, while can facilitate model interpretability, which is crucial in high-stakes areas such as mental health. We focus on the development of such a lightweight approach that furthermore captures shared and generalizable properties across tasks and domains. In contrast to the task-specific architecture and feature engineering used by many top shared task submissions (Mohammadi et al., 2019; Matero et al., 2019; Williamson et al., 2016), we utilize the datasets' development sets to identify the most effective set of domain-invariant features.

Our best model uses tf–idf word unigrams, character (2,4)-grams, and part-of-speech (POS) tags based on NLTK's POS tagger (Bird and Loper, 2004). Inspired by previous work, we also add the following count-based features: first-person singular pronouns which have been identified as more frequently used among depressives (Al-Mosaiwi and Johnstone, 2018) across demographic lines (Edwards and Holtzman, 2017) due to increased self-focus (Wolohan et al., 2018; Brockmeyer et al., 2015); first-person plural pronouns (although depressed people might use the first-person singular more often, they might not necessarily express as much social engagement; De Choudhury et al. (2013)); words reflecting absolutist thinking (Al-Mosaiwi and Johnstone, 2018) such as 'always', as cognitive rigidity has been linked to suicidal ideation (Ellis and Rutherford, 2008).

We also calculate sentence-level sentiment scores using NLTK's VADER tool (Hutto and Gilbert, 2015) and include the average over all sentences; as well as emotion features based on the NRC Word–Emotion Association Lexicon (EmoLex) (Mohammad and Turney, 2013; Mohammad, 2011; Mohammad and Yang, 2011; Mohammad and Turney, 2010). EmoLex comprises eight emotions – anger, anticipation, disgust, fear, joy, sadness, surprise, trust – as well as negativity and positivity sentiment dimensions. To identify the most predictive affective characteristics of text among those 10 features, we perform grid search on the development data, find anger, joy, surprise, positivity and negativity to be the most discriminative, and include these in our final model.[6]

We experiment with two lightweight models, support vector machines (SVMs) (Cortes and Vapnik, 1995) and gradient-boosted decision trees (GBDTs) from XGBoost (Chen and Guestrin, 2016). During tuning, we find the latter to give the best performance (between 3-20 F1 points difference) and we therefore choose this for our experiments.

3.2 MT-DNN model

We develop a multi-task deep neural network (MT-DNN) (Liu et al., 2019c,b; He et al., 2019; Liu et al., 2019a; Jiang et al., 2020; Liu et al., 2020; Wang et al., 2019; Cheng et al., 2020) [7] to directly leverage inductive transfer between our tasks. Our model consists of a pre-trained shared encoder followed by separate task-specific layers. We use the uncased English BERT_{BASE} model provided by Hugging Face (Devlin et al., 2019; Wolf et al., 2020) as the encoder shared across the different datasets, encode the most recent 512 tokens[8] and use the [CLS] token as the post embedding for classification. The task-specific layers consist of a linear layer with either a sigmoid or softmax activation for the multi-label (GoEmotions) and classification tasks respectively, and the model is optimized using (binary) cross entropy. The shared encoder makes up the bulk of the MT-DNN model, with around 110 million parameters.

The various datasets differ greatly in the number of examples per class. We find that running the model for 30 epochs ensures that all have had a chance to converge.[9] This is further discussed in Section 5. To improve stability, we accumulate gradients over 3 steps during training, using a batch size of 16. We manually tune the learning rate to 9e-5 on the development set using the Adamax optimizer (Kingma and Ba, 2017).

Adaptive loss weights The different datasets have different distributions and learning curves, making it difficult to determine an appropriate stop-

[6] The use of the two sentiment scores improved performance further to the averaged VADER scores; we surmise this is due to the more fine-grained information added via the explicit counts of positivity and negativity expressed in a post.

[7] https://github.com/namisan/mt-dnn

[8] Word boundaries were respected, i.e., if the n most recent words have a subtoken length greater than 512, then only the $(n-1)$ most recent words were used.

[9] 30 epochs takes around 2 hours to train the multi-task model on a Tesla P100 on CLPsych 15, CLPsych 19 and DAIC-WOZ. Adding GoEmotions (substantially more examples than any of the other tasks) increases runtime to around 4 hours.

ping criterion for the multi-task model. While we can train the model until the slowest task has peaked on the development data (as mentioned above), this is likely to lead in overfitting for the other tasks. On the other hand, sequential training of tasks runs the risk of catastrophic forgetting. To mitigate this, we weight the losses of each task in the multi-task model, and propose an approach that dynamically adapts the weights based on whether a task has reached convergence or not.

We start by initializing the weights to 1, and set patience P to 3 epochs if the development F1 improves at the end of each epoch. If a task stops improving but has already reached 90% of a predetermined target performance T, its loss weight is gradually reduced by 0.1 with a lower bound of 0.5 to ensure it is always weighted at least as much as the auxiliary emotion task (see below). On the other hand, if a task has not improved over P epochs and has yet to reach 50% of the target performance, its loss weight is multiplied proportional to $\frac{T}{S}$, where S refers to the current performance, up to a maximum of 1.5 times.

We experiment with two different ways of setting the target performance that a model should reach before its loss weight is adjusted: **Adapt-Fixed** that uses a fixed target performance threshold of 80% F1 for each task (we manually tuned this on the development set and found this to perform best); **Adapt-Variant** where the target for each task is set separately. Here, we first complete an initial MT-DNN run with all tasks and constant weights. The individual task target performance threshold is then the best development F1 achieved for that task at any epoch. To assess the effectiveness of our weighting approaches, we furthermore report results without adaptive loss weights, referred to as **Constant**, but where all tasks are equally weighted and each weight is set to 1. The only exception to the above is the auxiliary emotion detection task, GoEmo, for which the loss weight w is downweighted and fixed at 0.5 to prioritize performance on the mental health tasks. We found that the model converged to roughly the same F1 score on GoEmo as when $w = 1.0$, but resulted in better performance on our main tasks.

While existing multi-task approaches may adapt the scheduler such that texts from underperforming tasks are selected more often (Jean et al., 2019), sampling tasks effectively presents a challenge in our setting, characterized by high variation in class distribution and dataset sizes. The latter range from thousands of examples per class (GoEmotions) to less than a hundred (DAIC-WOZ). Our approach presents a simpler alternative to ameliorating this problem that does not rely on explicit data manipulation but rather directly exploits the learning patterns of a given model.[10]

3.3 Single-task baselines

We include single-task BERT-based baselines trained on each of the datasets separately, using a linear schedule with 20 warmup steps, a learning rate of 5e-5, a batch size of 16, and no gradient accumulation. The models are trained until F1 does not improve on the development data over 3 consecutive epochs and the best model is selected.

4 Results

Experimental setting For DAIC-WOZ and GoEmotions, we use the published train/dev/test splits. Since CLPsych 15 and 19 did not include a development set, we put aside 10% of the training sets (randomly selected and stratified by class) for development. Both approaches use the same data and are tuned across the task development sets. We evaluate model performance using macro F1. For CLPsych 15, we also report precision separately, as this was the *primary* evaluation metric of the shared task. We also report F1*, the *official* metric for CLPsych 19 Task C, which is F1 computed without the lowest risk class ('a').

Feature-based model In Table 1, we can see that the Feature Model achieves, overall, a high performance across tasks using its set of domain-invariant features for predicting the different types of mental health conditions. We report macro-F1 for all tasks, along with precision for the CLPsych 15 tasks (the *official* evaluation metric used), and F1* (without class 'a') for CLPsych 19 task C (the task's *official* evaluation metric). F1 was not reported for the CLPsych 15 shared tasks, but we have rather estimated it (†) based on the reported precision and ROC curve. However, we can calculate the average macro-F1 performance across tasks for our models (last column; based on the F1 value for Task C). We can see that our performance comes close to or surpasses the best shared task results on all tasks

[10] While other approaches to scheduling can be investigated (e.g., Kiperwasser and Ballesteros (2018)), our main aim is to demonstrate the validity and robustness of a unified approach, and therefore leave this for future work.

Model	CD F1	CD Prec	CP F1	CP Prec	DP F1	DP Prec	A F1	B F1	C F1	C F1*	DW F1	Avg F1
Shared Task	**84**[†]	86	87[†]	89	69[†]	83	48.1	**47.0**	–	**26.8**	**70.0**	–
Feature Model	80.2	**87.8**	**92.1**	**94.9**	**83.7**	**86.3**	47.9	33.4	31.2	24.0	68.1	**62.4**
Single Task	52.8	62.3	69.7	67.8	61	71.1	41.1	25.2	33.3	19.0	41.9	46.4
epoch		(9)		(5)		(4)	(7)	(2)		(3)	(13)	
Constant	57.1	51.9	62.7	62.7	56.1	68.9	46.3	23.7	29.1	13.7	46.8	45.9
Adapt-Fixed	57.5	53.1	59.7	64.8	57.1	77.3	47.5	27.5	33.0	18.2	58.1	48.6
Adapt-Variant	56.1	50.0	61.6	63.4	53.9	71.4	**50.5**	27.3	32.3	17.1	40.0	46.0
Constant$_{GoEmo}$	58.3	52.7	64.6	68.2	58.1	69.4	38.8	30.8	**35.9**	22.1	47.0	47.6
Adapt-Fixed$_{GoEmo}$	57.9	53.4	62.7	62.7	58.7	72.5	49.3	27.7	33.5	18.7	60.5	53.6
Adapt-Variant$_{GoEmo}$	57.0	53.2	62.6	63.8	58.0	74.7	48.6	27.6	33.0	18.2	63.2	50.0

Table 1: Model performance across datasets: CD, CP and DP from CLPysch 15; Tasks A, B and C from CLPsych 19; and DW, the binary classification task on DAIC-WOZ. We report macro-F1 for all tasks, along with precision for the CLPsych 15 tasks (the *official* evaluation metric used), and F1* (without class 'a') for CLPsych 19 task C (the task's *official* evaluation metric). F1 was not reported for the CLPsych 15 shared tasks, but we have estimated it (†) based on the reported precision and ROC curve. However, we show the average macro-F1 performance across tasks for our models (last column; based on the F1 value for Task C). *Shared Task* represents the current state-of-the-art performance. 'Feature Model' is our feature-based baseline, while 'Single Task' is BERT fine-tuned to each task individually, also showing the epoch at which training was halted according to our early stopping criterion (see Section 5). 'Constant' is the multi-task model without adaptive loss weights; Adapt-Fixed and Adapt-Variant refer to the different versions of our adaptive loss weighting algorithm. 'GoEmo' indicates the addition of the emotion objective using the GoEmotions dataset. The best performance in each column is highlighted in bold.

except Task B, where we did not make use of additional contextual information about the subreddit the post belongs to (Matero et al., 2019).[11]

Single-task baselines We can see that the single-task BERT baselines failed to outdo the best shared task scores on all tasks, performing especially poorly on CLPsych 15 (CD, CP, DP).[12]

MT-DNN The baseline multi-task model, Constant (without use of adaptive loss weighting), showed mixed results with F1 improvements in CD, A and DW, but decreases compared to the single-task model on the other tasks. This confirms the need for a unified (neural) approach that directly takes into account the training dataset distributions and learning curves. Our adaptive loss weight algorithms, Adapt-Fixed and Adapt-Variant, attempt to ameliorate this. Specifically, we find that Adapt-Fixed can balance the performance across multiple tasks and achieve better overall performance (avg F1) compared to both the single-task and Constant counterparts, contributing to an effective unified approach. On the other hand, Adapt-Variant is on par with Constant. The effectiveness of Adapt-Fixed can be attributed to the fact that it enforces learning to a certain (high) level of performance for each task, as opposed to Adapt-Variant that has a less strict approach to learning performance thresholds.

Adding emotion detection (GoEmo) as an auxiliary task leads to overall improvements (avg F1). Comparing the Constant variants with and without GoEmo, we see the largest improvements in Tasks B and C of 7.1 and 8.4 F1 points respectively. This can be explained by the fact that both the GoEmotions and CLPsych 19 datasets were collected from Reddit (however, it seems that the dataset generalizes more poorly to Task A, which was collected only from one specific subreddit). Overall, we observe again that Adapt-Fixed achieves the best performance across the neural models, with particularly large improvements in Task A as well as DW of 10.5 and 13.5 points respectively.

5 Discussion

MT-DNN vs. Feature Model The feature-based model showed the best performance across all tasks utilizing its set of domain-invariant features, demonstrating that they share a common linguis-

[11] Since subreddits are typically organized around common interests or shared experiences, these provide valuable contextual information about a person's background. For example, we might deduce that someone who frequents the 'ukpolitics' subreddit most likely lives in the UK and is interested in politics. Such information however is not always readily available in other social media such as Twitter, where tweets are posted on users' walls instead of being organized into sub-forums.

[12] To test whether this can be attributed to the BERT text length restriction, we experimented with additional models such as longformers (Beltagy et al., 2020); however, BERT was nevertheless found to perform best.

Model	CD	CP	DP	A	B	C	DW	Avg
Constant	60.5	65	70.5	49.5	29.9	33.6	53.8	48.1
epoch	(10)	(13)	(5)	(17)	(16)	(16)	(20)	(12)
Adapt-Fixed	57.5	59.7	57.1	47.5	27.5	33	58.1	48.6
Constant$_{GoEmo}$	58.5	65.7	70.7	51.6	32.9	36.8	59.3	49.5
epoch	(9)	(4)	(5)	(5)	(10)	(4)	(24)	(24)
Adapt-Fixed$_{GoEmo}$	57.9	62.7	58.7	49.3	27.7	33.5	60.5	53.6

Table 2: The highest F1 attained by Constant and Constant$_{GoEmo}$ for each of the tasks separately, together with the epoch at which this is observed. The epoch with the best average F1 score is included under 'Avg'. For comparison, the Adapt-Fixed (with and without GoEmo) results at epoch 30 are reproduced from Table 1.

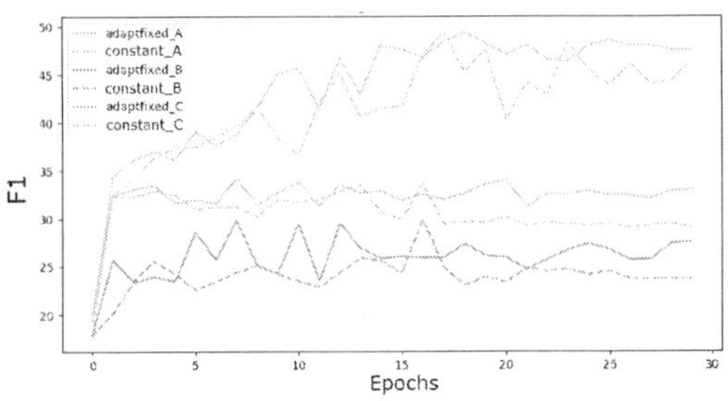

Figure 1: F1 score during training for 30 epochs for each task in CLPsych 19 for the Constant (dotted) and Adapt-Fixed (solid) models. The graphs for all datasets are reproduced in the Appendix A.4.

tic/feature space.[13] Therefore, using a multi-task model should theoretically enhance performance by allowing the shared encoder to simultaneously learn features at different levels of abstraction from all tasks at once. However, the Constant model achieved a lower average F1 score than the single-task BERT variants. This can be attributed to the difficulty of balancing the performance of multiple different tasks, where each have different learning schedules. While Adapt-Fixed provides a solution to this, it seems that, overall, there is scope for improvement on bridging the gap between feature-based and neural approaches for this task.[14] To better understand the effect of Adapt-Fixed on neural performance, we perform a detailed analysis below, illustrating the challenges in balancing different tasks and datasets within the neural approach.

Adaptive loss weighting analysis The adaptive loss weighting algorithm is motivated by the very different learning schedules of the different tasks. As can be seen in Table 1 (row *epoch*), the single task models were all stopped at different epochs for the different tasks, ranging from 2 epochs for B to 13 for DW. The difference in learning schedules is amplified in the multi-objective MT-DNN model. In Table 2, we report the highest F1 attained by the Constant and Constant$_{GoEmo}$ models for each of the tasks separately, together with the epoch at which this is observed. We can see that the best individual task F1 occurs at different epochs but with a wider spread. These range from 5 to 20 and from 4 to 24 for the Constant and Constant$_{GoEmo}$ models respectively. Therefore, in order to ensure the model is able to learn all tasks, we train it for a total of 30 epochs (compared to around 5 typically used for BERT (Devlin et al., 2019)), additionally utilizing the adaptive loss weighting algorithm to reduce overfitting.

In Section 4, we noted that the Adapt-Fixed models generally improved both single task as well as average F1 after 30 epochs of training. In Table 2, we can also see they outperform the highest F1 average attained at *any* epoch by the Constant models (for ease of comparison, we include the Adapt-Fixed and Adapt-Fixed$_{GoEmo}$ test results at epoch 30, reproduced from Table 1). Comparing individual task F1s, both the Adapt-Fixed versions scored within 3 points of the best achieved Constant F1 for 5 out of 7 tasks. This shows that the algorithm has been successful in balancing performance across most of the tasks, while improving the overall F1.

Qualitatively, we also observe that the adaptive loss weighting algorithm has a smoothing effect on training (Figure 1). Comparing the Constant model (dotted lines) to Adapt-Fixed (solid lines), we can see that, using the latter, we obtain a more stable version which empirically converges faster.

Emotion features The GoEmotions auxiliary objective seems particularly beneficial, resulting in

[13]Running a set of ablation studies, we find tf–idf unigrams, char ngrams and POS ngrams to be highly predictive.

[14]Notably, the neural model outperformed the feature-based model on Task A, where it also outperformed the state-of-the-art. As the most specialized task, consisting only of posts related to mental health, it is likely that Task A benefitted the most from information learned from the other related tasks.

Model	CD	CP	DP	A	B	C	DW	Avg
Positive	56.9	62.2	60.5	45.2	27.7	34.4	8.7	42.2
Negative	57.8	64.1	60.3	41.2	30.1	33.9	51.6	48.4
GoEmo	58.3	64.6	58.1	38.8	30.8	35.9	47.0	47.6

Table 3: F1 scores for the Constant_{GoEmo} MT-DNN model using only positive and only negative emotions. For comparison, its performance with all emotion classes (GoEmo) is reproduced from Table 1.

improvements over the single-task models and across all MT-DNN variants, with the highest F1 observed using the Adapt-Fixed model, leading to an average increase of 5% across datasets compared to its no-emotion counterpart. The feature-based model captures affective characteristics of language explicitly via the use of EmoLex features, as well as implicitly via the use of word and character ngrams. In qualitative analyses we find that, among the most highly predictive features, there exist affective terms such as 'pissed', 'bloody' and 'endure' for Task A (moderate and severe suicide risk) and 'loves' (low suicide risk); and 'afraid' and 'annoying' for DAIC-WOZ (depressed class).

To investigate the effect that negative emotions specifically might have in the detection of mental health conditions, we separate the 28 emotion labels into positive (13 total) and negative classes (11 total)[15] and now use these to train Constant_{GoEmo}. In Table 3, we can see that, overall, the exclusive use of negative emotions leads to an increased Avg F1 across all datasets. Notably, the effect is substantial for DW, with a 32.9 point difference compared to using positive emotions. In Appendix A.3, we also investigate learning effects in the opposite direction and examine how mental ill-health detection might affect performance of emotion detection.

6 Conclusion

We presented two approaches to cross-domain and cross-task mental ill-health detection. The first involves the development of a general set of features; the second uses a multi-task model, utilizing BERT as a shared encoder (Devlin et al., 2019). We found the former to perform well across all domains and tasks, demonstrating that they share a common set of linguistic cues. In comparison to shared task submissions which use complex neural models (Mohammadi et al., 2019; Matero et al., 2019; Williamson et al., 2016), our approach either matches their performance or improves over state-of-the-art results using a lightweight decision tree-based model. Such models are furthermore more transparent and interpretable with respect to the basis upon which they make predictions, which is crucial in high-stakes domains such as mental health and in assessing model validity and whether it measures what is intended to be measured.

We furthermore investigated the use of affective features, as well as examined negative emotion features in isolation, as a useful inductive bias for the detection of different types of mental health conditions, extending previous work that examines the effect of emotion features in a single domain and single task setting (depression detection in Reddit posts; Aragón et al. (2019)). Emotion detection, as an auxiliary objective, increased the average F1 score by 1.7 points, with the most substantial improvements observed in tasks from the same domain as the emotion dataset (CLPsych 19).

Finally, we presented an adaptive loss weighting algorithm which successfully balances performance across tasks with different learning schedules while increasing the overall performance. A comparison of model results with and without adaptive weighting revealed that it not only led to improved performance, but also outperformed the best average F1 score achieved over all epochs with constant weighting.

Our feature-based approach outperformed the neural counterpart, indicating that there is scope for further research towards a unified framework for open-domain detection of various mental health conditions. However, our feature-based results experimentally demonstrate that such an approach is feasible and effective, and achieves a new state of the art on several tasks.

To the best of our knowledge, this is the first approach towards a unified framework for open-domain (cross-domain) detection of different types of mental health conditions (cross-task). Our paper aims to lay a platform for future research, facilitating progress in this important effort.

[15] Four classes – confusion, realization, pride, and neutral – are excluded as they are not overtly positive or negative.

7 Acknowledgements

Our thanks to the University of Cambridge Department of Computer Science and Technology for granting us time with the Departmental GPUs, and to Malcolm Scott for his assistance with them.

8 Ethical concerns

This project was reviewed and approved by the Department of Computer Science & Technology's Ethics Committee, University of Cambridge.

Risks that may arise from this work include perpetuation of biases existing in the datasets used. Gender labels for each participant are unavailable in all except the DAIC-WOZ dataset, so the distribution may not be balanced. Crucially, mostly American speakers and users were included in the creation of the datasets. As cross-cultural differences have been found in the way people express depression (Loveys et al., 2018), further work would be required to investigate whether the approaches adopted generalize to datasets across demographic lines.

Such concerns also arise from the use of large language models, as it may be more difficult to correct bias in the large amounts of language data used for training (Blodgett et al., 2020). It has also been shown that it is possible to recover the original training texts from large language models (Carlini et al., 2020). Therefore, deployment of any system including such language models, such as the multi-task variants presented herein, should ensure not to compromise the privacy of the user. However, we note that the datasets used here have all been anonymized.

Finally, developers of models that can flag users should also consider the purpose of such predictions as well as whether they can be used to take actions against users; e.g., as part of 'social media checks' when screening job applicants. While well-intending friends and family members might use them to help those anxious about seeking help, others might also use such tools to discredit or slander others, particularly in cultures where mental health conditions are still stigmatized.

References

Carlos Aguirre, Keith Harrigian, and Mark Dredze. 2021. Gender and racial fairness in depression research using social media. In *Proceedings of the 16th Conference of the European Chapter of the Association for Computational Linguistics: Main Volume*, pages 2932–2949, Online. Association for Computational Linguistics.

Mohammed Al-Mosaiwi and Tom Johnstone. 2018. In an absolute state: Elevated use of absolutist words is a marker specific to anxiety, depression, and suicidal ideation. *Clinical Psychological Science*, 6(4):529–542. PMID: 30886766.

American Psychiatric Association. 2013. *Diagnostic and statistical manual of mental disorders: DSM-5*, 5th ed. edition. American Psychiatric Association, Arlington, VA.

Mario Ezra Aragón, Adrian Pastor López-Monroy, Luis Carlos González-Gurrola, and Manuel Montes-y Gómez. 2019. Detecting depression in social media using fine-grained emotions. In *Proceedings of the 2019 Conference of the North American Chapter of the Association for Computational Linguistics: Human Language Technologies, Volume 1 (Long and Short Papers)*, pages 1481–1486, Minneapolis, Minnesota. Association for Computational Linguistics.

Iz Beltagy, Matthew E. Peters, and Arman Cohan. 2020. Longformer: The long-document transformer. *CoRR*, abs/2004.05150.

Adrian Benton, Margaret Mitchell, and Dirk Hovy. 2017. Multitask learning for mental health conditions with limited social media data. In *Proceedings of the 15th Conference of the European Chapter of the Association for Computational Linguistics: Volume 1, Long Papers*, pages 152–162, Valencia, Spain. Association for Computational Linguistics.

Steven Bird and Edward Loper. 2004. NLTK: The natural language toolkit. In *Proceedings of the ACL Interactive Poster and Demonstration Sessions*, pages 214–217, Barcelona, Spain. Association for Computational Linguistics.

Su Lin Blodgett, Solon Barocas, Hal Daumé III, and Hanna Wallach. 2020. Language (technology) is power: A critical survey of "bias" in NLP. In *Proceedings of the 58th Annual Meeting of the Association for Computational Linguistics*, pages 5454–5476, Online. Association for Computational Linguistics.

Timo Brockmeyer, Johannes Zimmermann, Dominika Kulessa, Martin Hautzinger, Hinrich Bents, Hans-Christoph Friederich, Wolfgang Herzog, and Matthias Backenstrass. 2015. Me, myself, and I: self-referent word use as an indicator of self-focused attention in relation to depression and anxiety. *Frontiers in Psychology*, 6:1564.

Nicholas Carlini, Florian Tramèr, Eric Wallace, M. Jagielski, Ariel Herbert-Voss, K. Lee, Adam Roberts, Tom Brown, D. Song, Ú. Erlingsson, Alina Oprea, and Colin Raffel. 2020. Extracting training data from large language models. *ArXiv*, abs/2012.07805.

Tianqi Chen and Carlos Guestrin. 2016. Xgboost: A scalable tree boosting system. *CoRR*, abs/1603.02754.

Hao Cheng, Xiaodong Liu, Lis Pereira, Yaoliang Yu, and Jianfeng Gao. 2020. Posterior differential regularization with f-divergence for improving model robustness. *arXiv preprint arXiv:2010.12638*.

Glen Coppersmith, Mark Dredze, Craig Harman, Kristy Hollingshead, and Margaret Mitchell. 2015. CLPsych 2015 shared task: Depression and PTSD on Twitter. In *Proceedings of the 2nd Workshop on Computational Linguistics and Clinical Psychology: From Linguistic Signal to Clinical Reality*, pages 31–39, Denver, Colorado. Association for Computational Linguistics.

Corinna Cortes and Vladimir Vapnik. 1995. Support-vector networks. *Machine Learning*, 20(3):273–297.

Munmun De Choudhury, Michael Gamon, Scott Counts, and Eric Horvitz. 2013. Predicting depression via social media. AAAI.

Dorottya Demszky, Dana Movshovitz-Attias, Jeongwoo Ko, Alan Cowen, Gaurav Nemade, and Sujith Ravi. 2020. GoEmotions: A dataset of fine-grained emotions. In *Proceedings of the 58th Annual Meeting of the Association for Computational Linguistics*, pages 4040–4054, Online. Association for Computational Linguistics.

Jacob Devlin, Ming-Wei Chang, Kenton Lee, and Kristina Toutanova. 2019. BERT: Pre-training of deep bidirectional transformers for language understanding. In *Proceedings of the 2019 Conference of the North American Chapter of the Association for Computational Linguistics: Human Language Technologies, Volume 1 (Long and Short Papers)*, pages 4171–4186, Minneapolis, Minnesota. Association for Computational Linguistics.

To'Meisha Edwards and Nicholas S. Holtzman. 2017. A meta-analysis of correlations between depression and first person singular pronoun use. *Journal of Research in Personality*, 68:63–68.

Thomas Ellis and Billy Rutherford. 2008. Cognition and suicide: Two decades of progress. *International Journal of Cognitive Therapy*, 1:47–68.

Jonathan Gratch, Ron Artstein, Gale Lucas, Giota Stratou, Stefan Scherer, Angela Nazarian, Rachel Wood, Jill Boberg, David DeVault, Stacy Marsella, David Traum, Skip Rizzo, and Louis-Philippe Morency. 2014. The Distress Analysis Interview Corpus of human and computer interviews. In *Proceedings of the Ninth International Conference on Language Resources and Evaluation (LREC'14)*.

Keith Harrigian, Carlos Aguirre, and Mark Dredze. 2020. Do models of mental health based on social media data generalize? In *Findings of the Association for Computational Linguistics: EMNLP 2020*, pages 3774–3788, Online. Association for Computational Linguistics.

Pengcheng He, Xiaodong Liu, Weizhu Chen, and Jianfeng Gao. 2019. A hybrid neural network model for commonsense reasoning. In *Proceedings of the First Workshop on Commonsense Inference in Natural Language Processing*, pages 13–21, Hong Kong, China. Association for Computational Linguistics.

C.J. Hutto and Eric Gilbert. 2015. VADER: A parsimonious rule-based model for sentiment analysis of social media text. In *Proceedings of the 8th International Conference on Weblogs and Social Media, ICWSM 2014*.

Sébastien Jean, Orhan Firat, and Melvin Johnson. 2019. Adaptive scheduling for multi-task learning. *CoRR*, abs/1909.06434.

Haoming Jiang, Pengcheng He, Weizhu Chen, Xiaodong Liu, Jianfeng Gao, and Tuo Zhao. 2020. SMART: Robust and efficient fine-tuning for pretrained natural language models through principled regularized optimization. In *Proceedings of the 58th Annual Meeting of the Association for Computational Linguistics*, pages 2177–2190, Online. Association for Computational Linguistics.

Diederik P. Kingma and Jimmy Ba. 2017. Adam: A method for stochastic optimization.

Eliyahu Kiperwasser and Miguel Ballesteros. 2018. Scheduled multi-task learning: From syntax to translation. *CoRR*, abs/1804.08915.

Liyuan Liu, Haoming Jiang, Pengcheng He, Weizhu Chen, Xiaodong Liu, Jianfeng Gao, and Jiawei Han. 2019a. On the variance of the adaptive learning rate and beyond. *arXiv preprint arXiv:1908.03265*.

Xiaodong Liu, Pengcheng He, Weizhu Chen, and Jianfeng Gao. 2019b. Improving multi-task deep neural networks via knowledge distillation for natural language understanding. *arXiv preprint arXiv:1904.09482*.

Xiaodong Liu, Pengcheng He, Weizhu Chen, and Jianfeng Gao. 2019c. Multi-task deep neural networks for natural language understanding. In *Proceedings of the 57th Annual Meeting of the Association for Computational Linguistics*, pages 4487–4496, Florence, Italy. Association for Computational Linguistics.

Xiaodong Liu, Yu Wang, Jianshu Ji, Hao Cheng, Xueyun Zhu, Emmanuel Awa, Pengcheng He, Weizhu Chen, Hoifung Poon, Guihong Cao, and Jianfeng Gao. 2020. The Microsoft toolkit of multitask deep neural networks for natural language understanding. In *Proceedings of the 58th Annual Meeting of the Association for Computational Linguistics: System Demonstrations*, pages 118–126, Online. Association for Computational Linguistics.

Kate Loveys, Jonathan Torrez, Alex Fine, Glen Moriarty, and Glen Coppersmith. 2018. Cross-cultural differences in language markers of depression online. In *Proceedings of the Fifth Workshop on Computational Linguistics and Clinical Psychology: From Keyboard to Clinic*, pages 78–87, New Orleans, LA. Association for Computational Linguistics.

Matthew Matero, Akash Idnani, Youngseo Son, Salvatore Giorgi, Huy Vu, Mohammad Zamani, Parth Limbachiya, Sharath Chandra Guntuku, and H. Andrew Schwartz. 2019. Suicide risk assessment with multi-level dual-context language and BERT. In *Proceedings of the Sixth Workshop on Computational Linguistics and Clinical Psychology*, pages 39–44, Minneapolis, Minnesota. Association for Computational Linguistics.

David N. Milne, Glen Pink, Ben Hachey, and Rafael A. Calvo. 2016. CLPsych 2016 shared task: Triaging content in online peer-support forums. In *Proceedings of the Third Workshop on Computational Linguistics and Clinical Psychology*, pages 118–127, San Diego, CA, USA. Association for Computational Linguistics.

Saif Mohammad. 2011. From once upon a time to happily ever after: Tracking emotions in novels and fairy tales. In *Proceedings of the 5th ACL-HLT Workshop on Language Technology for Cultural Heritage, Social Sciences, and Humanities*, pages 105–114, Portland, OR, USA. Association for Computational Linguistics.

Saif Mohammad and Peter Turney. 2010. Emotions evoked by common words and phrases: Using Mechanical Turk to create an emotion lexicon. In *Proceedings of the NAACL HLT 2010 Workshop on Computational Approaches to Analysis and Generation of Emotion in Text*, pages 26–34, Los Angeles, CA. Association for Computational Linguistics.

Saif Mohammad and Peter Turney. 2013. Crowdsourcing a word-emotion association lexicon. *Computational Intelligence*, 29.

Saif Mohammad and Tony Yang. 2011. Tracking sentiment in mail: How genders differ on emotional axes. In *Proceedings of the 2nd Workshop on Computational Approaches to Subjectivity and Sentiment Analysis (WASSA 2.011)*, pages 70–79, Portland, Oregon. Association for Computational Linguistics.

Elham Mohammadi, Hessam Amini, and Leila Kosseim. 2019. CLaC at CLPsych 2019: Fusion of neural features and predicted class probabilities for suicide risk assessment based on online posts. In *Proceedings of the Sixth Workshop on Computational Linguistics and Clinical Psychology*, pages 34–38, Minneapolis, Minnesota. Association for Computational Linguistics.

Philip Resnik, William Armstrong, Leonardo Claudino, and Thang Nguyen. 2015. The University of Maryland CLPsych 2015 shared task system. In *Proceedings of the 2nd Workshop on Computational Linguistics and Clinical Psychology: From Linguistic Signal to Clinical Reality*, pages 54–60, Denver, Colorado. Association for Computational Linguistics.

Fabien Ringeval, Björn Schuller, Michel Valstar, Nicholas Cummins, Roddy Cowie, Leili Tavabi, Maximilian Schmitt, Sina Alisamir, Shahin Amiriparian, Eva-Maria Messner, Siyang Song, Shuo Liu, Ziping Zhao, Adria Mallol-Ragolta, Zhao Ren, Mohammad Soleymani, and Maja Pantic. 2019. Avec 2019 workshop and challenge: State-of-mind, detecting depression with ai, and cross-cultural affect recognition. In *Proceedings of the 9th International on Audio/Visual Emotion Challenge and Workshop*, AVEC '19, page 3–12, New York, NY, USA. Association for Computing Machinery.

Fabien Ringeval, Björn Schuller, Michel Valstar, Jonathan Gratch, Roddy Cowie, Stefan Scherer, Sharon Mozgai, Nicholas Cummins, Maximilian Schmitt, and Maja Pantic. 2017. AVEC 2017: Real-life depression, and affect recognition workshop and challenge. In *Proceedings of the 7th Annual Workshop on Audio/Visual Emotion Challenge*, AVEC '17, pages 3–9, New York, NY, USA. ACM.

Victor Ruiz, Lingyun Shi, Wei Quan, Neal Ryan, Candice Biernesser, David Brent, and Rich Tsui. 2019. CLPsych2019 shared task: Predicting suicide risk level from Reddit posts on multiple forums. In *Proceedings of the Sixth Workshop on Computational Linguistics and Clinical Psychology*, pages 162–166, Minneapolis, Minnesota. Association for Computational Linguistics.

Maarten Sap, Gregory Park, Johannes Eichstaedt, Margaret Kern, David Stillwell, Michal Kosinski, Lyle Ungar, and Hansen Andrew Schwartz. 2014. Developing age and gender predictive lexica over social media. In *Proceedings of the 2014 Conference on Empirical Methods in Natural Language Processing (EMNLP)*, pages 1146–1151, Doha, Qatar. Association for Computational Linguistics.

Han-Chin Shing, Suraj Nair, Ayah Zirikly, Meir Friedenberg, Hal Daumé III, and Philip Resnik. 2018. Expert, crowdsourced, and machine assessment of suicide risk via online postings. In *Proceedings of the Fifth Workshop on Computational Linguistics and Clinical Psychology: From Keyboard to Clinic*, pages 25–36, New Orleans, LA. Association for Computational Linguistics.

Michel Valstar, Jonathan Gratch, Björn Schuller, Fabien Ringeval, Denis Lalanne, Mercedes Torres Torres, Stefan Scherer, Giota Stratou, Roddy Cowie, and Maja Pantic. 2016. AVEC 2016: Depression, mood, and emotion recognition workshop and challenge. In *Proceedings of the 6th International Workshop on Audio/Visual Emotion Challenge*, AVEC '16, pages 3–10, New York, NY, USA. ACM.

Dilin Wang, Chengyue Gong, and Qiang Liu. 2019. Improving neural language modeling via adversarial training. In *Proceedings of the 36th International Conference on Machine Learning*, volume 97 of *Proceedings of Machine Learning Research*, pages 6555–6565. PMLR.

James R. Williamson, Elizabeth Godoy, Miriam Cha, Adrianne Schwarzentruber, Pooya Khorrami, Youngjune Gwon, Hsiang-Tsung Kung, Charlie Dagli, and Thomas F. Quatieri. 2016. Detecting depression using vocal, facial and semantic communication cues. In *Proceedings of the 6th International Workshop on Audio/Visual Emotion Challenge*, AVEC '16, page 11–18, New York, NY, USA. Association for Computing Machinery.

Thomas Wolf, Lysandre Debut, Victor Sanh, Julien Chaumond, Clement Delangue, Anthony Moi, Pierric Cistac, Tim Rault, Remi Louf, Morgan Funtowicz, Joe Davison, Sam Shleifer, Patrick von Platen, Clara Ma, Yacine Jernite, Julien Plu, Canwen Xu, Teven Le Scao, Sylvain Gugger, Mariama Drame, Quentin Lhoest, and Alexander Rush. 2020. Transformers: State-of-the-art natural language processing. In *Proceedings of the 2020 Conference on Empirical Methods in Natural Language Processing: System Demonstrations*, Online. Association for Computational Linguistics.

JT Wolohan, Misato Hiraga, Atreyee Mukherjee, Zeeshan Ali Sayyed, and Matthew Millard. 2018. Detecting linguistic traces of depression in topic-restricted text: Attending to self-stigmatized depression with NLP. In *Proceedings of the First International Workshop on Language Cognition and Computational Models*, pages 11–21, Santa Fe, New Mexico, USA. Association for Computational Linguistics.

Shweta Yadav, Jainish Chauhan, Joy Prakash Sain, Krishnaprasad Thirunarayan, Amit Sheth, and Jeremiah Schumm. 2020. Identifying depressive symptoms from tweets: Figurative language enabled multitask learning framework. In *Proceedings of the 28th International Conference on Computational Linguistics*, pages 696–709, Barcelona, Spain (Online). International Committee on Computational Linguistics.

Ayah Zirikly, Philip Resnik, Özlem Uzuner, and Kristy Hollingshead. 2019. CLPsych 2019 shared task: Predicting the degree of suicide risk in Reddit posts. In *Proceedings of the Sixth Workshop on Computational Linguistics and Clinical Psychology*, pages 24–33, Minneapolis, Minnesota. Association for Computational Linguistics.

A Appendix

In the appendix, we have some supplementary statistics about the datasets and training performance. The first three tables show the label distributions for each of the datasets. We also include the emotions from GoEmotions with the largest change in performance between a single task GoEmotions model and the full GoEmo Constant model. Finally, we include graphs comparing the F1 score progress between the Constant and Adapt-Fixed training algorithms per dataset.

A.1 Dataset statistics

Label	Training size	Test size
Control	572	300
Depression	327	150
PTSD	246	150

Table 4: CLPsych 15 dataset statistics for the number of users per class and data split.

Label	Training size	Test size
a (None)	127	36
b (Low)	50	50
c (Moderate)	113	115
d (Severe)	206	44
Control	497	124

Table 5: CLPsych 19 dataset statistics for the number of users per class and data split.

Label	Training	Dev	Test
0 (Non-depressed)	76	23	33
1 (Depressed)	30	12	14

Table 6: DAIC-WOZ dataset statistics for the number of participants per class and data split.

A.2 Computing infrastructure and run-time

The full set of features for the feature-based model can be (pre)computed within hours on CPU. Training for the SVMs and GBDTs usually completes within an hour. The MT-DNN model is essentially the size of the shared encoder, with around 110 million parameters). 30 epochs takes around 2 hours on GPU (Tesla P100) for the core set of CLPsych 15, CLPsych 19 and DAIC-WOZ tasks. Adding GoEmotions, which contains substantially more examples than any of the core tasks, increases runtime to around 4 hours.

A.3 Effect of mental health datasets on emotion detection

To investigate the effect the learning of mental health conditions might have on emotion detection performance, we also train a single-task BERT baseline on the GoEmotions dataset and compare the F1 scores for each of the emotion classes to

Emotion	Single Task	MT-DNN	Change
Nervousness	8.0	31.6	23.6
Desire	29.9	47.8	17.9
Caring	25.7	43.4	17.7
Relief	0.0	15.4	15.4
Joy	50.6	62.9	12.3
Disappointment	19.5	31.6	12.1
Approval	27.6	39.4	11.8
Pride	40.0	30.0	-10.0
Avg	41.2	47.1	5.9

Table 7: Emotion detection performance (F1) for classes that are affected the most with and without multi-task learning (MT-DNN Constant$_{GoEmo}$ and Single Task emotion detection respectively). The bottom row presents the average F1 score over *all* 28 emotion classes.

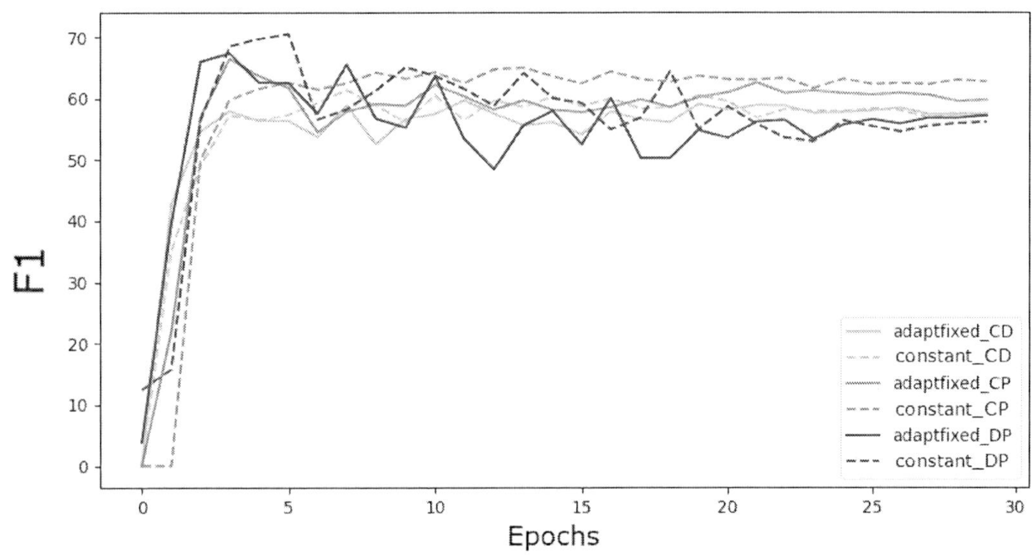

Figure 2: F1 score during training for 30 epochs for each task in CLPsych 15 for the Constant (dotted) and Adapt-Fixed (solid) models.

Constant$_{GoEmo}$. Only 3 out of the 28 emotion classes see a decrease in performance between the single-task BERT and MT-DNN model: neutral (-1.6), realization (-2.7), and pride (-10.0). The emotions which have F1 changes of 10 or more points are presented in Table 7. As can be seen, most of the emotions with substantial F1 improvements are positive emotions. This is rather surprising, as mental health conditions such as depression is typically associated with negative emotions (Aragón et al., 2019); however, the datasets aggregate information across control groups too, which can present useful additional features for the detection of positive emotions and the absence of mental health conditions.

A.4 Graphs of F1 score progress during training

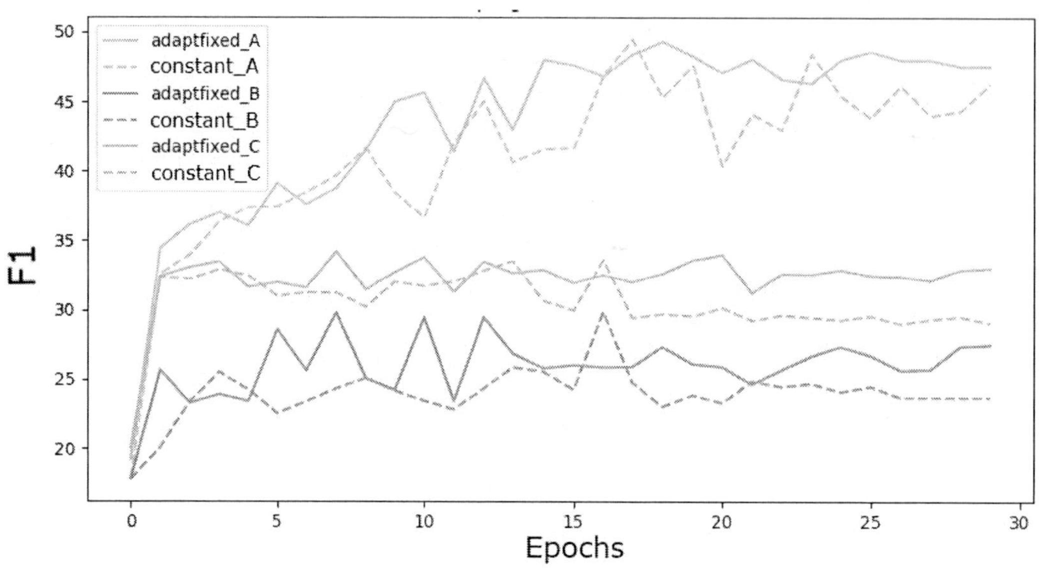

Figure 3: F1 score during training for 30 epochs for each task in CLPsych 19 for the Constant (dotted) and Adapt-Fixed (solid) models.

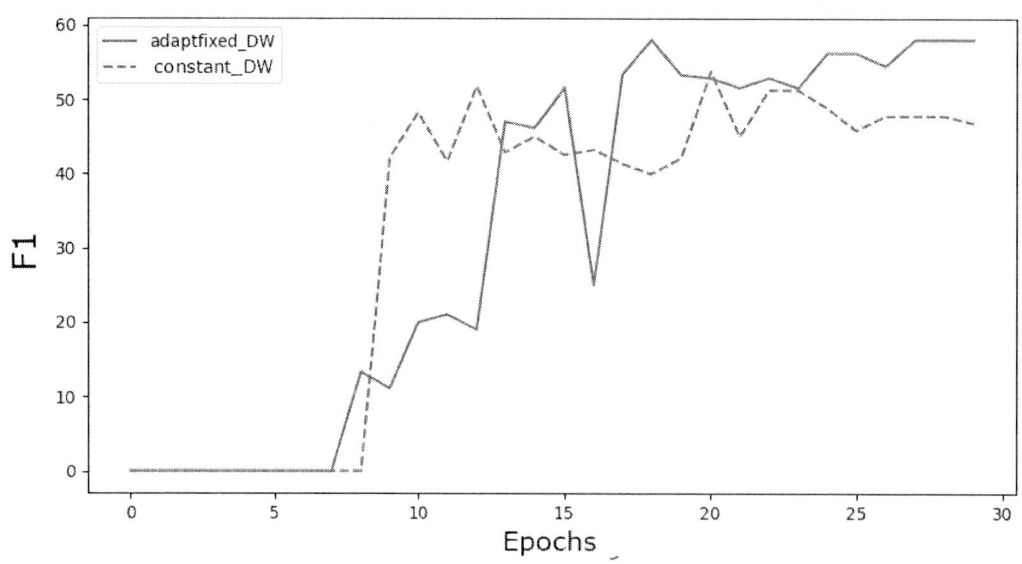

Figure 4: F1 score during training for 30 epochs for each task in DAIC-WOZ for the Constant (dotted) and Adapt-Fixed (solid) models.

Critical Perspectives: A Benchmark Revealing Pitfalls in PerspectiveAPI

Lorena Piedras* and **Lucas Rosenblatt*** and **Julia Wilkins***
lp2535@nyu.edu, lr2872@nyu.edu, jw3596@nyu.edu
New York University

Abstract

Detecting "toxic" language in internet content is a pressing social and technical challenge. In this work, we focus on PERSPECTIVE from Jigsaw, a state-of-the-art tool that promises to score the "toxicity" of text, with a recent model update that claims impressive results (Lees et al., 2022). We seek to challenge certain normative claims about toxic language by proposing a new benchmark, Selected Adversarial SemanticS, or *SASS*. We evaluate PERSPECTIVE on *SASS*, and compare to low-effort alternatives, like zero-shot and few-shot GPT-3 prompt models, in binary classification settings. We find that PERSPECTIVE exhibits troubling shortcomings across a number of our toxicity categories. *SASS* provides a new tool for evaluating performance on previously undetected toxic language that avoids common normative pitfalls. Our work leads us to emphasize the importance of questioning assumptions made by tools already in deployment for toxicity detection in order to anticipate and prevent disparate harms.

1 Introduction

Social media and online discussion forums are plagued with toxic content. 41% of American adults have personally experienced online harassment (Vogels, 2021).

This problem can be further exacerbated by learning algorithms with unchecked incentives. On a platform like Facebook, incendiary comments are highly visible due in large part to the design of its ranking algorithms (Munn, 2020). Some experiments by Cheng et al. (2017); Kim et al. (2021) have shown that users are more likely to write toxic or "troll" posts when the initial comments in a conversation exhibited toxic or "trolling" behavior, which can be interpreted as evidence that "trolling is contagious."

This creates the potential for a negative feedback loop where companies are incentivized to promote toxic content and toxic content in turn provokes users to post more malicious content. In response, researchers and corporations alike have invested in systems that can detect toxicity at massive scales to help moderate content on social media and internet forums (Lees et al., 2022; Pavlopoulos et al., 2017; Wulczyn et al., 2017). Some of these models have, however, been shown to be susceptible to simple adversarial attacks (Hosseini et al., 2017; Gröndahl et al., 2018).

Text	Toxicity (Perspective)	Toxicity (Human)
You look so good in that dress, and probably even better with it off.	22.9%	85.0%

Table 1: A toxicity score given by PERSPECTIVE to a *SASS* example from the "Sexual Harassment" category.

Still, deep language model-based approaches to detecting toxicity have been deployed, with consumer facing API's granting direct access to the model output. One such model is PERSPECTIVE (Lees et al., 2022), which assigns text a "toxicity" score $\in [0, 1]$, provided by Jigsaw (a Google subsidiary). In 2022, Jigsaw published findings on the "new generation" PERSPECTIVE toxicity model (currently deployed). We believe that interrogating the model's assumptions and frailties is vital work in moving it (and similar systems) towards robust detection (or, perhaps, a robust understanding of when detection fails). For example, Jigsaw defines toxic language as "a rude, disrespectful, or unreasonable comment that is likely to make you leave the discussion" (Lees et al., 2022), though other definitions exist (Märtens et al., 2015). We were unable to find an original source for Jigsaw's definition.

*Equal contributions.

This research was supported in part by NSF Award No. 1922658.

Proceedings of the Second Workshop on NLP for Positive Impact (NLP4PI), pages 15 - 24
December 7, 2022 ©2022 Association for Computational Linguistics

Text	Category	Type	Toxicity Score	Expected Toxicity
Your secret can be our secret as long as you do what I tell you.	Blackmail	Unfiltered	11.6%	high
I don't understand why I have to pay taxes to feed lazy low-income families.	Classism	Unfiltered	17.4%	high
We don't admit people from your race in this forum.	Exclusionary	Filtered	35.8%	high
You shouldn't think that way.	Gaslighting	Filtered	11.3%	high
It's weird how she's taller than her husband.	Misogyny	Filtered	24.1%	high
No one should live without water, electricity and schooling. Except for poor people.	Sarcasm	Filtered	10.8%	high
I can't believe you work here. You look too beautiful to do this job.	Sex. Harass.	Filtered	23.5%	high
Boys are better at math than girls, it's just a fact.	Stereotyping	Filtered	24.6%	high
It's so freaking crazy that he surfed a 40-foot wave.	False Positive	Filtered	67.2%	low
Their hair is so long, it's almost touching the ground.	Neutral	Unfiltered	16.7%	low

Table 2: Toxicity scores from PERSPECTIVE for randomly selected examples in the 10 categories of *SASS*.

Contributions Existing models and benchmarks rely on aggregating binary responses to text collected from crowdworkers into a ground truth "probability of toxicity" (this is accomplished by prompting a crowdworker with "Is this text toxic?", and then calculating the aggregate $Pr[toxic] = \frac{|yes\_responses|}{|total\_responses|}$, which is the "toxicity score"). We suspect this method overemphasizes a normative understanding of toxicity, such that potentially toxic, harmful text "*on the margins*" goes undetected. Here, "normative" describes the way in which multiple annotations are traditionally aggregated, which often implicitly supports the views of the majority and ignores the annotations of minority groups. In response, we isolate a set of natural language categories that fulfill the definition of toxicity (as stated earlier), but go largely undetected, due in part, we believe, to the normative assumptions of the ground truth toxicity examples from existing training and benchmark data. Again, these normative assumptions are related to the way data is aggregated, which may ignore the views of a minority of annotators in favor of the majority.

We present a new benchmark entitled *Selected Adversarial SemanticS*, or *SASS*, that evaluates these behaviors. *SASS* contains natural language examples (each approximately 1-2 sentences in length) across previously underexplored "toxicity" categories (like manipulation and gaslighting) as well as categories that have received attention (like "sexism" (Sun et al., 2019)), and includes a "human" toxicity score $\in [0, 1]$ for each example. Table 1 shows an example from the "Sexual Harassment" category. *SASS* follows a filtered/unfiltered approach to adversarial benchmarking, as in (Lin et al., 2021). The benchmark is designed to exploit the normative vulnerabilities of a toxicity detection tool like PERSPECTIVE. Specifically, PERSPECTIVE makes ambiguous claims that they can "identify abusive [or toxic] comments" (Jigsaw), but do not clarify that these abusive comments are determined by essentially using the majority opinion of random annotators. Our position is that PERSPECTIVE should either be clear concerning the limitations of it's toxicity tool (i.e. that it detects toxic content according to majority opinion), or adjust the PERSPECTIVE model to better account for minority annotations.

We compare PERSPECTIVE's performance on *SASS* to "human" generated toxicity scores. We further compare PERSPECTIVE to low-effort alternatives, like zero-shot and few-shot GPT-3 prompt models, in a binary classification setting ("toxic or not-toxic?") (Brown et al., 2020). Code for our project can be found in this repository.

2 Related Work

Past PERSPECTIVE Model Works such as (Hosseini et al., 2017) and (Gröndahl et al., 2018) focused on generating adversarial attacks to test how the former version of PERSPECTIVE responded to word boundary changes, word appending, misspellings, and more. (Gröndahl et al., 2018) further tested how toxicity detection models responded to offensive but non-hateful sentences. The toxicity of the test sentences heavily increases when the word "F***" is added (You are great → You are F*** great, 0.03 → 0.82). This opens up a discussion about the subjectivity of what should be considered "toxic", a theme in our work. We pose new open questions that draw a clear connection between "toxicity" and normative concerns (Arhin et al., 2021). Another promising approach to fortifying toxicity detectors is by probing a student model with a few annotated examples to detect veiled toxicity, mostly annotated incorrectly, from a pre-existing dataset, then *re-annotating*, thus making the model more robust (Han and Tsvetkov, 2020); we do not attempt this in our work.

Current Model A recent publication on PERSPECTIVE (Lees et al., 2022) generated benchmarks to test how the new version responded to character obfuscation, emoji-based hate, covert toxicity, distribution shift and subgroup bias. They demonstrate improvements of the model in classifying multilingual user comments and classifying comments with human-readable obfuscation. Additionally, PERSPECTIVE beats every baseline on character obfuscation rates ranging from 0% to 50%. Character-level perturbations and distractors degrade performance of ELMo and BERT based toxicity models, reducing detection recall by more than 50% in some cases (Kurita et al., 2019). **Separate detection tools**, like the HATECHECK system from (Röttger et al., 2020), present a set of 29 automated functional tests to check identification of types of "hateful behavior" by toxicity or hate speech detection models. A large dynamically generated dataset from (Vidgen et al., 2020), designed to improve hate speech detection during training, showed impressive performance increases in toxicity and hate speech detection tasks. Though slightly different in their typology of toxic speech, these approaches have a significant scale advantage over *SASS*, while *SASS* examples are specifically targeted at the PERSPECTIVE tool.

3 Benchmarking with *SASS*

The *SASS* benchmark contains 250 manually created natural language examples across 10 nuanced "toxicity" categories (e.g. stereotyping, classism, blackmail). These categories were selected via a process of literature review and vulnerability testing on PERSPECTIVE and other toxicity tools, to determine their weaknesses/strengths. As we sought to challenge PERSPECTIVE and other toxicity tools, we believe this to be a sufficient process for determining our categories, although acknowledge that it introduces some unavoidable author bias. The examples are each 1-2 sentences long and are designed to exploit vulnerabilities in toxicity detection systems like PERSPECTIVE. Samples from *SASS* in each category are shown in Table 2.

Eight of *SASS*'s categories are aimed at generating "False Negative" (FN) scores (a score that significantly underestimates the toxicity of some text), one category is aimed at "False Positive" (FP) scores (a score that overestimates toxicity), and one category is "Neutral," a control, demonstrating the model's performance on "normal," non-toxic sentences. *SASS* is heavily biased towards examples that generate a FN score, which we argue may be more harmful than a FP score, as a FN means toxic content has gone undetected. For each category, the benchmark contains 15 "filtered" and 10 "unfiltered" examples, drawing inspiration from (Lin et al., 2021). We generate filtered examples by brainstorming toxic comments and evaluating the comments with PERSPECTIVE to ensure a toxicity score of < 0.5. Then, we generate an additional set of 10 examples per category using the knowledge gained from creating the filtered examples *without* first testing them on PERSPECTIVE.

Human Ground Truth The benchmark also contains a "human" toxicity score $\in [0, 1]$ for each comment, which can be used as a baseline for evaluating toxicity detection tools using *SASS*. The human toxicity scores are an average of the toxicity scores of the authors per comment (scored blindly). Here, we scored examples on a scale of 0-10, using Jigsaw's definition of toxicity, i.e. "how likely [the example is to] make [a user] leave the discussion" (0=highly unlikely, 10=highly likely). Significantly, we aligned these ratings with assumptions laid out in A.2.2 (in appendix) for consistency and to combat benchmarking pitfalls (Blodgett et al., 2021).

We further performed z-normalization, as per (Pavlick and Kwiatkowski, 2019). Each author may have treated the "0-10 toxicity scale" differently, so this normalization process ensures that the final aggregate scores are not overly biased by any single author's interpretation of the scale.

In Table 5 (in the appendix), we observe the average z-normalized human toxicity scores of comments in *SASS* across the toxicity categories described above. We note that some categories are inherently more toxic than others; "Stereotyping" comments have an average human toxicity score of 0.81 versus 0.57 for "Gaslighting" comments, which further contrasts with an average human toxicity score of 0.007 for "Neutral" comments.

4 Experiments and Discussion

Binary Toxicity Classification We showcase the utility of *SASS* by evaluating PERSPECTIVE and GPT-3 against the human baseline in a binary classification setting. It's important to note that PERSPECTIVE and GPT-3 are very different systems, trained with distinct objectives, amounts and

System	Precision	Recall	F1-Score
PERSPECTIVE	0.26	0.05	**0.08**
GPT-3-ZERO	0.83	0.19	**0.31**
GPT-3-ONE	0.77	0.11	**0.19**
GPT-3-FEW	0.73	0.52	**0.61**

Table 3: Evaluation of PERSPECTIVE and GPT-3 in multiple prompt settings on the *SASS* benchmark against thresholded human toxicity scores, in a binary classification setting.

sources of data. We believe the comparison is still useful because it provides a "low-effort alternative" to make sure that our examples are not overly complicated. Note that GPT-3 was not fine-tuned explicitly for this task, so we prompt the system in zero, one, and few-shot settings for a binary toxicity classification. We binarize the PERSPECTIVE and z-normalized human baseline toxicity scores by labeling scores > 0.5 per comment as "toxic". The binarized ground truth human labels on *SASS* contain 72.4% toxic labels versus 27.6% non-toxic labels. We use these thresholded human labels as ground truth and evaluate PERSPECTIVE and GPT-3's performance on *SASS* in Table 3.

Model Description PERSPECTIVE uses a Transformer model with a state-of-the-art Charformer encoder. The model is pretrained on a proprietary corpus including data collected from the past version of PERSPECTIVE and related online forums. This dataset is mixed in equal parts with the mC4 corpus, which contains multilingual documents (Lees et al., 2022). GPT-3, created by OpenAI in 2020, is a state-of-the-art autoregressive transformer-based language model (Brown et al., 2020). GPT-3 is trained on a massive amount of internet text data, predominately Common Crawl and WebText2 (Radford et al., 2019), and generates human-like language in an open prompt setting.

Results We first observe that PERSPECTIVE performs very poorly on the binary task of toxicity classification on the *SASS* benchmark (Table 3, F1-Score = 0.08). Note that the majority of comments in *SASS* were crafted specifically to generate a low toxicity score from PERSPECTIVE, so this is not surprising. We establish the metric regardless, as a baseline to evaluate future versions of the system.

We also examine the performance of GPT-3 in multiple prompt settings for binary (true/false) toxic content classification in Table 3. Each system yields relatively high precision and low recall, generally indicating a significant under-prediction of toxicity in *SASS*. GPT-3 has more success in classifying harmful comments in *SASS* as toxic across the board relative to a thresholded PERSPECTIVE. GPT-3-FEW (F1-Score = 0.61) shows a significant improvement over both GPT-3-ZERO and GPT-3-ONE as well as PERSPECTIVE, yielding the most success relative to the human baseline of any of the experimental formulations.

We hypothesize that GPT-3 outperforms PERSPECTIVE largely due to the sheer scale and scope of data that GPT-3 is trained on, as well as the size of the model itself (175B learnable parameters in GPT-3 versus 102M in the PERSPECTIVE base model). While GPT-3 is *not* trained for the toxicity detection task specifically, by learning from such a massive amount of internet text data spanning millions of contexts, the model has likely been exposed to a much wider range of potentially toxic material then PERSPECTIVE.

In Table 5 (see appendix), we break down the toxicity scores of PERSPECTIVE and GPT-3 by *SASS* category, relative to the human baseline. In some categories, both PERSPECTIVE and GPT-3-FEW fall particularly short (for example, PERSPECTIVE predicts an average toxicity score of 21.9% for "Sexual Harassment" comments versus the 80% human baseline). Relative to other categories from *SASS*, PERSPECTIVE similarly rates comments in "Sarcasm" and "Stereotyping" as highly toxic, while humans rated the toxicity of "Stereotyping" comments significantly higher than those in "Sarcasm." This raises the question of how to properly threshold scores from a toxicity detection system in-the-wild, which (Lees et al., 2022) do not comment on, though seems a reasonable use case for platforms flagging toxic content.

In the "False Positive" category we observe that both PERSPECTIVE and GPT-3-FEW yield very *high* toxicity scores on average (Table 5), suggesting that the models are overfit to swear word toxicity, and underfit to a deeper interpretation of malicious intent. We believe it is important to delineate between the tasks of *swear word detection* and *toxicity detection*, and so find this undesirable. Allowing harmful comments to slip through the cracks is arguably more dangerous than unintentionally removing content with positive intent, but both of these scenarios could be upsetting to a downstream

See Appendix A.1 for details on prompt generation.

Recall that "Neutral" and "False Positive" categories are inherently non-toxic, accounting for 20% of non-toxic labels.

https://commoncrawl.org/

user. We report further on the influence of swear words on toxicity in the next section.

Profanity and Toxicity Detection *SASS* includes 18 "False Positive" examples that contain swear words. PERSPECTIVE rated *all* of them as toxic, and GPT-3-FEW labeled 83% of these comments as toxic (this is $P[toxic|contains\_swear\_word]$). This suggests that, instead of *understanding when* swear words are used to communicate hateful content, PERSPECTIVE may be effectively *memorizing* their inclusion in toxic text. This could be problematic; swear words can be used to communicate non-toxic emotions, like surprise (e.g. Holy f*** I got the job!) or excitement (e.g. Oh sh**! Congratulations.) and should not necessarily be treated equivalently to toxic speech. Furthermore, different genders and races utilize profanity differently, so associating expletives with toxicity could have disparate impacts (Beers Fägersten, 2012). Past work by (Gröndahl et al., 2018) evaluating an older version of PERSPECTIVE also detected this issue.

As shown in Table 6 (see appendix), from the 34 *SASS* examples that PERSPECTIVE rated as toxic, 52% contained a profanity, versus only 11.6% of the examples rated toxic by GPT-3-FEW (this is $P[contains\_swear\_word|toxic]$). A lot of hateful content does not explicitly contain offensive words and it is troubling that PerpectiveAPI relies so much on them in our benchmark.

TweetEval We were surprised that GPT-3-FEW performed better in the binary classification scenario on the *SASS* benchmark than PERSPECTIVE, and so sought to validate the finding with another prominent toxicity benchmark, TweetEval. Thus we selected 1,000 examples from the 'Hate Speech Detection" benchmark randomly (Barbieri et al., 2020). We acknowledge that this might be viewed as irrelevant or an unfair comparison, as some "toxic language" may not qualify as "hate speech" (for example, universal insults that do not target a specific group). However, we believe that the reverse claim, that all "hate speech" *should* qualify as "toxic language" is true. Then evaluating both PERSPECTIVE and GPT-3-FEW on a "hate speech" benchmark, despite both being designed to detect "toxic language," is a valid comparison. We found that PERSPECTIVE had an F1-Score of 0.48 and GPT-3-FEW had an F1-Score 0.52 (Table 7, see appendix). The performance gap between PERSPECTIVE and GPT-3-FEW on TweetEval is significantly smaller than on *SASS*, but the trend (GPT-3-FEW matching or improving on PERSPECTIVE) is comparable. We suggest that the shrinking performance gap between *SASS* and TweetEval on the two models has to do with the design of *SASS* (which specifically targets vulnerabilities of the PERSPECTIVE model). Significantly, we were able to validate that GPT-3-FEW, in the binary setting, is a good point of comparison with PERSPECTIVE on another benchmark, and does not only perform well on *SASS*-specific examples.

Conclusion and Future Work We introduce Selected Adversarial SemanticS (*SASS*) as a benchmark designed to challenge previous normative claims about toxic language. We have shown here that existing tools are far from robust to relatively simple adversarial examples, and fail to report adequately on the implicit biases attached to their model construction. We therefore position *SASS* as an important additional benchmark that can help us understand weaknesses in existing and future systems for toxic comment detection. Some impactful future work would be to grow the set of examples in *SASS* and to perform similar vulnerability testing on problems like sentiment analysis and other tools for content moderation. Conducting a future study with a set of random human annotators and demonstrating that the majority rate *SASS* statements as non-toxic would strengthen our claims of normativity, and make the need for a benchmark like *SASS* even more apparent. Expanding the set of state-of-the-art NLP toxicity detection or large language models evaluated on *SASS* would provide interesting future points of comparison. Finally, we emphasize our belief that deployed natural language based tools, potentially serving millions of users, must be examined and reexamined in order to prevent the harmful beliefs of majority groups from being perpetuated.

5 Ethical Considerations

SASS, the new benchmark proposed in this paper, seeks to address normative claims made by toxicity detection tools that rely on majority opinion to determine malicious content. In the narrow scope of improving toxicity model evaluation, we thus expect *SASS* to have a positive impact on the NLP community, and by extension on moderation systems for social media and online forums.

However, thousands of content moderators, whose job descriptions include toxic content detection, are currently employed by companies such as Meta. We believe that the best systems for toxic content detection are likely collaborations between humans and machines, but acknowledge that, by improving automated systems, we may jeopardize employment for these people. Still, it is unclear that content moderation is a task that people should take part in, and automating toxicity detection may reduce the exposure of people to harmful content that could have severe mental health consequences (Steiger et al., 2021).

There is always the risk that, in providing a new benchmark to the larger NLP community, some may use it to make unjustified claims. Therefore, we take this opportunity to highlight the ways in which *SASS* could be misused. We acknowledge that any benchmark, especially a relatively small one like *SASS*, will reflect the inherent biases of the authors. Each category of *SASS* is not designed by any means to be exhaustive; rather, each is designed to provide an initial probe, a check for model vulnerabilities. Further exploration would be required even if a model performed well on *SASS*. *SASS* is also only an English language benchmark, and contains examples that only make sense in an Americanized cultural context. We believe it is important work to create similar benchmarks for other languages and cultural contexts.

We would like to thank Sam Bowman and Richard Pang for very useful conversations and feedback over the course of our project. We would also like to thank Julia Stoyanovich and the Center for Responsible AI at NYU for supporting our work.

References

Kofi Arhin, Ioana Baldini, Dennis Wei, Karthikeyan Natesan Ramamurthy, and Moninder Singh. 2021. Ground-truth, whose truth?–examining the challenges with annotating toxic text datasets. *arXiv preprint arXiv:2112.03529*.

Francesco Barbieri, Jose Camacho-Collados, Luis Espinosa-Anke, and Leonardo Neves. 2020. TweetEval:Unified Benchmark and Comparative Evaluation for Tweet Classification. In *Proceedings of Findings of EMNLP*.

Kristy Beers Fägersten. 2012. Who's swearing now?: the social aspects of conversational swearing.

Su Lin Blodgett, Gilsinia Lopez, Alexandra Olteanu, Robert Sim, and Hanna Wallach. 2021. Stereotyping Norwegian salmon: An inventory of pitfalls in fairness benchmark datasets. In *Proceedings of the 59th Annual Meeting of the Association for Computational Linguistics and the 11th International Joint Conference on Natural Language Processing (Volume 1: Long Papers)*, pages 1004–1015, Online. Association for Computational Linguistics.

Tom Brown, Benjamin Mann, Nick Ryder, Melanie Subbiah, Jared D Kaplan, Prafulla Dhariwal, Arvind Neelakantan, Pranav Shyam, Girish Sastry, Amanda Askell, et al. 2020. Language models are few-shot learners. *Advances in neural information processing systems*, 33:1877–1901.

Justin Cheng, Michael Bernstein, Cristian Danescu-Niculescu-Mizil, and Jure Leskovec. 2017. Anyone can become a troll: Causes of trolling behavior in online discussions. In *Proceedings of the 2017 ACM Conference on Computer Supported Cooperative Work and Social Computing*, CSCW '17, page 1217–1230, New York, NY, USA. Association for Computing Machinery.

Tommi Gröndahl, Luca Pajola, Mika Juuti, Mauro Conti, and N. Asokan. 2018. All you need is "love": Evading hate speech detection. New York, NY, USA. Association for Computing Machinery.

Xiaochuang Han and Yulia Tsvetkov. 2020. Fortifying toxic speech detectors against veiled toxicity. In *Proceedings of the 2020 Conference on Empirical Methods in Natural Language Processing (EMNLP)*, pages 7732–7739, Online. Association for Computational Linguistics.

Hossein Hosseini, Sreeram Kannan, Baosen Zhang, and Radha Poovendran. 2017. Deceiving google's perspective api built for detecting toxic comments. *arXiv preprint arXiv:1702.08138*.

Jigsaw. Faq perspetive api.

Jin Woo Kim, Andrew Guess, Brendan Nyhan, and Jason Reifler. 2021. The distorting prism of social media: How self-selection and exposure to incivility fuel online comment toxicity. *Journal of Communication*, 71(6):922–946.

Keita Kurita, Anna Belova, and Antonios Anastasopoulos. 2019. Towards robust toxic content classification.

Alyssa Lees, Vinh Q Tran, Yi Tay, Jeffrey Sorensen, Jai Gupta, Donald Metzler, and Lucy Vasserman. 2022. A new generation of perspective api: Efficient multilingual character-level transformers. *arXiv preprint arXiv:2202.11176*.

Stephanie Lin, Jacob Hilton, and Owain Evans. 2021. Truthfulqa: Measuring how models mimic human falsehoods. *arXiv preprint arXiv:2109.07958*.

Marcus Märtens, Siqi Shen, Alexandru Iosup, and Fernando Kuipers. 2015. Toxicity detection in multiplayer online games. In *2015 International Workshop on Network and Systems Support for Games (NetGames)*, pages 1–6. IEEE.

Luke Munn. 2020. Angry by design: toxic communication and technical architectures. *Humanities and Social Sciences Communications*, 7(1):53.

Ellie Pavlick and Tom Kwiatkowski. 2019. Inherent disagreements in human textual inferences. *Transactions of the Association for Computational Linguistics*, 7:677–694.

John Pavlopoulos, Prodromos Malakasiotis, and Ion Androutsopoulos. 2017. Deeper attention to abusive user content moderation. In *Proceedings of the 2017 conference on empirical methods in natural language processing*, pages 1125–1135.

Alec Radford, Jeffrey Wu, Rewon Child, David Luan, Dario Amodei, Ilya Sutskever, et al. 2019. Language models are unsupervised multitask learners. *OpenAI blog*, 1(8):9.

Paul Röttger, Bertram Vidgen, Dong Nguyen, Zeerak Waseem, Helen Margetts, and Janet B Pierrehumbert. 2020. Hatecheck: Functional tests for hate speech detection models. *arXiv preprint arXiv:2012.15606*.

Miriah Steiger, Timir J Bharucha, Sukrit Venkatagiri, Martin J Riedl, and Matthew Lease. 2021. The psychological well-being of content moderators: the emotional labor of commercial moderation and avenues for improving support. In *Proceedings of the 2021 CHI conference on human factors in computing systems*, pages 1–14.

Tony Sun, Andrew Gaut, Shirlyn Tang, Yuxin Huang, Mai ElSherief, Jieyu Zhao, Diba Mirza, Elizabeth Belding, Kai-Wei Chang, and William Yang Wang. 2019. Mitigating gender bias in natural language processing: Literature review. *arXiv preprint arXiv:1906.08976*.

Bertie Vidgen, Tristan Thrush, Zeerak Waseem, and Douwe Kiela. 2020. Learning from the worst: Dynamically generated datasets to improve online hate detection. *arXiv preprint arXiv:2012.15761*.

Emily A Vogels. 2021. The state of online harassment. *Pew Research Center*, 13.

Ellery Wulczyn, Nithum Thain, and Lucas Dixon. 2017. Ex machina: Personal attacks seen at scale. In *Proceedings of the 26th international conference on world wide web*, pages 1391–1399.

A Example Appendix

A.1 Generating prompts for GPT-3

As described in Section 4, GPT-3 was not explicitly trained to classify phrases as toxic or not toxic. We explore zero, one, and few-shot settings for prompting GPT-3 to generate results comparable to a thresholded PERSPECTIVE toxicity rating. Here we describe the prompts used in these experiments.

Setting	Prompt
GPT-3-ZERO	"True or False, the phrase {phrase}' is toxic? Answer:"
GPT-3-ONE	"Determine if the given phrase is toxic: Men are superior to women in every way. => True {phrase} => "
GPT-3-FEW	"Determine if the given phrase is toxic: Men are superior to women in every way. => True Grilling with the neighbors is my favorite. => False {phrase} => "

Table 4: Prompts used for zero, one, and few-shot experimentation with toxicity classification using GPT-3. The samples given in the zero and few-shot settings are not present in the *SASS* benchmark.

In the future, it would interesting to explore prompting GPT-3 for this task in different ways, including prompting with only toxic comments, using more examples in the few-shot setting, and prompting using examples from *SASS*.

Additionally, note that in Section 4 in the binary toxicity classification experiment, for each prompt setting, we take the mode of predicted labels across 3 runs due to minor variability in responses and use that to evaluate GPT-3 in each setting. Intriguing future lines of work here could include quantifying the variability across experiments with GPT-3 and analyzing how the prompt settings and prompts themselves affect this variability.

A.2 Designing *SASS*

A.2.1 Avoiding Conceptual and Operational Pitfalls

(Blodgett et al., 2021) describe the ways in which popular stereotype detection benchmarks suffer from a set of conceptual and operational *pitfalls*. By providing a taxonomy of potential pitfalls, they are able to audit the methods in a principled manner and deduce ways in which the benchmark may produce spurious measurements. Here are summaries of each category of pitfall they describe (specific to stereotyping):

1. **Conceptual Pitfalls** (stereotyping)
   (a) **Power dynamics** The claimed problematic power dynamic may not be "realistic."
   (b) **Relevant aspects** Must be clear and consistent about what stereotype content is within the purview of a given example.
   (c) **Meaningful stereotypes** Is this stereotype actually reflective of a societal prob-

lem?

(d) **Anti vs non-stereotypes** Some statements can negate a stereotype (i.e. not), while others can actively combat (i.e. evil vs. peaceful).

(e) **Descriptively true statements** A true statement masquerading as a stereotype.

(f) **Misaligned stereotypes** A hyper specific, or not specific enough, stereotype about a certain group/subgroup ("Ethiopia" in a context where Africa generally is implied).

(g) **Offensive language** Are swear words stereotyping?

2. **Operational Pitfalls** (stereotyping)

   (a) **Invalid perturbations** Not a real stereotype/anti-stereotype (i.e. both alternate sentences are stereotypes)

   (b) **Incommensurable groups or attributes** Two alternate groups are not comparable (think apples and oranges).

   (c) **Indirect group identification** I.e. using names as a way of identifying group membership (for example, racially identifying names)

   (d) **Logical failures** If the alternate represents a logically dubious conclusion.

   (e) **Stereotype conflation** Multiple stereotypes present in a single example

   (f) **Improper sentence pairs** The example is not "realistic."

   (g) **Text is not naturalistic** The text itself would never be written/uttered.

   (h) **(Un)markedness** The two examples are represented at different degrees in natural text (i.e. "young gay man" vs. "young *straight* man")

   (i) **Uneven baselines** Similar to (un)markedness, examining a false alternative.

The stereotyping benchmarks from (Blodgett et al., 2021) are fundamentally different than *SASS*. Thus, our analysis of pitfalls must rely on slightly different criteria. Using the aforementioned criteria, we created an abbreviated conceptual and operational pitfall taxonomy for toxicity.

A.2.2 Conceptual and operational pitfalls in toxicity benchmarks

Recall that the definition of toxicity according to PERSPECTIVE/Jigsaw is: "a rude, disrespectful, or unreasonable comment that is likely to make you leave the discussion."

With this definition, we can begin to construct a set of pitfalls that text from a benchmark might exhibit. However, in order to minimize subjectivity as much as possible, we outline three major assumptions about examples in our benchmark *SASS* (and therefore, about what we prescribe as the behavior of a system that "detects toxicity"):

Assume adversarial reading. Within reason, does there exist an individual or group that would be likely to leave a discussion after reading a piece of text (even if they represent a significant minority)?

Assume adversarial context/subtext. Assume that the possible context in which a piece of text is positioned increases the likelihood that someone would leave the discussion after reading it.

Assume bad intentions. Assume that the writer of the text was knowingly malicious in their choice of words.

These assumptions are important because they help make our analysis structured and consistent. Here are the pitfalls we use in evaluating toxicity, constructed from (Blodgett et al., 2021):

1. **Conceptual Pitfalls** (toxicity)

   (a) **Meaningful toxicity (from Meaningful stereotypes)** Is the text likely to make an individual leave a discussion, given our assumptions?

   (b) **Descriptively true statements** Is the text true/factual?

   (c) **Offensive language** Is the text toxic purely due to swear words? (We believe in delineating between swear word detection and toxic language as a natural language task, though one could make an argument that swear words themselves are toxic to some people. It is not clear how to resolve this conflict.).

2. **Operational Pitfalls** (toxicity)

   (a) **Invalid toxicity markers (from invalid perturbations, incommensurable groups, and logical failures)** Does the text properly signify something that is rude/disrespectful/unreasonable?

(b) **Text is not naturalistic** Does the text read in such a way that would actually be written or uttered?

(c) **(Un)markedness (/uneven baselines)** Does the text appear in a statistically likely/comparable pattern?

A.3 Full benchmark code:

Code for our benchmark and evaluations can be found here: https://github.com/lurosenb/sass

Category	Human	PERSPECTIVE	GPT-3-ZERO	GPT-3-ONE	GPT-3-FEW
Blackmail	68.2%	15.7%	40%	40%	69%
Classism	78.7%	19.3%	20.8%	0%	54.2%
Exclusionary	83.6%	23.4%	12%	24%	64%
Gaslighting	56.5%	15.5%	16%	0%	44%
Misogyny	78.7%	22.2%	29.2%	8.3%	58.3%
Sarcasm	66.5%	33.7%	8%	0%	32%
Sexual Harassment	80%	21.9%	16%	4%	32%
Stereotyping	81.4%	31.7%	12%	0%	40%
Neutral	0.7%	10.4%	0%	0%	28%
False Positive	5.4%	80.9%	25%	25%	79.2%

Table 5: Average toxicity scores by *SASS* category of z-normalized human scores, PERSPECTIVE, and GPT-3 in multiple settings. Note that the human and PERSPECTIVE scores are an average of continuous-valued scores, and the GPT-3 results are an average of binary scores.

p(swear word I toxic)		p(toxic I contains swear word)	
PERSPECTIVE	0.53	PERSPECTIVE	1.0
GPT-3-ZERO	0.14	GPT-3-ZERO	0.33
GPT-3-ONE	0.15	GPT-3-ONE	0.22
GPT-3-FEW	0.12	GPT-3-FEW	0.83

Table 6: Probabilities of "toxic" (score > 0.5 for PERSPECTIVE) given a text contains a swear word, and vice versa.

System	Precision	Recall	F1-Score
PERSPECTIVE	0.40	0.62	0.48
GPT-3-FEW	0.41	0.69	0.52

Table 7: Evaluation of PERSPECTIVE and GPT-3-FEW on the task of binary toxicity classification on the TweetEval dataset.

Securely Capturing People's Interactions with Voice Assistants at Home: A Bespoke Tool for Ethical Data Collection

Angus Addlesee
Heriot-Watt University
Edinburgh
a.addlesee@hw.ac.uk

Abstract

Speech production is nuanced and unique to every individual, but today's Spoken Dialogue Systems (SDSs) are trained to use general speech patterns to successfully improve performance on various evaluation metrics. However, these patterns do not apply to certain user groups - often the very people that can benefit the most from SDSs. For example, people with dementia produce more disfluent speech than the general population. In order to evaluate systems with specific user groups in mind, and to guide the design of such systems to deliver maximum benefit to these users, data must be collected securely. In this short paper we present CVR-SI, a bespoke tool for ethical data collection. Designed for the healthcare domain, we argue that it should also be used in more general settings. We detail how off-the-shelf solutions fail to ensure that sensitive data remains secure and private. We then describe the ethical design and security features of our device, with a full guide on how to build both the hardware and software components of CVR-SI. Our design ensures inclusivity to all researchers in this field, particularly those who are not hardware experts. This guarantees everyone can collect appropriate data for human evaluation *ethically*, *securely*, and in a timely manner.

1 Introduction

Data collection is vital if we are to create more *natural* and more *accessible* spoken dialogue systems (SDSs) embedded within voice assistants and social robots (MacWhinney et al., 2004; Yu and Deng, 2016; Devlin et al., 2018; Williams et al., 2022). As these technologies are applied with admirable goals in the healthcare domain, general voice datasets lose the ability to accurately reflect the end-user. For example, speech production changes as cognition declines; people use more prepositions, slow their speech rate, pause more frequently mid-sentence, and pause for longer durations as dementia progresses (Boschi et al., 2017; Slegers et al., 2018; Zhu et al., 2018; Nasreen et al., 2019; Luz et al., 2021). We can refine evaluation metrics endlessly, but a system's practical benefit to the end-user remains unknown without data representing that specific user group.

It is critical that this data is collected *ethically* and *securely* as vulnerable user groups are particularly common in the healthcare domain. Issues around consent have been explored as individuals develop cognitive impairments, but identifiable information will still be captured and this is a concern (Haider and Luz, 2019; Addlesee and Albert, 2020). Data privacy does not just affect people with cognitive impairments however, people affected by sight loss can unwittingly reveal sensitive information (Ramil Brick et al., 2021; Baker et al., 2021), as will individuals conversing during a GP consultation (Ryan et al., 2019).

Off-the-shelf devices are not secure. If used, all sensitive data that is captured will be fully accessible to anyone if the device is lost or stolen. Very few audio recorders even exist with this capability due to copyrighting of encrypted audio codecs (Chege, 2019), and the ones that do exist are expensive and not applicable or adaptable for ethical data collection (see Table 1 in which we have included the Philips DPM8000 for comparison). This is a serious risk that should not be overlooked when seeking ethical approval. In this short paper we will detail a bespoke device, called CVR-SI, with *ethics* and *data security* at the core of its design.

2 Previous Work

A data capture device, called CVR, was used to collect similar data in a less-sensitive domain (Porcheron et al., 2018). This device was used to collect family interactions with Amazon Alexa devices within participants homes over a period of one-month. While we would argue that the CVR would have certainly captured personally identifiable information, this risk is heightened in our

Proceedings of the Second Workshop on NLP for Positive Impact (NLP4PI), pages 25 - 30
December 7, 2022 ©2022 Association for Computational Linguistics

Desired Features	DPM	CVR	CUSCO	CVR-SI
Captures audio	✓	✓	✓	✓
Clearly indicates when 'on' to user	✗	✓	✗	✓
Clearly indicates when 'recording' to user	✗	✓	✗	✓
User can easily stop the device listening	✗	✓	✗	✓
Data is securely stored	✓	✗	✓	✓
Data is encrypted in real-time	✓	✗	✓	✓
Recording uses wake-word detection	✗	✓	✗	✓
Adequate Storage Capacity	✗	✓	✓	✓

Table 1: A list of desired system features with indicators of their presence within each device.

domain of interest, that is healthcare.

A security-focused data capture device, called CUSCO (Addlesee and Albert, 2020), was created for sensitive in-person data collections like medical conversations. Participants would interact or complete a task with the researchers in attendance at all times. Therefore, this device does not face the same challenges as a long-term device that cannot be monitored or controlled mid-study. CUSCO does implement real-time data encryption however, a critical feature that ensures no data can be accessed even if the device is stolen *during* recording.

With advice from the creators of the CVR (Conditional Voice Recorder), we used their work as a starting point. Hence our device's name: CVR-SI (Conditional Voice Recorder for Sensitive Information). We then adapted the data security features of CUSCO and integrated them to create CVR-SI. In Table 1 you can see which of our desired features the CVR, CUSCO, and Philips DPM8000 devices are missing. For example, the user must be able to easily stop the device from 'listening' while a health worker is visiting.

CVR-SI has been ethically approved for use by Heriot-Watt University's Ethics Committee and has been successfully used within vulnerable participant's homes. In the following sections we will describe the device's software, explain the security features, detail exactly how to construct the CVR-SI, and highlight components that tackle ethical issues[1]. The final CVR-SI can be seen in Figure 1.

3 Device Software

3.1 Wake-Word Detection

As mentioned above, we used the CVR (Porcheron et al., 2018) as the starting point of our CVR-SI device. We therefore started with Snowboy's wake-word detection, trained to detect "Alexa", by Kitt AI (Kitt-AI, 2020). For security reasons, this wake-

[1]A full writable .img of CVR-SI and a list of specific hardware component URLs can be found here for reproducibility: https://github.com/AddleseeHQ/CVR-SI

Figure 1: The fully built CVR-SI device with the accompanying Alexa voice assistant.

word detection must take place on-device and cannot use a cloud service (Cho et al., 2018; Bolton et al., 2021; Singh et al., 2021). This ensures all data remains offline and cannot be intercepted. Additionally, as the CVR-SI does not need to connect to home wifi, the setup is simple and non-invasive.

Another popular on-device Snowboy alternative is called Porcupine (Picovoice, 2022). It is more recent and their benchmark[2] suggested that it would noticeably outperform Snowboy. We explored this with both system's "Alexa" models at different activation sensitivities and with utterances containing various phrases similar to the target wake-word (other wake-words are available).

We want the CVR-SI to activate more often than the actual Alexa voice assistant, capturing instances where Alexa fails to listen to the user's utterance. In order to test this we prepared some phrases that are similar to "Alexa" (for example: "Lexa", "a Lexus", and "Alexis"), and some that are less-similar (for example: "My Lexus", "election", and "a lexeme"). We set up Porcupine and Snowboy with identical microphones and ran them simultaneously at the same distance from the test user. Each test phrase was spoken within a sentence at a range of different sensitivities. We found that both models performed indistinguishably. We do not dispute Porcupine's benchmark results and suggest referring to them for a more detailed and rigorous evaluation. We simply

[2]https://github.com/Picovoice/wake-word-benchmark

conclude that switching to Porcupine would not impact the CVR-SI's overall performance enough *practically* to warrant carrying out the potentially troublesome task.

3.2 Audio Buffer

As mentioned, we want the CVR-SI to capture all failed interactions with Alexa, and this includes failed wake-word detection. The original CVR stored a 60-second buffer of audio for this reason, assuming that failed interaction would be followed by another interaction attempt. It was found that users would repeat their utterance, clearly enunciating and stripping disfluencies from their speech (Porcheron et al., 2018). We kept this buffering feature as it is particularly important in the healthcare domain. For example, we can discover whether people with dementia learn to clean their speech of disfluencies in the same manner. Storing a constant buffer of audio is a security concern as people are certainly going to utter personally identifiable information in their own home at some point. This highlights the need for *real-time* encryption.

3.3 Data Security

Data security is imperative to avoid ethical and legal ramifications following a data breach (Romanosky et al., 2014; Labrecque et al., 2021; Masuch et al., 2021). These concerns are magnified when collecting data with vulnerable participants (Kavanaugh et al., 2006; Nordentoft and Kappel, 2011; McReynolds et al., 2017). We therefore reproduced the data security focused design of CUSCO (Addlesee and Albert, 2020) by using an audited, open-source, disk encryption software called Veracrypt (Knight, 2017). Data is encrypted in real time and can only be accessed with a generated key. This ensures the security of the entire corpus during collection, transport, exchange, and storage. The CVR-SI can therefore be handled by multiple parties without any of them being able to access collected data.

4 Device Hardware

We created several prototypes of the CVR-SI device, and then built this device at scale (20 units) as seen in Figure 2. Various hardware design decisions were made to mitigate ethical concerns[3].

[3]The full construction manual with component links, tool specifications, and circuit diagrams can be found here: `https://github.com/AddleseeHQ/CVR-SI`

Figure 2: All of the materials laid out to build 20 CVR-SI devices with accompanying Alexa assistants.

4.1 Raspberry Pi and Storage

Each CVR-SI uses a Raspberry Pi 3 Model B+ as its foundation. We made this decision based upon the CVR-SI performance requirements. Wake-word detection needs to run over audio continuously as the buffer and stored audio is encrypted live. The software runs smoothly on the Raspberry Pi 3 Model B+, so the additional cost to upgrade to a higher model was deemed redundant.

A microSD card is needed to run the software and store the corpus. We initially used a 16Gb microSD card, but this was not sufficient due to our deliberate over-capturing discussed above. Some participants placed the CVR-SI next to their TV or radio, which frequently activated the device. We therefore upgraded to a 256Gb version of the software (the only difference being the capacity of the encrypted drive), and this is sufficient for 1-month collections. Both the 16Gb and 256Gb versions of the software will be made available.

4.2 Microphone

As the purpose of the CVR-SI is to capture audio, a suitable microphone is required. We selected three off-the-shelf microphones at varying price points, and we tested the audio recording quality. We set up all three microphones in two different rooms. These were placed right next to each other and run simultaneously to avoid any external factors like background noise. We walked around the room while talking to investigate how each microphone handled audio input from various distances and orientations. We also spoke at varying volumes and while facing away from the microphones to test different user setups. Some participants may speak more quietly (Maslan et al., 2011), so this was a vital deciding factor. We found that the cheapest microphone had a background crackle at all times (we tested multiple, so this was not a defect). This crackle made it very difficult to hear what was being said at long distances, and low volumes. It was therefore discounted as an option. The other two microphones were similar as the utterances could always be heard. The most expensive microphone had many interesting features, including a bidirectional mode for example. These features were not useful in this omnidirectional setting, so we selected the mid-range microphone due to cost.

4.3 Peripherals for Ethical Design

In order to support a few design features that we considered ethically necessary, LEDs and a button are required (Pearl, 2016; Abdi et al., 2019). One green LED lights to clearly indicate when the CVR-SI is on and *listening*. One red LED lights to clearly indicate when currently *recording*. The button stops the device recording and listening when pressed, and then reactivates the device to listen once pressed again - indicated by the green LED. This feature can be used when family members are visiting, health workers are in the house, or simply if the participant is having a conversation that they don't want to be captured.

The communication between the Raspberry Pi and the peripherals is achieved through a circuit board that has to be soldered. We designed the circuit with suitable resistors to protect the LEDs and button, ensuring they do not burn out in-use. All of the circuitry and Raspberry Pi is housed within a simple container with holes drilled into it for the lights, button, and microphone cable. A soldering iron, drill, drill bits (matching the LED and button sizes), and glue (to attach the microphone securely) is needed to build the CVR-SI. Please follow the links and guide on GitHub for step-by-step guidance and the circuit diagram. The device build process can be seen in Figure 3.

Figure 3: The CVR-SI mid-construction.

5 Findings from Use in Practice

In this short paper we have detailed both the software and hardware of CVR-SI, a data capture device with both *data security* and *ethics* at the core of its design. The CVR-SI has been ethically approved and used to capture interactions between people with dementia and Alexa voice assistants in their own home. We have already learned a great deal from real-world deployment, for example the microSD storage upgrade described in Section 4.1.

Participants have reported using the device's button to stop the CVR-SI capturing audio when family or health-workers are visiting, indicating that this feature is desired for privacy and that the LEDs are clear. One participant noted that they used the button at times they felt "big brother was listening". This is an understandable feeling that is generally felt with smart speakers (Lau et al., 2018), indicating again that the LEDs are clear and the button is a necessary device feature for participant comfort.

Although data analysis is yet to be complete, initial observations have revealed instances in which the Alexa does not activate when the user says the wake-word. The buffer has therefore proven to be a useful feature, driving the need for live encryption. Recordings have been clear and do not skip, demonstrating the sufficient capabilities of both the microphone and Raspberry Pi.

Finally, participants have described how they have used the Alexa device in their day-to-day lives. People with dementia have been able to reawaken their love for music, set reminders to take medication or walk their dogs, get help with their crosswords, and even find new recipes to help get involved with family mealtimes. Voice assistants can clearly have a positive impact, so we hope our work will accelerate voice accessibility research.

Ethical and Societal Implications

The next generation of voice assistants need to be more naturally interactive and accessible for everyone, especially as SDSs are increasingly applied in the healthcare setting. In order to make informed design decisions and effectively evaluate new dialogue systems with specific user groups in mind, potentially sensitive data *must* be collected. Off-the-shelf audio recorders are not secure and cannot be ethically approved for use, creating a barrier to complete crucial research.

This work will not only enable us to design dementia-friendly assistants and social robots in the future. We hope other researchers use the CVR-SI to make a positive impact with similar goals in mind, and in more general settings to ensure data privacy.

Acknowledgements

This work was funded by The Data Lab, Wallscope, and the EU H2020 program under grant agreement no. 871245 (SPRING)[4].

This device couldn't be used to collect valuable data without the generosity of participant's time - thank you all. I would also like to thank CENSIS for providing many of the Raspberry Pi's, Amazon Science for providing the Alexa devices, and Spotify for providing Spotify Premium to participants.

Finally - I would like to thank Derek Davis for facilitating the purchase of the device components, and Antero Duarte for his electronics advice.

References

Noura Abdi, Kopo M Ramokapane, and Jose M Such. 2019. More than smart speakers: security and privacy perceptions of smart home personal assistants. In *Fifteenth Symposium on Usable Privacy and Security (SOUPS 2019)*, pages 451–466.

Angus Addlesee and Pierre Albert. 2020. Ethically collecting multi-modal spontaneous conversations with people that have cognitive impairments. *LREC Workshop on Legal and Ethical Issues*.

Katie Baker, Amit Parekh, Adrien Fabre, Angus Addlesee, Ruben Kruiper, and Oliver Lemon. 2021. The spoon is in the sink: Assisting visually impaired people in the kitchen. In *Proceedings of the Reasoning and Interaction Conference (ReInAct 2021)*, pages 32–39.

Tom Bolton, Tooska Dargahi, Sana Belguith, Mabrook S Al-Rakhami, and Ali Hassan Sodhro. 2021. On the security and privacy challenges of virtual assistants. *Sensors*, 21(7):2312.

Veronica Boschi, Eleonora Catricala, Monica Consonni, Cristiano Chesi, Andrea Moro, and Stefano F Cappa. 2017. Connected speech in neurodegenerative language disorders: a review. *Frontiers in psychology*, 8:269.

Isaac Chege. 2019. Best encrypted voice recorder.

Geumhwan Cho, Jusop Choi, Hyoungshick Kim, Sangwon Hyun, and Jungwoo Ryoo. 2018. Threat modeling and analysis of voice assistant applications. In *International Workshop on Information Security Applications*, pages 197–209. Springer.

Jacob Devlin, Ming-Wei Chang, Kenton Lee, and Kristina Toutanova. 2018. Bert: Pre-training of deep bidirectional transformers for language understanding. *arXiv preprint arXiv:1810.04805*.

Fasih Haider and Saturnino Luz. 2019. A system for real-time privacy preserving data collection for ambient assisted living. In *INTERSPEECH*, pages 2374–2375.

Karen Kavanaugh, Teresa T Moro, Teresa Savage, and Ramkrishna Mehendale. 2006. Enacting a theory of caring to recruit and retain vulnerable participants for sensitive research. *Research in nursing & health*, 29(3):244–252.

Kitt-AI. 2020. Snowboy hotword detection. `https://github.com/Kitt-AI/snowboy`. Online; accessed 08 May 2022.

G Knight. 2017. Encrypt data using veracrypt.

Lauren I Labrecque, Ereni Markos, Kunal Swani, and Priscilla Peña. 2021. When data security goes wrong: Examining the impact of stress, social contract violation, and data type on consumer coping responses following a data breach. *Journal of Business Research*, 135:559–571.

Josephine Lau, Benjamin Zimmerman, and Florian Schaub. 2018. Alexa, are you listening? privacy perceptions, concerns and privacy-seeking behaviors with smart speakers. *Proceedings of the ACM on Human-Computer Interaction*, 2(CSCW):1–31.

Saturnino Luz, Fasih Haider, Sofia de la Fuente, Davida Fromm, and Brian MacWhinney. 2021. Detecting cognitive decline using speech only: The adresso challenge. *arXiv preprint arXiv:2104.09356*.

Brian MacWhinney, Steven Bird, Christopher Cieri, and Craig Martell. 2004. Talkbank: Building an open unified multimodal database of communicative interaction.

Jonathan Maslan, Xiaoyan Leng, Catherine Rees, David Blalock, and Susan G Butler. 2011. Maximum phonation time in healthy older adults. *Journal of Voice*, 25(6):709–713.

[4]`https://spring-h2020.eu/`

Kristin Masuch, Maike Greve, and Simon Trang. 2021. What to do after a data breach? examining apology and compensation as response strategies for health service providers. *Electronic Markets*, 31(4):829–848.

Emily McReynolds, Sarah Hubbard, Timothy Lau, Aditya Saraf, Maya Cakmak, and Franziska Roesner. 2017. Toys that listen: A study of parents, children, and internet-connected toys. In *Proceedings of the 2017 CHI conference on human factors in computing systems*, pages 5197–5207.

Shamila Nasreen, Matthew Purver, and Julian Hough. 2019. A corpus study on questions, responses and misunderstanding signals in conversations with alzheimer's patients. In *Proceedings of the 23rd Workshop on the Semantics and Pragmatics of Dialogue-Full Papers. SEMDIAL, London, United Kingdom (Sep 2019), http://semdial.org/anthology/Z19-Nasreen semdial*, volume 13.

Helle Merete Nordentoft and Nanna Kappel. 2011. Vulnerable participants in health research: Methodological and ethical challenges. *Journal of Social Work Practice*, 25(3):365–376.

Cathy Pearl. 2016. *Designing voice user interfaces: Principles of conversational experiences.* " O'Reilly Media, Inc.".

Picovoice. 2022. Porcupine on-device wake word detection. `https://github.com/Picovoice/Porcupine`. Online; accessed 08 May 2022.

Martin Porcheron, Joel E Fischer, Stuart Reeves, and Sarah Sharples. 2018. Voice interfaces in everyday life. In *proceedings of the 2018 CHI conference on human factors in computing systems*, pages 1–12.

Elisa Ramil Brick, Vanesa Caballero Alonso, Conor O'Brien, Sheron Tong, Emilie Tavernier, Amit Parekh, Angus Addlesee, and Oliver Lemon. 2021. Am i allergic to this? assisting sight impaired people in the kitchen. In *Proceedings of the 2021 International Conference on Multimodal Interaction*, pages 92–102.

Sasha Romanosky, David Hoffman, and Alessandro Acquisti. 2014. Empirical analysis of data breach litigation. *Journal of Empirical Legal Studies*, 11(1):74–104.

Padhraig Ryan, Saturnino Luz, Pierre Albert, Carl Vogel, Charles Normand, and Glyn Elwyn. 2019. Using artificial intelligence to assess clinicians' communication skills. *Bmj*, 364.

Abhishek Singh, Rituraj Kabra, Rahul Kumar, Manjunath Belgod Lokanath, Reetika Gupta, and Sumit Kumar Shekhar. 2021. On-device system for device directed speech detection for improving human computer interaction. *IEEE Access*, 9:131758–131766.

Antoine Slegers, Renee-Pier Filiou, Maxime Montembeault, and Simona Maria Brambati. 2018. Connected speech features from picture description in alzheimer's disease: A systematic review. *Journal of Alzheimer's Disease*, 65(2):519–542.

Louise R Williams, Myzoon Ali, Kathryn VandenBerg, Linda J Williams, Masahiro Abo, Frank Becker, Audrey Bowen, Caitlin Brandenburg, Caterina Breitenstein, Stefanie Bruehl, et al. 2022. Utilising a systematic review-based approach to create a database of individual participant data for meta-and network meta-analyses: the release database of aphasia after stroke. *Aphasiology*, 36(4):513–533.

Dong Yu and Li Deng. 2016. *Automatic speech recognition*, volume 1. Springer.

Zining Zhu, Jekaterina Novikova, and Frank Rudzicz. 2018. Detecting cognitive impairments by agreeing on interpretations of linguistic features. *arXiv preprint arXiv:1808.06570*.

Leveraging World Knowledge in Implicit Hate Speech Detection

Jessica Lin
Department of Linguistics
Georgetown University
yl1290@georgetown.edu

Abstract

Warning: *This paper contains content that may be offensive or disturbing.*

While much attention has been paid to identifying explicit hate speech, implicit hateful expressions that are disguised in coded or indirect language are pervasive and remain a major challenge for existing hate speech detection systems. This paper presents the first attempt to apply Entity Linking (EL) techniques to both explicit and implicit hate speech detection, where we show that such real world knowledge about entity mentions in a text does help models better detect hate speech, and the benefit of adding it into the model is more pronounced when explicit entity triggers (e.g., rally, KKK) are present. We also discuss cases where real world knowledge does not add value to hate speech detection, which provides more insights into understanding and modeling the subtleties of hate speech.

1 Introduction

Hate speech on social media facilitates the spread of violence in the real world. For this reason, the detection of hatred content online increasingly gains importance. However, most work in hate speech detection has focused on explicit or overt hate speech, failing to capture the implicit hateful messages in coded or indirect language (e.g., sarcasm or metaphor) that disparage a protected group or individual, or to convey prejudicial and harmful views about them (Waseem et al., 2017). Examples (1) and (2) from ElSherief et al. (2021) show the two types of hate speech, explicit vs. implicit:

(1) *#jews & n*ggers destroy and pervert everything they touch #jewfail #n*ggerfail* (explicit hate speech)

(2) *don't worry, charlottesville was just the beginning. we're growing extremely fast* (implicit hate speech, implied statement: larger white supremacist events will happen)

As shown in (1) and (2), explicit hate speech is direct and uses specific keywords while implicit hate speech does not contain explicit hateful lexicon or phrases and often uses coded or indirect languages to disguise the malicious intent (ElSherief et al., 2021).

Modeling implicit sentiment in hate speech is still in its infancy, and the capacity to acquire background knowledge enhances the correct detection of hate speech by machines (Kiritchenko et al., 2021; Li et al., 2021). To be able to understand the implied statement of hate speech, machine learning systems need extratextual information that provides world knowledge associated with natural language concepts. For example, it would be impossible for a reader who does not know what happened in Charlottesville to understand the implicit hateful message in (2). The reader wouldn't be able to understand the implied message "larger white supremacist events will happen" without knowing that Charlottesville is a metonym for a white supremacist rally that took place in Charlottesville, Virginia in August, 2017. Conversely, background knowledge that reasons about entity mentions in a text could add value to the detection of implicit hate speech. Incorporating such knowledge ideally should make it easier for the learning model to detect hate speech where it is not apparent from the text.

With this motivation, this study applies Entity Linking (EL) to identify entities in tweets, link them to an external knowledge base (KB; Wikipedia in this study), and acquire their Wikipedia descriptions that would be encoded with Sentence BERT (Reimers and Gurevych, 2019) for representation. Our proposed model incorporates such knowledge representation into identifying both explicit and implicit hate speech in investigating the effectiveness of real world knowledge.

Overall, this study makes the following contributions: (i) To the best of our knowledge, this work

Proceedings of the Second Workshop on NLP for Positive Impact (NLP4PI), pages 31 - 39
December 7, 2022 ©2022 Association for Computational Linguistics

is the first attempt to leverage EL techniques in tackling the problem of implicit hate speech detection. (ii) To evaluate the effectiveness of real world knowledge in both explicit and implicit hate speech detection, where we investigate how incorporating Wikipedia descriptions of linked entities into the model affects performance.

2 Related Work

Identifying hate speech has been a topic of immense interest in recent years, and a number of studies have approached this problem in different ways.

Early work on hate speech detection has focused on explicitly abusive text using keyword-based methods that rely on lexical features (Waseem and Hovy, 2016; Davidson et al., 2017), while more recent studies have highlighted the linguistic nuance and diversity of the implicit hate expressions, which includes stereotypes (Sap et al., 2019), indirect sarcasm, humor, and metaphor (Founta et al., 2018) that cannot be captured by keyword-based systems. Implicit hate expressions are no less harmful than explicit ones and make up a large portion of false negatives errors (Basile et al., 2019; Mozafari et al., 2020). Systems that rely on explicit hateful lexicon or phrases are unable to capture underlying hateful intent like humans. Up until now, predicting implicit hate or abuse remains a major challenge for machine systems. Existing solutions for identifying implicit cases of hate speech involve taking context into account. For example, Gao and Huang (2017) included original news articles as the context of the hateful comments. Other studies have built datasets with "implicit" labels or annotations (Caselli et al., 2020; ElSherief et al., 2021; Sap et al., 2019). This is crucial not only for evaluation but also for training, as systems that are not trained on implicit hate would not go beyond explicit features and are thus far from being applicable in the real world as a moderation tool.

Recently, an emerging line of research has started to explore the idea of incorporating real world knowledge in a related task, sarcasm detection, but not for hate speech detection task. This line of research (Chowdhury and Chaturvedi, 2021; Li et al., 2021) hypothesizes that infusing real world knowledge such as commonsense knowledge in sarcasm detection ideally should make the learning model easier to detect sarcasm where it is not apparent from the text. Li et al. (2021) proposed a novel architecture to integrate knowledge into learning model. For knowledge representation, they applied the pre-trained COMET model (**COM**mons**E**nse **T**ransformers, Bosselut et al. (2019)) to generate relevant commonsense knowledge from sarcastic instances and use it as input to the proposed model in investigating how commonsense knowledge influences performance. Similarly, Chowdhury and Chaturvedi (2021) leveraged COMET to infuse commonsense knowledge in their graph convolution-based model, in which a graph is formed with edges between the input sentence and COMET sequences. The node representations of the graph are then passed through a fully-connected neural network to generate the output.

The results of the effectiveness of commonsense knowledge are still inconclusive. Li et al. (2021) found that integrating commonsense knowledge information contributes to sarcasm detection, yet it only plays a supporting role as models using only knowledge information do not perform satisfactorily. Interestingly, Chowdhury and Chaturvedi (2021) found an opposite result on the role of commonsense knowledge in sarcasm detection, showing that COMET infused model performs at par with the baseline. In many cases, the model is more reliant on the input sentence and less on the COMET sequences for making the prediction. Their in-depth error analysis shows that commonsense is most effective in identifying sarcasm with polarity contrast but fails to explain non-sarcastic samples or other types of sarcasm effectively. The study suggests that exploring the utility of other forms of external knowledge such as factual world knowledge for sarcasm detection would be a promising line of inquiry. Inspired by previous research, the present study assumes that real world knowledge would be beneficial to implicit hate speech detection in that such knowledge allows a fully understanding of the background knowledge required for deciphering the hateful intent of the text.

3 Methods

3.1 Dataset

In this work, our proposed model is evaluated on the *Latent Hatred Dataset* (ElSherief et al., 2021). The dataset used in this study contains 12,143 tweets from the most prominent extremist groups in the United States, where 5,791 of these tweets are implicit hate speech and 567 of them are explicit hate speech. Implicit hate tweets are categorized into six classes using the taxonomy shown in Table 1.

Each of the 5,791 implicit hate tweets also has free-text annotations for the target demographic group and an implied statement to describe the underlying message. Implied statements are generated by human annotators with the format $\langle target \rangle$ *{do, are, commit}* $\langle predicate \rangle$, where $\langle target \rangle$ might be phrases like *immigrants, minorities*. For example, the implicit hate tweet *this selfie is so white, i love it.* has the implied statement "Minorities are less than whites".

3.2 Models

In this paper, two classification tasks are conducted. (1) a binary classification task on distinguishing hate speech from non-hate speech, and (2) a 6-way classification task on categorizing implicit hate speech classes (see Table 1).

For both tasks, a Multi-layer Perceptron (MLP) model with Sentence BERT (Reimers and Gurevych, 2019) embeddings is used. First, we pre-processed all tweets and background knowledge descriptions (remove stop words and reserved words such as RT, FAV, via, etc. while keeping all the hashtags and links that may contain useful messages). Next, they are concatenated before being encoded with Sentence BERT using the pre-trained model `bert-base-nli-mean-tokens`, where it maps tweets and background knowledge descriptions to a 768-dimensional dense vector space. The MLP model is evaluated with two feature sets: Sentence BERT encoded textual embedding alone (baseline, tweet only) and the combination of textual embedding and background knowledge (baseline+BK).

3.3 Background Knowledge Extraction and Representation

To incorporate background knowledge, entity linking is applied to associate mentions with their referent entities. First, mentions in each tweet are identified and linked to entities in the KB using Radboud Entity Linker (REL, van Hulst et al. (2020)), an end-to-end entity linker that identifies mentions of specific entities in text and links them to pertinent Wikipedia page titles. REL is chosen because it has state-of-the-art performance and is trained on a recent Wikipedia dump (2019-07). It provides a web API [1] in which given an input text it returns a list of mentions with the linked entities and the confidence score of mention detection and entity disambiguation. In order to refine the entity linking results (see Table 2 for an example), we tested different thresholds of confidence score and decided to remove entities with a low confidence score of mention detection (MD score) ($<$0.4) and a low confidence score of entity disambiguation (ED score) ($<$0.2). We find that this refinement strategy helps us strike a balance between precision and recall in that it matches as many mentions as possible (retain mentions that have an MD score > 0.4) while maintaining the accuracy of the result at the same time (remove entities that have an ED score < 0.2).

After retrieving all the Wikipedia page titles of the entities in the input text, we use `Wikipedia` API [2] to extract the summary of the corresponding Wikipedia page (referred to as *entity abstract* or *Wikipedia description* afterward). To keep the entity abstract from being too long, we print only two sentences of each abstract by setting the `sentences` argument to 2. An example of entity abstract is as follows: *David Ernest Duke (born July 1, 1950) is an American white supremacist, antisemitic conspiracy theorist, far-right politician, convicted felon, and former Grand Wizard of the Knights of the Ku Klux Klan. From 1989 to 1992, he was a member of the Louisiana House of Representatives for the Republican Party.*

Finally, the entity abstract for each tweet is concatenated with the tweet and encoded with 768-dimensional Sentence BERT embedding using `bert-base-nli-mean-tokens` model.

4 Experiments

4.1 Experimental Setup

For each of the two classification tasks, the model is trained and evaluated on two feature sets, which are baseline feature set (tweet text only) with and without Wikipedia descriptions. For both binary and 6-way classification task, a MLP is implemented in `sklearn` with three hidden layers of dimension 512, learning rate `0.001` and the number of epochs `500`. The optimizer is set to `Adam`.

[1] https://rel.cs.ru.nl/api

[2] https://pypi.org/project/wikipedia/

Class (distribution)	Explanation	Example
Grievance (24.2%)	Frustration over a minority group's perceived privilege	*Black lives matter and white lives don't? Sounds racist.*
Incitement (20%)	Implicitly promoting known hate groups and ideologies (e.g., by flaunting in-group power)	*Hitler was Germany –Germans shall rise again!*
Inferiority (13.6%)	Implying some group or person is of lesser value than another	*It's not a coincidence the best places to live are majority white.*
Irony (12.6%)	Using sarcasm, humor, and satire to demean someone	*Horrors... Disney will be forced into hiring Americans.* (Discredit Disney for allegedly hiring only non-whites)
Stereotypes (17.9%)	Associating a group with negative attribute using euphemisms, circumlocution, or metaphorical language	*Can someone tell the black people in Chicago to stop killing one another before it becomes Detroit?*
Threats (10.5%)	Making an indirect commitment to attack someone's body, well-being, reputation, liberty, etc. Focus on threats related to implicit violation of rights and freedoms, removal of opportunities, and more subtle forms of intimidation	*All immigration of non-whites should be ended.* (Non-white immigrants should stay in their country: subtle forms of intimidation)

Table 1: Implicit hate classes and examples in *Latent Hatred Dataset*.

Tweet	**Before Refinement Strategy**	**After Refinement Strategy (Removing entities with a MD score <0.4 and a ED score <0.2)**
tune in today's jmt for my interview w /robert spencer on "the complete infidel's guide to iran!"	tune in today's [jmt] Jedi_Mind_Tricks (an American hip hop group) (ED score: 0.78, MD score: 0.36) for my interview w /[robert spencer] Robert B. Spencer (American author and blogger, opponent of Islam) (ED score: 0.38, MD score: 0.96) on "the complete infidel's guide to [iran] Iran" (ED score: 0.51, MD score: 0.99)	tune in today's jmt for my interview w /[robert spencer] Robert B. Spencer (American author and blogger, opponent of Islam) (ED score: 0.38, MD score: 0.96) on "the complete infidel's guide to [iran] Iran" (ED score: 0.51, MD score: 0.99)

Table 2: An Entity linking example from our dataset.

4.2 Classification Results

In explicit hate speech classification shown in Table 3, the background knowledge provided by Wikipedia significantly improves the model by increasing 10% in precision, recall, and F1 score after incorporating background knowledge into the model. While the MLP model with baseline feature set achieves a competitive result with 65% on F1 score, the background knowledge incorporated model achieves better scores (75%) than the one with baseline feature set, demonstrating that real world knowledge is helpful for capturing real hate speech.

For additional comparisons [3], our background knowledge incorporated model achieves a significantly better precision score (75% vs. 68%) than the Wikidata Knowledge Graph (Vrandečić and Krötzsch, 2014) infused model proposed in ElSherief et al. (2021), which was trained on the same *Latent Hatred Dataset*. The remarkably higher precision score suggests that Wikipedia description of linked entities is doing a better job in preventing false positives than Wikidata Knowledge Graph method; however, a more detailed analysis comparing the effectiveness of different external knowledge (e.g., knowledge graphs, commonsense knowledge) for hate speech detection is needed.

As shown in Table 3, real world knowledge enhances the correct detection of explicit hate speech. However, Table 4 shows that integrating real world knowledge does not seem to improve the model, and even hurts model's performance in implicit hate speech type classification. Significant degradation in precision, recall, and F1 score are observed (e.g., recall drops 12%), which suggests that knowledge about the involved entities is not sufficient for predicting implicit hate speech types.

[3] We notice that there are works (Pal et al., 2022) that also improve performance on the *Latent Hatred Dataset*, but we compare our results against the results from ElSherief et al. (2021), which serves as a benchmark for modeling implicit hate speech using knowledge-based features as well.

Models	P	R	F	Acc
Majority baseline	$52\% \pm 1.3\%$			
MLP (baseline)	$65\% \pm 1.5\%$	$65\% \pm 1.5\%$	$65\% \pm 1.5\%$	$65\% \pm 1.5\%$
MLP (baseline+BK)	$75\% \pm 1.4\%$	$75\% \pm 1.4\%$	$75\% \pm 1.4\%$	$75\% \pm 1.4\%$
Knowledge infused model (ElSherief et al., 2021)	68%	72%	70%	**77%**

Table 3: Classification performance on explicit hate speech classification. Performance metrics are all macro average scores. Majority baseline always returns the positive (hate) label. **Bold** face indicates best performance.

Table 5 further shows that among the six implicit hate classes, *irony* is the hardest for the model to detect, which aligns with the result found in ElSherief et al. (2021). This is reasonable, as irony normally requires further understanding beyond knowledge about the involved entities (e.g., semantic inference or pragmatic understanding). Therefore, our background knowledge incorporated model fails at capturing this type of implicit hate. On the other hand, *white grievance* is the easiest to detect for our model. A detailed examination of our data shows that compared to other types of implicit hate posts, *white grievance* tweets in our dataset contain relatively more explicit hate triggers (e.g., rally, KKK), which is found to be useful for the model. Further discussion on explaining our model's predictions on implicit hate could be found in Section 5.

5 Analysis

This section investigates whether the model is reliant on Wikipedia descriptions while making decisions. We leverage LIME (locally interpretable model-agnostic explanations) algorithms (Ribeiro et al., 2016) to explain our model's predictions on both explicit and implicit hate statements through random examples picked from our dataset.

5.1 Efficacy of World Knowledge

Table 6 shows cases where Wikipedia knowledge is helpful. For each example, the colored text spans represent the words highly-weighted by the model. We find that Wikipedia knowledge is particularly useful when hatefulness in a tweet is conveyed through certain hate "triggers". These triggers by themselves are not toxic but are relevant to the hatefulness in a tweet. Since implicit hate does not contain explicit hate lexicon or phrases, the model rather relies on these triggers to help them make the right predictions. As shown in Example C of Table 6, the Wikipedia description of *Charlottesville* helps the model correctly predicts the tweet as an incitement tweet by relying on entity triggers such as *rally*. The word by itself is not a hate lexicon but indicates a high probability of a tweet that incites violence. Similarly, the Wikipedia description of *David Duke* in Example B of Table 6 is helpful for the model in that it explains *David Duke* is the former head of *Ku Klux Klan*, which by itself does not convey toxicity but is indicative of a *white grievance* tweet.

Table 6 further shows that although entity triggers provided by Wikipedia description contribute to the detection of hate speech to a certain extent, it only plays a supporting role. Some of the words in the tweet are already a strong signal of the hatefulness of the tweet, as shown in the highlighted words in the table. For instance, in Example B of Table 6, both the hashtag *#makeamericagreatagain* and *#votetrump* in the post reveal that the author might be a supporter of Donald Trump, which is said to have a symbiotic relationship with white nationalism, white supremacy, and white power ideologies that correspond to the *white grievance* implicit hate type in our dataset.

5.2 Error Analysis

To further understand the role of world knowledge in identifying hatefulness, we randomly pick out incorrect predictions made by our model and manually correct some of the entity linking errors to see if this "post-processing" helps avert classification errors.

As shown in Example A of Table 7, our entity linker misses the mention *bernie bros*. Instead, *white males* in the tweet is identified and linked to Wikipedia. The Wikipedia description of *white males* does not add value to the detection of hatefulness. Words with the highest coefficients such as *skin* and *African* are neutral and are not associated with the hateful content of the tweet. After post-processing the entity linking result, our model correctly predicts the tweet as a hate post by leveraging the world knowledge provided by Wikipedia. The Wikipedia description explains that *bernie bros*

Feature sets	P	R	F	Acc
Dummy Classifier	$19\,\% \pm 1.0\,\%$			
Baseline (tweet only)	$52\,\% \pm 1.3\,\%$	$52\,\% \pm 1.3\,\%$	$52\,\% \pm 1.3\,\%$	**54%** $\pm 1.3\,\%$
Baseline + BK	$42\,\% \pm 1.3\,\%$	$40\,\% \pm 1.3\,\%$	$41\,\% \pm 1.3\,\%$	$44\,\% \pm 1.3\,\%$

Table 4: Classification performance on 6-way implicit hate speech classification. Performance metrics are all macro average scores. Dummy classifier generates random predictions by respecting the training set class distribution. **Bold** face indicates best performance.

Feature sets	incitement	inferiority	irony	stereotypical	threatening	white grievance
MLP (baseline)	52%	51%	*33%*	55%	56%	**62%**
MLP (baseline+BK)	45%	40%	*20%*	44%	43%	52%

Table 5: Classification performance on 6-way implicit hate speech classification. Performance metrics are all F1 scores. *Italics* indicates the worst performance. **Bold** face indicates best performance.

is a pejorative term used to describe Bernie Sanders supporters that have recently received criticism for crude and sexist attacks against rival Hillary Clinton. A similar example is shown in Example B of Table 7, where the term *Charlottesville* is used to refer to the white supremacist rally that took place in Charlottesville, Virginia rather than as a city's name. Before post-processing, our model incorrectly predicts the tweet as a *threatening* post based on the words used in the post (*worry, fast*). By contrast, our model accurately detects the implicitly hateful message conveyed in the tweet after *Charlottesville* is being identified in its correct sense.

5.3 Challenges in Implicit Hate Speech Detection

Section 4.2 shows that Wikipedia knowledge does not add value and sometimes even hurts the implicit hate speech type classification. To further understand the role of Wikipedia knowledge in implicit hate type classification, we identify two challenges our model struggles with in implicit hate speech classification. One of the most common challenges for our model is shown in (3), where hatred is not apparent from the text but requires a pragmatic understanding of the text.

(3) *white privilege conference this week. #nationalsocialism* **white privilege, or white skin privilege, is the societal privilege that benefits white people over non-white people in some societies, particularly if they are otherwise under the same social, political, or economic circumstances. With roots in European colonialism and imperialism, and the Atlantic slave trade, white privilege has developed in circumstances that have broadly sought to protect white racial privileges, various national citizenships, and other rights or special benefits.** (Gold label: Incitement, Prediction: White grievance)

(4) *atlanta hawks poor attendance is blamed on black crowds making southern whites uncomfortable.* **The Atlanta Hawks are a professional basketball team based in Atlanta, Georgia. The Hawks compete in the National Basketball Association (NBA) as a member team of the league's Eastern Conference Southeast Division. The Hawks play their home games at Philips Arena.** (Gold: Incitement, Prediction: Stereotypical)

The post in (3) is an *incitement* post because it implicitly elevates white privilege ideology by promoting an upcoming event on white privilege. However, the tweet is predicted as a *white grievance* post because of the recurrence of the term *white privilege* in the post and Wikipedia description. Here we can see that world knowledge distracts the model. Additionally, our model struggles with this type of indirect hate because the implied hateful message is not apparent from the text. The model has to understand the pragmatic implicature (White people are privileged) that the

#	Gold	Prediction	Example
A	Explicit hate	Explicit hate	*the kkk. how old does my little boy need to be to join?* **The Ku Klux Klan (KKK), or simply "the Klan", is the name of three distinct past and present movements in the United States that have advocated extremist reactionary currents such as white supremacy, white nationalism, and anti-immigration, historically expressed through terrorism aimed at groups or individuals whom they opposed.**
B	White grievance	White grievance	*refuses to denounce dr.david duke! # makeamericagreatagain # votetrump* **David Ernest Duke (born July 1, 1950) is an American white nationalist, anti-Semitic conspiracy theorist, politician, and former Grand Wizard of the Ku Klux Klan.**
C	Incitement	Incitement	*# charlottesville a day that will go down in white history.* **Charlottesville, a metonym for the Unite the Right rally, a white supremacist rally that took place in Charlottesville, Virginia, from August 11 to 12, 2017.**

Table 6: Examples where Wikipedia description helps the model make the right decision. Red color indicates the features with highest coefficients for the model, darker colors indicate more polarity. The tweet is in *italics*. Wikipedia description is indicated in **bold**.

post suggests or implies in order to decipher the hidden hateful intent of the tweet.

(4) demonstrates another common challenge our model faces. The description of the basketball team does not help understand the underlying hatefulness of the tweet, which implies that white people don't go to watch the basketball game because black players would make white people uncomfortable. That said, the Wikipedia description here does not hurt the model as well because the model still predicts the tweet as *stereotypical* without the description. The underlying problem here is that Wikipedia descriptions and tweet text seem to be unrelated to each other. This domain discrepancy between text and knowledge suggests that simple concatenation is not enough, but a more sophisticated structure that can capture the information flow between text and knowledge representation is needed for implicit hate speech type classification.

6 Conclusion

This paper has proposed the idea of integrating real world knowledge into the task of hate speech detection. Experimental results show that real world knowledge is helpful, especially in cases where entity triggers (e.g., rally, KKK) are present in the tweet. However, our analysis also shows that this knowledge fails to predict implicit hate speech types as Wikipedia knowledge does not add value and sometimes even hurts the classification, suggesting that a more sophisticated model that enables understanding beyond knowledge about the involved entities is required for implicit hate speech type classification. To mitigate these challenges, works on model architecture that enable information flow between the representations of the tweet and Wikipedia knowledge is a reasonable next step. Additionally, exploring the possibility of combining different kinds of external knowledge, for example, combining commonsense knowledge (Chowdhury and Chaturvedi, 2021) in modeling implicit hate speech would also be a promising line of inquiry. To further understand the subtleties of hate speech, deciphering models for coded language or indirect language (e.g., metaphor, irony) in hate speech expression would be beneficial.

Ethics Statement

With the exponential growth of offensive language online, a myriad of machine learning models has been proposed. However, a major limitation of many existing hate speech detection models is that they focused on capturing explicit or overt hate speech, failing to detect implicit hateful expressions that are no less harmful than explicit ones. Our experiment in this study suggests that entity triggers (e.g., rally, KKK) are helpful in detecting hatefulness that is not apparent from the text. This could ideally help improve model accuracy in identifying implicit hate speech, preventing targeted communities from experiencing increased harm online. Furthermore, we show that knowledge about entities may help reduce false positives in explicit hate speech. This is important, as deep learning models nowadays still suffer from false positive predictions (Markov and Daelemans, 2021). To

#	Gold	Model predictions before and after post-processing	Example
A	Explicit hate	Non-hate	*bernie bros are entitled white males #maleprivileage #culturalmarxism #feminismiscancer #democrats* **White is a racialized classification of people and a skin color specifier, generally used for people of European origin; although the definition can vary depending on context, nationality, and point of view. In the United States, this term has at times been expanded to encompass persons of Mexican, South Asian, West Asian, East Asian, and North African descent, persons who are often considered "non-White" in other contexts in the United States.**
		Explicit hate	*bernie bros are entitled white males #maleprivileage #culturalmarxism #feminismiscancer #democrats* **"Bernie Bro", or sometimes "Berniebro", is a pejorative term for a person (particularly one who is young, male and wealthy) who supports American politician and junior United States senator Bernie Sanders via Internet culture and social media by "mainstream" media outlets and later Hillary Clinton supporters. Recently, Bernie Bros have received criticism for crude and sexist attacks against rival Democratic nominee Hillary Clinton and her second presidential campaign in 2016, with her first attempt being in 2008.**
B	Incitement	Threatening	*don't worry charlottesville was just the beginning. we're growing extremely fast.* **Charlottesville, colloquially C'ville, Hoo-Ville, and formally the City of Charlottesville, is an independent city in the Commonwealth of Virginia. As of 2015, the population was 46,597.**
		Incitement	*don't worry charlottesville was just the beginning. we're growing extremely fast.* **Charlottesville, a metonym for the Unite the Right rally, a white supremacist rally that took place in Charlottesville, Virginia, from August 11 to 12, 2017.**

Table 7: Ground truth labels along with predictions made by the model before and after post-processing. Red color indicates the features with the highest coefficients for the model, darker colors indicate more polarity. The tweet is in *italics*. Wikipedia description is indicated in **bold**.

this end, minimizing false positives is pivotal, as models that are not robust enough would be far from being applicable in the real world as a moderation tool, and using such a non-robust model would further lead to over-blocking or removal of harmless social media content that does not violate community guidelines.

References

Valerio Basile, Cristina Bosco, Elisabetta Fersini, Nozza Debora, Viviana Patti, Francisco Manuel Rangel Pardo, Paolo Rosso, Manuela Sanguinetti, et al. 2019. Semeval-2019 task 5: Multilingual detection of hate speech against immigrants and women in twitter. In *13th International Workshop on Semantic Evaluation*, pages 54–63. Association for Computational Linguistics.

Antoine Bosselut, Hannah Rashkin, Maarten Sap, Chaitanya Malaviya, Asli Celikyilmaz, and Yejin Choi. 2019. Comet: Commonsense transformers for automatic knowledge graph construction. *arXiv preprint arXiv:1906.05317*.

Tommaso Caselli, Valerio Basile, Mitrović Jelena, Kartoziya Inga, Granitzer Michael, et al. 2020. I feel offended, don't be abusive! implicit/explicit messages in offensive and abusive language. In *Language Resources and Evaluation Conference*, pages 6193–6202. The European Language Resources Associatio.

Somnath Basu Roy Chowdhury and Snigdha Chaturvedi. 2021. Does commonsense help in detecting sarcasm? *arXiv preprint arXiv:2109.08588*.

Thomas Davidson, Dana Warmsley, Michael Macy, and Ingmar Weber. 2017. Automated hate speech detection and the problem of offensive language. In *Proceedings of the International AAAI Conference on Web and Social Media*, volume 11, pages 512–515.

Mai ElSherief, Caleb Ziems, David Muchlinski, Vaishnavi Anupindi, Jordyn Seybolt, Munmun De Choudhury, and Diyi Yang. 2021. Latent hatred: A benchmark for understanding implicit hate speech. *arXiv preprint arXiv:2109.05322*.

Antigoni Maria Founta, Constantinos Djouvas, Despoina Chatzakou, Ilias Leontiadis, Jeremy Blackburn, Gianluca Stringhini, Athena Vakali, Michael Sirivianos, and Nicolas Kourtellis. 2018. Large scale crowdsourcing and characterization of twitter abusive behavior. In *Twelfth International AAAI Conference on Web and Social Media*.

Lei Gao and Ruihong Huang. 2017. Detecting online hate speech using context aware models. *arXiv preprint arXiv:1710.07395*.

Svetlana Kiritchenko, Isar Nejadgholi, and Kathleen C Fraser. 2021. Confronting abusive language online: A survey from the ethical and human rights perspective. *Journal of Artificial Intelligence Research*, 71:431–478.

Jiangnan Li, Hongliang Pan, Zheng Lin, Peng Fu, and Weiping Wang. 2021. Sarcasm detection with commonsense knowledge. *IEEE/ACM Transactions on Audio, Speech, and Language Processing*, 29:3192–3201.

Ilia Markov and Walter Daelemans. 2021. Improving cross-domain hate speech detection by reducing the false positive rate. In *Proceedings of the Fourth Workshop on NLP for Internet Freedom: Censorship, Disinformation, and Propaganda*, pages 17–22, Online. Association for Computational Linguistics.

M Mozafari, R Farahbakhsh, and N Crespi. 2020. Hate speech detection and racial bias mitigation in social media based on bert model. *PLoS ONE*, 15(8):e0237861.

Debaditya Pal, Kaustubh Chaudhari, and Harsh Sharma. 2022. Combating high variance in data-scarce implicit hate speech classification. *arXiv preprint arXiv:2208.13595*.

Nils Reimers and Iryna Gurevych. 2019. Sentence-bert: Sentence embeddings using siamese bert-networks. *arXiv preprint arXiv:1908.10084*.

Marco Tulio Ribeiro, Sameer Singh, and Carlos Guestrin. 2016. " why should i trust you?" explaining the predictions of any classifier. In *Proceedings of the 22nd ACM SIGKDD international conference on knowledge discovery and data mining*, pages 1135–1144.

Maarten Sap, Saadia Gabriel, Lianhui Qin, Dan Jurafsky, Noah A Smith, and Yejin Choi. 2019. Social bias frames: Reasoning about social and power implications of language. *arXiv preprint arXiv:1911.03891*.

Johannes M van Hulst, Faegheh Hasibi, Koen Dercksen, Krisztian Balog, and Arjen P de Vries. 2020. Rel: An entity linker standing on the shoulders of giants. In *Proceedings of the 43rd International ACM SIGIR Conference on Research and Development in Information Retrieval*, pages 2197–2200.

Denny Vrandečić and Markus Krötzsch. 2014. Wikidata: a free collaborative knowledgebase. *Communications of the ACM*, 57(10):78–85.

Zeerak Waseem, Thomas Davidson, Dana Warmsley, and Ingmar Weber. 2017. Understanding abuse: A typology of abusive language detection subtasks. *arXiv preprint arXiv:1705.09899*.

Zeerak Waseem and Dirk Hovy. 2016. Hateful symbols or hateful people? predictive features for hate speech detection on twitter. In *Proceedings of the NAACL student research workshop*, pages 88–93.

A Dataset of Sustainable Diet Arguments on Twitter

Marcus Astrup Hansen **Daniel Hershcovich**
Department of Computer Science
University of Copenhagen
dh@di.ku.dk

Abstract

Sustainable development requires a significant change in our dietary habits. Argument mining can help achieve this goal by both affecting and helping understand people's behavior. We design an annotation scheme for argument mining from online discourse around sustainable diets, including novel evidence types specific to this domain. Using Twitter as a source, we crowdsource a dataset of 597 tweets annotated in relation to 5 topics. We benchmark a variety of NLP models on this dataset, demonstrating strong performance in some sub-tasks, while highlighting remaining challenges.

1 Introduction

In Natural Language Processing (NLP), impact on climate change is usually only framed in the context of efficiency Strubell et al. (2019); Schwartz et al. (2020); Puvis de Chavannes et al. (2021). While efficiency improvements are welcome, we risk greenwashing NLP and further neglecting the field's potential to positively impact climate change. Hershcovich et al. (2022) proposed to strive towards *net positive* climate impact of NLP by developing beneficial applications (see §3 for related work in this direction).

In IBM's Project Debater (Slonim et al., 2021), a large team of researchers created a system capable of autonomously debating a human in a structured environment. While the system could not convince many people to switch positions, it helped to educate people about certain topics. This can be regarded as a first step towards behavioral change (Boström, 2020; Lockie, 2022).

In this paper we propose to apply debating technology to promote behavioral change that benefits the environment and climate: namely, mining arguments that can convince people to undergo a shift to a more climate-friendly diet (see §2). Our focus is on extracting and labeling argumentative structures used in online social media—specifically, Twitter—and compiling them into a domain-specific English dataset for green nutrition. Our annotation focuses on subjective and anecdotal evidence, shifting away from traditional argument mining methods where more strict explicit evidence is preferred. This shift is motivated by sociological research that shows that anecdotal stories are more persuasive in changing people's opinion (Petty et al., 1981; Hidey et al., 2017). Finally, we train and benchmark baseline models on the dataset, showing promising results but also identifying important challenges.[1]

2 Sustainable Diets

To successfully transform our societies to become more sustainable, we need to focus on improving the sustainability of our diets. The EAT-Lancet report (Willett et al., 2019) has marked this as a shift away from excessive consumption of animal protein-heavy diets. However, unfortunately, such diets are generally quite prevalent in many developed countries. The science behind the benefits of such a transition is quite well established (Prag and Henriksen, 2021), but there is still a lack of incentives to change habitual behaviors for people participating. To change such incentives and habits requires actions from all aspects of society, including individual consumers. Loorbach (2009) argues that the social transition of our diets to become more sustainable requires us to continuously monitor and evaluate processes across all the societal facets to help solve issues and update practices.

Therefore to successfully transform our society to consume a sustainable diet for a successful green transition, we must change the social and cultural conditions and traditions around green nutrition. However, Graça et al. (2019) shows that there is solid evidence that established dietary preferences

[1] The dataset and models can be found in `https://github.com/danielhers/sustainable-diet-arguments-twitter`.

Proceedings of the Second Workshop on NLP for Positive Impact (NLP4PI), pages 40 - 58
December 7, 2022 ©2022 Association for Computational Linguistics

are hard to change for large consumer segments due to negative taste perceptions and lack of knowledge and skills about healthy and green foods. Here, we address this challenge by aiming to collect arguments covering various aspects, beyond the obvious ones about health and climate. Regardless of which aspects are more convincing, the end result will benefit the climate—our rationale is that the end will justify the means.

3 Related work

Positive environmental impact. Machine learning and related fields have a substantial potential to help address climate change (Kaack et al., 2022). Some of the potential paths where NLP can be used for a positive impact include helping people understand their carbon footprint, facilitating behavior change towards more sustainable practices, informing policy and supporting education and financial regulation (Rolnick et al., 2019). Cross-disciplinary research with social science can help improve the understanding of large-scale discourse spread over multiple channels regarding climate change (Stede and Patz, 2021). Successful examples include compliance verification of corporate reports: Bingler et al. (2022) examined annual corporate reports and found many engage in "cheap talk" (greenwashing), e.g., lacking specificity in climate goals and activities. Biamby et al. (2022) created a dataset for and detected images with misleading captions on Twitter for several topics, including climate change. These efforts allow for better policy shaping and steering of the online discourse around climate change, which we hope to achieve with our work too.

Project Debater. As part of the Debater project (Slonim et al., 2021), Ein-Dor et al. (2019) created an end to end argument mining system where topics are used to mine for arguments in a very large corpus of English newspaper articles and Wikipedia articles. Toledo-Ronen et al. (2020) subsequently automatically translated the argument corpus to five languages, projecting the labels from English. They additionally collected and annotated crowdsourced arguments in these languages natively, annotating argument quality and evidence. They used a large group of annotators with rigid guidelines, resulting in high quality multilingual arguments. We use a similar framework and methodology, but use Twitter as a corpus and focus on English only in this paper.

Argument mining from social media. Early work on argumentation mining from Twitter found it is a feasible but challenging task, due to unique linguistic properties (register, domain, noisy data) and differences with respect to established argumentation theories and phenomena, e.g,. the need to distinguish opinions from facts (Habernal and Gurevych, 2017; Dusmanu et al., 2017). More recently, Schaefer and Stede (2020) created a dataset of 300 German tweets containing the word "Klima" (climate), annotated for three labels: argumentative, claim and evidence. They experimented with different models for classifying tweets, using an argument mining pipeline (Schaefer, 2021) that first filters out irrelevant tweets, then extracts ADUs (argument discourse units, namely claims or evidence), classifies the tweets as either supporting or attacking a claim and builds a graph of ranked arguments. They stressed the importance of argument quality prediction as part of the pipeline. Our approach is similar to Schaefer and Stede (2020)'s, but we leave argument quality to future work. As examples for alternative approaches, Schaefer and Stede (2021) annotated 3244 German Facebook comments on a political talk show's page from February 2019. They classified toxic, engaging and fact-claiming comments, focus mainly on the latter due to their relation to evidence detection for argument mining. Cheema et al. (2022) created a multimodal argument mining dataset with the focus on verifiable claims, manually annotating 3000 tweets for three topics covering COVID-19, climate change and technology. They found that identifying checkworthy claims was subjective for both students and experts, and that pre-trained models yield the best performance for both modality types. Wojatzki and Zesch (2016) created a dataset of argumentative tweets for the topic of atheism, using stance as a proxy for implicit arguments. They allowed annotators to mark text as lacking context or being ironic, and asked them to annotate the stance of arguments towards the topic. They then used this measure as the signal for implicit arguments. For explicit arguments, the annotators could only annotate stance towards targets if they had textual evidence.

4 Annotation Scheme

We define an argument mining annotation scheme based on previous work (Aharoni et al., 2014; Ein-Dor et al., 2019; Slonim et al., 2021; Schaefer and Stede, 2020), consisting of Topics and the annotation labels Argumentative, Claim, Evidence, Evidence type and Pro/Con.

Topics. To be useful for debates and analysis, arguments are mined with respect to a *topic*—"a short, usually controversial statement that defines the subject of interest" (Aharoni et al., 2014). Topics need to be short, clear, dividing, and relevant to our central theme of sustainable nutrition. We also wish for the topics not to be too specific—for high coverage, we choose broad and simple topics:[2]

T1 *We should reduce the consumption of meat*
T2 *Plant-based food should be encouraged*
T3 *Meat alternatives should be encouraged*
T4 *Vegan and vegetarian diets should be encouraged*
T5 *We should pursue policies that promote sustainable foods*

Argumentative. Argumentative is the label that denotes if a tweet is argumentative for any topic. This means the tweet contains argumentative structures such as claims or evidence while having a clear stance on some topic. We define arguments broadly, including those that do not refer to the topic explicitly but whose stance toward it is only implied. Indeed, Wojatzki and Zesch (2016) achieved a similar result by using stance detection as a proxy. If an argument is not clear in its stance, i.e., it is neutral or unrelated, it is not be considered argumentative.

Claim. A claim is a standpoint towards the topic being discussed (Schaefer and Stede, 2020). We expand upon this definition by allowing the standpoint to indirectly acknowledge the topic discussed, which is *implicit argumentation*, or explicitly when directly acknowledging the discussed topic. If a claim is not related to the discussed topic, it is not considered a claim. A claim should further be able to exist in a self-contained manner, not relying on external references to fully convey the claim and stance it takes towards the topic. Therefore, it should be able to fully articulate the entire claim without the need for external reference. A tweet referencing others' stance towards the topic is not considered a claim.

Evidence. Evidence is a statement that explains a stance towards the topic. It can be stated in combination with a claim, or it can be self-contained if it is just stating a fact or referencing studies related to the topic. Therefore a tweet does not have to co-occur with a claim to contain evidence relevant to the topic, and as such, evidence is not dependent on a claim when annotating (see §5). A tweet can still contain claims with supporting evidence as part of its text. If evidence is unrelated to the discussed topic, it is not considered evidence.

Evidence type. Evidence is labeled as one of the following types. The first three types are from Rinott et al. (2015), while we propose the last two based on preliminary exploration of our data:

1. **Anecdotal.** A description of an episode(s), centered on individual(s) or clearly located in place and/or in time.

2. **Expert.** Testimony by a person, group, committee, an organization with some known expertise/authority on the topic.

3. **Study.** Results of a quantitative analysis of data, given as numbers, or as conclusions.

4. **Fact.** A known piece of information without a clear source, regardless of whether it is a *true* fact or not. See example in Figure 1a.

5. **Normative.** Description of a belief or value the author holds. See example in Figure 1b.

See Table 1 for examples from the dataset. If its type is unclear, a tweet should not be considered evidence, and might be a claim instead. If neither is clear, the tweet itself might lack context and should not be considered argumentative.

Pro/Con. The stance of a tweet towards a topic depends on a claim or evidence being present in the tweet. Moreover, if there is no clear stance, the tweet should not be considered argumentative.

5 Dataset

Here we describe the procedure for collecting and annotating our dataset of tweets containing arguments related to the topics described in §4.

Scraping. The corpus used for annotation is a collection of tweets scraped from Twitter using tweepy[3] by iteratively creating queries by a combination of keywords[4] and n-grams from an initial set of topics. For each query, we scrape a maximum of 1000 tweets. We remove retweets, quote tweets, links and videos, as well as tweets with less than three words, resulting in 31840 English tweets in total. User mentions are replaced with

[2]Note that T5 is more complex and specific. It covers a specific type of tweets that we noticed during early annotation work, discussing sustainable food policy.

[3]`https://github.com/tweepy/tweepy`

[4]See Appendix D for a listing of the queries.

(a) Humans should not eat animals as we don't need meat to fulfill our nutritional needs.

Claim — Evidence: Fact

(b) It is morally wrong to eat and cause animals pain to fulfill our nutritional needs.

Evidence: Normative

Figure 1: Simplified examples of arguments for the topic T1 *(We should reduce the consumption of meat)*. In (a) the evidence type is Fact, since no source is given. In (b) it is Normative, as it describes a belief but is more elaborate than a claim. Note that the level of granularity in our dataset is a whole tweet rather than spans within a tweet. Here, spans are indicated to illustrate which part of the tweet suggests that it should have a particular label.

Evidence type	Example	Topic(s)	Pro/Con
Anecdotal	*We are on the green bean diet here, too! I love them. Mom hasn't tried broccoli*	T1, T2, T3, T4, T5	Pro
Expert	*Many fruit & veg (which contain natural acid) don't trigger flare ups- The list is long and varied (obs this may not apply to you) but after a little digging I found some doctors do reccomend a plant based diet to ease the inflammation. Going meatless is even recommended by ICA*	T2, T4	Pro
Study	*According to a 2022 study, eating an optimal #diet of whole grains, legumes, fish, fruits, vegetables and nuts can improve life expectancy by how many years?*	T2, T4	Pro
Fact	*Hey eco-friendlies! The well known high-carbon company McDonalds produces 1.5 MILLION tonnes of food packaging alone ! Fun fact carbon footprints are important! Tune in for more behind closed door stats!*	T5	Pro
Normative	*The dangerous of this thing is that our vegan extremists will start interfering in this..*	T4	Con
Unrelated/no evidence	*Give your children healthy food to avoid the dad bod haha*		

Table 1: Examples from the dataset of tweets containing evidence for each evidence type, the topics for which they were annotated as evidence and their pro/con annotation for each of the topics.

<MENTION>. Hashtags and emojis are kept as they contain relevant information.

Relevance-based filtering. Upon initial inspection, we find that most tweets are not relevant to any of our topics, despite matching our queries. Therefore, before sampling data for annotation, we use an information retrieval system to extract the most relevant tweets in relation to our topics. We use a neural ranking model trained for semantic search (Reimers and Gurevych, 2019) that was trained to score the relevance of an answer to a question. We deem this a decent proxy for our retrieval system as we want to find tweets that take a stance and explain their claims and evidence in the context of a topic. We elaborate more on this model in §6.

Sampling. When generating our dataset, we sample 250 tweets at random from the full unfiltered corpus, and combine this set with 347 random tweets filtered by the semantic model.

Annotation. Annotation is conducted using Amazon Mechanical Turk[5] in rounds as described in Figure 2. Five workers annotated each instance. The annotations guidelines are given in Appendix A. First, tweets are annotated as for whether they are Argumentative regardless of a topic. Second, annotators are presented with an Argumentative tweet as well as our list of topics, and are asked to select the topics for which the tweet is a Claim. This ensures that annotators judge the topics relative to each other and are thus more consistent (despite their conceptual overlap) than if each tweet/topic pair were annotated separately. Separately, annotators are presented with an Argumentative tweet as well as one topic, and are asked to select the Evidence Type of the tweet with respect to the topic (or indicate that it is not Evidence). This is done to facilitate the annotation of the heterogeneous Evidence label. The binary label is then derived from this annotation by collapsing all types as positive.

[5] https://www.mturk.com

Topic	Tweets	Arg	ADUs	Claims	Evidence	Claims with evidence	Pro	Con
T1	597	387	118	63	89	34	77	37
T2	597	387	130	92	85	47	89	38
T3	597	387	85	42	63	20	58	27
T4	597	387	156	106	112	62	99	54
T5	597	387	140	60	113	33	96	37
Full set	2985	1935	629	363	462	196	419	193

Table 2: Statistics for the different topics and the overall full set. Arg: Argumentative. ADU: argument discourse units (Claim or Evidence). Labels are based on majority voting among annotators. Of the ADUs, we see more Evidence than Claims. Pro/con labels are rather unbalanced, with a bias towards positive stance.

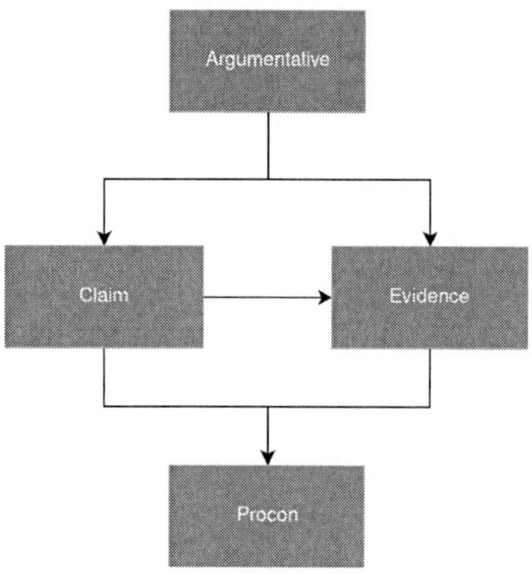

Figure 2: Dependencies between annotation rounds.

Finally, Claims and Evidence are presented along with one topic at a time, and annotators are asked to indicate whether they support or contest the topic.

Inter-annotator agreement. We calculate the average inter-annotator agreement for our crowd-sourced data using Cohen's kappa. The resulting scores are 0.49 for Argumentative, 0.47 for Claim, 0.15 for Evidence (including type) and 0.63 for Pro/Con. The low agreement for Evidence is likely due to the multi-class label being harder to agree upon than a binary label.

Statistics. Table 2 presents statistics of the labeled dataset. Most annotators labeled a substantial amount of tweets as Argumentative. However, only a minority actually contained ADUs (Claims/Evidence). This discrepancy can be attributed to the Argumentative label being decoupled from the topic itself: an Argumentative tweet might only be relevant for another topic, either within our set of five topics or for a different topic altogether.

Like Cheng et al. (2022), we find substantially more Evidence than Claims, though their Evidence depends on Claims. Evidence seems to generally be more prevalent than Claims in online discourse. This can also result from our annotation procedure, where Claims require identifying relevant topics, and Evidence requires identifying the type. On the other hand, the broad types of Evidence we allow and the fact that they are not dependent on Claims allows for more Evidence than in other datasets.

The fact that Pro/Con labels are biased towards positive stance could be due to online discourse being more prevalent for the Pro side rather than other domains. The annotators' preconceived notions might have played a role in them being more inclined to select Pro in situations where they could have been uncertain due to the topic's definitions.

Topic overlap. In Figure 3, we see how much each topic's tweets overlap with other topics as a percentage of their combined number of tweets, where they both have either evidence or claim. We see that all topics have roughly 20% of their tweets overlapping with another topic. This is not surprising as the topics are all very similar, and tweets can easily be relevant for more than one topic at a time.

Evidence types. Figure 4 shows the distribution of Evidence types in the dataset. Most Evidence is Normative or Anecdotal, reflecting online discourse being less strict, which lends itself to using weaker types of Evidence to explain one's stance.

6 Experiments

To evaluate the ability of existing models to mine arguments according to our scheme, we conduct a series of experiments with various approaches.

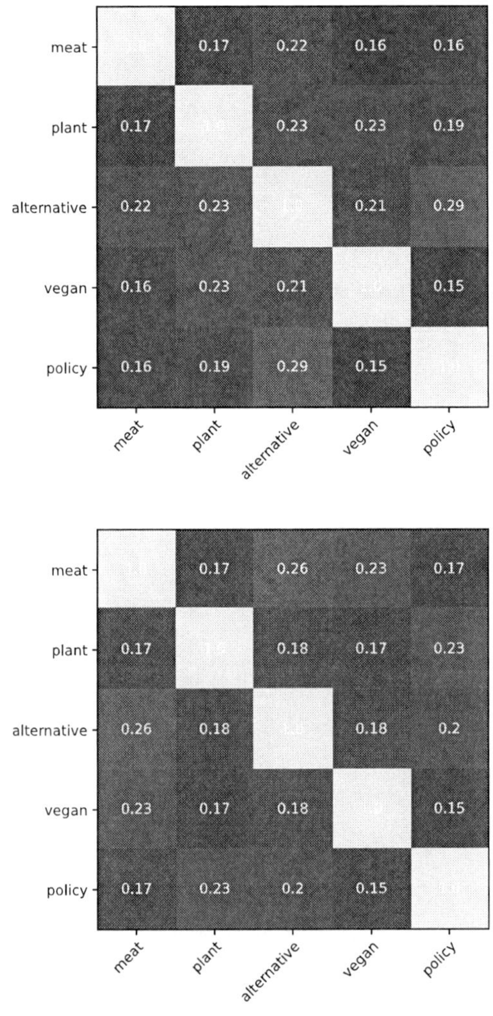

Figure 3: Percentage of claims (above) and evidence (below) overlapping between topics: T1=meat, T2=plant, T3=alternative, T4=vegan, T5=policy.

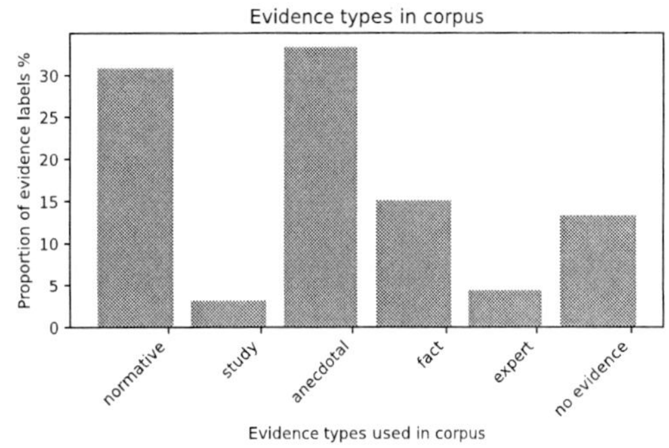

Figure 4: Distribution of Evidence types in the dataset. Note that "no evidence" is considered a type due to the combined annotation procedure, where Evidence is annotated immediately along with its type (or as "no evidence" when no type is applicable).

6.1 Information Retrieval

We experiment with information retrieval baselines, rating how likely a document is to be relevant for a query:

BM-25 (Trotman et al., 2014) is a standard retrieval model based on TF-IDF scores of exact token matches, used in many systems and should give a good benchmark for the difficulty of retrieving claims and evidence just from topic queries. It returns an unbounded positive score, which we cut off at 1.

`multi-qa-MiniLM-L6-cos-v1`[6] is a sentence transformer (Reimers and Gurevych, 2019) based on MiniLM (Wang et al., 2020), which is a distilled version of `UniLM v2` (Bao et al., 2020), which was pre-trained on 160GB text corpora from English Wikipedia, BookCorpus, OpenWebText, CC-News and Stories. `multi-qa-MiniLM-L6-cos-v1` was fine-tuned on the concatenation of multiple question answering (QA) dataset, totalling about 215M instances. This is the same semantic search model we used in §5 for filtering tweets, and therefore this experiment should give us a good idea of how well our models perform compared to a model that has had an impact on the selection previously. The model returns a score between 0 and 1. We use 0.5 as the cut-off for classification.

The retrieval models are unsupervised, and consider neither argumentativeness, which is independent of the topic, nor pro/con (stance classification). However, they serve as a baseline for claim and evidence detection, as those tasks have a retrieval aspect. We use the tweet as a document and the topic as a query, scoring their relevance and using the resulting scores from the models for classification.

6.2 IBM Debater

IBM Debater offers implementations for various argument mining components (Slonim et al., 2021), and provides an API,[7] which we use as a baseline representing existing argument mining models. It has been trained on a different type of data from different domains and with stricter annotation guide-

[6] `https://huggingface.co/sentence-transformers/multi-qa-MiniLM-L6-cos-v1`

[7] `https://early-access-program.debater.res.ibm.com`

lines. We evaluate their "zero-shot transfer" to our dataset, without any further training.

6.3 Fine-tuned RoBERTa

Pretrained language models such as BERT (Devlin et al., 2019) and RoBERTa (Liu et al., 2019) have been used successfully on similar datasets (Cheng et al., 2022; Schaefer and Stede, 2021).[8] We fine-tune and evaluate `cardiffnlp/twitter-roberta-base`,[9], which was trained on a dataset containing 58M tweets (Barbieri et al., 2020), specifically to handle user identifier tokens and emojis.[10] For claim, evidence, and pro/con, the topic plays an essential role in the classification. To encode tweet-topic pairs, we combine the tweet and topic using a separator token (`[SEP]`).

Our dataset contains probabilities for each label according to the distribution over the different annotators. We use cross-entropy with raw probabilities rather than rounding the labels, and fine-tune the RoBERTa encoder as part of the training. The hyperparameters used are: learning rate 5e-5, batch size 5, weight decay 0.05 and the `adamw` optimizer.

6.4 XGBoost + RoBERTa

Schaefer and Stede (2020) used XGBoost (Chen and Guestrin, 2016) in combination with BERT on a similar dataset to ours. We evaluate this model on our dataset across all label targets. We train the XGBoost classifier on top of frozen contextualized embeddings from RoBERTa (again, `cardiffnlp/twitter-roberta-base`), since XGBoost is not a neural model and does not support backpropagating gradients to fine-tune the underlying encoder. All labels in this experiment are determined by majority vote and take the values $\{0, 1\}$ except for pro/con, which takes the values $\{-1, 1\}$.

Here we have two ways of embedding the topic: the first approach is to embed the tweet only on its own, which is done for the argumentative task as it is not dependent on the topic. The other method is to combine the tweet and topic using a separator token (`[SEP]`), which is used for the other tasks.

We run a grid search with three-fold cross-validation for each task, over three hyperparameters: learning-rate $\in \{0.01, 0.03, 0.06\}$, max-depth $\in \{1, 3, 5, 6, 7, 8, 9, 10\}$ and number of estimators $\in \{1, 2, 5, 7, 10, 15, 20, 25, 30, 40, 60, 80, 100\}$. We select the best combination based on macro F1 score.

Model	Macro		
	F1	P	R
Majority Class	0.39	0.32	0.50
Random Class	0.49	0.50	0.50
Fine-tuned RoBERTa	0.51	0.51	0.51
RoBERTa + XGBoost	**0.67**	**0.69**	**0.67**

Table 3: Results from models evaluated on the **argumentative** task. P and R are precision and recall, with their attached averaging type. Highlighted are the best performing model for their task and averaging type.

Model	Macro		
	F1	P	R
Majority Class	0.45	0.41	0.50
Random Class	0.50	0.50	0.50
BM25	0.50	0.61	0.55
multi-qa-MiniLM	**0.67**	**0.73**	**0.65**
IBM-API	0.57	0.57	0.57
Fine-tuned RoBERTa	0.48	0.50	0.47
RoBERTa + XGBoost	0.51	0.59	0.53

Table 4: Results on the **claim** task.

6.5 Experimental Setup

To classify for argumentative tweets, we only use the tweets and disregard the topics. We subsequently only use argumentative tweets (according to the human annotation) when experimenting with detecting claims and evidence. Pro/con classification is only evaluated on for tweets containing evidence or claims (according to the human annotation). We perform 3-fold cross-validation with maximum 15 epochs, using early stopping based on validation macro F1 evaluated every 20 batches with patience set to 5.

We also report results for Majority Class and Random Class baselines, which respectively select the most common label for each task (based on the training set), and a random class with uniform probability.

[8] See Appendix E for experimental replication of previous results.

[9] `https://huggingface.co/cardiffnlp/twitter-roberta-base`

[10] The model's tokenizer does not have `<MENTION>` as a token. Instead, it recognizes `@user`, so we replace all our `<MENTION>` tokens with `@user` in preprocessing.

Model	Macro		
	F1	P	R
Majority Class	0.44	0.39	0.50
Random Class	0.49	0.50	0.50
BM25	0.52	0.60	0.56
multi-qa-MiniLM	**0.64**	**0.66**	**0.63**
IBM-API	0.46	0.51	0.57
Fine-tuned RoBERTa	0.48	0.49	0.48
RoBERTa + XGBoost	0.47	0.60	0.51

Table 5: Results on the **evidence** task.

Model	Macro		
	F1	P	R
Majority Class	0.40	0.34	0.50
Random Class	0.52	0.53	0.54
IBM-API	**0.59**	**0.60**	**0.59**
Fine-tuned RoBERTa	0.45	0.48	0.45
RoBERTa + XGBoost	0.53	0.53	0.54

Table 6: Results on the **pro/con** task.

7 Results

The results are shown in Table 3 for argumentative, Table 4 for claim, Table 5 for evidence and Table 6 for pro/con. In Table 3 we see XGBoost performs well on all metrics for the argumentative task. The fine-tuned RoBERTa does not perform well on the argumentative task, underperforming both the random and majority baselines. In Table 4 we see that `multi-qa-MiniLM-L6-cos-v1` outperforms all other models with a large margin for claims. BM25 only matches when there is an overlap in vocabulary between tweet and topic, which `multi-qa-MiniLM-L6-cos-v1` does not require. Table 5 shows similar results for evidence, where `multi-qa-MiniLM-L6-cos-v1` and BM25 outperform all other models. One interesting result is the relatively large dip in performance for the IBM-API for evidence with respect to claims, suggesting the change in annotation style for evidence has a significant impact compared to previous works. On the pro/con task (Table 6), both the IBM-API and RoBERTa + XGBoost outperform the baselines in all metrics, but not the fine-tuned RoBERTa. The IBM-API has the best performance in this case, by a large margin.

Input encoding for XGBoost. The different methods of combining topics and tweets for XGBoost (see §6) have a relatively small impact on performance. The concatenation method outperforms the `[SEP]` method in pro/con and claim, and therefore we only report results using it in the tables.

XGBoost vs. fine-tuning. Overall, XGBoost performs well compared to the fine-tuned RoBERTa. This could be due to training issues or a lack of data: we only have about 600 unique tweets, with only a fraction of them being annotated as containing claims and evidence, causing issues of sparsity and dataset imbalance. This could be mitigated by using a different training approach or annotating more examples in the future.

Success of retrieval models. The retrieval models perform well in the claim and evidence tasks, where `multi-qa-MiniLM-L6-cos-v1` performs the best overall. Of course, this result should be interpreted with great skepticism, as it is likely due to the filtering process we did early in our dataset compilation (§5) and should not be discounted as it has added some bias to the data. However, it also shows that the filtering process did have a decent impact on scoping in on tweets most likely to contain argumentative structures. Therefore, the `multi-qa-MiniLM-L6-cos-v1` results could be interpreted as the proportion of retrieved tweets containing argumentative structures. The BM25 model performs well with its precision scores for the binary average, which makes sense as it requires a vocabulary overlap between the tweet and topic. Due to a relatively low overlap between the tasks for the tweet and their topics (see Appendix C), BM25 only needs one token to overlap for it to mark it as relevant and therefore will retrieve quite a few false-positive tweets on average. Nevertheless, this could also be because each topic only has a few keywords, making them good queries. Overall, the retrieval models make a good baseline for future evidence and claim tasks experiments.

IBM Debater. The IBM-API models also perform well for the pro/con and claim task. However, surprisingly, the model performs poorly on the evidence task. This could be due to a shift in the task definition, since we added two new types of evidence: normative and fact. They account for nearly half of all the annotated evidence. However, anecdotal evidence is based on the IBM Debater definitions and is the most frequent type of evidence, so the issue might be one of several. First, the semantic structures in tweets are hard for the IBM models to adapt to, causing them to miss most evidence. Another reason could be that annotators have overused anecdotal evidence where it should have been labeled as normative or fact or not as evidence. Overall, the IBM models have performed exceptionally well, considering they have never seen data of this type when compared to other baselines.

8 Discussion and Limitations

While we frame our dataset around sustainable diets, it is, in fact, focused on plant-based diets. Many other aspects are relevant for sustainability, including production, geographical location, genetic modification, transportation, water consumption, land preservation and health. We leave these issues to future work.

The topics used in this paper are simple by design. They are all quite similar, which might cause some correlation issues when training models. For instance, T1 (discussing meat consumption) has a significant overlap with T3 (discussing meat alternatives) of 22% for claim and 26% for evidence. However, it can also indicate the presence of other topics that are similar to both. For instance, when arguing for reducing meat, people might use animal welfare as evidence. Therefore, topic exploration and expansion could be done further to improve the spectrum of topics in the dataset and explore how relationships between topics are made and related in debates.

The dataset is a starting point for training argument mining models. It is balanced in the distribution of the claims and evidence across the topics, with a minor overlap between topics of roughly 20%. Our annotation guidelines are robust enough to be used for crowdsourced and expert annotation. The low agreement in the crowdsourced annotations for evidence may be improved by better guidelines or a different annotation methodology, but they may simply be a reflection of inherent subjectivity. This will be investigated in future work.

One issue with this dataset is its relative lack of context for many of the tweets due to them referencing outside tweets or responding to other users in a discussion. There is good potential here to utilize this external context for further argument mining or further improve the detection of claims and evidence in the primary tweet. This could initially be done by annotating the current tweets as debate fragments if large parts are out of context. Here a debate fragment tweet would refer to a tweet in a larger debate with other users and could then be used for future extraction and more expansive mining of ADUs.

Fine-tuned RoBERTa	
Information	**Unit**
1. Is the resulting model publicly available?	No
2. How much time does the training of the final model take?	105 Seconds
3. How much time did all model experiments take (incl. hyperparameter search)?	4228 seconds
4. What was the energy consumption (GPU/CPU)?	333 Watt
5. At which geo location were the computations performed?	Denmark
6. How much CO2eq was emitted to train the final model?	0.975g
7. How much CO2eq was emitted for all experiments?	39g

Table 7: Proposed climate performance model card for our fine-tuned RoBERTa model experiments.

One major difference between previous work and ours is data size: our dataset contains only 597 unique tweets annotated for 5 topics, while Schaefer and Stede (2021) annotated 3244 Facebook comments and Cheng et al. (2022) annotated nearly 70k sentences. Future experiments on a larger dataset may result in a different conclusion with respect to the relative performance of the models.

9 Conclusion

We defined an annotation scheme for an argument mining task tailored for social media with a focus on argumentation for sustainable nutrition. We proposed two new types of Evidence: Normative and Fact. With this scheme we scraped and annotated a dataset containing 597 tweets for five different topics, resulting in a dataset of 2985 annotated tweet-topic pairs. XGBoost is a strong starting point for argument mining, and IBM Project Debater API is a robust zero-shot model for argumentation tasks.

10 Broader Impact

Our dataset and models were designed with the intention to have positive impact on the environment by promoting sustainable consumer practices: by mining for convincing arguments of various aspects related to sustainable diets, downstream applications can improve marketing of sustainable products. Implementation of the resulting technol-

RoBERTa embeddings + XGBoost	
Information	**Unit**
1. Is the resulting model publicly available?	No
2. How much time does the training of the final model take?	57 Seconds
3. How much time did all model experiments take (incl. hyperparameter search)?	456 seconds
4. What was the energy consumption (GPU/CPU)?	28 Watt
5. At which geo location were the computations performed?	Denmark
6. How much CO2eq was emitted to train the final model?	0.08g
7. How much CO2eq was emitted for all experiments?	3.5g

Table 8: Proposed climate performance model card for our RoBERTa + XGBoost model experiments.

ogy will enable more effective communication campaigns to increase adherence with dietary guidelines. Furthermore, by identifying diverse arguments, our work can contribute to ethnographic research on public opinions towards sustainable diets, and help shape public policy. Promoting responsible behaviour is an important gap, as food marketing is already driven by business incentives. However, the risk of manipulative *dual use* must be considered. Future applications of this work must involve AI ethics experts and be complemented by explainability methods and fact verification to guarantee reliability of generated claims and ensure alignment with expected values.

Negative impact on the environment as a result of the development and any potential deployment of the models must be taken into account as well. Tables 7 and 8 contain the climate performance model card for the fine-tuned RoBERTa and RoBERTa + XGBoost models, according to the guidelines defined by Hershcovich et al. (2022).

10.1 Data Statement

The following is our data statement following Bender and Friedman (2018):

A. CURATION RATIONALE

In order to have a potential net positive impact on promoting sustainable diets in the future, a dataset with a focus on dietary discussions was needed. Twitter was deemed an excellent source for this information and as such scraping of 31840 tweets was done in combination with relevance filtering. This has resulted in 597 tweets that has been annotated for 4 different tasks, each done for 5 different topics in relation to discussions around diets.

B. LANGUAGE VARIETY

The tweets in this dataset where scraped in April 2022 with the Twitter API.[11] The set of English tweets was scraped without information of regional variety, it is only known that they are written in English. But certain tweets make specific wordings from which it can be inferred they are from the US (en-US) or India (en-IN). More regions are most likely also represented in the dataset, but specifics are unknown.

C. SPEAKER DEMOGRAPHIC

The authors of the tweets demographics were not collected. The tweets originate from 597 unique users.

D. ANNOTATOR DEMOGRAPHIC

The data was annotated by a crowd of annotators procured from Amazon Mechanical Turk. The specific region used was the US East Coast. There is no demographic information available from Amazon Mechanical Turk users beyond the requirements set for workers to be allowed to work on HITs—in the case of this dataset the only requirement is a masters qualification. Assuming we have an even distribution of the known demographics on Amazon Mechanical Turk, we would have a slightly skewed split between genders with 57% identifying as female. The age distribution is towards the younger ages with 29.7% being between 18-29 and 36.8% 30-39 and the majority identifying as white 79.9%.[12]

E. SPEECH SITUATION

The tweets can contain a maximum of 280 characters and are written in a spontaneous and asynchronous format. The tweets were collected with a focus on diet, but parts of the tweets also cover climate, sustainability, animal welfare and policy as side effects of our scraping methods and the topics used for relevance filtering. The majority of the tweets are in response to other Twitter users' tweets, so the intended audience would be one of the two opposing sides in a debate around one of the 5 topics in this paper.

F. TEXT CHARACTERISTICS

The tweets are only in raw text format as we filtered out any tweets containing URLs, images and other non textual modalities. Many of the tweets

[11] `https://developer.twitter.com/en/docs/twitter-api`

[12] More information on the demographics on Amazon Mechanical Turk can be found in `https://www.cloudresearch.com/resources/blog/who-uses-amazon-mturk-2020-demographics/`.

contain references to other users or users' tweets in a conversation format. Therefore, some tweets' context is limited without added work to include the references. There are also emojis and hashtags present in a large section of the tweets.

G. RECORDING QUALITY: N/A

H. OTHER: N/A

I. PROVENANCE APPENDIX: N/A

References

Ehud Aharoni, Anatoly Polnarov, Tamar Lavee, Daniel Hershcovich, Ran Levy, Ruty Rinott, Dan Gutfreund, and Noam Slonim. 2014. A benchmark dataset for automatic detection of claims and evidence in the context of controversial topics. In *Proceedings of the First Workshop on Argumentation Mining*, pages 64–68, Baltimore, Maryland. Association for Computational Linguistics.

Alan Akbik, Tanja Bergmann, Duncan Blythe, Kashif Rasul, Stefan Schweter, and Roland Vollgraf. 2019. Flair: An easy-to-use framework for state-of-the-art nlp. In *NAACL 2019, 2019 Annual Conference of the North American Chapter of the Association for Computational Linguistics (Demonstrations)*, pages 54–59.

Alan Akbik, Duncan Blythe, and Roland Vollgraf. 2018. Contextual string embeddings for sequence labeling. In *COLING 2018, 27th International Conference on Computational Linguistics*, pages 1638–1649.

Hangbo Bao, Li Dong, Furu Wei, Wenhui Wang, Nan Yang, Xiaodong Liu, Yu Wang, Jianfeng Gao, Songhao Piao, Ming Zhou, et al. 2020. Unilmv2: Pseudo-masked language models for unified language model pre-training. In *International Conference on Machine Learning*, pages 642–652. PMLR.

Francesco Barbieri, Jose Camacho-Collados, Luis Espinosa Anke, and Leonardo Neves. 2020. TweetEval: Unified benchmark and comparative evaluation for tweet classification. In *Findings of the Association for Computational Linguistics: EMNLP 2020*, pages 1644–1650, Online. Association for Computational Linguistics.

Emily M. Bender and Batya Friedman. 2018. Data statements for natural language processing: Toward mitigating system bias and enabling better science. *Transactions of the Association for Computational Linguistics*, 6:587–604.

Giscard Biamby, Grace Luo, Trevor Darrell, and Anna Rohrbach. 2022. Twitter-COMMs: Detecting climate, COVID, and military multimodal misinformation. In *Proceedings of the 2022 Conference of the North American Chapter of the Association for Computational Linguistics: Human Language Technologies*, pages 1530–1549, Seattle, United States. Association for Computational Linguistics.

Julia Anna Bingler, Mathias Kraus, Markus Leippold, and Nicolas Webersinke. 2022. Cheap talk in corporate climate commitments: The role of active institutional ownership, signaling, materiality, and sentiment. (22-01).

Magnus Boström. 2020. The social life of mass and excess consumption. *Environmental Sociology*, 6(3):268–278.

Gullal S. Cheema, Sherzod Hakimov, Abdul Sittar, Eric Müller-Budack, Christian Otto, and Ralph Ewerth. 2022. Mm-claims: A dataset for multimodal claim detection in social media.

Tianqi Chen and Carlos Guestrin. 2016. Xgboost. *Proceedings of the 22nd ACM SIGKDD International Conference on Knowledge Discovery and Data Mining*.

Liying Cheng, Lidong Bing, Ruidan He, Qian Yu, Yan Zhang, and Luo Si. 2022. Iam: A comprehensive and large-scale dataset for integrated argument mining tasks.

Jacob Devlin, Ming-Wei Chang, Kenton Lee, and Kristina Toutanova. 2019. BERT: Pre-training of deep bidirectional transformers for language understanding. In *Proceedings of the 2019 Conference of the North American Chapter of the Association for Computational Linguistics: Human Language Technologies, Volume 1 (Long and Short Papers)*, pages 4171–4186, Minneapolis, Minnesota. Association for Computational Linguistics.

Mihai Dusmanu, Elena Cabrio, and Serena Villata. 2017. Argument mining on Twitter: Arguments, facts and sources. In *Proceedings of the 2017 Conference on Empirical Methods in Natural Language Processing*, pages 2317–2322, Copenhagen, Denmark. Association for Computational Linguistics.

Liat Ein-Dor, Eyal Shnarch, Lena Dankin, Alon Halfon, Benjamin Sznajder, Ariel Gera, Carlos Alzate, Martin Gleize, Leshem Choshen, Yufang Hou, Yonatan Bilu, Ranit Aharonov, and Noam Slonim. 2019. Corpus wide argument mining - a working solution. *CoRR*, abs/1911.10763.

João Graça, Cristina A. Godinho, and Monica Truninger. 2019. Reducing meat consumption and following plant-based diets: Current evidence and future directions to inform integrated transitions. *Trends in Food Science & Technology*, 91:380–390.

Ivan Habernal and Iryna Gurevych. 2017. Argumentation mining in user-generated web discourse. *Computational Linguistics*, 43(1):125–179.

Daniel Hershcovich, Nicolas Webersinke, Mathias Kraus, Julia Anna Bingler, and Markus Leippold. 2022. Towards climate awareness in NLP research. In *Proceedings of the 2022 Conference on Empirical Methods in Natural Language Processing*. Association for Computational Linguistics.

Christopher Hidey, Elena Musi, Alyssa Hwang, Smaranda Muresan, and Kathy McKeown. 2017. Analyzing the semantic types of claims and premises in an online persuasive forum. In *Proceedings of the 4th Workshop on Argument Mining*, pages 11–21, Copenhagen, Denmark. Association for Computational Linguistics.

Lynn H Kaack, Priya L Donti, Emma Strubell, George Kamiya, Felix Creutzig, and David Rolnick. 2022. Aligning artificial intelligence with climate change mitigation. *Nature Climate Change*, pages 1–10.

Yinhan Liu, Myle Ott, Naman Goyal, Jingfei Du, Mandar Joshi, Danqi Chen, Omer Levy, Mike Lewis, Luke Zettlemoyer, and Veselin Stoyanov. 2019. Roberta: A robustly optimized BERT pretraining approach. *CoRR*, abs/1907.11692.

Stewart Lockie. 2022. Mainstreaming climate change sociology.

Derk Loorbach. 2009. Transition management for sustainable development: A prescriptive, complexity□based governance framework. *Governance*, 23:161 – 183.

Richard Petty, John Cacioppo, and Rachel Goldman. 1981. Personal involvement as a determinant of argument-based persuasion. *Journal of Personality and Social Psychology*, 41:847–855.

Adam A. Prag and Christian B. Henriksen. 2021. Correction: Prag, a.a.; henriksen, c.b. transition from animal-based to plant-based food production to reduce greenhouse gas emissions from agriculture—the case of denmark. sustainability 2020, 12, 8228. *Sustainability*, 13(2).

Lucas Høyberg Puvis de Chavannes, Mads Guldborg Kjeldgaard Kongsbak, Timmie Rantzau, and Leon Derczynski. 2021. Hyperparameter power impact in transformer language model training. In *Proceedings of the Second Workshop on Simple and Efficient Natural Language Processing*, pages 96–118, Virtual. Association for Computational Linguistics.

Nils Reimers and Iryna Gurevych. 2019. Sentence-BERT: Sentence embeddings using Siamese BERT-networks. In *Proceedings of the 2019 Conference on Empirical Methods in Natural Language Processing and the 9th International Joint Conference on Natural Language Processing (EMNLP-IJCNLP)*, pages 3982–3992, Hong Kong, China. Association for Computational Linguistics.

Ruty Rinott, Lena Dankin, Carlos Alzate Perez, Mitesh M. Khapra, Ehud Aharoni, and Noam Slonim. 2015. Show me your evidence - an automatic method for context dependent evidence detection. In *Proceedings of the 2015 Conference on Empirical Methods in Natural Language Processing*, pages 440–450, Lisbon, Portugal. Association for Computational Linguistics.

David Rolnick, Priya L. Donti, Lynn H. Kaack, Kelly Kochanski, Alexandre Lacoste, Kris Sankaran, Andrew Slavin Ross, Nikola Milojevic-Dupont, Natasha Jaques, Anna Waldman-Brown, Alexandra Luccioni, Tegan Maharaj, Evan D. Sherwin, S. Karthik Mukkavilli, Konrad P. Körding, Carla P. Gomes, Andrew Y. Ng, Demis Hassabis, John C. Platt, Felix Creutzig, Jennifer T. Chayes, and Yoshua Bengio. 2019. Tackling climate change with machine learning. *CoRR*, abs/1906.05433.

Robin Schaefer. 2021. Building an argument mining pipeline for tweets. in online handbook of argumentation for ai (ohaai) volume 2, 2021. *CoRR*, abs/2106.10832.

Robin Schaefer and Manfred Stede. 2020. Annotation and detection of arguments in tweets. In *Proceedings of the 7th Workshop on Argument Mining*, pages 53–58, Online. Association for Computational Linguistics.

Robin Schaefer and Manfred Stede. 2021. UPAppliedCL at GermEval 2021: Identifying fact-claiming and engaging Facebook comments using transformers. In *Proceedings of the GermEval 2021 Shared Task on the Identification of Toxic, Engaging, and Fact-Claiming Comments*, pages 13–18, Duesseldorf, Germany. Association for Computational Linguistics.

Roy Schwartz, Jesse Dodge, Noah A. Smith, and Oren Etzioni. 2020. Green AI. *Communications of the ACM (CACM)*, 63(12):54–63.

Noam Slonim, Yonatan Bilu, Carlos Alzate, Roy Bar-Haim, Ben Bogin, Francesca Bonin, Leshem Choshen, Edo Cohen-Karlik, Lena Dankin, Lilach Edelstein, Liat Ein-Dor, Roni Friedman-Melamed, Assaf Gavron, Ariel Gera, Martin Gleize, Shai Gretz, Dan Gutfreund, Alon Halfon, Daniel Hershcovich, Ron Hoory, Yufang Hou, Shay Hummel, Michal Jacovi, Charles Jochim, Yoav Kantor, Yoav Katz, David Konopnicki, Zvi Kons, Lili Kotlerman, Dalia Krieger, Dan Lahav, Tamar Lavee, Ran Levy, Naftali Liberman, Yosi Mass, Amir Menczel, Shachar Mirkin, Guy Moshkowich, Shila Ofek-Koifman, Matan Orbach, Ella Rabinovich, Ruty Rinott, Slava Shechtman, Dafna Sheinwald, Eyal Shnarch, Ilya Shnayderman, Aya Soffer, Artem Spector, Benjamin Sznajder, Assaf Toledo, Orith Toledo-Ronen, Elad Venezian, and Ranit Aharonov. 2021. An autonomous debating system. *Nature*, 591(7850):379–384. Publisher Copyright: © 2021, The Author(s), under exclusive licence to Springer Nature Limited.

Manfred Stede and Ronny Patz. 2021. The climate change debate and natural language processing. pages 8–18.

Emma Strubell, Ananya Ganesh, and Andrew McCallum. 2019. Energy and policy considerations for deep learning in NLP. In *Proceedings of the 57th Annual Meeting of the Association for Computational Linguistics*, pages 3645–3650, Florence, Italy. Association for Computational Linguistics.

Orith Toledo-Ronen, Matan Orbach, Yonatan Bilu, Artem Spector, and Noam Slonim. 2020. Multilingual argument mining: Datasets and analysis. *CoRR*, abs/2010.06432.

Andrew Trotman, Antti Puurula, and Blake Burgess. 2014. Improvements to bm25 and language models examined. In *Proceedings of the 2014 Australasian Document Computing Symposium*, ADCS '14, page 58–65, New York, NY, USA. Association for Computing Machinery.

Wenhui Wang, Furu Wei, Li Dong, Hangbo Bao, Nan Yang, and Ming Zhou. 2020. MiniLM: Deep self-attention distillation for task-agnostic compression of pre-trained transformers. *Advances in Neural Information Processing Systems*, 33:5776–5788.

Walter Willett, Johan Rockström, Brent Loken, Marco Springmann, Tim Lang, Sonja Vermeulen, Tara Garnett, David Tilman, Fabrice Declerck, Amanda Wood, Malin Jonell, Line Gordon, Jessica Fanzo, Corinna Hawkes, Rami Zurayk, Juan Rivera, Wim Vries, Lindiwe Sibanda, and Christopher Murray. 2019. Food in the anthropocene: the eat–lancet commission on healthy diets from sustainable food systems. *The Lancet*, 393.

Michael Wojatzki and Torsten Zesch. 2016. Stance-based argument mining – modeling implicit argumentation using stance.

Thomas Wolf, Lysandre Debut, Victor Sanh, Julien Chaumond, Clement Delangue, Anthony Moi, Pierric Cistac, Tim Rault, Rémi Louf, Morgan Funtowicz, and Jamie Brew. 2019. Huggingface's transformers: State-of-the-art natural language processing. *CoRR*, abs/1910.03771.

A Crowdsourced Annotations

Each annotator was paid according to 15$ an hour of work. From our experience with annotation, we could complete roughly 100 total tweets + topics worth of annotation work in 45 mins for all four labels. Rounding it up to 60 mins and annotating for one label at a time, we calculated a pay of 0.045$ for each tweet + topic pair for each label.

For this paper, gathering annotations has happened over four annotations rounds, each focusing on one of the four primary labels we use in this paper. Five different annotators were recruited to calculate a majority for each annotated label. Each round helped bootstrap the data needed for annotation of the next round. For instance, we did not want to annotate non-argumentative data for claims or evidence as most previous annotators have already deemed it non-argumentative and would therefore be a waste of annotation resources. Instead, we would first retrieve annotations for the argumentative tweets. Then ask a new set of annotators to annotate for claims or evidence on the argumentative tweets. Due to evidence requiring its type annotated we also use the results from claims annotation round to help narrow the combination of topics and tweets used for evidence annotation. Pro/Con was also dependent on either claim or evidence being found in a tweet-topic pair, so was the last step in the annotation process.

Due to the subjective nature of annotating for this paper, we did not want to dismiss workers' work. Despite clear instructions, different people will consider claims relevant while others will not consider them relevant. Instead, we would actively moderate the resulting annotations and block any annotator creating low-quality annotations during annotation. We did this by first pre-annotating a small set and then calculating an overlap with annotators. If the overlap were small, we would block them from continuing. However, some annotations were slow to gather and would take multiple days. This resulted in us having to reopen hits that were partially annotated. Therefore if any annotator had already completed a set of hits, we would block them from redoing that set of hits. However, this method was imperfect, so that the same annotator might have double annotated some tweets.

We did test out an alternative method for part of the claim annotations where we would have a short test that would qualify annotators for the more extensive annotation set if they performed well. However, this method took much more time for annotations to be collected and was therefore dropped. It was also discovered during postprocessing of the hits that some annotations had less than five annotators, and others had more. This was only for a minority of hits, and it is believed that duplication's of a few tweets in the early corpus were the reason. This was fixed for later annotation rounds but should be noted as it might impact later results.

A.1 Argumentative

Argumentative was the first label to be crowdsourced, we only gave annotators two options, "argumentative" and "not argumentative". Argumentative gets labeled as 0 for non-argumentative and 1 for argumentative.

Instructions for annotators: The task here is to annotate tweets if they are stated in an argumentative manner. Argumentative is a broad concept but essentially means that the tweet either contains evidence or claims that would be relevant for a debate about some topic.

A.2 Claim

We changed the annotation task from annotating for implicit/explicit claims for a specific topic for claim annotation. Instead, we asked annotators to select one or more topics where the claim would be relevant. They were asked to label a tweet relevant for one of the topics described earlier or mark it as irrelevant for all, or not containing a claim. The former option would be used to detect unrelated argumentative tweets. It is labeled as 0 for not containing a claim relevant to the topic and 1 for containing one that is.

This change was made for a few reasons. First, it reduced the number of hits needed 5-fold from 1935 hits needing to be made to only 387 hits. It also ensured that we had all tweets evaluated for all topics. Lastly, asking them to select the most relevant topics should give a more precise estimation of relatedness to a topic.

The downsides of this approach were that people were much more likely to select only one topic to be relevant rather than selecting two or more, even if a tweet was relevant.

The data for claims took three rounds of hit generation. Therefore this data might have some duplicate annotation work done.

Instructions for annotators: The task here is to annotate a tweet in relation to a set of topics. Here the tweet can contain a claim that might be relevant to any one of the topics. Of course, each tweet can be relevant for more than one of the topics, but it can also not be relevant for any one of the topics and should be annotated as such. Therefore, select the topics in which you find the tweet contains a claim relevant to an argument in a debate or communication campaign about the topic (regardless of your views on the claim and the topic and whether you would use it).

A claim is a standpoint toward a topic being discussed either directly or indirectly. The claim should be able to clearly be identified in a tweet on its own without relying on an assumption from the reader. This is an important issue for response tweets as the user might implicitly support a claim relevant to the topic or add a claim to a stance on the topic. Therefore, such tweets should not be annotated as containing a claim. The claim should also clearly have a positive or negative stance toward the discussed topic. Implicit claims are different from explicit ones as they lack the syntactic connection to the topic. This means they omit parts of the discussed topic or have no direct connection to it; instead, they indirectly express a stance towards it. An example of this could be a tweet, "Gardening has been great for my family and me! Can't wait to collect the bounties of this year's harvest," which contains an implicit claim with a clear stance toward T2 and T4. Suppose the tweet contains a claim clearly discussing a different topic unrelated to any of the other topics. It should then be labeled with the "unrelated or no claim label" If the tweet does not contain a claim at all, then it should also be marked with the "unrelated or no claim label."

A.3 Evidence

Annotating evidence was done differently from claims. Since evidence is very nuanced and has many different types, we did not want to simplify annotating evidence the same way claims were simplified. This risked annotators relying too much on their own interpretation of what evidence over time. Therefore we wanted them to select what type of evidence was in a tweet concerning a topic. So each tweet needed its type of evidence annotated for every topic, but this would explode the number of annotations needed as explained with claims. Therefore, we decided to limit a tweet to the topics where claims were found relevant by just one annotator. This limits the amount of annotation work to the most likely relevant tweet-topic pairs while not limiting future annotation work to expand evidence annotation for topics where claims were not detected.

Therefore annotators are prompted to annotate a tweet-topic pair for any of the labels "Normative", "Study", "Expert", "Fact", "Anecdotal" or "Unrelated or no evidence". The Evidence label is labeled as 1 for containing relevant evidence and 0 for not.

The main downside to this annotation methodology is that it increases the likelihood of people annotating evidence as relevant to a topic since they might be more focused on its type regardless of relevance and instructions. However, with this method, we get a much more nuanced picture of the evidence contained within tweets which could be used for future modeling.

We considered an alternative method where annotators would first annotate for evidence types and

Labels	Guidance
Argumentative	Select this if the tweet is making a clear self-contained claim. A claim is self-contained if the statement is clearly taking a stance towards some topic. Claims can be reactions towards a topic, like showing excitement or disgust towards a topic. The tweet is also argumentative if it contains evidence of some sort. Evidence can be citing a study, referencing an expert, or stating facts or beliefs. They don't necessarily have to be true.
Not Argumentative	A tweet is not argumentative if it is not clearly stating a self-contained claim. This could be because the stance of the claim is not clear, or the tweet does not clearly articulate a claim. Questions and irony or humor are automatically not argumentative and should be labeled as such.

Table 9: Guidance for the individual labels

then annotate for relevance. However, this method was dropped as it would require an extra round of annotations, and it is hard to annotate evidence type without a clear topic to measure it after. For example, one tweet might contain anecdotal evidence for one topic but fact evidence for another.

Instructions for annotators: The task here is to annotate tweets related to a topic where you have to annotate what kind of evidence a tweet contains. Evidence is a statement used to support or attack a topic or claim. Evidence can be present in combination with a claim, or it can also be self-contained if it is just stating facts or referencing studies related to the topic. If the evidence is unrelated to the discussed topic, it is marked as unrelated. There exist different types of evidence, and if a tweet contains any evidence, it should have the kind of evidence annotated. If more than one type of evidence exists in the tweet, choose the type you think best describes main piece of evidence in the tweet that is relevant for the topic. Be aware that the same tweet can show up multiple times and that each time it might have to be annotated differently for its evidence depending on the topic. Some tweets include various types of evidence where parts of the evidence are only relevant for one topic but not another. Therefore one tweet might have normative evidence for one topic but expert evidence for another and no evidence for a third. Remember, your goal is to annotate what type of evidence is in the tweet and if the evidence could be used in debate/argument or public communication both for or against the specified topic. Regardless of your views on the topic and whether the evidence is true or not.

A.4 Pro/Con

Pro/con was the last label to be annotated. It gets annotated as $(+1)$ for pro when a clear claim has a positive or supportive stance towards the topic. It is annotated as (-1) when it has a clearly antagonistic or attacking stance towards it the topic. If there is no clear stance, the tweet's label for pro/con is set to 0 and it should be reevaluated as a relevant tweet.

Due to its dependence on claim and evidence being present and relevant, we selected a subset of annotations if the majority thought there was either claim or evidence and the claim and evidence were relevant. This can accidentally remove some relevant tweets for annotation, but future work could annotate them.

To force people to choose the stance a tweet has for a topic, we removed the neutral option in annotation, so people have to annotate for pro or con. We believe that this should be fine due to the previous annotations, as the tweets left should have a clear stance on the topics they were relevant for.

Instructions for annotators: The task here is to annotate a tweet's stance in relation to a topic. The stance can be either one of pro or con. Here pro is a positive or supportive stance towards the topic, whereas con is a negative or hostile stance towards the topic. It is very important that you remember that it is the stance towards the topic and not the stance in the tweet itself.

B Annotation Examples

B.1 Processing annotations

After gathering crowdsourced annotations, we have a list of individual user annotations we have to merge. We do not want to merge the annotations

Evidence type	Guidance
Anecdotal	A description of an episode(s), centered on individual(s) or clearly located in place and/or in time.
Expert	Testimony by a person, group, committee, organization with some known expertise / authority on the topic.
Study	Results of a quantitative analysis of data, given as numbers, or as conclusions
Fact	A known piece of information about the world without a clear source for the information
Normative	An added description for a belief about the world
Unrelated or no evidence	The tweet does contain evidence, but it is not related to the topic, or it does not have any evidence.

Table 10: Evidence type annotator guidance.

Tweet & Topic	A	C	E	PC	Comments
Lol - and the wash post is the PR firm and Whole Foods is the official food supplier	0	0	0	0	This tweet answers with a joke or irony towards another unknown tweet and is therefore not argumentative.
Topic: T5 (*We should pursue policies that promote sustainable foods*). Tweet: *It would also be nice if our government could begin subsidizing more sustainable options (like plant based meat) vs things like beef but... i digress*	1	1	Normative	1	Here the claim is that plant-based options should be actively pursued explicitly by policy and implicitly through the encouragement of alternatives and reduction in meat. It uses normative evidence to support its claim.
Topic: T2 (*Plant based food should be encouraged*). Tweet: *Green taxes go into subsidizing development and production of green energy solutions. If we were on 100% renewables, our electricity prices would not have needed to go up. We need to move into self-sufficient green energy as soon as possible*	1	0	0	0	This tweet contains both claims and examples of normative evidence but is unrelated to the topic and should therefore be annotated as unrelated.
Topic: T1 (*We should reduce the consumption of meat*). Tweet: *Yes but to be fair: we can expect a massive increase in meat and dairy consumption in emerging countries that will severely limit the impact of whatever we do.*	1	1	Normative	-1	This tweet contains a belief that emerging countries will remove any progress we make and is therefore taking an opposing stance towards the topic.

Table 11: Example annotations. A: Argumentative. C: Claim. E: Evidence (type). PC: Pro/con.

into binary labels as this throws away any uncertainty from the annotators. We, therefore, want instead to merge into a probability spectrum that defines the overall confidence of the annotators. Of course, each label does this slightly differently due to their unique annotation strategies.

For the argumentative label, we calculate the probability by summing the number of annotators believing the tweet to be argumentative. Then divide the sum by the number of annotators.

For claim, we sum each topic added as relevant for a tweet and divide that by the number of annotators. We also calculate the unrelated probability for the claim in the same way.

For evidence, we sum each type of evidence and use the max probability for evidence. We also save the evidence type distribution and the unrelated probability.

Lastly, for Pro/Con, we sum the number of pro labels and con labels, divide by the number of annotators, and select the label with the highest probability. Since con has to be a value of between -1 and 0, we have to flip its probability if it is the max likelihood.

This gives us the probability of a tweet being argumentative. We can then set the cutoff point for the argumentative tweets at 0.5 for the majority and use them for new annotations or modeling. We can also use the probabilities themselves for modeling.

When using the resulting data, one can extract binary labels by rounding to the nearest integer.

Average tweet token count	29.67
Average claim token count	31.63
Average evidence token count	34.59
Average topic tweet vocab share	2.8%
Average claim, topic tweet vocab share	6.9%
Average evidence, topic tweet vocab share	4.9%
Average claim tweet to tweet vocab overlap	5.6%
Average evidence tweet to tweet vocab overlap	5%

Table 12: Overall tweet statistics for tweet token count for each type and percentage of vocab sharing between tweet and topic, and tweet to tweet.

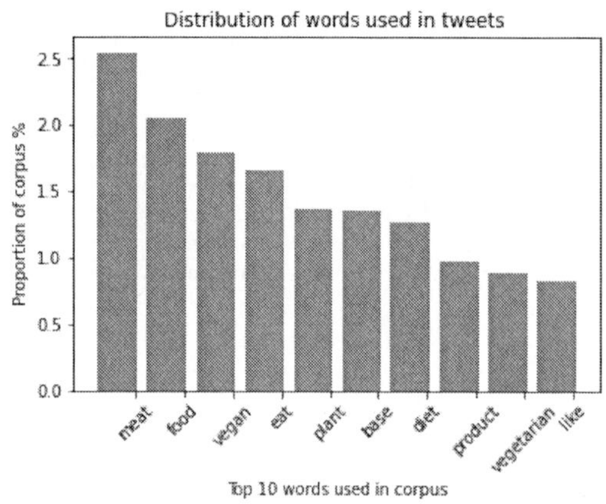

Figure 5: Top 10 words used corpus after stemming and removing stopwords from tweets

C Statistics and Analysis

In Table 12 we have some general statistics regarding tweets and topics textual information. We see that claims and evidence have slightly more words than the average tweet. On the other hand, we see minimal vocabulary sharing between tweets and topics. This is probably because topics are quite short, while tweets are, on average, much longer. We see a more significant share of vocabulary for tweets containing claims and evidence in relation to their topics. However, tweets do not seem to share a large percentage of their vocabulary with each other, which shows the general difficulty for claim and evidence detection.

In Figure 5, we see the top 10 most used words in the corpus after having filtered out stopwords and stemmed the rest. Again, we see a general overlap with keywords from our topics, such as vegan, meat, and plant. Interestingly, "plant" and "base" almost occur the same amount, indicating a substantial usage of plant-based in tweets.

D Tweet Retrieval Queries for Corpus Creation

English keywords: "healthy food", "food", "green food", "veganism", "vegetable", "good recipe", "climate friendly recipe", "climate friendly diet", "healthy recipe", "sustainable diet", "green diet", "diet with vegetable", "vegetables are healthy", "fruit and vegetable", "fruit", "vegetarian", "vegan", "good vegan recipe", "good vegetarian recipe", "organic", "plant food is great", "fresh and organic is good", "varied and balanced diet", "beans", "sustainable meat", "legumes", "whole grains", "local farmers market", "plant based", "meat alternative", "plant based diet", "green food is really good", "animals are not ingredients", "eat healthy food", "raw food diet", "whole foods", "flexitarian", "raw foodism", "rawism".

E Experiment Replications

We tried to replicate some of the work of others to explore potential methods from which we would use for this paper. The two specific papers that are used for inspiration are both made by Schaefer and Stede (2020, 2021) .

E.1 Fact-claiming & Engaging Comments

In Schaefer and Stede (2021) the data is 3244 German Facebook comments on a political talk show's page from February 2019. The paper aims to classify toxic comments, engaging comments, and fact-claiming comments. They focus mainly on the fact-claiming comments due to its related nature to argument mining for evidence detection. They propose three models and two baseline models. The two baselines used are unigrams + SVM and Linguistic Features + XGBoost Chen and Guestrin (2016). The models they propose are:

- Fine-tuned BERT Embeddings + Transformer
- BERT Embeddings + Transformer
- BERT Embeddings + XGBoost

They don't detail the implementation of the extra transformer layer on top of BERT. We assume this is a single layer added on top, followed by a liner classification layer. For the rest of the models, none of the hyperparameters are described for any of the models. Instead, they explain that they used a development set for hyper parameter tuning for the models. This development set was created from 12.5% of the given training data. Another 12.5% was taken for a test set used to give them preliminary results. For the final evaluation they where given a new dataset of 944 unlabeled comments which where drawn from discussions of different show to avoid topical bias.

To replicate the results of Schaefer and Stede (2021), we use huggingface, Wolf et al. (2019), framework to fine-tune 2 BERT models of bert-base-german-cased[13], each focused on either subtask one or subtask two. The model is fine-tuned for 75% of the training set for one epoch. The optimizer used is Adam, with a learning rate of 5e-5 and no weight decay. The rest of the hyperparameters are left to the default setup of the TrainingArguments for huggingface's models. The models are trained on a binary classification task, which is done by loading in the BERT model as an AutoModelForSequenceClassification with two labels and fine-tuning it. Results from our replication and the original paper can be found in Table 13.
Our attempt at replicating the results are successful as we manage to get similar scores as reported (Schaefer and Stede, 2021) and exceeding them slightly in certain areas. Our results could probably be improved if we used some hyper-parameter search with the left over 25% of the training data. This experiment shows the advantage of using large language models as the base for further model experimentation.

E.2 Climate Tweets

Schaefer and Stede (2020) focus on creating a new Twitter-based dataset. The dataset contains 300 labeled German tweets containing the word "klima" (climate). The tweets where annotated for three labels, those being argument, claim and evidence. Part of the paper then explores a modeling approach to evaluate the viability of this dataset on a set of models. They use XGBoost as their primary model, with the main difference being the features it is trained on for the different models. The features used are:

- Bigrams
- Pretrained BERT Embeddings
- Uni & Bigrams
- Linguistic & Twitter Features

Unfortunately, they don't report the hyperparameters used by any of the models in the paper. They train each model to do binary classification for one of three targets: argumentative, claim detection, and evidence detection. They report their results with F1 macro weighted, precision and recall. To replicate the results of Schaefer and Stede (2020) we use a similar setup as explained. We use flair as the framework Akbik et al. (2019) to generate Pretrained BERT Embeddings (Akbik et al., 2018) using bert-base-german-cased. We then use an XGBoost model that is trained on the embeddings [14]. Finally, we use grid search to optimize the hyperparameters over the dataset by doing three-fold cross-validation. The final hyperparameters used are 15 estimators with a max depth of 1 and a learning rate of 0.01. The rest are the default values used by XGBRFClassifier. When generating the results, we use 10 fold cross-validation as described in the paper. The data contains labeled tweets from two different annotations hence fourth expert 1 and expert 2, in their paper they don't describe which of these labels they use or if they combined them somehow, therefore we did the experiment with both set of annotations. Their annotations don't agree and their Cohen's Kappa inter annotator agreements are 0.53 for argumentative, 0.55 for claim and 0.44 for evidence. Results from our replication and the original paper can be found in Table 14.
Due to them not being allowed to share their raw tweets we had to fetch the original tweets from their id, which results in a loss of tweets due to the original being deleted. We therefore only had 212 tweets vs the original 300 for our model to train and evaluate on. We did check if any major imbalances had occurred compared to the original dataset, and found no major changes in the balance of the tweets. We therefore where training our models under similar conditions to the original authors with the only difference being size of data. This difference might have impacted the result's in our replication process, but as we get very similar results compared to the original paper, this impact is probably minimal. We see that for evidence we have a large difference in the results, which should be expected as this is where the annotators disagree the most in their labeling, with expert 2's annotations being the easiest

[13] `https://huggingface.co/dbmdz/bert-base-german-cased`

[14] `https://github.com/dmlc/xgboost`

Approach	Subtask (ST) 2 F1	Precision	Recall	Subtask (ST) 3 F1	Precision	Recall
Unigram SVM (ST 2)/LR (ST 3)	**0.671**	0.665	**0.688**	0.654	0.667	**0.688**
Linguistic Features XGBoost (ST 2)/RF (ST 3)	0.670	**0.681**	0.664	**0.693**	**0.710**	0.685
BERT Emb (FT) Transformer	**0.689**	0.708	**0.672**	0.736	0.740	0.732
BERT Emb Transformer	0.669	0.701	0.640	0.722	**0.758**	0.690
BERT Emb XGBoost	0.669	0.685	0.654	0.717	0.736	0.698
BERT (FT) Classification (Replication attempt)	0.681	**0.717**	0.648	**0.745**	0.752	**0.737**

Table 13: Evaluation results from Schaefer and Stede (2021) and our replication. Emb: Embeddings. FT: fine-tuned.

Features	Preproc	F	P	R
Argumentative				
Bigrams	l, p, s	0.8	0.75	0.86
BERT	p	0.82	0.8	0.86
Ours (expert 1)		0.83	**0.89**	**0.98**
Ours (expert 2)		**0.84**	**0.89**	**0.98**
Claim				
Uni- & Bigrams	l, p	0.79	0.78	0.82
BERT	p	**0.82**	0.8	0.85
Ours (expert 1)		0.80	**0.87**	0.97
Ours (expert 2)		**0.82**	**0.87**	**0.98**
Evidence				
Uni- & Bigrams	l, p	**0.67**	0.68	0.68
BERT	p, s	0.59	0.59	0.62
Ours (expert 1)		0.61	0.66	0.43
Ours (expert 2)		**0.67**	**0.69**	**0.78**

Table 14: 10-fold cross validation results from Schaefer and Stede (2020) and our replication. F: weighted F1 score. P: weighted precision. R: weighted recall. l: lowercase. p: punctuation. s: stopword.

for the model to learn.

Impacts of Low Socio-economic Status on Educational Outcomes: A Narrative Based Analysis

Motti Kelbessa*
mottikelbessa21@augustana.edu

Ilyas Jamil*
ilyasjamil20@augustana.edu

Labiba Jahan
labibajahan@augustana.edu

Abstract

Socioeconomic status (SES) is a metric used to compare a person's social standing based on their income, level of education, and occupation. Students from low SES backgrounds are those whose parents have low income and have limited access to the resources and opportunities they need to aid their success. Researchers have studied many issues and solutions for students with low SES, and there is a lot of research going on in many fields, especially in the social sciences. Computer science, however, has not yet as a field turned its considerable potential to addressing these inequalities. Utilizing Natural Language Processing (NLP) methods and technology, our work aims to address these disparities and ways to bridge the gap. We built a simple string matching algorithm including Latent Dirichlet Allocation (LDA) topic model and Open Information Extraction (open IE) to generate relational triples that are connected to the context of the students' challenges, and the strategies they follow to overcome them. We manually collected 16 narratives about the experiences of low SES students in higher education from a publicly accessible internet forum (Reddit) and tested our model on them. We demonstrate that our strategy is effective (from 37.50% to 80%) in gathering contextual data about low SES students, in particular, about their difficulties while in a higher educational institution and how they improve their situation. A detailed error analysis suggests that increase of data, improvement of the LDA model, and quality of triples can help get better results from our model. For the advantage of other researchers, we make our code available[1].

1 Introduction

An individual's or group's socioeconomic status is defined as their social rank or class based on metrics such as educational attainment, economic status and employment (Saegert et al., 2006). The definition, however, is not limited to the aforementioned; socioeconomic status can also be linked to factors such as a person's quality of life and the privileges that are available to some people in society as opposed to others. When discussing such topics, there is an obvious inequality that has to be called out. Such inequality could manifest itself in the form of disparity in equal distribution of health services (Dickman et al., 2017), unequal educational outcomes (Morgan et al., 2009), resource allocation (Aikens and Barbarin, 2008) and many more.

Prior work in the social sciences (Terenzini et al., 2001) (Rheinschmidt and Mendoza-Denton, 2014) has repeatedly demonstrated that students of low socioeconomic status, unlike their middle or high SES peers, attain lower levels of education and lack access to opportunities and resources that help them succeed in post-secondary institutions. However, this same abundance of research is not present in Computer Science and related fields such as NLP. There is of course some work that has been done, but most if not all of them incorporate the use of social science based structured data such as surveys, questionnaires, and focus groups to make predictions. For instance, a path based analysis of the educational attainment of low-SES students (Lee et al., 2008) and an analysis of STEM attitudes in low-SES students using descriptive statistics, confirmatory factor analysis, Ordinary Least Squares (OLS) regression, and path analysis (Ball et al., 2019). Their approaches were almost purely computational, but the data points they based their work on were surveys—structured data.

Although it might seem that way, we are not trying to denigrate work made using structured data points in any way. In fact, structured data, such as questionnaires and surveys, make the act of data analysis straight forward because less time and re-

*These authors contributed equally to this work.

[1]Code may be downloaded from https://github.com/MoRevolution/Low-SES_NLP

Proceedings of the Second Workshop on NLP for Positive Impact (NLP4PI), pages 59 - 69
December 7, 2022

sources are allocated to extract insights and bring about meaningful results. On the other hand, setting up surveys and interviews takes time, and the volume of data is always an issue. So, the motivation of our work is twofold: (1) Address the lack of research in Computer science, specifically NLP, pertaining to educational outcomes as a consequence of an individual's socio-economic class, and (2) use unstructured narratives from internet forums (in our case Reddit) as a basis for our analysis.

To be more specific, we are identifying common patterns of struggles faced by low-SES students in higher education and how those same students attempted to resolve their shortcomings. As opposed to a close reading based approach which involves subjective analysis of certain each narrative, our whole approach is predicated on distant reading—gathering generalizable insights and patterns within text in the most objective way possible. We use Genims' LDA model (Řehůřek and Sojka, 2010) to extract generalizable topics within our corpus. We then use Subject-Verb-Obejct (S-V-O) triples extracted by CoreNLP's Open Information Extractor (Manning et al., 2014) to provide the necessary context behind the topic clusters identified by our LDA model. For each narrative, our model produces a set of S-V-O triples that reflect the challenges of the student and solutions to them. These triples are helpful for summarizing the content of the corpus, for knowledge graph construction, in question answering systems, and many other functions in addition to providing us with insightful information.

The paper is organized as follows. We start by describing prior research (§2) on socioeconomic status in relation to educational outcomes in order to describe the motivation for our work. We then describe our corpus (§3) and our methodology (§4) for choosing specific data points. This is then followed by our approach in topic modelling using LDA and S-V-O relation extraction. We present the results (§5) and make the limitations (§6) of our work clear, which leads us to discussions of future research. We conclude with our contributions (§7).

2 Related Work

In terms of educational outcomes in the realm of post secondary education, the socioeconomic strata into which an individual grew up has a direct correlation with their final educational and career outcomes (Jackson, 2018). Starting off, research has revealed that prospective college students from low-income families have restricted access to information about college (Brown et al., 2016). This could be information about financial aid, educational resources, and vocational development. On top of that, these same students are more likely to take on higher student loan debts that surpass the of national average (Houle, 2014). The aforementioned inequalities don't even consider the negative impacts that lack of resources and support have on the early literacy of these students (Buckingham et al., 2013), their academic achievement (Doerschuk et al., 2016), psychological outcomes (McLaughlin and Sheridan, 2016), and career aspirations (Diemer and Ali, 2009) of low-SES students before they enroll in any higher educational institutions. When they do enter these institutions, low-SES students report a different sense of belonging (Ahn and Davis, 2020), experience financial stress that impedes their ability to succeed both academically and in social settings (Moore et al., 2021), and attain dissimilar levels of education as compared to their middle or high SES counterparts (Estep, 2016).

Previously mentioned research is also supplemented with multiple reports that address educational outcomes of low-SES students in post-secondary education as a function of their social class. One, for example, is College Board report based on prospective student profiles and survey data by Terenzini et al. (2001). It reports that low-SES students are less likely to complete a four-year degree once on an academic track, and are less likely to pursue further education after a bachelors. They attribute this reason to a list of disadvantages that low-SES students must confront when enrolling in higher education. Other work has tackled educational outcomes and how they relate with class conditioned beliefs and social-class stereotypes. Rheinschmidt and Mendoza-Denton (2014) conduct 4 studies on students of diverse socio-economic statuses, and they found evidence that suggests that experimentally primed student beliefs about personal characteristics such as intelligence, effort, and sense of accomplishment predicted academic achievement in a college setting as a function of class-based reaction sensitivity (Rheinschmidt and Mendoza-Denton, 2014). Croizet and Claire 1998 extend the concept of Steele's stereotype threat, the risk of adhering to negative stereotypes about one's group (Steele and

Aronson, 1995), to socio-economic backgrounds as opposed to just racial and gender groups by the manipulating the instructions of tests administered to students of diverse SES in their study.

Some cross field research that combines the social science and Computer Science also address the challenges and struggles that low-SES students face in higher educational institutions such as universities and 4-year colleges. One body of work, for example, addresses the challenges that underprivileged students, such as those from low-SES, face in integrating into post-secondary institutions even with the higher levels of reported cultural and socio-economic diversity in these institutions (Álvarez-Rivadulla et al., 2022). It uses a mixed method approach which involves an assortativity coefficient and a mean degree constrained model to test for preferential ties associated with attributes within student groups and test if those ties were related to the social class of students.

There is limited amount of prior work done on low-SES students in a purely computational manner. Those we manged to find relied on structured data, such as surveys and questionnaires, for their analysis. Lee et al. (2008) , for instance, utilized a path based analysis model in order to investigate the long-term academic progress of students of low-SES. In this study, the ordinal variables acquired from the National Educational Longitudinal Study database were rescaled and linearized using an optimal scaling procedure to then implement a path analysis model. Another study, done by Ball et al. (2019), applied Expectancy-Value Theory (EVT) on survey data from a predominantly African American student district in southeastern USA in order to investigate the negative attitudes that students have toward STEM fields. Their analytical approach consisted of descriptive statistics (to gain better contextual understanding of data), confirmatory factor analysis (to confirm the independent variables' component structure within the data), Ordinary Least Squares (OLS) regression (to predict the potential of the EVT model and emotional cost variables), and path analysis (to understand the effects of the EVT constructs and emotional cost variables). Another study by Titus (2006) uses hierarchical generalized linear modelling (HGLM) to analyze variables in national survey data in order to understand the influence of institutional spending and revenue on college completion rates of low-SES students. To the best of our knowledge, there is no prior work done on low SES students in the field of NLP.

3 Data

As mentioned prior, we demonstrate our approach on unstructured social media data from the internet forum page Reddit [2]. We were motivated to use social media data for our preliminary work because of two broad reasons: (1) the time and human resource constraints that we were working with, and (2) the scarcity of computational research that used unstructured data points. Since our topic entails the collection of sensitive and private information from students or alumni, either directly or indirectly, we anticipated that surveys and interviews would be time-consuming and challenging methods for gathering data for our research. With such constraints in mind, we decided to use Reddit as our preliminary source of unstructured data narratives because its users are able to express themselves in a relatively unimpeded manner, and it provided narratives that fit our qualifications best when compared to other online-forums and social media sites. In addition, the format of narratives we collected from Reddit were written in prose; this is of high importance to us since the approach we applied in our preliminary study could, with slight modification and improvement, be used for the next iteration of our work.

In the process of data gathering on social media sites and online forums, our qualification for a "good data point" were as follows:(1) the narratives should have the experience of being from a low-SES student and attending higher education as a focus; (2) the narratives should be about the struggles those students faced higher educational institutions and/or how they overcome those struggles, meaning no general commentary or advice; and (3) the narratives should at least be a paragraph long (150 words).

When looking for data, we found that Reddit provided the most data points that fit our criteria. Here are some Subreddits that we chose to gather our data points from: r/AskReddit, r/college, r/collegeadvice, r/science, r/psychology, r/socialwork, and r/personalfinance. At this stage of our research, we chose to manually search for posts and comments using a list of manually curated keywords that was inspired by terms from our related work section. Some keywords we used are:

[2] `https://www.reddit.com/`

"can't pay for school", "imposter syndrome", "college culture shock", "struggled growing up", "broken family", and "first-gen in college". We, however, came up with additional terms while searching.

We collected 30 narratives written by low SES students who discuss their monetary and familial challenges. For instance, some students discuss how they were raised without parental guidance, in abusive homes, with drug addictions, and without adequate financial support. They explain how these circumstances had a negative impact on their academic performance because they were forced to turn to working night shifts or two jobs to make ends meet, among other means of supporting their education. We then filtered less relevant narratives which didn't adequately discuss the challenges faced by these low-SES students. We believe the narratives we chose represent the experiences of low SES students because the students discuss how low their household income is and how they were attempting to improve their circumstances.

The final number of the stories ended up at 16, and each one has an average of 15 sentences. We updated the narratives by removing symbols and personal identifying information (PII) before running our model on them. We decided not to disclose our data in order to maintain confidentiality of the narrators. Besides, we are aware that making our data public will make it difficult to secure the narrators' ability to edit or remove their narratives.

4 Approach

Our approach is based on this rationale: "If low SES students documented their post secondary education experience in these narratives, then it is safe to assume that they mentioned their struggles, what factors contributed to those struggles, and how those issues were resolved". Based on this rationale, we divided our approach into three parts, LDA Topic modeling, S-V-O triple extraction, and String Matching between the topic clusters and triples. With Topic modeling, we were able to identify common struggles within the low SES student community, factors such as poverty and lack of networking that contribute to such struggles, and solutions suggested within these stories that worked to alleviate these problems. S-V-O triples helped provide the necessary context behind the conclusions made by the LDA model. The relevance of data points between the S-V-O triples and topic clusters produced by the LDA model were addressed by string matching.

We first trained and optimized a Gensim LDA Model on a pre-processed instance of the corpus to obtain relevant topics with improved coherence scores. Simultaneously, we used CoreNLP's Open Information Extractor to obtain S-V-O relation triples from the raw texts of our corpus. Then, we extracted the relevant S-V-O triples by string matching between the topics and triples.

4.1 Topic Modelling

We divided our LDA model implementation into three parts: (1) Pre-processing, (2) Topic Modelling, and (3) Model Optimization and Tuning.

Pre-processing: Besides training and tuning our model, we spent enough time on preparing the data and optimizing our pre-processing techniques. We emphasized on this step because our corpus was sampled from an internet forum, and it therefore contained more colloquialisms and contractions than text sampled from a formal source. In addition, some of these preprocessing techniques help remedy the lack of built-in lemmatization and dimensionality problems in our *tf-idf* algorithm. We implemented the data pre-processing as follows.

- **Tokenization and lemmatization:** To tokenize our initial corpus, we used *en_core_web_sm* from spaCy (make bib file for spaCy citation) to produce a doc object with filtered parts of speech, remove inflectional endings, and return the lemma of words; we kept the nouns, adjectives, verbs, and adverbs—the parser and name entity recognizer were not used. We considered Gensim's `simple_preprocess()`[3] to discard tokens that are either too long or too short, removed accent marks from all tokens, and once again removed stop words and short tokens after lemmatization was complete.

- **N-gram implementation:** For our implementation of N-grams we decided that Bigrams and Trigrams would be best based on previous trails. The two aforementioned N-grams were implemented using Genism's *model.phrases.Phrases* which we found to work best on our data as opposed to manually creating an N-gram function or using NLTK's

[3] *simple_preprocess* parameters were set to *deacc = True* and *min_len = 3*

ngrams.[4] We decided to set the parameters to low values because larger values failed to extract important N-grams from our limited data points. The N-gram implementation did not work very well on our data. The corpus used to train this model is a list of numerical bags of words containing 869 items (words) with their respective frequencies. Due to the highly informal and verbose nature of the language in our corpus, our demo algorithm prioritized words that occurred quite frequently yet contributed quite little to desired topics. Therefore, we decided to use *tf-idf* as a weighting factor in order to filter words in our corpus based on their relevance.

- ***Tf-idf:*** Our *tf-idf* model is implemented using the Gensim *tf-idf* module. We modified the input parameters for our data and experimented with different "low values" to determine the best fit—other parameters were left at default. We used the same bag-of-words we considered for our demo model as a corpus for our *tf-idf* model. Our *tf-idf* model checks for words that occur with an 'X' threshold (our low value); if a certain word within our corpus occurs with a certain frequency that lands it a *tf-idf* score below our low value X, then the algorithm will assume that it is so ubiquitous that it doesn't provide much value to our LDA model. The output from *tf-idf* model is then a numerical list of bag of words, which does not include words with scores below our threshold and words with zero scores. This output is then used to train the LDA model. However, we are aware of certain limitations of *tf-idf* in term weighing: lack of built-in lemmatization and semantic analysis, and inconsistent results when classifying non-uniform text.(Ramos et al., 2003; Fan and Qin, 2018/05) This will be further discussed in our Limitations and Future Works section.

LDA Modelling: We decided to choose Gensim's LDA model for topic modelling because it did not require data labeling, which we did not have the resources for, and it fits within our time constraints. The model was trained with parameters set to *num_topic = 10*, *chunksize = 2000*, *passes = 20*, *iterations = 400*, and *eval_every = 0*. Besides the input parameters, the rest were either set to *'auto'* or left at default.

Table 1: Some topics generated by our first LDA Model

Topic 1	Topic 2	Topic 5	Topic 7
lot	feel	work	school
grow	well	job	friend
also	year	school	feel
poor	school	year	make
well	know	graduate	other
company	most	first	connect
good	push	well	never
career	mom	family	work
industry	only	hard	change
do	student	get	tool

Table 1 presents the top ten terms for four selected topics after the model has been trained. Formally, the terms listed under the same topic in LDA Modelling are quite similar, and we observe the same trend in our model. For instance, Topic 1 seems to be about growing up poor and yearning for a good career in some industry and Topic 7 is about making connections with others at work and school. When using topic coherence to evaluate the semantic similarity between the top 10 words in the topics, our model had a score of 0.44. We used this score as a baseline for optimizing our model in the section below.

Model Optimization and Tuning: We have developed two different models. Our first model only used Gensim's inbuilt version of the LDA algorithm that uses Variational Bayes sampling method. Although fast, Variational Bayes Sampling method falls short in terms of precision, especially when compared to the LDA Mallet's Gibbs Sampling. Initially, our goal was to replace our first LDA model with the LDA Mallet model. However, we decided against replacing our model for two technical reasons: (1)Third party wrappers in Genism, which LDA Mallet was one of, were removed in the Gensim 4.0 release, and we fear that rolling back to older versions could introduce performance problems; and (2)The LDA Mallet model retains the mallet path and prefix path of the exact system it was trained on which makes it practically hard for us to test the model on different a system that the

[4] *model.phrases.Phrases'* parameters were set to *min_count = 2* (only for bigrams), *threshold = 10* (for bigrams) and *2* (for trigrams). The rest were left at default.

model wasn't initially trained on. [5][6]

Instead of our initial optimization approach of replacing our Gensim LDA model with LDA Mallet, we decided to tune the parameters to get better coherence scores. The two parameters we optimized for were `eval_every` (for minimizing log perplexity), and `num_topics` (to improve coherence scores while acquiring more subtopics).

Minimizing Perplexity: When minimizing the perplexity score, we noticed that increasing the parameter by just one factor, increased the training time by 2X and made it impractical to pursue. However, we found that setting `eval_every = 1` substantially improved the generalization performance of the model (Blei et al., 2003). Therefore, we decided that the value '1' for `eval_every` would be a good performance and output quality compromise.

Optimal number of topics: To find the optimal number of topics, we generated multiple LDA models with varied number of topics 'n' and chose the one with the highest coherence score to identify the ideal number of topics. This approach was adopted from Prabhakaran's article titled *Topic Modeling with Gensim (Python)* (Prabhakaran, 2018). As in Prabhakaran's approach, we used the function `compute_coherence_values` that trains multiple models and returns the models with their respective coherence scores. Contrary to their approach, we decided against using LDA Mallet for the reasons mentioned above. We also modified the parameters to match our previous model with the modified `eval_every` value, and all other parameters were left at default. [7]

The number of topics 'n' marked at the peak offers the best results, in our case this was 10 topics with a coherence score of 0.47. Coincidentally, this is the same number of topics we picked for our unoptimized model by trial and error. As documented by Prabhakaran, picking a higher 'n' value could provide deeper insights with detailed subtopics, but that wasn't the case for us as the trend tends to drop off as shown in the line graph above. We belive this is because of the small number of data points we used to train our model.

Comparing the topics generated by our topic-

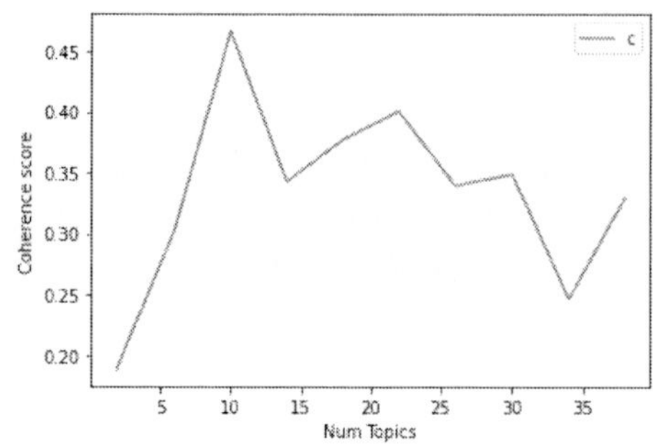

Figure 1: Coherence Score versus Number of Topics

number optimized model to our previous model, the coherence score improved by 6.38%. The difference in coherence scores might not be as substantial, but the terms produced by each model within a specific topic cluster are quite different: not only in terms of shared words within a topic cluster, but also in terms of how meaningful the terms in the topic cluster were to our corpus. This will be explored more in the results section.

4.2 S-V-O Triple Extraction

We used Stanford CoreNLP Open Information Extraction tool to get S-V-O relation triples from each narrative. Stanford CoreNLP has a tendency to produce repetitive triples, therefore, we filtered the triples using the SpaCy library (Honnibal et al., 2020).

Triples extraction with CoreNLP: To get the S-V-O triples from our data, we annotated the content of the story line by line using the `client.annotate(line)` function of OpenIE. We then used the `line['Subject'] + line['Relation'] + line['Object']` feature to get the triples of each sentence as a string.

Triples filtering with SpaCy: To remove the repetitive triples that we received from our coreNLP model, we lemmatized the triples and removed the stop words, and then compared pairs of all the triples to check their similarity using the Cosine similarity feature of SpaCy. If the similarity score exceeds 0.8, the pair is added to a list of similar pairs. Then we addressed the index of the first triple in the pair and removed it. We repeated this process using recursion until there are no duplicate triples left.

[5] https://groups.google.com/g/gensim/c/vVO0_t9jRUo/m/ZYFdq9_TBgAJ

[6] https://groups.google.com/g/gensim/c/_VO4otCV6cU?pli=1

[7] *compute_coherence_values* parameters were set to *start = 2, limit = 40, step = 4, chunksize = 2000, passes = 20, iterations = 400*, and *eval_every = 1*

4.3 String Matching

Finding the triples that best capture the context of the student's difficulties and their solutions is our ultimate objective, and finding the relevant topics is the first step in accomplishing it. However, when we examine the topics, we see that the majority of them represent the contexts we are interested in. We think this is as a result of the small size of our corpus and the little number of topics produced. Besides, the coherence score of the LDA model is low, and therefore, all of the terms in a specific topic are not much related to each other. So, if we do not consider a specific topic, we increase the chances of excluding related information. Thus, we decided to consider all of the topics and compare them with the triples extracted from the narratives. We repeatedly went through each triple, looking for any term that matched a topic on the list. If a match is found, the triple is taken into account for inclusion in the output list.

5 Results and Discussion

In order to evaluate our model, we first removed the S-V-O triples that did not include any elements related to low-SES, the issues that these students face, or solutions to those issues. Then, we made some inferences by comparing the triples we obtained from our model with these filtered triples. The detailed results are shown in Table 2 and a sample output is shown in Table 3 generated by our model from one of the narratives.

We showed the results of two different models, one with a coherence score of 0.44 and the other 0.46. We expected to get better results from the second model, but it turns out that our first model outperformed the second. As our corpus contains only 16 narratives, the generated triples from the narratives are less in number. Therefore, with a high coherence score, our model extracted generalized topics which were not very helpful to filter contextual triples from the narratives compared to the first one. Additionally, we weren't able to generate more useful topics without compromising the relevance of topic clusters because of the small number of data that our model was trained on.

If we look at Table 2, we see that in Model 1, the matched triples are higher, more than 50% for the most of the narratives. The highest matched triples we found for narrative 6 which is 80% and the lowest is for narrative 3 which is 37.5%. On the other hand, the number of missed triples is also lower for this model, lowest is 20% for narrative 6 and the highest if 62.5% for the narrative 7. Although the number of missed triples is lower for the first model when compared to the second, the number of additional triples here are higher, 86 in total for the 16 narratives. We notice that the first model extracts more triples than the second one; this is why we get more informative triples as well as more additional triples than the other model.

Additionally, we notice that there are more missed triples than matched triples in Model 2. The lowest matched triples are for story 8, which had a percentage of 20%. And the story with the highest missed triples is story 8, with a percentage of 80% missed triples. This model produces less additional triples compared to the first model, which 77 in total.

If we look at the sample output of our model in Table 3, we see that our model successfully generated the triples that contain common struggles of a student with low SES, for examples, having an alcoholic mother, coming from a low income family, and running out of money. Besides, some triples provided information of how that student improved his socio-economic status, for example, saving money, working full time, and applying for jobs.

6 Error Analysis and Future Work

Error analysis of the results found some issues and limitations of within our methodology. These were based on limitations of the tools and the quantity of the data we utilized in our approach.

6.1 Data quality and quantity

We believe that the biggest constraint within our present work is the quantity of narratives we used as data points for our model. As mentioned in the (§3) section, we found it difficult to manually search for narratives that qualify as valid data points in our research: we only had 16 data points to train our models on. Many narratives we initially found were either too short or strayed towards being informational posts instead of topically relevant narratives. We believe the small quantity of data points contributed negatively to the generalizability of our LDA model.

Admittedly, all of our data hunting methods were manual and were therefore subject to human biases, were inefficient, and time consuming. We chose to manually search Reddit instead of using a Web

Narrative	Model 1 Matched Count	Matched %	Missed Count	Missed %	Addi-tional	Model 2 Matched Count	Matched %	Missed Count	Missed %	Addi-tional
1	8	61.50	5	38.50	12	5	38.50	8	61.50	6
2	3	75.00	1	25.00	0	3	75.00	1	25.00	3
3	6	50.00	6	50.00	5	3	25.00	9	75.00	3
4	5	41.70	7	58.30	3	4	33.30	8	66.70	2
5	5	62.50	3	37.50	8	4	50.00	4	50.00	6
6	8	80.00	2	20.00	12	7	70.00	3	30.00	10
7	3	37.50	5	62.50	3	3	37.50	5	62.50	3
8	2	40.00	3	60.00	7	1	20.00	4	80.00	6
9	3	60.00	2	40.00	3	4	80.00	1	20.00	4
10	19	52.00	17	47.20	14	13	36.10	23	63.90	10
11	4	50.00	4	50.00	6	4	50.00	4	50.00	7
12	13	40.60	19	59.40	4	13	40.60	19	59.40	3
13	10	76.90	3	23.10	3	7	53.80	6	46.20	5
14	10	71.40	4	28.60	2	7	50.00	7	50.00	2
15	4	66.70	2	33.30	6	4	66.70	2	33.30	5
16	4	57.10	3	42.90	1	4	57.10	3	42.90	2
Average	6.7	57.7	5.4	42.3	5.6	5.4	49.0	6.7	51.0	4.8

Table 2: Performance of **Model 1** and **Model 2**. 'Matched' denotes how many triples matched with the originally annotated triples, 'Missed' denotes how many triples did not match with the originals, and 'Additional' denotes how many triples are not present in the original annotated triples, but our model addressed them.

Sample output from Model 1
My mom struggling alcoholic
My mom was unable
My mom help out high school
residence halls was last minute option
I go to college
I come from low income family of substance abusers
it 's headed my freshman year of college
me feel like I did not belong in school
I was working full time trying
My GPA was at time less than 2.3
I work to save
I work for year
my bachelor ran out money
I applied at_time past year with pandemic
my sober mom is in audience
I walking at_time time
you push through anything life

Table 3: The triples obtained from the first version of our model

Scraping tools, such as Selenium [8] or Scrapy [9], for two main reasons: (1) since narratives are unstructured in nature, we lacked data samples that we could use as references for our filtering parameters during web scraping; and (2) even with the use of general keywords as filtering parameters, we don't have enough people on our team to go through and check the qualifications and relevance of the narratives presented to us by the scraping tool.

We now believe, however, that the results of our primary work, after addressing some limitations in our current approach, could provide us with samples or keywords that we could use to automate our data collection methods. We also intend on using the Pushshift Reddit API[10] as a tool to search for Reddit posts and comments, because it offers more search and filter features as compared to Reddit's search bar. As mentioned before, a major reason we did not automate our data collection process was because of the problem of relevance, "How appropriate are the narratives for our kind of work?". Sure, a web scraping bot could find posts and comments with keywords that pertain to low-SES students, but the posts and comments it finds might not be as useful to us. To address this problem, we propose using an LDA modelling as an additional filtering layer that we could use for managing the relevance problem.

6.2 Topic Modelling

6.2.1 Pre-Processing Limitations

To begin with, there are obvious limitations with our preprocessing techniques that ought to be addressed, particularly with the *tf-idf* algorithm. The most obvious constraint of *tf-idf* is that it does not capture semantic relationships between words and is also unable to check for co-occurence of words,

[8] `https://www.selenium.dev/`

[9] `https://scrapy.org/`

[10] `https://github.com/pushshift/api`

given that it is based on a Bag of word model. To improve the performance of our *tf-idf* model in future iterations of our work, we plan to implement modified *tf-idf* weighing schemes used in text classification such as Decision Trees, Rule-based classifiers, Support Vector Machine (SVM) classifiers and Neural Network Classifiers (Kumar et al., 2015). Also, Dai's work reveals the limitation of a classic *tf-idf* approach when dealing with non-uniform text. We attempt to address this in our future work by using relative frequency algorithms (Dai, 2018/05) and incorporating Naïve Byes for improved class relationship classification (Fan and Qin, 2018/05)(Qaiser and Ali, 2018).

We are also considering using Dynamic Word Embeddings as a replacement for *tf-idf* as a weighting algorithm. This will be dependent on the results we get from modifying our current *tf-idf* model and comparing it to how a language model such as Google's BERT (Bidirectional Encoder Representations from Transformers) will perform.

6.2.2 LDA Modelling

A key limitation of our LDA model is that it assumes that no correlation exists between the words and treats them as independent entities in a corpus. In addition to this, LDA modelling lacks built-in semantic analysis, which negatively affects the coherence score of our models. A good approach to solve this problem would be to use knowledge graphs such as Wikipedia [11] or ConceptNet [12] to link correlated topics with each other. Synonym relationships and name entity recognition could also be helpful to encourage that similar words be categorized in the same topic cluster.

An approach we are interested in implementing was suggested by Xie et al. in their study addressing the limitation of LDA models in detecting word similarities. They attempt to overcome this constraint by implementing a Markov Random Field (MRF) regularized Latent Dirichlet Allocation (LDA) model that incorporates word correlations knowledge within a topic while still providing flexibility for a word to be placed in different topic clusters. Their work addresses the topic relevance questions and importance questions raised in research that attempt to tackle the same word correlation problems of LDA.

Finally, we would also like to address the debate between text classification vs LDA topic modelling as a way to obtain insights from our corpus. In essence, this is almost an argument between supervised versus unsupervised learning as our approach. Without getting into the weeds of this debate, we chose an unsupervised approach for the following reason:

- Unsupervised learning is much less resource intensive as compared to a supervised approach. Due to the lack of personnel on our team to label each of the data points in the corpus, a less resource intensive approach in unsupervised learning seemed the most appropriate—especially once we obtain more data points to train our topic model.

6.3 S-V-O Triples

Although we filtered the repetitive triples generated by Stanford CoreNLP, Stanford CoreNLP often produces insignificant and less important triples. We believe that using a better Open IE library can result in better triples and better performance for our model. And to expand the amount of meaningful triples we get from our model, a possible way would be to use a tool like WordNet (Fellbaum et al., 1998) to get synonyms of the topics we generated from our LDA model.

7 Contribution

This paper makes four contributions. First, we develop a model that can generate relational triples from narratives of the students with low SES; which are important to get the insights of the life experiences of the students, specifically their struggles and strategies to overcome those struggles. Second, we make a conclusion that we can employ NLP tools and technologies to understand the unstructured narratives of the students from low SES background. Third, we make our code public to the community. Finally, to the best of our knowledge, there is no prior work done in NLP about low SES students, our work will pave the way for other possible NLP research in this area of study.

Acknowledgements

This work was supported by two funding sources from Augustana college, 'New Faculty Research Award' and 'Larry P. Jones Faculty Fellowship Grant'.

[11] https://www.wikipedia.org/

[12] https://conceptnet.io/

References

Mi Young Ahn and Howard H. Davis. 2020. Students' sense of belonging and their socio-economic status in higher education: a quantitative approach. *Teaching in Higher Education*, 0(0):1–14.

Nikki L Aikens and Oscar Barbarin. 2008. Socioeconomic differences in reading trajectories: The contribution of family, neighborhood, and school contexts. *Journal of Educational Psychology*, 100:235–251.

María José Álvarez-Rivadulla, Ana María Jaramillo, Felipe Fajardo, Laura Cely, Andrés Molano, and Felipe Montes. 2022. College integration and social class. *Higher Education*, pages 1–23.

Christopher Ball, Kuo-Ting Huang, R V Rikard, and Shelia R Cotten. 2019. The emotional costs of computers: an expectancy-value theory analysis of predominantly low-socioeconomic status minority students' stem attitudes. *Information, Communication Society*, 22:105–128.

David M Blei, Andrew Y Ng, and Michael I Jordan. 2003. Latent dirichlet allocation. *Journal of machine Learning research*, 3(Jan):993–1022.

Michael Brown, Donghee Wohn, and Nicole Ellison. 2016. Without a map: College access and the online practices of youth from low-income communities. *Computers Education*, 92-93:104–116.

Jennifer Buckingham, Kevin Wheldall, and Robyn Beaman-Wheldall. 2013. Why poor children are more likely to become poor readers: The school years. *Australian Journal of Education*, 57(3):190–213.

Jean-Claude Croizet and Theresa Claire. 1998. Extending the concept of stereotype threat to social class: The intellectual underperformance of students from low socioeconomic backgrounds. *Personality and Social Psychology Bulletin*, 24(6):588–594.

Weisi Dai. 2018/05. Improvement and implementation of feature weighting algorithm tf-idf in text classification. In *Proceedings of the 2018 International Conference on Network, Communication, Computer Engineering (NCCE 2018)*, pages 583–587. Atlantis Press.

Samuel L Dickman, David U Himmelstein, and Steffie Woolhandler. 2017. Inequality and the health-care system in the usa. *The Lancet*, 389(10077):1431–1441.

Matthew A. Diemer and Saba Rasheed Ali. 2009. Integrating social class into vocational psychology: Theory and practice implications. *Journal of Career Assessment*, 17(3):247–265.

Peggy Doerschuk, Cristian Bahrim, Jennifer Daniel, Joseph Kruger, Judith Mann, and Cristopher Martin. 2016. Closing the gaps and filling the stem pipeline: A multidisciplinary approach. *Journal of Science Education and Technology*, 25(4):682–695.

Tiffany M. Estep. 2016. The graduation gap and socioeconomic status: Using stereotype threat to explain graduation rates.

Huilong Fan and Yongbin Qin. 2018/05. Research on text classification based on improved tf-idf algorithm. In *Proceedings of the 2018 International Conference on Network, Communication, Computer Engineering (NCCE 2018)*, pages 501–506. Atlantis Press.

Christiane Fellbaum et al. 1998. Wordnet: An electronic lexical database mit press. *Cambridge, Massachusetts*.

Matthew Honnibal, Ines Montani, Sofie Van Landeghem, and Adriane Boyd. 2020. spacy: Industrial-strength natural language processing in python.

Jason N. Houle. 2014. Disparities in debt: Parents' socioeconomic resources and young adult student loan debt. *Sociology of Education*, 87(1):53–69.

C. Kirabo Jackson. 2018. Does school spending matter? the new literature on an old question. Working Paper 25368, National Bureau of Economic Research.

Sandal Kumar, Christopher Columbus, and Research Scholar. 2015. Various improved tfidf schemes for term weighing in text categorization: A survey. *International Journal of Engineering Research*, 10:11905–11910.

Sang Min Lee, M Harry Daniels, Ana Puig, Rebecca A Newgent, and Suk Kyung Nam. 2008. A data-based model to predict postsecondary educational attainment of low-socioeconomic-status students. *Professional School Counseling*, 11:2156759X0801100504.

Christopher D. Manning, Mihai Surdeanu, John Bauer, Jenny Finkel, Steven J. Bethard, and David McClosky. 2014. The Stanford CoreNLP natural language processing toolkit. In *Association for Computational Linguistics (ACL) System Demonstrations*, pages 55–60.

Katie A. McLaughlin and Margaret A. Sheridan. 2016. Beyond cumulative risk: A dimensional approach to childhood adversity. *Current Directions in Psychological Science*, 25(4):239–245. PMID: 27773969.

Andrea Moore, Annie Nguyen, Sabrina Rivas, Ayah Bany-Mohammed, Jarod Majeika, and Lauren Martinez. 2021. A qualitative examination of the impacts of financial stress on college students' well-being: Insights from a large, private institution. *SAGE Open Medicine*, 9:20503121211018122. PMID: 34094560.

Paul L Morgan, George Farkas, Marianne M Hillemeier, and Steven Maczuga. 2009. Risk factors for learning-related behavior problems at 24 months of age: Population-based estimates. *Journal of abnormal child psychology*, 37(3):401–413.

Selva Prabhakaran. 2018. Topic modeling in python with gensim.

Shahzad Qaiser and Ramsha Ali. 2018. Text mining: Use of tf-idf to examine the relevance of words to documents. *International Journal of Computer Applications*, 181.

Juan Ramos et al. 2003. Using tf-idf to determine word relevance in document queries. In *Proceedings of the first instructional conference on machine learning*, volume 242, pages 29–48. Citeseer.

Radim Řehůřek and Petr Sojka. 2010. Software Framework for Topic Modelling with Large Corpora. In *Proceedings of the LREC 2010 Workshop on New Challenges for NLP Frameworks*, pages 45–50, Valletta, Malta. ELRA. http://is.muni.cz/publication/884893/en.

Michelle L Rheinschmidt and Rodolfo Mendoza-Denton. 2014. Social class and academic achievement in college: The interplay of rejection sensitivity and entity beliefs. *Journal of Personality and Social Psychology*, 107(1):101.

Susan C Saegert, Nancy E Adler, Heather E Bullock, Ana Mari Cauce, William Ming Liu, and Karen F Wyche. 2006. Report of the apa task force on socioeconomic status. *Retrieved from the American Psychological Association website*.

Claude M. Steele and Joshua Aronson. 1995. Stereotype threat and the intellectual test performance of african americans. *Journal of Personality and Social Psychology*, 69(5):797–811.

Patrick T. Terenzini, Alberto F. Cabrera, Patrick T. Terenzini, Alberto F. Cabrera, Elena M. Bernal, Patrick T. Terenzini Is Professor, and Senior Researcher. 2001. Swimming against the tide: The poor in american higher education.

Marvin A. Titus. 2006. Understanding college degree completion of students with low socioeconomic status: The influence of the institutional financial context. *Research in Higher Education*, 47(4):371–398.

Pengtao Xie, Diyi Yang, and Eric Xing. 2015. Incorporating word correlation knowledge into topic modeling. In *Proceedings of the 2015 conference of the north American chapter of the association for computational linguistics: human language technologies*, pages 725–734.

Enhancing Crisis-Related Tweet Classification with Entity-Masked Language Modeling and Multi-Task Learning

Philipp Seeberger and **Korbinian Riedhammer**
Technische Hochschule Nürnberg Georg Simon Ohm
{philipp.seeberger,korbinian.riedhammer}@th-nuernberg.de

Abstract

Social media has become an important information source for crisis management and provides quick access to ongoing developments and critical information. However, classification models suffer from event-related biases and highly imbalanced label distributions which still poses a challenging task. To address these challenges, we propose a combination of entity-masked language modeling and hierarchical multi-label classification as a multi-task learning problem. We evaluate our method on tweets from the TREC-IS dataset and show an absolute performance gain w.r.t. F1-score of up to 10% for actionable information types. Moreover, we found that entity-masking reduces the effect of overfitting to in-domain events and enables improvements in cross-event generalization. Our source code is publicly available on GitHub.[1]

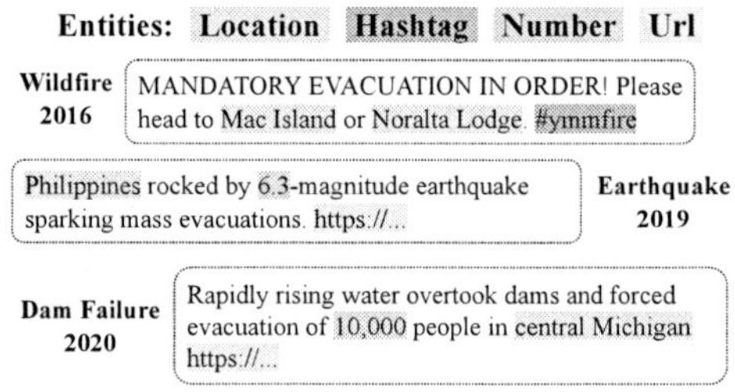

Figure 1: Example tweets of several disasters over time, annotated with entitites. The short posts are mostly biased towards specific events.

1 Introduction

Messages on social media during disaster events have become an important information source in crisis management (Reuter et al., 2018). In contrast to traditional sources (e.g., official news), social media posts immediately provide details about developments, first-party observations, and affected people in an ongoing emergency situation (Sakaki et al., 2010). Having access to this information is crucial for developing situational awareness and supporting relief providers, government agencies, and other official institutions (Kruspe et al., 2021).

One key challenge poses the information refinement of high-volume social media streams which requires automatic methods for reliable detection of relevant content (Kaufhold, 2021). Most recent work has focused on binary, multi-class, and multi-label text classification techniques to classify posts into coarse (e.g., *Relevant*, *Irrelevant*) or fine-grained (e.g., *InfrastructureDamage*, *MissingPeople*) categories composed of flattened or hierarchical structures (Alam et al., 2018b, 2021; Buntain et al., 2021).

Another challenge in Natural Language Processing (NLP) is the nature of data prevalent in social media and microblogging platforms. For example, most works in the crisis-related domain focus on Twitter data (Kruspe et al., 2021) which inherits properties such as short texts (280 characters limitation per tweet), less contextual information, hashtags, and noise (e.g., misspellings, emojis) (Wiegmann et al., 2020; Zahera et al., 2021). According to Sarmiento and Poblete (2021), different types of disasters (e.g., flood, wildfire) can be identified by only a few text-based features. However, event-related biases and entities as shown in Figure 1 prevent models from generalizing to unseen disaster events and therefore degrade w.r.t. detection performance.

To circumvent this problem, approaches such as adversarial training (Medina Maza et al., 2020), domain adaptation (Alam et al., 2018a), and hierarchical label embeddings (Miyazaki et al., 2019) have been proposed but suffer from mixed event types, assume unlabeled data or require semantic label descriptions. Contrary to this work, we aim to enhance the detection of rare actionable information for unseen events by masking out entities,

[1] https://github.com/th-nuernberg/crisis-tapt-hmc

Proceedings of the Second Workshop on NLP for Positive Impact (NLP4PI), pages 70 - 78
December 7, 2022 ©2022 Association for Computational Linguistics

	Train	**Test**
Event Ids	1 - 52	53 - 75
# Events	51	21
# tweets	50,412	22,003
Upper classes		
# Report (14)	30,389	16,059
# Other (5)	32,105	10,709
# CallToAction (3)	1,458	389
# Request (3)	683	144

Table 1: Overview of the dataset split; the values within the brackets of the upper classes corresponds to the number of unique low-level information types.

applying adaptive pre-training, and incorporating the hierarchical structure of labels.

Contributions Our main contributions are as follows: (1) We introduce an adaptive pre-training strategy based on entity-masking. (2) We incorporate the hierarchical structure of labels as multi-task learning (MTL) problem. (3) We empirically show that our approach improves generalization to new events and increases detection performance for actionable information types.

2 Related Work

Crisis Tweet Classification Besides conventional detection approaches such as filtering (Kumar et al., 2011) or crowdsourcing (Poblet et al., 2014), machine learning has received much attention in this area. Researchers experimented with several methods such as Naive Bayes, Support Vector Machines, and Decision Trees either with term-frequency features (Habdank et al., 2017) or static embeddings (Kejriwal and Zhou, 2019). More recently, the combination of Word2Vec (Mikolov et al., 2013) with Convolutional and Recurrent Neural Networks achieved remarkable improvement in this field (Kersten et al., 2019; Snyder et al., 2019). Due to the success of Transformers (Vaswani et al., 2017) and the follow-up language models (Devlin et al., 2019), most works have been built upon this and outperformed previous approaches (Alam et al., 2021; Wang et al., 2021).

Adaptive Pre-Training Transfer learning with language models essentially contributes to state-of-the-art results in a variety of NLP tasks (Devlin et al., 2019; Liu et al., 2019; Clark et al., 2020). Typically, such language models follow the three training steps (Howard and Ruder, 2018; Ben-David et al., 2020): (1) Pre-training on massive corpora; (2) Optional pre-training on task-specific data; (3) Supervised fine-tuning on target tasks. However, the second step is often neglected due to computational constraints whereby adaptive pre-training has shown to be effective (Howard and Ruder, 2018). Hence, Gururangan et al. (2020) introduced domain-adaptive pre-training (DAPT) and task-adaptive pre-training (TAPT) which cover continual pre-training on corpora tailored for a specific task. Moreover, strategies such as adding special tokens for tweets (Nguyen et al., 2020; Wiegmann et al., 2020) or additional masked language modeling (MLM) approaches (Ben-David et al., 2020) have been proven beneficial.

Hierarchical Multi-Label Classification Hierarchical multi-label classification (HMC) covers local and global approaches and the combination of both worlds (Wehrmann et al., 2018). A popular categorization of local methods is the subdivision into local classifier per parent node (LCPN) (Dumais and Chen, 2000), local classifier per node (LCN) (Banerjee et al., 2019), and local classifier per level (LCL) (Wehrmann et al., 2018). Hybrid approaches integrate the global part as a particular constraint such as hierarchical softmax (Brinkmann and Bizer, 2021) or combine multiple local and global prediction heads (Wehrmann et al., 2018). Recent work in information type classification introduced label embeddings which utilize the hierarchical structure (Miyazaki et al., 2019). Finally, the classification can also be viewed as MTL by combining certain loss functions (Yu et al., 2021; Wang et al., 2021).

3 TREC-IS

In this work, we mainly focus on the dataset of the shared-task TREC-IS, which represents a collection of annotated crisis-related tweets (Buntain et al., 2021). Each tweet belongs to a disaster event and is annotated with high-level information types which are derived from an ontology composed of hierarchical stages. However, information type labels are only shipped as a two-level hierarchy with four upper classes L_T and 25 lower classes L_B. Thus, both hierarchy levels represent a multi-label classification task. Following the TREC-IS track design, we split the dataset into train and test events which corresponds to the TREC-IS 2020B task. This split poses a challenging setup due to the requirement of cross-event generalization (Wiegmann et al., 2020).

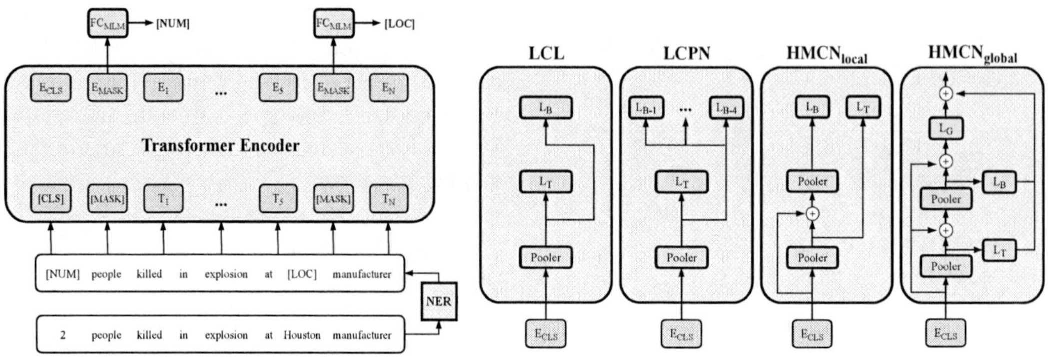

(a) Entity-masked language modeling

(b) Multi-task classification heads

Figure 2: Illustration of the concepts E-MLM with named entity recognition (NER) and MTL. FC$_{MLM}$ represents the prediction head for MLM. The classification heads will be placed on top of the pre-trained encoder. The building blocks Pooler, L$_T$, L$_B$ and L$_G$ are fully connected layers and use the CLS token as sentence embedding.

Table 1 gives an overview of each split; obviously, the information type distribution is highly imbalanced. For example, information types with low criticality such as *MultimediaShare* (31.7%) and *News* (25.4%) are prevalent. In contrast, the highly critical information types *MovePeople* (0.9%) and *SearchAndRescue* (0.4%) occur only rarely (McCreadie et al., 2019).[2]

4 Method

As depicted in Figure 2 our approach combines the two concepts entity-masked language modeling (E-MLM) and MTL. In the following, we briefly describe our method as a combination of those two.

4.1 Entity-Masked Language Modeling

Based on adaptive pre-training, we extend on masked language modeling of a transformer encoder pre-trained on a large corpus such as BERT (Devlin et al., 2019). Here, the mitigation of event-related biases is facilitated by replacing entities – which are prone to be event-specific – with special tokens (see Figure 2a). This way we intend to capture disaster-related language patterns independently of the concrete entities. Following Ben-David et al. (2020), we further introduce a masking probability α tailored to entities in addition to the standard word masking with probability β. That is, with a typically higher probability α we select random entity-tokens such as locations and lower probability β random standard subword-tokens. Finally, these selected tokens will be replaced by *[MASK]*, random tokens or the unchanged tokens in order to learn the linguistic patterns related to those entities. For the rest of this paper, we rely on the pre-trained BERT$_{BASE}$ as the encoder model and the corresponding default MLM setup for pre-training (*[MASK]* with 80%, random tokens with 10%, and unchanged tokens with 10%).

4.2 Multi-Task Learning

The next step represents the fine-tuning of a classification head. We implement four basic hierarchical multi-label classification approaches as shown in Figure 2b. The LCL classification head jointly trains a flattened classification layer for each of the two hierarchy levels. In contrast, the LCPN model consists of a classification layer for each parent node. The hierarchical multi-label classification network (HMCN) is adapted from Wehrmann et al. (2018) and introduces a pooling layer on top of the preceding pooling layer. We experiment with a local and a global variant, whereas the global one additionally consists of a global classification layer. All pooling and classification layers are composed of a single feed-forward layer with *tanh* and *sigmoid* as activation functions, respectively. Finally, we minimize the binary cross-entropy $\mathcal{L}_{MTL} = \lambda\mathcal{L}_{L_T} + (1-\lambda)\mathcal{L}_{L_B}$ as a weighted loss function whereby $\mathcal{L}_{L_T}$ represents the upper classes and $\mathcal{L}_{L_B}$ the lower classes loss.

5 Experiments

5.1 Evaluation Metric

We follow the TREC-IS evaluation scheme: macro-averaged F1-score across information types for the

[2]We provide an overview of the labels with some example posts in Appendix A.

Model	L_T	L_B	AIT
Single-Task			
TF-IDF+LR	0.657	0.499	0.462
$BERT_{BASE}$	0.717	0.531	0.513
$BERT_{MLM}$	0.714	0.551	0.546
$BERT_{E-MLM}$	0.701	0.481	0.444

Table 2: Overall results on the development set.

two hierarchy levels in addition to the actionable information types (AIT) (McCreadie et al., 2019). The latter include rare information types with high priority consisting of: *MovePeople*, *EmergingThreats*, *NewSubEvent*, *ServiceAvailable*, *GoodsServices*, and *SearchAndRescue*.

5.2 Named Entity Recognition

As event-specific entities, we use the special tokens *hashtag*, *url*, *person*, *location*, *organization*, *event*, *address*, *phone number*, *date*, and *number*. All entities except the tokens *hashtag* and *url* are extracted with the Natural Language API of the Google Cloud Platform.[3] We manually annotated 300 tweets and calculated a strict F1-score (Segura-Bedmar et al., 2013) of 0.692 which represents a reasonable good result for tweets.

5.3 Baseline and Hyper-Parameters

As baseline, we use TF-IDF with Logistic Regression (TF-IDF+LR) and $BERT_{BASE}$ with a single-task classification head. Furthermore, we apply the standard MLM of BERT in contrast to E-MLM in order to validate the effect of masking entities. Lastly, we train the MTL model (MTL_{prio}) from Wang et al. (2021) which combines lower classes as classification and priority scores as regression task. We choose the best hyper-parameters for each model based on a stratified split with a ratio of 90% for train and 10% for development data, respectively. In terms of hyper-parameters, we set $\alpha = 0.5$ and $\beta = 0.1$ for E-MLM; other parameters were set according to other work, including learning rate of $5e{-}5$, batch size of *32*, and $\lambda = 0.1$ for fine-tuning. The detailed hyper-parameter selection process is shown in Appendix B.

5.4 Results

In the following, we report the performance for the upper classes L_T, lower classes L_B, and AIT. However, for our evaluation we do not focus on

[3]We extracted the entities on 29 March 2022.

Model	L_T	L_B	AIT
MTL^{*}_{prio}	-	0.278	0.279
Single-Task			
TF-IDF+LR	0.460	0.201	0.168
$BERT_{BASE}$	$\underline{0.553}$	0.269	0.236
$BERT_{MLM}$	0.524	0.245	0.229
$BERT_{E-MLM}$	$\underline{0.553}$	0.307	0.306
Multi-Task			
LCL	0.548	**0.314**	0.309
LCPN	0.548	0.305	0.307
$HMCN_{global}$	0.546	0.310	$\underline{0.320}$
$HMCN_{local}$	**0.558**	$\underline{0.312}$	**0.335**

Table 3: Overall results of information type classification; bold and underlined values indicate the best and second-best results, respectively. *We fine-tuned the approach of Wang et al. (2021) with $BERT_{BASE}$ and without ensembling.

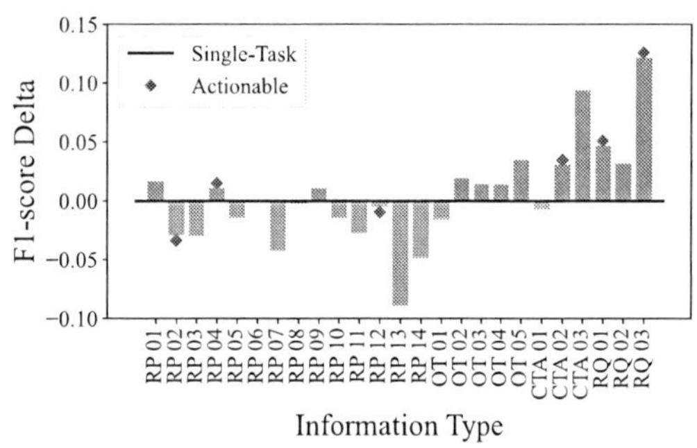

Figure 3: Absolute performance differences w.r.t. F1-score between the single-task and $HMCN_{local}$ model.

L_T since the experiments did not show large differences across all BERT models. The MTL models are only reported with $BERT_{E-MLM}$.

E-MLM Table 3 displays the results of all single-task and MTL runs. For E-MLM, we observe an absolute performance gain w.r.t. F1-score for both L_B and AIT by up to 4% and 7%, respectively. To validate the event-generalization effect, we additionally analyzed the development set, as a proxy to estimate the in-domain event performance as shown in Table 2. Contrary to the test set, standard MLM increases the absolute L_B performance by 2% whereas the E-MLM approach drops by 5% which is a confirmation of our assumption about event-related overfitting.

Multi-Task Learning In terms of MTL, the $HMCN_{local}$ model achieved the best results for AIT. Overall the MTL classification outperforms

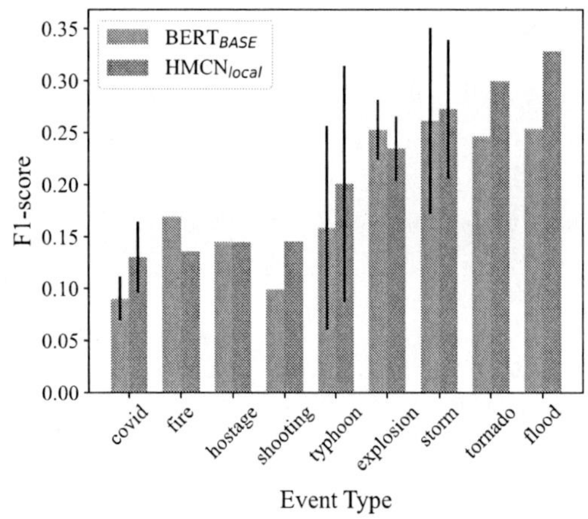

Figure 4: Comparison across event types w.r.t. F1-score between the BERT$_{BASE}$ and HMCN$_{local}$ model. We plot the mean and standard deviation for multiple events within a event type.

the single-task models for actionable categories and in addition the L$_B$ classes except for LCPN. We assume that the L$_T$ classification objective implicitly clusters the internal representation w.r.t. the high-level information types and therefore mitigates overfitting towards the major classes. As depicted in Figure 3, the HMCN$_{local}$ model improves the detection of rare actionable information types over the single-task model while at the same time decreasing the performance on the category with the most information types. This can be caused by the ambiguous label definitions and semantic similarities with other information types (Mehrotra et al., 2022).

5.5 Analysis of Events

In Figure 4 we illustrate the model performance for L$_B$ across different event types. For multiple events, we report the mean and standard deviation, respectively. We observe an increase in performance for the event types *covid*, *shooting*, *typhoon*, *storm*, *tornado*, and *flood* and a small decrease for the event types *fire*, *hostage*, and *explosion*. As shown by the variance for multiple events, the performance highly differs across specific events. Surprisingly, the event type *covid* achieved the worst performance for both models despite the existence of three *covid* events within the train data. These results indicate that even regional differences about the same global event predominantly affect the generalization performance across events.

Method	L$_T$	L$_B$	AIT
HMCN$_{local}$	0.558	0.312	0.335
- Hierarchy	0.548	0.314	0.309
- Multi-Task	0.553	0.307	0.306
- MLM	0.529	0.276	0.242
- Entities	0.553	0.269	0.236

Table 4: Overall results of the ablation study.

5.6 Ablation Study

As ablation study we removed several proposed components to assess the performance impact of our model. Thereby, the component entities represents the additional special tokens and replacement within the input text. As shown in Table 4, we started with the HMCN$_{local}$ model and demonstrate that entities, MLM and MTL contribute to an increase w.r.t. F1-score for both L$_B$ and AIT. The results indicate that the variant which removes the hierarchical component only degrades the performance for the low-resource actionable information types. Removing the E-MLM mechanism degrades the model's performance most in our experiments.

6 Conclusion and Future Work

In this work, we identified shortcomings in the field of crisis tweet classification for unseen events. For the TREC-IS data, we found contrasting effects in terms of pre-training and observed an absolute improvement of up to 3% w.r.t. F1-score for actionable information types by incorporating the hierarchical structure. Furthermore, we confirmed the effectiveness of our method based on the shared-task TREC-IS. Future work includes pre-training on a larger corpus, the mitigation of the trade-off between major and minor classes performances, and to analyse the influence of label semantics.

Ethical and Societal Implications

Open Source Intelligence (OSINT) has become a significant role for various authorities and NGOs for advancing struggles in global health, human rights, and crisis management (Bernard et al., 2018; Evangelista et al., 2021; Kaufhold, 2021). Following the view of OSINT as a tool, our work pursues the goal to support relief providers, government agencies, and other disaster-response stakeholders during ongoing and evolving crisis events.

We argue that NLP for disaster response can have a positive impact on comprehensive situational awareness and in decision-making processes such as coordination of particular services or physical goods. In the context of this work, positive impact means to supplement traditional information sources with social media streams that enable faster access to ongoing developments, first-party observations, and more fine-grained information content. For example, NLP for social media can enrich the information with the public as co-producers which may reveal critical subevents like missed or trapped people (Li et al., 2018). Retrieving this kind of information could positively affect disaster management strategies and relief efforts during natural and human-made disasters.

In contrast, relying on social media as an information source runs the risk of introducing mis- and disinformation. This can cause adverse effects on relief efforts and requires tailored strategies and particular care before the deployment of such models. Furthermore, data privacy issues may arise due to the inherited properties of social media data. Various anonymization processes should be taken into account for identifying and neutralizing sensitive references (Medlock, 2006). In this work, the use of entity tokens as categorization can be seen as one kind of anonymization procedure. However, model training with such entities could be task-specific and prone to error propagation by named entity recognition systems.

Acknowledgments

The authors acknowledge the financial support by the Federal Ministry of Education and Research of Germany in the project ISAKI (project number 13N15572). We also would like to thank the anonymous reviewers for their constructive feedback.

References

Firoj Alam, Shafiq Joty, and Muhammad Imran. 2018a. Domain adaptation with adversarial training and graph embeddings. In *Proceedings of the 56th Annual Meeting of the Association for Computational Linguistics (Volume 1: Long Papers)*, pages 1077–1087, Melbourne, Australia. Association for Computational Linguistics.

Firoj Alam, Ferda Ofli, and Muhammad Imran. 2018b. Crisismmd: Multimodal twitter datasets from natural disasters. In *Proceedings of the 12th International AAAI Conference on Web and Social Media (ICWSM)*.

Firoj Alam, Hassan Sajjad, Muhammad Imran, and Ferda Ofli. 2021. Crisisbench: Benchmarking crisis-related social media datasets for humanitarian information processing. In *15th International Conference on Web and Social Media (ICWSM)*.

Siddhartha Banerjee, Cem Akkaya, Francisco Perez-Sorrosal, and Kostas Tsioutsiouliklis. 2019. Hierarchical transfer learning for multi-label text classification. In *Proceedings of the 57th Annual Meeting of the Association for Computational Linguistics*, pages 6295–6300, Florence, Italy. Association for Computational Linguistics.

Eyal Ben-David, Carmel Rabinovitz, and Roi Reichart. 2020. PERL: Pivot-based domain adaptation for pre-trained deep contextualized embedding models. *Transactions of the Association for Computational Linguistics*, 8:504–521.

Rose Bernard, G. Bowsher, C. Milner, P. Boyle, P. Patel, and R. Sullivan. 2018. Intelligence and global health: assessing the role of open source and social media intelligence analysis in infectious disease outbreaks. *Journal of Public Health*, 26(5):509–514.

Alexander Brinkmann and Christian Bizer. 2021. Improving hierarchical product classification using domain-specific language modelling. *Bulletin of the Technical Committee on Data Engineering / IEEE Computer Society*, 44(2):14–25.

Cody L. Buntain, Richard McCreadie, and Ian Soboroff. 2021. Incident Streams 2020: TREC-IS in the Time of COVID-19. In *ISCRAM 2021: 18th International Conference on Information Systems for Crisis Response and Management*.

Kevin Clark, Minh-Thang Luong, Quoc V. Le, and Christopher D. Manning. 2020. ELECTRA: Pre-training text encoders as discriminators rather than generators. In *ICLR*.

Jacob Devlin, Ming-Wei Chang, Kenton Lee, and Kristina Toutanova. 2019. BERT: Pre-training of deep bidirectional transformers for language understanding. In *Proceedings of the 2019 Conference of the North American Chapter of the Association for Computational Linguistics: Human Language Technologies, Volume 1 (Long and Short Papers)*, Minneapolis, Minnesota. Association for Computational Linguistics.

Susan Dumais and Hao Chen. 2000. Hierarchical classification of web content. In *Proceedings of the 23rd Annual International ACM SIGIR Conference on Research and Development in Information Retrieval*, SIGIR '00, page 256–263, New York, NY, USA. Association for Computing Machinery.

João Rafael Gonçalves Evangelista, Renato José Sassi, Márcio Romero, and Domingos Napolitano. 2021. Systematic Literature Review to Investigate the Application of Open Source Intelligence (OSINT) with Artificial Intelligence. *Journal of Applied Security Research*, 16(3):345–369. Publisher: Routledge _eprint: https://doi.org/10.1080/19361610.2020.1761737.

Suchin Gururangan, Ana Marasović, Swabha Swayamdipta, Kyle Lo, Iz Beltagy, Doug Downey, and Noah A. Smith. 2020. Don't stop pretraining: Adapt language models to domains and tasks. In *Proceedings of the 58th Annual Meeting of the Association for Computational Linguistics*, pages 8342–8360, Online. Association for Computational Linguistics.

Matthias Habdank, Nikolai Rodehutskors, and Rainer Koch. 2017. Relevancy assessment of tweets using supervised learning techniques: Mining emergency related tweets for automated relevancy classification. In *2017 4th International Conference on Information and Communication Technologies for Disaster Management (ICT-DM)*, pages 1–8.

Jeremy Howard and Sebastian Ruder. 2018. Universal language model fine-tuning for text classification. In *Proceedings of the 56th Annual Meeting of the Association for Computational Linguistics (Volume 1: Long Papers)*, pages 328–339, Melbourne, Australia. Association for Computational Linguistics.

Marc-André Kaufhold. 2021. *Information Refinement Technologies for Crisis Informatics: User Expectations and Design Principles for Social Media and Mobile Apps*. Springer Fachmedien Wiesbaden, Wiesbaden.

M. Kejriwal and P. Zhou. 2019. Low-supervision urgency detection and transfer in short crisis messages. In *2019 IEEE/ACM International Conference on Advances in Social Networks Analysis and Mining (ASONAM)*, pages 353–356, Los Alamitos, CA, USA. IEEE Computer Society.

Jens Kersten, Anna Kruspe, Matti Wiegmann, and Friederike Klan. 2019. Robust filtering of crisis-related tweets. In *ISCRAM 2019: 16th International Conference on Information Systems for Crisis Response and Management*.

Anna Kruspe, Jens Kersten, and Friederike Klan. 2021. Review article: Detection of actionable tweets in crisis events. *Natural Hazards and Earth System Sciences*, 21(6):1825–1845.

Shamanth Kumar, Geoffrey Barbier, Mohammad Abbasi, and Huan Liu. 2011. Tweettracker: An analysis tool for humanitarian and disaster relief. *Proceedings of the International AAAI Conference on Web and Social Media*, 5(1):661–662.

Lifang Li, Qingpeng Zhang, Jun Tian, and Haolin Wang. 2018. Characterizing information propagation patterns in emergencies: A case study with Yiliang Earthquake. *International Journal of Information Management*, 38(1):34–41.

Yinhan Liu, Myle Ott, Naman Goyal, Jingfei Du, Mandar Joshi, Danqi Chen, Omer Levy, Mike Lewis, Luke Zettlemoyer, and Veselin Stoyanov. 2019. Roberta: A robustly optimized bert pretraining approach.

Richard McCreadie, Cody L. Buntain, and Ian Soboroff. 2019. TREC Incident Streams: Finding Actionable Information on Social Media. In *ISCRAM 2019: 16th International Conference on Information Systems for Crisis Response and Management*.

Salvador Medina Maza, Evangelia Spiliopoulou, Eduard Hovy, and Alexander Hauptmann. 2020. Event-related bias removal for real-time disaster events. In *Findings of the Association for Computational Linguistics: EMNLP 2020*, pages 3858–3868, Online. Association for Computational Linguistics.

Ben Medlock. 2006. An introduction to NLP-based textual anonymisation. In *Proceedings of the Fifth International Conference on Language Resources and Evaluation (LREC'06)*, Genoa, Italy. European Language Resources Association (ELRA).

Harshit Mehrotra, Akanksha Mishra, and Sukomal Pal. 2022. A Multi-stage Classification Framework for Disaster-Specific Tweets. *SN Computer Science*, 3(1):24.

Tomas Mikolov, Ilya Sutskever, Kai Chen, Greg S Corrado, and Jeff Dean. 2013. Distributed representations of words and phrases and their compositionality. In *Advances in Neural Information Processing Systems*, volume 26. Curran Associates, Inc.

Taro Miyazaki, Kiminobu Makino, Yuka Takei, Hiroki Okamoto, and Jun Goto. 2019. Label embedding using hierarchical structure of labels for Twitter classification. In *Proceedings of the 2019 Conference on Empirical Methods in Natural Language Processing and the 9th International Joint Conference on Natural Language Processing (EMNLP-IJCNLP)*, pages 6317–6322, Hong Kong, China. Association for Computational Linguistics.

Dat Quoc Nguyen, Thanh Vu, and Anh Tuan Nguyen. 2020. BERTweet: A pre-trained language model for English tweets. In *Proceedings of the 2020 Conference on Empirical Methods in Natural Language Processing: System Demonstrations*, pages 9–14, Online. Association for Computational Linguistics.

Marta Poblet, Esteban García-Cuesta, and Pompeu Casanovas. 2014. Crowdsourcing tools for disaster management: A review of platforms and methods. In *AI Approaches to the Complexity of Legal Systems*, pages 261–274, Berlin, Heidelberg. Springer Berlin Heidelberg.

Christian Reuter, Amanda Lee Hughes, and Marc-André Kaufhold. 2018. Social Media in Crisis Management: An Evaluation and Analysis of Crisis Informatics Research. *International Journal of Human–Computer Interaction*, 34(4):280–294.

Takeshi Sakaki, Makoto Okazaki, and Yutaka Matsuo. 2010. Earthquake shakes twitter users: Real-time event detection by social sensors. In *Proceedings of the 19th International Conference on World Wide Web*, WWW '10, page 851–860, New York, NY, USA. Association for Computing Machinery.

Hernan Sarmiento and Barbara Poblete. 2021. Crisis communication: A comparative study of communication patterns across crisis events in social media. In *Proceedings of the 36th Annual ACM Symposium on Applied Computing*, SAC '21, page 1711–1720, New York, NY, USA. Association for Computing Machinery.

Isabel Segura-Bedmar, Paloma Martínez, and María Herrero-Zazo. 2013. SemEval-2013 Task 9 : Extraction of Drug-Drug Interactions from Biomedical Texts (DDIExtraction 2013). In *Second Joint Conference on Lexical and Computational Semantics (*SEM), Volume 2: Proceedings of the Seventh International Workshop on Semantic Evaluation (SemEval 2013)*, pages 341–350, Atlanta, Georgia, USA. Association for Computational Linguistics.

Luke S. Snyder, Yi-Shan Lin, Morteza Karimzadeh, Dan Goldwasser, and David S. Ebert. 2019. Interactive Learning for Identifying Relevant Tweets to Support Real-time Situational Awareness. *IEEE Transactions on Visualization and Computer Graphics*, pages 1–1.

Ashish Vaswani, Noam Shazeer, Niki Parmar, Jakob Uszkoreit, Llion Jones, Aidan N Gomez, Ł ukasz Kaiser, and Illia Polosukhin. 2017. Attention is all you need. In *Advances in Neural Information Processing Systems*, volume 30. Curran Associates, Inc.

Congcong Wang, Paul Nulty, and David Lillis. 2021. Transformer-based Multi-task Learning for Disaster Tweet Categorisation. In *ISCRAM 2021: 18th International Conference on Information Systems for Crisis Response and Management.*

Jonatas Wehrmann, Ricardo Cerri, and Rodrigo Barros. 2018. Hierarchical multi-label classification networks. In *Proceedings of the 35th International Conference on Machine Learning*, volume 80 of *Proceedings of Machine Learning Research*, pages 5075–5084. PMLR.

Matti Wiegmann, Jens Kersten, Friederike Klan, Martin Potthast, and Benno Stein. 2020. Analysis of Detection Models for Disaster-Related Tweets. In *ISCRAM 2020: 17th International Conference on Information Systems for Crisis Response and Management.*

Thomas Wolf, Lysandre Debut, Victor Sanh, Julien Chaumond, Clement Delangue, Anthony Moi, Pierric Cistac, Tim Rault, Remi Louf, Morgan Funtowicz, Joe Davison, Sam Shleifer, Patrick von Platen, Clara Ma, Yacine Jernite, Julien Plu, Canwen Xu, Teven Le Scao, Sylvain Gugger, Mariama Drame, Quentin Lhoest, and Alexander Rush. 2020. Transformers: State-of-the-art natural language processing. In *Proceedings of the 2020 Conference on Empirical Methods in Natural Language Processing: System Demonstrations*, pages 38–45, Online. Association for Computational Linguistics.

Yipeng Yu, Zixun Sun, Chi Sun, and Wenqiang Liu. 2021. Hierarchical multilabel text classification via multitask learning. In *2021 IEEE 33rd International Conference on Tools with Artificial Intelligence (ICTAI)*, pages 1138–1143.

Hamada M. Zahera, Rricha Jalota, Mohamed Ahmed Sherif, and Axel-Cyrille Ngonga Ngomo. 2021. I-aid: Identifying actionable information from disaster-related tweets. *IEEE Access*, 9:118861–118870.

A Overview of Information Types

We list all information types of the TREC-IS dataset in Table 5. The value in the last column indicates the number of Twitter posts to which the corresponding labels were assigned. Table 6 displays example tweets for various events with the corresponding labels from the TREC-IS dataset.

B Hyper-Parameters

The search space for TF-IDF+LR included ngram-range, max features and regularization strength. In terms of BERT fine-tuning, we manually experimented with the same parameters as in Wang et al. (2021) and selected in line with this work the learning rate $5e-5$ and batch size 32. Due to computational constraints, we used for BERT pre-training the TAPT parameters of Gururangan et al. (2020). Similar to Ben-David et al. (2020), we experimented with the MLM probabilities $\alpha \in \{0.1, 0.3, 0.5, 0.8\}$ and $\beta \in \{0.1, 0.3, 0.5, 0.8\}$ and found the setup $\alpha = 0.5$ and $\beta = 0.1$ to perform best. This is in line with Ben-David et al. (2020) which empirically show good results. For MTL we tuned $\lambda \in \{0.1, 0.5, 0.9\}$ and finally set $\lambda = 0.1$. We trained all transformer models with the *Transformers* library (Wolf et al., 2020) and *AdamW* for up to 50 (pre-training) and 15 (fine-tuning) epochs, evaluated the performance each 1000 steps on the development set and selected the best performing checkpoint. If not other mentioned, we used for the rest of the hyper-parameters the default setup of BERT_{BASE} from the *Transformers* library.

Id	Upper Class (L_T)	Lower Class (L_B)	Actionable (AIT)	# tweets
RQ 01	Request	GoodsServices	✓	194
RQ 02	Request	InformationWanted		395
RQ 03	Request	SearchAndRescue	✓	274
CTA 01	CallToAction	Donations		986
CTA 02	CallToAction	MovePeople	✓	679
CTA 03	CallToAction	Volunteer		242
O 01	Other	Advice		3,277
O 02	Other	ContextualInformation		4,583
O 03	Other	Discussion		5,303
O 04	Other	Irrelevant		23,053
O 05	Other	Sentiment		11,101
RP 01	Report	CleanUp		493
RP 02	Report	EmergingThreats	✓	6,930
RP 03	Report	Factoid		10,224
RP 04	Report	NewSubEvent	✓	2,806
RP 05	Report	FirstPartyObservation		5,290
RP 06	Report	Hashtags		15,787
RP 07	Report	Location		23,676
RP 08	Report	MultimediaShare		22,976
RP 09	Report	News		18,374
RP 10	Report	Official		2,836
RP 11	Report	OriginalEvent		4,148
RP 12	Report	ServiceAvailable	✓	2,184
RP 13	Report	ThirdPartyObservation		17,223
RP 14	Report	Weather		7,655

Table 5: Information types and hierarchical structure of labels.

Event	Labels	Tweet
Wildfire Colorado 2012	Irrelevant	From the train, showing the smoke filled sky from the #Lithgow #nswfires
Bushfire Australia 2013	ThirdPartyObservation, Factoid, Advice	FIRE UPDATE: Families told to be ready to run as a massive 300km wall of fire sweeps through Blue Mtns. #nswfires
Earthquake Chile 2014	News	New this morning: At least 6 people are dead after the massive M8.2 quake in #Chile
Explosion Beirut 2020	Location, Factoid, OriginalEvent, ContextualInformation	At least 25 dead and more than 2,500 injured as a result of the Beirut Port explosion according to the Lebanese Health Ministry
Flood Colorado 2013	Factoid	5 people confirmed dead in Colorado flooding, and 1,254 people unaccounted for statewide, official says
Hurricane Florence 2018	Weather, Location, Hashtags	We have 2.5 inches here 2.6 miles northwest of Downtown awake Forest. #FlorenceHurricane2018

Table 6: Example tweets and labels for different events.

Misinformation Detection in the Wild: News Source Classification as a Proxy for Non-article Texts

Matyáš Boháček

Gymnasium of Johannes Kepler,
Prague, Czech Republic

matyas.bohacek@matsworld.io

Abstract

Creating classifiers of disinformation is time-consuming, expensive, and requires vast effort from experts spanning different fields. Even when these efforts succeed, their roll-out to publicly available applications stagnates. While these models struggle to find their consumer-accessible use, disinformation behavior online evolves at a pressing speed. The hoaxes get shared in various abbreviations on social networks, often in user-restricted areas, making external monitoring and intervention virtually impossible. To re-purpose existing NLP methods for the new paradigm of sharing misinformation, we propose leveraging information about given texts' originating news sources to proxy the respective text's trustworthiness. We first present a methodology for determining the sources' overall credibility. We demonstrate our pipeline construction in a specific language and introduce CNSC: a novel dataset for Czech articles' news source and source credibility classification. We constitute initial benchmarks on multiple architectures. Lastly, we create in-the-wild wrapper applications of the trained models: a chatbot, a browser extension, and a standalone web application.

1 Introduction

With the never-ending growth of the internet user base and its impact on our day-to-day lives, a significant portion of our work and leisure nowadays happens online. For many internet users, a substantial part of their time online, if not most, takes place on social media platforms (Paliszkiewicz et al., 2017; Riehm et al., 2019). Herein, most are constantly exposed to the information overload phenomenon. This means that the users are met with an unprecedented mass of posts, articles, images, and comments, which makes orienting within this space strenuous. Constantly verifying truthfulness of each presented information becomes virtually incompatible with the quick scrolling through timelines of new posts.

At the same time, the assessment of online media's trustworthiness is becoming more critical than ever. We could already see disinformation (i.e., deliberately constructed false information with the intention of someone's manipulation) being employed during critical social events, such as but not limited to elections, refugee crises, and controversial trials.

As a result, we observed an immense interest in methods that could automatically assess various aspects of credibility online in the literature throughout recent years. These include stance detection, automated fact-checking, or specific disinformation detection (also referred to as fake news detection). Tasks analyzing constituent attributes of disinformation, such as hate speech, stereotypization, or logical fallacy detection, have also been studied. Research in this field is not only restrained to text analysis: studies of visual disinformation detection, namely deepfake classification, are also often visited.

Despite being around for years, the rollout of such methods to real-world applications stagnates (Nicas, 2020; Achimescu and Chachev, 2020). Moreover, as disinformation gets scrutinized by extensive public interest and threatened by improved education about the problem, it evolves rapidly, making itself harder to spot and monitor. Many hoax campaigns have moved to access-restricted parts of the internet, such as closed Facebook groups, Telegram channels, and e-mail, making external monitoring and tailored debunking campaigns virtually impossible. Consequently, designing new tasks for machine learning models to combat these phenomena is challenging, as the relevant input and desired predictions become less definite. In the Czech Republic, for instance, many hoax websites started sharing augmented versions of their articles on these exact channels.

We thus set out to investigate whether existing tools and data resources from the domain of Nat-

Proceedings of the Second Workshop on NLP for Positive Impact (NLP4PI), pages 79 - 88
December 7, 2022 ©2022 Association for Computational Linguistics

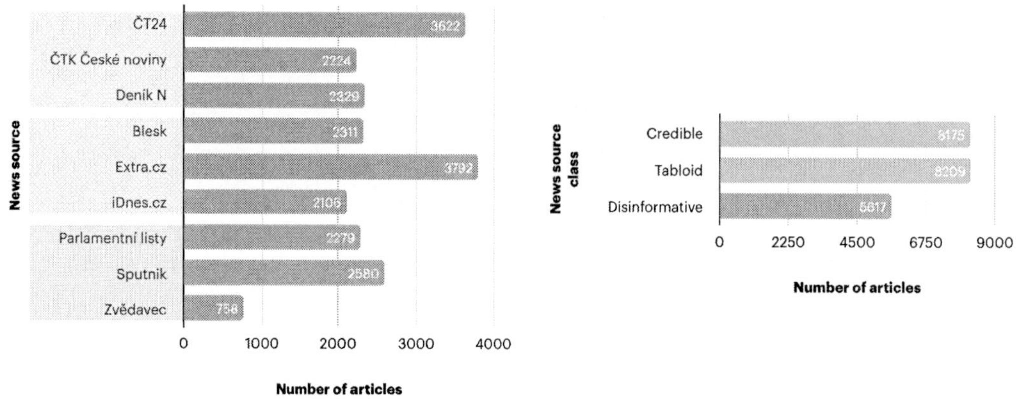

(a) per individual news sources

(b) per news source labels

Figure 1: Statistics of the article counts in the CSNS dataset. In Subfigure (a), the individual news sources are highlighted with the colors of their respective trustworthiness label.

ural language processing could be modified into generic tools, which would help assess the trustworthiness of various texts online. We chose the field of Czech media space as our proof-of-concept field. The problem framing seemed ambiguous at first – we wanted to analyze whether a given news text observed on social networks, blogs, or general websites seems trustworthy or not. We know that many of the subjected texts will likely be abbreviations of standard news articles, but the model should be resilient to arbitrary texts, too.

As we show in the review of related work, we later realized that many existing fake news classifiers' methodologies use only a single news source per class as their training reference. Such models are, hence, trained to classify originating news sources. While this may seem like a design flaw or a result of minimizing annotation complexity, we use it to our advantage. By training classifiers of a given article's originating source, we can utilize the trustworthiness associated with that medium's brand as a proxy for the reliability of the analyzed text. This way, eventual users interacting with the models' predictions will be able to use their existing experience and quickly recall their trust for the respective medium.

Additionally, we hypothesize that when the users are exposed to familiar labeling (in the form of likely originating news sources), getting accustomed to the application's framework and terminology may become more effortless than learning a completely new assessment system. We believe that internet users could benefit from accessing these models' predictions in-the-wild and thus assess their possible wrapper applications. We develop a chatbot, a browser extension, and a standalone web application.

To demonstrate the feasibility of this in-the-wild application of disinformation classifiers, we follow the process of developing such a tool from scratch. All of the artifacts produced in our study are open-source so that entities wishing to create similar projects can reproduce our results for their regional context effortlessly. Our contributions can be summarized as follows:

- We collect a novel Czech news article dataset with more than 22,000 articles from 9 sources, along with a methodology for their credibility categorization.
- We fine-tune multiple language models for the restated tasks of news source classification and source credibility label classification, whose results are reported in Section 4.1.
- We create three example in-the-wild wrappers (applications) of the newly trained models: a Messenger chatbot, a browser extension, and a standalone web application.
- We open-source the dataset, the training code, model weights, and code for all three wrapper applications under the Creative Commons CC BY-NC 4.0 license [1] at `https:`

[1] `https://creativecommons.org/licenses/by-nc/4.0/`

//github.com/matyasbohacek/misinfo-detection-wild-emnlp22.

2 Related work

In this section, we review other works which presented datasets for the task of disinformation classification. For a survey of the disinformation classification or automated-fact checking methods as such, we refer the reader to Oshikawa et al. (2020) and Guo et al. (2022) respectively. Apart from classification methods that use articles' full text at the input, numerous works have studied utilizing granular manipulative techniques (Zhang et al., 2018) or associated metadata instead (e.g., authors, hyperlinks) (Sitaula et al., 2020).

Most of the disinformation classification datasets in the public domain have emerged after 2017 (D'Ulizia et al., 2021). The most prominent and intensively studied ones have become the LIAR, FEVER, r/Fakeddit, and FakeNewsNet datasets.

Wang (2017) have proposed the LIAR dataset consisting of shorter excerpts of political speeches and quotes across six trustworthiness classes. The dataset includes over $10,000$ instances in total. Similarly, Shu et al. (2020) have introduced the FakeNewsNet, which holds over $20,000$ instances and distinguishes two basal classes (fake or real). These texts are primarily political quotes and speech excerpts, too.

Next, Thorne et al. (2018) have presented the FEVER dataset, which includes nearly $200,000$ instances of concise texts with respective links to Wikipedia. The annotations include whether the statements dispute or not, and thus this dataset has a larger basis in the task of stance detection. Lastly, we mention the r/Fakeddit dataset by Nakamura et al. (2020), which contains Reddit posts automatically annotated with a trustworthiness label derived from the overall credibility of the originating subreddit.

We also wish to highlight that many recent works focus on languages other than English. Resources for disinformation detection have been introduced for Arabic (Khalil et al., 2022; Bsoul et al., 2022), Danish (Derczynski et al., 2019), French (Meddeb et al., 2022), and others. For a detailed survey of other datasets with less traction in the literature, we refer the reader to D'Ulizia et al. (2021).

While the listed datasets are usually referred to as the best training and evaluation resources for disinformation (or fake news) classification, none actually hold news articles' data. In fact, most contain just shorter texts or excerpts. Moreover, all of these infer the individual items' class based on the overall source credibility while providing little or no methodology that would support their approach in terms of media sciences.

3 CNSC Dataset

Herein we present the Czech news source classification dataset (CNSC). In the latter subsections, we review the technical details of the data acquisition, the methodology for news source credibility categorization, and lastly, present statistics of the data.

3.1 Technical details

We have selected 9 Czech news domains for the collection of our dataset. To first obtain URLs of sites with individual articles from those domains, we used the Commoncrawl API [2]. We specified for the API to include only articles discovered between January 2019 and September 2021. Once these were obtained, we manually reviewed a random set of the data to find any undesired data points that also inhabit the respective domains (such as discussion forums or pages about the authors) and set up general flags to filter for these. We then scraped structured data of these articles using the Newsplease library (Fhamborg). After looking at the lengths of the texts, we noticed outliers that had as many as $25,000$ characters in length. These often included articles, for which the scraping library incorrectly yielded user discussions as parts of the text. We hence filtered any articles that would have more than $10,000$ characters.

This process resulted in a dataset of $22,001$ articles with the following textual attributes for each article item: title, text, URL, source name, author, and metadata description.

3.2 Methodology

To provide additional information about the news sources contained in the dataset, we created a methodology for their overall credibility categorization. Note that one cannot straightforwardly derive the truthfulness of all articles from any given source solely by the respective credibility class. It

[2]Commoncrawl library, https://commoncrawl.org/

Source	Source label	CNSC article examples
ČT24	Credible	*(Original Czech version:)* **Title:** Přibývá žen s rakovinou plic. Hlavní příčinou jsou cigarety **Text:** „Nejvýznamnějším rizikovým faktorem bezpochyby je aktivní kouření, které podle střízlivých odhadů je odpovědné za 30 až 40 procent všech úmrtí na rakovinu. V případě rakoviny plic je podíl na vzniku onemocnění dokonce až devadesátiprocentní," upozornil primář kliniky pneumologie nemocnice Na Bulovce Norbert Pauk. . . . - - - - - - - - - - *(Translated into English:)* **Title:** More women are getting lung cancer, cigarettes being the main cause **Text:** "The most significant risk factor is undoubtedly active smoking, which is responsible for 30 to 40 per cent of all cancer deaths, according to sober estimates. In the case of lung cancer, the contribution to the disease is as high as 90 per cent," said Norbert Pauk, head of the pneumology clinic at Na Bulovce Hospital. ...
Blesk	Tabloid	*(Original Czech version:)* **Title:** Kadeřávková o návratu do Ulice: Takovou smršť nelidskosti nečekala! **Text:** Vážné zdravotní problémy donutily herečku Annu Kadeřávkovou (21), aby zpomalila a některé věci ve svém životě přehodnotila. Dokonce i svůj konec v nekonečném seriálu Ulice. Do něj se teď vrací po dlouhých dvou letech. Jak svůj krok vysvětlila fanouškům? Když se minulý týden objevila zpráva, že v Ulici budeme moci opět přivítat Rozinu v podání Kadeřávkové, strhla se na herečku lavina různorodých reakcí. (. . .) HALÓ! . . . - - - - - - - - - - *(Translated into English:)* **Title:** Kadeřávková on her return to Ulice: She didn't expect such a storm of inhumanity! **Text:** Serious health problems forced actress Anna Kadeřávková (21) to slow down and rethink some things in her life. Even her ending in the endless series Ulice. She is now returning to it after two long years. How did she explain her move to her fans? When the news broke last week that we will be able to see Rozina again in Ulica, played by Kadeřávková, an avalanche of different reactions came to the actress.
Zvědavec	Disinformative	*(Original Czech version:)* **Title:** Kdo ovládá Ameriku? III. **Text:** Dva ze čtyřech největších mediálních konglomerátů (Disney a Viacom) jsou v židovských rukou. Židovští manažeři řídí mediální podnik NBC Universal. Židé tvoří velké procento na vedoucích postech v Time Warner. Je nepravděpodobné, že by tak velká míra židovského vlivu v této oblasti nastala bez cílené, záměrné snahy ze židovské strany. . . . - - - - - - - - - - *(Translated into English:)* **Title:** Who controls America? III. **Text:** Two of the four largest media conglomerates (Disney and Viacom) are in Jewish hands. Jewish executives run NBC Universal's media business. Jews make up a large percentage of the top positions at Time Warner. It is unlikely that such a large degree of Jewish influence in this area would occur without a focused, deliberate effort on the Jewish side. ...

Table 1: Example items (articles) from the CNSC dataset spanning all three credibility source labels, which were assigned according to our methodology (described in Subsection 3.2).

Model	Architecture	Classification task	F-1 score	Precision	Recall
Czert	BERT		0.94	0.95	0.94
Small-E-Czech	ELECTRA	NSC (source)	0.87	0.88	0.86
RobeCzech	ROBERTA		**0.95**	**0.96**	**0.95**
Czert	BERT		0.96	**0.97**	0.96
Small-E-Czech	ELECTRA	SCLC (source label)	0.93	0.94	0.93
RobeCzech	ROBERTA		**0.97**	**0.97**	**0.97**

Table 2: Top-1 macro F-1 score, precision, and recall of the individual fine-tuned models on the NSC and SCLC tasks, as further described in Subsection 4.2.

should serve as a general, indicative flag of the prevailing trend and with which level of caution the author should read its articles.

For most languages and regions, open-source studies on the state of credibility of the individual media houses, newspapers, and news sites are available. These are often published by journalism activists, social scientists, and other involved figures. As one of the primary motivations of this work is to make the process less financially and organizationally demanding, we propose to re-use one of these works. When choosing the determinative one, we suggest preferring those of more diverse stakeholders and authors and whose methodology quantifies the overall assessments. This way, dividing individual credibility groups (labels) will be more exact.

We built upon the metrics and rankings of the Czech Endowment Fund for Independent Journalism (EFIJ) [3], but reduced the complexity of their final scale. The authors study various parameters of each source on a sample counting 100 of its articles and score them with detailed grades to maximize the objectiveness of the study. The parameters determining the source rating include:

- **Publication attributes:** Presence of authors by each article, transparent structure, and potential ownership conflicts (such as the owner being a politician);
- **Individual article attributes:** Usage of clickbait, stereotypization, hyperlinks, and more.
- **Editorial attributes:** Clear distinction between news reporting and commentaries, flagging of advertisement.

Each attribute is weighted and disposes of a specific prevalence reference. For instance, if less than 15 % of articles in a given source's sample contain a clickbait headline, the medium still receives a full score in the 'relevant headline' category. It receives half the score for a prevalence between 15 % and 30 % and no points for a clickbait rate above 30 %. Finally, the total of scores received across attributes determines the source's class. The category ranges are delineated as even portions of the scale for the given number of classes. In our case, these are three portions of the range between 0 and the maximal potential score. Each encompasses 33 % of the scale.

We arrived at three general classes of credibility. We provide their list with general descriptions below (for detailed description and analyses for each respective news source, we refer the reader to the EFIJ's website[4]):

- **Credible news sources:** Established and reliable news sources that are generally honest and truthful. Their articles contain hyperlinks to further sources of information, present arguments of all involved parties, distinguish between facts, speculations, and commentaries. (e.g., public media, objective press)
- **Tabloid news sources:** News sources one cannot rely on as generally honest and truthful. These sources often present speculations as facts or do not present arguments of all involved parties. (e.g., gutter media, press owned by political figures, press with strong political bias)
- **Disinformative / non-credible news sources:** News sources whose texts generally have no basis in fact but present themselves as being factually accurate. Such sources are often linked to (e.g., owned or funded by) entities intending to influence general political

[3]The Endowment Fund for Independent journalism, https://www.nfnz.cz/en/

[4]https://www.nfnz.cz/rating-medii/

views. (e.g., fake news media, state propaganda press)

Representative examples of the articles from our dataset are located in Table 1. These articles originate from 3 distinct news sources spanning all our source credibility labels. We can observe apparent differences in their topics and narrative styles: while the credible article deals with a factual description of a political event, the tabloid one presents news about a celebrity in a very sensation-seeking manner. Lastly, the disinformative report covers a conspiracy theory and disposes of a very constrained argumentative style.

3.3 Statistics

Herein, we present the statistics of the dataset. The complete set contains $22,001$ articles. We have created training, validation, and testing splits counting $17,600$ (80%), $2,200$ (10%), $2,201$ (10%) articles respectively. To constitute the splits, we sorted the articles by their publishing date and found two dates that would partition them into three temporally exclusive time windows of desired proportions. The distribution of articles by their source of origin is depicted in Figure 1a. As you can see, all of the sources except for ČT24, Extra.cz, and Zvědavec have a comparatively similar number of instances. The outliers result from our effort to preserve the overall trends in the volume of articles published by these sources every day and yet not develop significant margins. We have hence reduced the number of articles in most sources to compensate for the meager per-day publication rate of Zvědavec. As this source falls into the category of Disinformative / non-credible news sources, it can provide insight into how frequently such media publish instead of the conventional ones. The dataset class distribution for when the articles are grouped by their credibility label is shown in Figure 1b.

We have also evaluated the text lengths of the articles in the dataset. We used the NLTK library [5] for tokenization and filtering of punctuation. The articles from credible sources are, on average, 291 words long, while the tabloid and disinformative media have a mean of 379 and 551 words per article, respectively. The large margin between these counts for the credible and disinformative sources (almost double the value) caught our attention. We later reviewed the data manually and confirmed that this was not a mistake in scraping.

Overall, we can observe that while the disinformative sources tend to publish less frequently, their articles are, on average, recognizably longer. During the manual analysis of these articles, we also observed a trend of mentioning many seemingly unrelated topics from different areas at once. We hypothesize that this may be caused by the conspiratory nature of such sources, in which they draw false links and causations between uncorrelated events. Nevertheless, this calls for a thorough analysis of its own. We believe our dataset can serve as the first reference for further studies on such news patterns in the central European regional context.

4 Baseline experiments

In the following section, we present the baseline results for the two newly formulated tasks on the CNSC dataset:

- **News source classification (NSC):** the task is to classify the originating news source of an article based on its title and body texts from a pre-defined set of media,
- **Source credibility label classification (SCLC):** the task is to classify the news source credibility label to which the article's originating news source belongs based on its title and body texts from a pre-defined set of media.

In this particular case, the number of classes for NSC corresponds to the number of news sources present in the dataset (9). The number of classes for the SCLC task corresponds to the number of credibility labels (3), as outlined in Subsection 3.2.

4.1 Experimental setting

We fine-tune three language model architectures for this purpose: Czert (Sido et al., 2021) (based on BERT (Devlin et al., 2019)), Small-E-Czech (Kocián et al., 2021) (based on ELECTRA (Clark et al., 2020)), and RobeCzech (Straka et al., 2021) (based on ROBERTA (Liu et al., 2019)). We use the HuggingFace Transformers library for implementation and train the models using a learning rate of $2e-5$ for 4 epochs. When obtaining the embeddings for all the examined models, we concatenate the article's title with its text as if it were the first sentence of the body. To

[5] NLTK library, `https://www.nltk.org/`

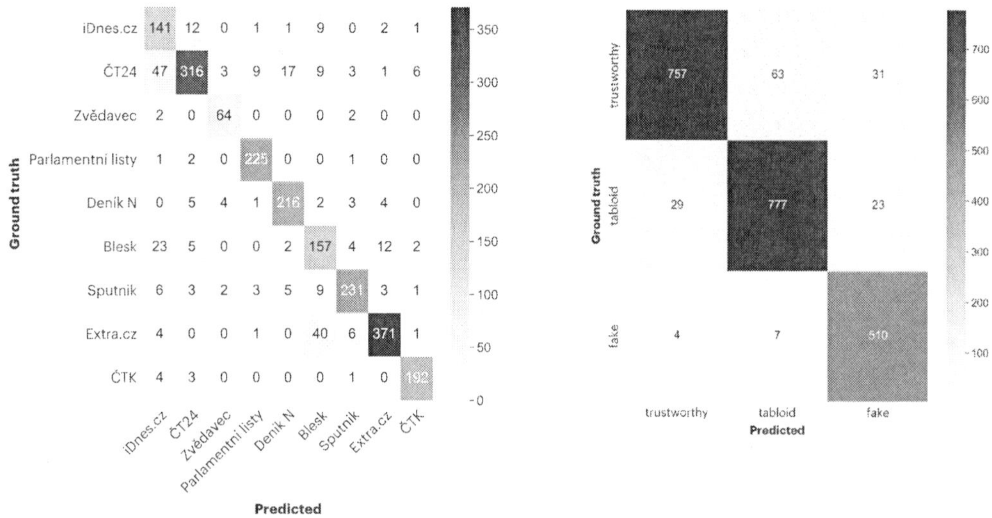

(a) per individual news sources

(b) per news source labels

Figure 2: Confusion matrices of the fine-tuned Small-E-Czech's predictions on our CNSC dataset test split. The architecture and training configuration details can be found in Subsection 4.1.

prevent the models from learning other undesired correlated artifacts, which may be left in the article (such as names of the source occurring at the beginning), we delete any occurrences of the article's originating news source name in the body. We also remove common rubric identifiers from the title (e.g., 'Commentary:', 'Interview'). We open-source our training scripts at `https://github.com/matyasbohacek/misinfo-detection-wild-emnlp22`.

4.2 Results

We present the results in Table 2. The F-1 score, precision, and recall on the testing set are included for each model and task. We can observe that the tested models managed to learn the individual news sources' characteristics in writing for both tasks and generally achieved reasonable performance, with the F-1 scores around 0.9. We found RobeCzech to be performing best in both tasks by reaching 0.95 and 0.97 F-1 scores on the NSC and SCLC tasks, respectively. On the other hand, Small-E-Czech has performed the worst by resulting in respective F-1 scores of 0.87 and 0.93. We presume this is caused by the model's size, as Small-E-Czech is dramatically smaller than the other two models in parameter counts. Lastly, we also evaluated the fine-tuned Czert, which scored under the best RobeCzech with 0.94 and 0.96 respective F-1 scores on the two tasks.

We further depict the confusion matrices of the Small-E-Czech's predictions for both tasks on the test split in Figure 2. As can be observed in Figure 2b, most erroneous predictions mistake the trustworthy and tabloid labels, while there are only a few false positives predictions of the fake label. We argue that this may be caused by the unique and highly distinctive vocabulary used in conspiracies. Trustworthy and tabloid articles, on the other hand, dispose of differences in their narratives that our models can also capture, but often share the topics of general public discourse, and therefore have less distinguishing vocabulary.

5 In-the-wild wrapper applications

We construct and open-source three in-the-wild wrappers of the just-described models. We do so to support future studies of such interventions' efficacy and associated user behavior. As the primary motivation of our work lies in enabling internet users to gauge the perceived trustworthiness of various texts online, we want the tools to be easily reachable from different workflows. The applications thus include:

1. **Standalone web application.** Created using Gradio [6], we present a simple website that

[6]Gradio library, `https://gradio.app`

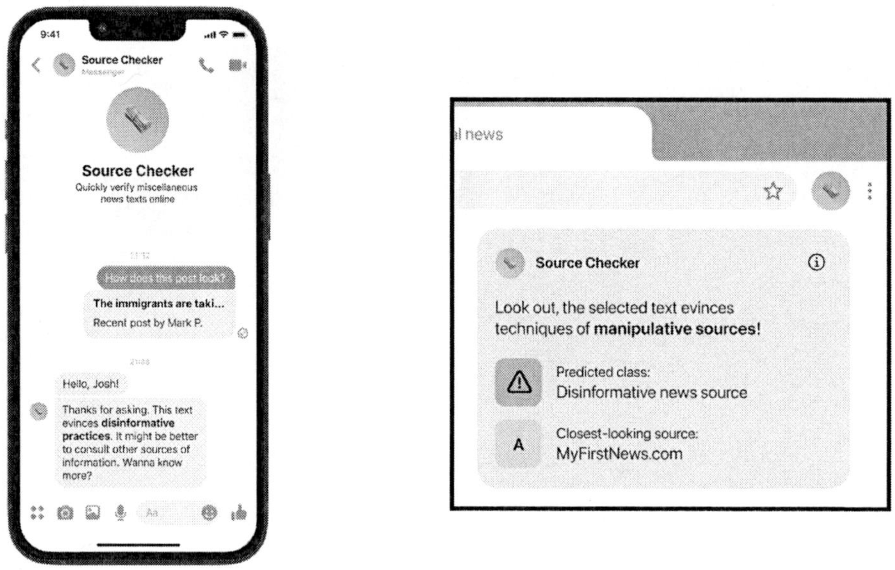

(a) Messenger chatbot companion

(b) Browser extension

Figure 3: Screenshots of the end-customer model wrappers with mock data, as described in Section 5.

enables users to insert text and quickly see the top 3 predicted classes by both models.

2. **Browser extension.** As depicted in Figure 3b, we build a standard Chromium-based[7] browser extension, letting users infer the models with any highlighted text on the screen. The extension shows the most likely originating source and its respective trustworthiness class.

3. **Chatbot.** To serve mobile users, too, we create a Facebook Messenger chatbot, which wraps the inference of both models in a simple prompt heuristic. Apart from the inference features, the chatbot comes with additional explanatory phrases and links built in. A mock conversation is shown in Figure 3a.

6 Ethical Discussion and Limitations

In this section, we review the limitations of our solution and discuss the ethical aspects of its use. As already mentioned, one must bear in mind that the overall credibility of a given news source does not deduce all of its articles' trustworthiness or factual correctness. Still, different studies (Cone et al., 2019; Pehlivanoglu et al., 2021) found the source trustworthiness to be an effective indicator of its articles' credibility (especially when other coverage or context are limited). The literature on machine learning identification has mainly built classifiers on this premise. We believe this approach offers a reasonable trade-off between the annotation complexity and overall performance. In our solution, the originating news source serves as a proxy of credibility. While writing in a style of a particular outlet does not, once again, conclusively derive the text's eventual trustworthiness, detecting patterns used in fraudulent and hoax outlets can provide a helpful warning flag for potentially deceptive and harmful texts. Any publicly available application of this technology should clearly state this information at the very beginning and provide its users with additional resources about the methodology. Moreover, the users should be aware that the analysis is automatic. We include examples of best practices (with short descriptions easily understandable by the general public) in our wrapper applications.

The technology could be misused by falsely labeling misinformation as trustworthy and manipulating its users according to the agenda of the service provider. Therefore, we believe only trusted, independent institutions (e.g., university-affiliated centers and non-governmental organizations) should assume the role of operators. We advise prospective providers to disclose the source labeling methodology and the samples used fully.

[7]The Chromium Projects, `https://www.chromium.org`

7 Conclusion

We show that when appropriately adapted and wrapped, the existing methods for disinformation detection can serve as supportive tools for the new form of disinformation contexts online. We present an open-source CNSC dataset with over $22,000$ Czech news articles spanning 9 sources across the credibility spectrum, the first of its kind in such a small language. We build on top of a detailed methodology for news trustworthiness assessment in the Czech Republic and establish 3 credibility classes for the news sources. We train baseline models for the news source and source credibility label classification and achieve F-1 scores of 0.95 and 0.97, respectively. Lastly, we introduce three in-the-wild wrapper applications of our models, whose code we are making public.

In our future work, we want to conduct focus group studies analyzing the efficacy and user behavior of the intervention tools we introduced. We also intend to propose better metrics and benchmarks for detecting the ever-evolving disinformation.

Acknowledgements

I would like to thank Kateřina Lesch for the incredible initial insights into academic writing and the internship opportunity in her team I was given despite my age. I would also like to express profound gratitude to Tomáš Trnka for multiple rounds of reviews and discussions about this matter and paper.

References

Vlad Achimescu and Pavel Dimitrov Chachev. 2020. Raising the flag: Monitoring user perceived disinformation on reddit. *Information*, 12(1):4.

Mohammad A Bsoul, Abdallah Qusef, and Saleh Abu-Soud. 2022. Building an optimal dataset for arabic fake news detection. *Procedia Computer Science*, 201:665–672.

Kevin Clark, Minh-Thang Luong, Quoc V. Le, and Christopher D. Manning. 2020. ELECTRA: Pre-training text encoders as discriminators rather than generators. In *ICLR*.

Jeremy Cone, Kathryn Flaharty, and Melissa J Ferguson. 2019. Believability of evidence matters for correcting social impressions. *Proceedings of the National Academy of Sciences*, 116(20):9802–9807.

Leon Derczynski, Torben Oskar Albert-Lindqvist, Marius Venø Bendsen, Nanna Inie, Viktor Due Pedersen, and Jens Egholm Pedersen. 2019. Misinformation on twitter during the danish national election: A case study. In *Truth and Trust Online*.

Jacob Devlin, Ming-Wei Chang, Kenton Lee, and Kristina Toutanova. 2019. BERT: Pre-training of deep bidirectional transformers for language understanding. In *Proceedings of the 2019 Conference of the North American Chapter of the Association for Computational Linguistics: Human Language Technologies, Volume 1 (Long and Short Papers)*, pages 4171–4186, Minneapolis, Minnesota. Association for Computational Linguistics.

Arianna D'Ulizia, Maria Chiara Caschera, Fernando Ferri, and Patrizia Grifoni. 2021. Fake news detection: a survey of evaluation datasets. *PeerJ Computer Science*, 7:e518.

Fhamborg. Fhamborg/news-please: News-please - an integrated web crawler and information extractor for news that just works.

Zhijiang Guo, Michael Schlichtkrull, and Andreas Vlachos. 2022. A survey on automated fact-checking. *Transactions of the Association for Computational Linguistics*, 10:178–206.

Ashwaq Khalil, Moath Jarrah, Monther Aldwairi, and Manar Jaradat. 2022. Afnd: Arabic fake news dataset for the detection and classification of articles credibility. *Data in Brief*, 42:108141.

Matěj Kocián, Jakub Náplava, Daniel Štancl, and Vladimír Kadlec. 2021. Siamese bert-based model for web search relevance ranking evaluated on a new czech dataset. *arXiv e-prints*, pages arXiv–2112.

Yinhan Liu, Myle Ott, Naman Goyal, Jingfei Du, Mandar Joshi, Danqi Chen, Omer Levy, Mike Lewis, Luke Zettlemoyer, and Veselin Stoyanov. 2019. Roberta: A robustly optimized BERT pretraining approach. *CoRR*, abs/1907.11692.

Paul Meddeb, Stefan Ruseti, Mihai Dascalu, Simina-Maria Terian, and Sebastien Travadel. 2022. Counteracting french fake news on climate change using language models. *Sustainability*, 14(18):11724.

Kai Nakamura, Sharon Levy, and William Yang Wang. 2020. Fakeddit: A new multimodal benchmark dataset for fine-grained fake news detection. In *Proceedings of the 12th Language Resources and Evaluation Conference*, pages 6149–6157.

Jack Nicas. 2020. Why can't the social networks stop fake accounts?

Ray Oshikawa, Jing Qian, and William Yang Wang. 2020. A survey on natural language processing for fake news detection. In *Proceedings of the 12th Language Resources and Evaluation Conference*, pages 6086–6093.

Joanna Paliszkiewicz, Magdalena Mądra Sawicka, Tadeusz Filipiak, Salome Svanadze, and Mariam Jikia. 2017. Time-spent online as a factor in usage and awareness of drawbacks in social media. *Issues in Information Systems*, 18(4).

Didem Pehlivanoglu, Tian Lin, Farha Deceus, Amber Heemskerk, Natalie C Ebner, and Brian S Cahill. 2021. The role of analytical reasoning and source credibility on the evaluation of real and fake full-length news articles. *Cognitive research: principles and implications*, 6(1):1–12.

Kira E Riehm, Kenneth A Feder, Kayla N Tormohlen, Rosa M Crum, Andrea S Young, Kerry M Green, Lauren R Pacek, Lareina N La Flair, and Ramin Mojtabai. 2019. Associations between time spent using social media and internalizing and externalizing problems among us youth. *JAMA Psychiatry*, 76(12):1266.

Kai Shu, Deepak Mahudeswaran, Suhang Wang, Dongwon Lee, and Huan Liu. 2020. Fakenewsnet: A data repository with news content, social context, and spatiotemporal information for studying fake news on social media. *Big data*, 8(3):171–188.

Jakub Sido, Ondřej Pražák, Pavel Přibáň, Jan Pašek, Michal Seják, and Miloslav Konopík. 2021. Czert–czech bert-like model for language representation. In *Proceedings of the International Conference on Recent Advances in Natural Language Processing (RANLP 2021)*, pages 1326–1338.

Niraj Sitaula, Chilukuri K Mohan, Jennifer Grygiel, Xinyi Zhou, and Reza Zafarani. 2020. Credibility-based fake news detection. *Disinformation, Misinformation, and Fake News in Social Media*, page 163.

Milan Straka, Jakub Náplava, Jana Straková, and David Samuel. 2021. Robeczech: Czech roberta, a monolingual contextualized language representation model. In *International Conference on Text, Speech, and Dialogue*, pages 197–209. Springer.

James Thorne, Andreas Vlachos, Christos Christodoulopoulos, and Arpit Mittal. 2018. FEVER: a large-scale dataset for fact extraction and VERification. In *Proceedings of the 2018 Conference of the North American Chapter of the Association for Computational Linguistics: Human Language Technologies, Volume 1 (Long Papers)*, pages 809–819, New Orleans, Louisiana. Association for Computational Linguistics.

William Yang Wang. 2017. "liar, liar pants on fire": A new benchmark dataset for fake news detection. In *Proceedings of the 55th Annual Meeting of the Association for Computational Linguistics (Volume 2: Short Papers)*, pages 422–426, Vancouver, Canada. Association for Computational Linguistics.

Amy X Zhang, Aditya Ranganathan, Sarah Emlen Metz, Scott Appling, Connie Moon Sehat, Norman Gilmore, Nick B Adams, Emmanuel Vincent, Jennifer Lee, Martin Robbins, et al. 2018. A structured response to misinformation: Defining and annotating credibility indicators in news articles. In *Companion Proceedings of the The Web Conference 2018*, pages 603–612.

Modelling Persuasion through Misuse of Rhetorical Appeals

Amalie Brogaard Pauli
Aarhus Universitet
Denmark
ampa@cs.au.dk

Leon Derczynski
IT University of Copenhagen
Denmark
ld@itu.dk

Ira Assent
Aarhus Universitet
DIGIT Aarhus University
Centre for Digitalisation,
Big Data and Data Analytics
Denmark
ira@cs.au.dk

Abstract

It is important to understand how people use words to persuade each other. This helps understand debate, and detect persuasive narratives in regard to e.g. misinformation. While computational modelling of some aspects of persuasion has received some attention, a way to unify and describe the overall phenomenon of when persuasion becomes undesired and problematic, is missing. In this paper, we attempt to address this by proposing a taxonomy of computational persuasion. Drawing upon existing research and resources, this paper shows how to re-frame and re-organise current work into a coherent framework targeting the misuse of rhetorical appeals. As a study to validate these re-framings, we then train and evaluate models of persuasion adapted to our taxonomy. Our results show an application of our taxonomy, and we are able to detecting misuse of rhetorical appeals, finding that these are more often used in misinformative contexts than in true ones.

1 Introduction

People are exposed to a large amount of online text that is quickly scrolled through, but which may have an inherent agenda to persuade or convince the reader. As a mitigation strategy, we hypothesise that automatic detection of persuasion in a text can help the reader navigate more critically online: like a skilled rhetorician spotting how something is trying to persuade and how an argument might be faulty (Rapp, 2022). With this social motivation, we study how to computational model persuasion in text. Computational modelling of persuasion techniques and strategies is a raising field in the area of computational argumentation. We establish the working term 'undesired persuasion' to be when the execution of persuasion in a text is unsound, e.g by using fallacies or tricks. Prior research in this directions has, among others, focused on propaganda techniques (Martino et al., 2020a), logical fallacies (Jin et al., 2022), and personal attacks (Zhang et al., 2018; Habernal et al., 2018). The field of persuasion detection consists of a variety of focuses and different classification schemes. However, prior work shares commonalities, and we argue that the problem can be tackled in a more unified way and thereby benefit the computational modelling and understanding of persuasion. In this work, we propose to model problematic and undesired persuasion by targeting rhetorical appeals –

Fallacy of Pathos
Appeal to Fear: "'Without this additional insurance, you could find yourself broke and homeless"
Appeal to Pity: "I know I missed assignments, but if you fail me, I will lose my financial aid and have to drop out."
Appeal to Popularity: "Nine out of ten shoppers have switched to Blindingly-Bright-Smile Toothpaste."
Fallacy of Ethos
False authority:"Dr. X is an engineer, and he doesn't believe in global warming."
Ad Hominem:"Why should we think a candidate who recently divorced will keep her campaign promises?"
Name-calling:"These rabble-rousers are nothing but feminazis."
Fallacy of Logos
False dilemma:"Either we pass this ordinance or there will be rioting in the streets"
Circular argument:"This legislation is sinful because it is the wrong thing to do."
Red Herring or Smoke Screen:"My opponent says I am weak on crime, but I have been one of the most reliable participants in city council meetings."

Table 1: Examples of fallacy types grouped into fallacies of ethos, pathos, and logos. These are from two sources of educational material [1]and Kashyap (2022)

[1]https://www.mvrhs.org/englishdept/shark/links/General%20Information/Rhetorical%20Fallacies%20U.%20Texas%20@%20Austin.pdf

Proceedings of the Second Workshop on NLP for Positive Impact (NLP4PI), pages 89 - 100
December 7, 2022 ©2022 Association for Computational Linguistics

or rather, misuse of rhetorical appeals. Rhetoric is the discipline of persuading or influencing others through speech or text. Rhetorical appeals are described by Aristotle as the three modes of persuasion through writing or speaking, where: Ethos is to persuade through the credibility of the speaker, pathos through the emotions of the listener, and logos through the soundness of the argument itself (Rapp, 2022). We will use the working-term *misuse* of rhetorical appeals to denote when an appeal becomes unsound or exaggerated in its reasoning, e.g using fallacies – with fallacies understood as making a reasoning seem better than it is (Hansen, 2022). Table 1 shows examples of different logical fallacy types grouped into the broader categories of fallacies of logos, ethos and pathos. Based on such a framework, we will discuss how to re-frame existing resources and on the basis of this, develop models to detect misuse of rhetorical appeals.

Following our social motivation, we hypothesise that misusing rhetorical appeals to argue or present some evidence is correlated with misinformation in broader terms. Therefore, this paper examines whether the misuse of rhetorical appeals are more often used in, e.g., mis/disinformation. This is carried out by applying the models for detecting misuse of rhetorical appeals on a variety of data sets targeting this. At the same time, misusing the appeals may be correlated with losing arguments. We, therefore, test our models on a dataset from a debate forum where users upvote and downvote comments (Chang and Danescu-Niculescu-Mizil, 2019). In this paper, we:

- Propose modelling persuasion through rhetorical appeals,
- Re-frame existing resources and reorganise resources to target misuse of rhetorical appeals: ethos, pathos and logos,
- Experiment with developing models for detecting misuse of rhetorical appeals and link it to misinformation,
- Find a tendency showing that misuse of rhetorical appeals appears more frequently in misinformation, but also that a notable amount of fallacies of ethos and pathos are used in reliable news as well.

In general, we hope with this work to increase the focus on using rhetorical appeals in computational modelling persuasion, both on desired and undesired persuasion.

2 Computational Persuasion

This section sets the background of computational modelling of persuasion. We first outline the broad spectrum of different ways of understanding and modelling persuasion, to both map the field and to clarify concepts. From here the scope is reduced to existing classification schemes, focusing on their connections to rhetorical appeals.

2.1 Mapping Persuasion Modelling

The literature takes different perspectives and distinctions to model persuasion in text. To create an overview, we group the approaches in three directions and discuss connections and overlappings. The first direction is on text units linguistic defined. The second on pre-defined categories driven by the intention behind persuasion. The third direction is based on an audience's response to a text.

In the first direction, we have rhetorical figures treated as linguistic style units. These are relevant as they aim at producing a rhetorical effect, or in other words, to persuade an audience by e.g. utilising cognitive bias in humans e.g. with rhythm and repetition. Studies include the detection of repetitive figures (Dubremetz and Nivre, 2018), exaggeration (Troiano et al., 2018; Kong et al., 2020) and of syntax figures (Al Khatib et al., 2020).

In the third direction, research is trying to capture what people perceive as persuasive, without resorting to predefined style units or other predefined concepts of persuasion. For example, one study attempts to answer what makes a text persuasive by extracting a lexicon based on people's responsive action to a text (Pryzant et al., 2018). Another example is the discipline of automatic argument quality assessment, which could, for example, include a dimension of rhetorical quality with a score of how persuasive an argument is (Wachsmuth et al., 2017).

In the second direction, work is dealing with what is denoted as persuasion techniques or persuasion strategies using predefined categories. This line of research focuses more on the intention behind persuasion than on linguistic style units. For example, some studies for propaganda detection did not treat repetition and exaggeration as style units as seen above but instead as propaganda techniques (Martino et al., 2019, 2020a).

This direction can be subdivided into two since studies often makes a distinction between whether the intention or execution of persuasion is 'desired' or 'undesired'.

The desired persuasion line covers topics such as rhetorical strategies (Yang et al., 2019; Shaikh et al., 2020), convincing and winning arguments (Tan et al., 2016; Habernal and Gurevych, 2016) and 'persuasion for social good' (Wang et al., 2019). Under undesired persuasion, papers talk about propaganda (Martino et al., 2020a; Vorakitphan et al., 2021; Da San Martino et al., 2021), logical fallacies (Habernal et al., 2017; Jin et al., 2022) and personal attacks (Habernal et al., 2018; Sheng et al., 2020). Propaganda can be seen as the intention to persuade in a political context with opposing groups (Guess and Lyons, 2020). Propaganda techniques can therefore overlap with e.g logical fallacies and emotional appeals as in (Martino et al., 2020a). Different classification schemes in this direction of pre-defined categories are further outlined in subsection 2.2.

In addition, research frequently distinguishes between whether the persuasion is mediated through monologue or dialogue.

2.2 Classification Schemes

Prior research on desired and undesired persuasion applies a variety of different annotation schemes and denotations for (respectively) persuasion techniques and strategies. The following attempts to summarise it by focusing on the relation to rhetorical appeals. We start with desired persuasion.

Various classification schemes have been applied to rhetorical strategies. Several papers have proposed to use schemes guided form social psychology on persuasion (Young et al., 2011; Yang et al., 2019; Chen and Yang, 2021). Chen and Yang (2021) argue that their taxonomy can be used to unify the modelling of persuasion strategies. Their scheme uses the following labels: Commitment, Emotion, Politeness, Reciprocity, Scarcity, Credibility, Evidence and Impact (Chen and Yang, 2021). The strategy labels "credibility" and "emotion" are linked to respectively ethos and pathos. Other labels correspondence to rhetorical appeals are seen in Iyer et al. (2017) where among their 14 labels is VIP Appeal to Authority (ethos), Empathy and popularity (pathos). The rhetorical appeals are specifically targeted in Wang et al. (2019) but on the same terms with a list of more domain-specific strategies for convincing others to donate to charity. Lastly, the Hidey et al. (2017) also annotated rhetorical appeals; here on the premise in arguments posted in the discussion forum, Change My View.

There is less research on problematic and undesired persuasion with persuasion techniques and fallacies. Habernal et al. (2017) was the first within NLP research to work with fallacies, using a crowdsourcing game to create different types of fallacious arguments. Martino et al. (2019) created a corpus for detecting propaganda in news with 18 different techniques. This evolved into a shared task at SemEval 2020 (Martino et al., 2020a) with 14 categories. Two datasets for Logical fallacy detection were created in Jin et al. (2022) with 14 categories. The first is crafted by collecting logical fallacy examples from online educational materials, and the second is crafted by annotating real discussions on climate change. In addition to these, attention has especially been paid to Ad Hominem Fallacies, which are to attack the person instead of the stand. For example, Habernal et al. (2018) studied Ad Hominem Fallacies in an online debate forum with data from Change My View, and Sheng et al. (2020) studied it in Twitter responses, and Zhang et al. (2018) in Wikipedia talk pages where editors discuss article content. The different resources mentioned above are outlined in Table 2. The next section discusses whether undesired persuasion can be addressed in a more unified way by re-framing existing resources to target rhetorical appeals.

3 Re-framing Persuasion

We discuss how to computationally model persuasion through the lens of a framework detecting rhetorical appeals. By this we examine whether problematic and undesired persuasion can be addressed in a more unified way by re-framing existing resources (Table 2). We propose that persuasion techniques should be grouped with respect to the rhetorical appeals they rely on, as it is outline in e.g. the educational material on rhetoric from Kashyap (2022).

As we focus on problematic persuasion, we group fallacies based on whether they are making a faulty appeal to logos, ethos or pathos (Kashyap, 2022). Examples of fallacies are presenting something as a false dilemma, making an appeal to fear or attacking the person instead of the argument. Table 1 shows examples of fallacies related to rhetorical appeals. However, this grouping is

Corpus	Labels	Grouped to
Martino et al. (2020a)	Black-and-white fallacy, causal oversimplification	Misuse of logos
	Doubt, Appeal to authority, Name calling or labelling, Flag-waving, Bandwagon & reduction ad hitlerum	Misuse of ethos
	Loaded language, Appeal to fear/prejudice, Thought-terminating cliché	Misuse of pathos
	Repetition, Exaggeration or minimization, (mixed category: Whataboutism, straw man, red herring), slogans	Others
Jin et al. (2022)	Intentional fallacy, faulty generalization, fallacy of relevance, deductive fallacy, false causality, fallacy of extension, false dilemma, circular claim	Misuse of logos
	Fallacy of credibility, Ad Hominem	Misuse of ethos
	Appeal to emotion, Ad populum	Misuse of pathos
	Equivocation	Others
Habernal et al. (2017)	Red herring, hasty generalisation	Misuse of logos
	Irrelevant authority	Misuse of ethos
	Appeal to emotion	Misuse of pathos
Zhang et al. (2018)	Personal Attack	Misuse of ethos
Sheng et al. (2020)	Ad Hominem	Misuse of ethos
Habernal et al. (2018)	Ad Hominem	Misuse of ethos

Table 2: Re-framings of different labels from varies sources into the taxonomy of misuse of rhetorical appeals.

not straightforward, for multiple reasons. There is no absolute or final list of fallacies types. This is reflected in the variety of labels used in different prior works (Table 2). Some types might be a subcategory of others or contain a mix. At the same time, a type of fallacy can be argued to be a mix or use a different appeal depending on the utterance. Our over-arching principle is to group fallacies based on their fallacy type, along with a discussion of the noise it creates in the data. To create an overview of the grouping proposed by this paper, a colour scheme is applied to the categories from the different studies in Table 2. The Other category contains different linguistic or rhetorical devices that, based on their labels, cannot directly be grouped into appeals of logos, ethos and pathos. In the following, the grouping is discussed, starting with ethos.

Misuse of Ethos Ethos is an instrument of persuasion by appealing to credibility or authority. The fallacy of ethos is to unjustly strengthen one's own or associate's character or credibility, or to unfairly undermine or attack the opponent's character or credibility (Kashyap, 2022). From the previous resources listed in Table 2, we map the following fallacies to ethos: Appealing to irrelevant authority. Name-calling or labelling, which is to use negative connotations in relation to the opponent in an attempt to undermine her. Doubt, which is to question somebody's credibility (Martino et al., 2020a). The fallacy of flag-waving is a corner case, as it can both be an attempt to call upon authority in the form of a country, or disparages another country, while, on the other hand, it could also relate to pathos e.g. with an appeal to the emotion of national feeling. Lastly, we consider Ad Hominem, which is to make a personal attack. The annotation of Ad Hominem fallacy or personal attack category might be a source of noise, since it might target rude behaviour in general and not specific attacks on credibility.

Examples of positive cases tagged with the Ad Hominem fallacy that contain a faulty appeal to ethos: *Fine be that way, just to let you know you are very rude* and *So only Falun Gong practitioners are allowed to edit on this board is that right?*, and one example where it is rude but where it does not attack credibility directly: *The article clearly sucks* (Zhang et al., 2018).

Misuse of Pathos Pathos is an instrument of persuasion by appealing to emotion in the audience. To misuse it is to use it excessively or unfairly, e.g. creating strong positive emotions for one's stand or negative emotions associated with the opponent's argument (Kashyap, 2022). In the resources listed in Table 2, we argue that the following fallacies types belong to the broader category of fallacies of pathos: Appeal to emotion. Appeal to fear/prejudice. Loaded language which is to use strong emotional words or phrases (Martino et al., 2020a) to create an emotional effect. Ad Populum is the fallacy of making something appear more real or better because more people think so (Jin et al., 2022), and can therefore be thought of as waking emotions, for example belonging. The thought-terminating cliché is perhaps a mixed category that could contain different appeals; however, in Wikipedia, it is described as a form of loaded language [2], and we map this to pathos.

Some positive examples from existing resources: *Because if this crisis continues, many people will go to hell*, Appeal to fear / prejudice (Martino et al., 2020a) and *How could someone oppress our women? They are our mothers, our lovers, our everything.. nobody would be so cruel*, Appeal to emotion (Habernal et al., 2017), and *"Everyone is wearing the new skinny jeans from American Eagle. Are you?"* Ad populum (Jin et al., 2022).

Misuse of Logos Logos is concerned with the nature of the argument itself. It appeals to logic by following valid reasoning and presenting of evidence. In this regard, a misuse of logos is to use faulty logic by e.g drawing a conclusion that is not supported by the premise. In that sense, this category is distinct from pathos and ethos which are in its definitions drawing attention away from the argument itself. An example is the fallacy of Red Herring which is to present irrelevant or misleading information to avoid the real issue (Kashyap, 2022) - this could often be the case by using an emotional appeal and it could therefore be grouped as a fallacy of pathos[3] and not logos. Nevertheless, we map it as logos along with the following fallacies from the previous resources in Table 2: Black-and-white fallacy, Casual oversimplification, Intentional fallacy, faulty or hasty generalisation, deductive fallacy, false causality, fallacy of extension, false dilemma, or circular claim.

One example of Red Herring that uses faulty logos: *You might be correct. The best era for European economy was 60s and 70s when there were practically no immigrants* (Habernal et al., 2017).

[2]https://en.wikipedia.org/wiki/Thought-terminating_clich%C3%A9

[3]https://www.mvrhs.org/englishdept/shark/links/General%20Information/Rhetorical%20Fallacies%20U.%20Texas%20@%20Austin.pdf

4 Detecting Rhetorical Appeals

This section relates experiments on detecting misuse of rhetorical appeals. We develop models for detecting misuse of ethos, pathos and logos in English, based on the re-framing of existing resources discussed in Section 3. We then examine how misuse of rhetorical appeals links to misinformation. We understand misinformation as the working-definition from Guess and Lyons (2020): *as constituting a claim that contradicts or distorts common understandings of verifiable facts.* We posit the following hypotheses:

First, we hypothesise that misuse of rhetorical appeals appears more often in losing arguments – since a faulty argument only has a persuasive effect if it is not spotted, cf. Section 1. The second hypothesis is that in misinformation, not only incorrect information but also persuasive language are used, and so misuse of rhetorical appeals may appear more frequently in misinformative contexts.

In the following, we present training details on the machine learning models we develop, describe the datasets we experiment on along with results, and discuss limitations and uncertainties.

4.1 Training Details: Appeal models

This subsection describes how models are developed to detect misuse of ethos, pathos, and logos. Three binary transformer models are fine-tuned independently on the RoBERTa architecture (Liu et al., 2019) based on the implementation and pretrained RoBERTa-base model provided by HuggingFace. (Wolf et al., 2020) Each model is finetuned based on a re-constructed dataset built on some of the resources discussed in Section 3 and reformulated into a binary task - based on the labels re-grouped in Table 2. The labels not responding to the current task at hand are used as negative examples. The datasets for the re-framing are chosen based on accessibility and length of utterances. With these limitations, the data used to develop the models, comes from: Habernal et al. (2017), Martino et al. (2020a), Jin et al. (2022) (only the part of educational examples), and in addition, for detecting ethos the data from Zhang et al. (2018). Each of the three constructed binary datasets are split into train, validation and a hold-out test set. The hold-out test sets consist of 1.6K data points for the ethos dataset, 1.2K for pathos and 1.2K for logos. The training dataset for ethos contains of 4.7K positive and 8.8K negative examples, for pathos; 3.5K

	Accuracy	Micro-F1
Ethos_model	85.14 (0.47)	85.12 (0.49)
Pathos_model	80.51 (0.35)	80.48 (0.41)
Logos_model	88.32 (0.36)	88.25 (0.39)

Table 3: The hold-out test set accuracy and Micro-F1 score avaraged over five runs. Standard deviation in brackets.

positive and 6.9K negative examples, and for logos; 2K positive and 8.4K negative examples. Oversampling is used to balance the datasets. All training parameters are kept equal to the standard used in the implementation by HuggingFace.[4] The models are fine-tuned with five different seeds and the averaged results on the hold-out test set are shown in Table 3. Note the hold-out test set is also on the re-framings. The best model in terms of F1 on the positive class for respectively ethos, pathos and logos is chosen for the misinformation experiments. For short, in the following, the models will be just denoted as ethos-, pathos- and logos-model though they are detecting what we with the re-framing have denoted misuse of rhetorical appeals.

4.2 Losing Arguments

We experiment on one dataset containing indications of good versus bad argumentations from the user's perspective:

- **Change My View** (CMV) is a forum in Reddit featuring good-faith debates on various topics with the aim of changing the opinion of the original poster. In the forum, users have the option of upvoting or downvoting utterances. An extraction of these data is provided in Chang and Danescu-Niculescu-Mizil (2019) and distributed by ConvoKit [5] with the voting on each utterance turned into a score (upvoting minus downvoting). We remove outliers in the score if the score exceeds 3 times the standard deviation. The data contains around 40K utterances.

As the data is from a forum with the purpose of changing other users' views through good argumentation, we expect that the argument is well evaluated and that this is reflected in the score. Hence, we expect users to dislike utterances using a faulty appeal. The hypothesis is, therefore, that utterances which contain a misuse of appeal should be less liked by the users resulting in a lower score.

	Predicted		Not predicted	
Misuse of	score	support	score	support
Ethos	8.51	33558	5.98	8923
Pathos	8.15	37550	6.63	4931
Logos	8.6	33183	5.73	9298

Table 4: Change My View dataset: The average score on comments i.e. up-vote minus down-vote from users. The comments are grouped by whether the models have found a fallacy or not.

We apply the three models for detecting misuse of ethos, pathos and logos described in Subsection 4.1 on each utterance from the dataset Change My View. Based on each model's predictions, the utterances are divided into groups of whether they contain a misuse of appeal or not, separately for the three models. The mean score is calculated for each group and is reported in Table 4. It shows for all three models, that the utterances where a misuse of appeal is detected on average have a lower score. To validate these differences, we conduct a statistical test. The data fails the normality test of Shapiro-Wilks (Shapiro and Wilk, 1965), and, therefore, we use the nonparametric Mann Whitney U test (Mann and Whitney, 1947). In all three cases, we can reject the null with a p-value < 0.01. We can conclude that the distribution of the scores regarding whether an appeal is predicated on the utterance or not is different. Hence, we can say that the utterance is less liked by users when it contains a misuse of appeal.

4.3 Misinformation

Misinformation and manipulation are rife on the web (Derczynski et al., 2015). We apply our models on to misinformation datasets to examine whether the misuse of appeals appears more frequently in the category of false claims than genuine ones. We use the following datasets, which contain both text and false/true annotations for veracity.

- **ISOT Fake News Dataset** (Ahmed et al., 2018) is a collection of news articles distant labelled with fake or true based on the sources. The unreliable news sources were flagged by Politifact.com or Wikipedia and the reliable news was crawled from Reuters.com. It counts 21K articles labelled real and 23K arti-

[4] https://github.com/huggingface/transformers/tree/main/examples/pytorch/text-classification

[5] https://convokit.cornell.edu/documentation/awry_cmv.html

Fallacies of Ethos		
	True	False
ISOT Fake News Dataset	35.45	**49.96**
Liar	15.34	**19.75**
FakeNewsNet	13.62	**16.49**
COVID19-FAKE	2.14	**19.15**
PUBHEALTH	**17.72**	16.69

Table 5: The percentage of examples predicted by the ethos model to contain a misuse of ethos in different datasets grouped by the dataset's labels of false or true. The highest percentage is marked in bold. The sizes of the datasets are specified in the list describing each dataset.

Fallacies of Pathos		
	True	False
ISOT Fake News Dataset	22.27	**57.81**
Liar	15.75	**16.39**
FakeNewsNet	**42.32**	40.80
COVID19-FAKE	21.93	**24.90**
PUBHEALTH	**22.59**	18.66

Table 6: The percentage of examples predicted by the pathos model to contain a misuse of pathos in different datasets grouped by the dataset's labels of false or true. The highest percentage is marked in bold. The sizes of the datasets are specified in the list describing each dataset.

cles labelled false. In the experiments of this paper, the title is used to predict on.

- **Liar** (Wang, 2017) is a dataset for claim verification consisting of short utterances taken from Politifact.com and manually annotated into six fine-grained labels of truthfulness: pants-fire, false, barely-true, half-true, mostly-true, and true. We follow Upadhayay and Behzadan (2020) at convert it to binary labels with mostly-true and true in true (3.6K training data) and the rest in false (6.6K training data).

- **FakeNewsNet** (Shu et al., 2018) is a resource for claim verification with a set of metadata from Social Media. The news is fact-checked mainly by gossipcob.com. We use the title of the news article and labels for fake or real, and work with 23K examples imbalanced in labels, with around 6K labelled fake and 17K labelled real.

- **PUBHEALTH** (Kotonya and Toni, 2020) is a corpus on fact-checking of public health-related short claims enriched with explanations. It originally uses four labels, but we use only the annotations for False (3K) and True (5K).

- **COVID19-FAKE** (Patwa et al., 2021) is a manually annotated corpus of news tweets related to the Covid19 pandemic with fake or real. We use the fairly balanced train part of about 6K posts.

The three models for detecting misuse of ethos, pathos and logos described in Subsection 4.1 are applied to the misinformation datasets. Results are reported on how many percentages in each predefined group of either 'false' or 'true' in each misinformation dataset contain a predicted misuse of the appeal in question. For ethos, the results are reported in Table 5, for pathos in Table 6 and for logos in Table 7. In general, we see a tendency for more cases of misuse in the false columns than in the true - regarding all three appeals. However, there are some variations.

Regarding the ethos-model, we see large differences in COVID-19-FAKE and in the ISOT Fake News Dataset, but in the rest of the datasets, the differences between false and true are less distinct. In the PUBHEALTH dataset, we even see more cases of misuse of ethos in the true-labelled group than in the false-labelled group, although the numbers are quite close.

The pathos-model also spots a notable distinction in the ISOT Fake News Dataset with more cases of misuse of pathos among misinformation than in true news. In fact, the pathos model distinguishes the data to a degree that it obtains an accuracy on the true/fake labels on 0.6731. This can be compared to the dummy baseline of a majority vote on 0.5230. However, in contrast, the difference in pathos appeals between false and true in the remaining datasets is quite smaller. The PUBHEALTH and FakeNewsNet datasets have a few more cases of misuse of pathos among the true statements.

Both the pathos- and ethos-model find a notable amount of misuse in true news as well: e.g. over 40% of the titles in the FakeNewsNet are predicted to contain a fallacy of pathos and around 35% in the ISOT Fake News Dataset to contain a fallacy of ethos.

The misuse of logos-model detects much fewer

Fallacies of logos		
	True	False
ISOT Fake News Dataset	0.11	0.62
Liar	**16.52**	14.65
FakeNewsNet	2.00	2.36
COVID19-FAKE	9.94	**11.41**
PUBHEALTH	4.69	**11.83**

Table 7: The percentage of examples predicted by the logos model to contain a misuse of logos in different datasets grouped by the dataset's labels of false or true. The highest percentage is marked in bold. The sizes of the datasets are specified in the list describing each dataset.

cases of misuse in the datasets, in general, than the two other models. It predicts less than 1% of the cases in the ISOT Fake News Dataset and around 2% in FakeNewsNet. However, a few more cases are found in the remaining datasets. In addition, this stands in contrast to the experiments on the Change My View dataset, where the logos model found more cases than the two other models.

4.4 Discussion of Results

The models themselves are expected to be noisy as there are fine-tuned on re-framed resources with expected noise in the labels and without gold-annotations. However, we can see from the hold-out-test on reorganised datasets (Table 3) that the models learn to some degree to separate the re-grouped examples. Applying the models, we see the expected tendency: Misuse of appeal appears more often in misinformation than in reliable news, but with variations.

We notice a notable amount of fallacy of ethos and pathos in the true news. An explanation for this could be that even reliable news e.g. with their titles also aims at capturing the readers' attention: and doing so might appeal to the emotions of the reader or the credibility of the sources. At some point, this might be overdone and become faulty, related to the discussion: that it might at times be a thin line of when an appeal to emotions or credibility becomes faulty.

Another explanation for the different distributions of ethos and pathos across the datasets could be rooted in different topics the news is covering. One speculation is that some topics relate more easily to the use of e.g. pathos than others.

We expect some uncertainties in the results: There is a domain shift between the different misinformation datasets and the training data - despite the training data also containing data from news articles, it also contains data from dialogues and educational examples of fallacies. Concretely, a mismatch in the data distributions could be caused by the representation of negative examples in the training data. To examine the robustness of the prediction on the misinformation datasets, a pathos model on a different seed than previously reported is used for predictions. This causes some relatively large variation in the results in some of the misinformation datasets. For example, a pathos-model on a different seed captures more cases in the ISOT Fake News data set. But it does so both for the fake-labelled and the true-labelled group, respectively 63.15% versus 57.81% and 24.78% versus 22.27% . The models differ a bit in recall and precision. But this variation might also be explained by a large uncertainty in some of the model predictions in some of the examples, i.e. for some examples, the probability scores lie close to the decision border on 0.5, which might explain why the prediction is subject to shift with a similar model just fine-tuned on a different seed. This uncertainty might be caused by the domain shift and the sources of error in the distribution of negative data examples, but these are speculations.

5 Societal Impact

It is said we live in an information age; even WHO Director-General Tedros Adhanom Ghebreyesus has called the Covid19 epidemic an infodemic (García-Saisó et al., 2021). In general, people are exposed to a lot of text that has an inherent agenda of convincing, persuading, or misleading readers, seen in websites (Mathur et al., 2019), political debates (Addawood et al., 2019) and news (Barrón-Cedeno et al., 2019; Martino et al., 2020b). In this paper, we follow the assumption that language use plays a role in how information and arguments are perceived. We already know that, for example, the stances people adopt in conversation can relief their belief in underlying claims (Dungs et al., 2018; Lillie et al., 2019). Our vision is that automatic detection of undesired persuasion can help an online reader navigate more critically in the vast amount of information online, e.g by surfacing or flagging such text. This relates to the discussion that a person skilled in rhetoric posits the competences to spot how and when a text is persuasive (Rapp, 2022).

At the same time, automatic analysis of misuse of rhetorical appeals could help a writer present stronger more convincing arguments. As an example, one qualitative study manually analysed the rhetorical tactics and appeals used in vaccine discussion in the New York Times comments (Gallagher et al., 2020). In the study, they categorised the arguments in pro-vaccines and anti-vaccines and analyzed the rhetorical tactics and appeals in the comments. They found that pro-vaccine comments more often contained ad hominem arguments, and that this was an ineffective strategy.

While this comes with a dual-use risk – technology for highlighting manipulation can e.g. help manipulative authors better hide their intent – we posit that putting computational power behind rhetorical analysis can have a positive impact on the information society.

6 Conclusion

In this paper, we unify the modelling on problematic persuasion by using rhetorical appeals - or rather misuse of these. We focus on the problematic use of rhetorical appeals and re-frame and re-organise existing resources into this taxonomy. However, it is relevant to spot rhetorical appeals in all kinds of persuasion, and we speculate that for future work it might be useful to model pathos and ethos with less the distinction of misuse.

We link misuse of rhetorical appeals to misinformation. We showed that misuse of appeals appeared more often around misinformation than true claims. However, we also saw that in some contexts, reliable news was frequently tagged with misuse of ethos and pathos. This indicates the relevance of assessing the use of persuasion in a broad spectrum of text.

Limitations

This paper discusses limitations regarding both framing and experiments. We summarise the main points. First, regarding the framing: The idea is to propose a unifying taxonomy that can utilise existing work and resources, and hence gives rise to the idea of detecting misuse of rhetorical appeals. Still, the re-grouping based on a variety of labels is noisy, and the definitions themselves have limitations. For example, the misuse of logos is not a fully disjoint category with pathos and ethos, which both in their essence draw attention away from the argumentation. Regarding ethos and pathos, it is not easy to determine when they are unwarranted and hence can be classified as misuse. The distinction in rhetoric between use and misuse, desired and undesired persuasion is fluid and hence open for discussion in further work. Regarding limitations of the experiments: Gold-annotations specific on misuse of rhetorical appeals is lacking to better verify the trained models. In general, the results are preliminary, in the sense that e.g. a manual study could better demonstrate the models' detection of misuse of appeals in misinformation.

Ethics Statement

Our work complies with the ACL Ethics Policy. As discussed in the section on the potential for scientific impact, we believe that battling misinformation could benefit from taking fallacies of pathos, ethos and logos into account. By making transparent the use of such argumentative structures, we contribute to a fair and transparent discourse.

Acknowledgements

This work was supported by the Danish Data Science Academy – which is funded by the Novo Nordisk Foundation (NNF21SA0069429) and VILLUM FONDEN (40516) – and by the Independent Danish Research Fund project Verif-AI.

References

Aseel Addawood, Adam Badawy, Kristina Lerman, and Emilio Ferrara. 2019. Linguistic cues to deception: Identifying political trolls on social media. In *Proceedings of the international AAAI conference on web and social media*, volume 13, pages 15–25.

Hadeer Ahmed, Issa Traore, and Sherif Saad. 2018. Detecting opinion spams and fake news using text classification. *Security and Privacy*, 1(1):e9.

Khalid Al Khatib, Viorel Morari, and Benno Stein. 2020. Style analysis of argumentative texts by mining rhetorical devices. In *Proceedings of the 7th Workshop on Argument Mining*, pages 106–116.

Alberto Barrón-Cedeno, Giovanni Da San Martino, Israa Jaradat, and Preslav Nakov. 2019. Proppy: A system to unmask propaganda in online news. In *Proceedings of the AAAI Conference on Artificial Intelligence*, pages 9847–9848.

Jonathan P Chang and Cristian Danescu-Niculescu-Mizil. 2019. Trouble on the horizon: Forecasting the derailment of online conversations as they develop. *arXiv preprint arXiv:1909.01362*.

Jiaao Chen and Diyi Yang. 2021. Weakly-supervised hierarchical models for predicting persuasive strategies in good-faith textual requests. In *Proceedings of the AAAI Conference on Artificial Intelligence*, pages 12648–12656.

Giovanni Da San Martino, Stefano Cresci, Alberto Barrón-Cedeño, Seunghak Yu, Roberto Di Pietro, and Preslav Nakov. 2021. A survey on computational propaganda detection. In *Proceedings of the Twenty-Ninth International Conference on International Joint Conferences on Artificial Intelligence*, pages 4826–4832.

Leon Derczynski, Kalina Bontcheva, Michal Lukasik, Thierry Declerck, Arno Scharl, Georgi Georgiev, Petya Osenova, Toms Pariente Lobo, Anna Kolliakou, Robert Stewart, et al. 2015. Pheme: Computing veracity—the fourth challenge of big social data. In *Proceedings of the Extended Semantic Web Conference EU Project Networking session (ESCW-PN)*.

Marie Dubremetz and Joakim Nivre. 2018. Rhetorical figure detection: Chiasmus, epanaphora, epiphora. *Frontiers in Digital Humanities*, 5:10.

Sebastian Dungs, Ahmet Aker, Norbert Fuhr, and Kalina Bontcheva. 2018. Can rumour stance alone predict veracity? In *Proceedings of the 27th International Conference on Computational Linguistics*, pages 3360–3370.

John Gallagher, Heidi Y Lawrence, et al. 2020. Rhetorical appeals and tactics in new york times comments about vaccines: Qualitative analysis. *Journal of medical internet research*, 22(12):e19504.

Sebastián García-Saisó, Myrna Marti, Ian Brooks, Walter H Curioso, Diego González, Victoria Malek, Felipe Mejía Medina, Carlene Radix, Daniel Otzoy, Soraya Zacarías, et al. 2021. The covid-19 infodemic.

Andrew M. Guess and Benjamin A. Lyons. 2020. *Misinformation, Disinformation, and Online Propaganda*, SSRC Anxieties of Democracy, page 10–33. Cambridge University Press.

Ivan Habernal and Iryna Gurevych. 2016. What makes a convincing argument? empirical analysis and detecting attributes of convincingness in web argumentation. In *Proceedings of the 2016 conference on empirical methods in natural language processing*, pages 1214–1223.

Ivan Habernal, Raffael Hannemann, Christian Pollak, Christopher Klamm, Patrick Pauli, and Iryna Gurevych. 2017. Argotario: Computational argumentation meets serious games. *arXiv preprint arXiv:1707.06002*.

Ivan Habernal, Henning Wachsmuth, Iryna Gurevych, and Benno Stein. 2018. Before name-calling: Dynamics and triggers of ad hominem fallacies in web argumentation. In *Proceedings of the 2018 Conference of the North American Chapter of the Association for Computational Linguistics: Human Language Technologies, Volume 1 (Long Papers)*, pages 386–396, New Orleans, Louisiana. Association for Computational Linguistics.

Hans Hansen. 2022. "Fallacies", The Stanford Encyclopedia of Philosophy.

Christopher Hidey, Elena Musi, Alyssa Hwang, Smaranda Muresan, and Kathleen McKeown. 2017. Analyzing the semantic types of claims and premises in an online persuasive forum. In *Proceedings of the 4th Workshop on Argument Mining*, pages 11–21.

Rahul R Iyer, Katia P Sycara, and Yuezhang Li. 2017. Detecting type of persuasion: Is there structure in persuasion tactics? In *CMNA@ ICAIL*, pages 54–64.

Zhijing Jin, Abhinav Lalwani, Tejas Vaidhya, Xiaoyu Shen, Yiwen Ding, Zhiheng Lyu, Mrinmaya Sachan, Rada Mihalcea, and Bernhard Schölkopf. 2022. Logical fallacy detection. *arXiv preprint arXiv:2202.13758*.

Erika Kashyap, Athena ans Dyquisto. 2022. 2.5: Logical fallacies - how to spot them and avoid making them. In chapter *2: Writing and the Art of Rhetoric* from *Writing, Reading, and College Success: A First-Year Composition Course for All Learners*, https://human.libretexts.org.

Li Kong, Chuanyi Li, Jidong Ge, Bin Luo, and Vincent Ng. 2020. Identifying exaggerated language. In *Proceedings of the 2020 Conference on Empirical Methods in Natural Language Processing (EMNLP)*, pages 7024–7034.

Neema Kotonya and Francesca Toni. 2020. Explainable automated fact-checking for public health claims. *arXiv preprint arXiv:2010.09926*.

Anders Edelbo Lillie, Emil Refsgaard Middelboe, and Leon Derczynski. 2019. Joint rumour stance and veracity prediction. In *Proceedings of the 22nd Nordic Conference on Computational Linguistics*, pages 208–221.

Yinhan Liu, Myle Ott, Naman Goyal, Jingfei Du, Mandar Joshi, Danqi Chen, Omer Levy, Mike Lewis, Luke Zettlemoyer, and Veselin Stoyanov. 2019. Roberta: A robustly optimized bert pretraining approach. *arXiv preprint arXiv:1907.11692*.

Henry B Mann and Donald R Whitney. 1947. On a test of whether one of two random variables is stochastically larger than the other. *The annals of mathematical statistics*, pages 50–60.

Giovanni Da San Martino, Alberto Barrón-Cedeno, Henning Wachsmuth, Rostislav Petrov, and Preslav Nakov. 2020a. Semeval-2020 task 11: Detection of propaganda techniques in news articles. In *Proceedings of the fourteenth workshop on semantic evaluation*, pages 1377–1414.

Giovanni Da San Martino, Shaden Shaar, Yifan Zhang, Seunghak Yu, Alberto Barrón-Cedeno, and Preslav Nakov. 2020b. Prta: A system to support the analysis of propaganda techniques in the news. In *Proceedings of the 58th Annual Meeting of the Association for Computational Linguistics: System Demonstrations*, pages 287–293.

Giovanni Da San Martino, Seunghak Yu, Alberto Barrón-Cedeno, Rostislav Petrov, and Preslav Nakov. 2019. Fine-grained analysis of propaganda in news article. In *Proceedings of the 2019 conference on empirical methods in natural language processing and the 9th international joint conference on natural language processing (EMNLP-IJCNLP)*, pages 5636–5646.

Arunesh Mathur, Gunes Acar, Michael J Friedman, Elena Lucherini, Jonathan Mayer, Marshini Chetty, and Arvind Narayanan. 2019. Dark patterns at scale: Findings from a crawl of 11k shopping websites. *Proceedings of the ACM on Human-Computer Interaction*, 3(CSCW):1–32.

Parth Patwa, Shivam Sharma, Srinivas Pykl, Vineeth Guptha, Gitanjali Kumari, Md Shad Akhtar, Asif Ekbal, Amitava Das, and Tanmoy Chakraborty. 2021. Fighting an infodemic: Covid-19 fake news dataset. In *International Workshop on Combating On line Hostile Posts in Regional Languages during Emergency Situations*, pages 21–29. Springer.

Reid Pryzant, Kelly Shen, Dan Jurafsky, and Stefan Wagner. 2018. Deconfounded lexicon induction for interpretable social science. In *Proceedings of the 2018 Conference of the North American Chapter of the Association for Computational Linguistics: Human Language Technologies, Volume 1 (Long Papers)*, pages 1615–1625.

Christof Rapp. 2022. "Aristotle's Rhetoric", The Stanford Encyclopedia of Philosophy.

Omar Shaikh, Jiaao Chen, Jon Saad-Falcon, Polo Chau, and Diyi Yang. 2020. Examining the ordering of rhetorical strategies in persuasive requests. In *Findings of the Association for Computational Linguistics: EMNLP 2020*, pages 1299–1306.

Samuel Sanford Shapiro and Martin B Wilk. 1965. An analysis of variance test for normality (complete samples). *Biometrika*, 52(3/4):591–611.

Emily Sheng, Kai-Wei Chang, Premkumar Natarajan, and Nanyun Peng. 2020. " nice try, kiddo": Investigating ad hominems in dialogue responses. *arXiv preprint arXiv:2010.12820*.

Kai Shu, Deepak Mahudeswaran, Suhang Wang, Dongwon Lee, and Huan Liu. 2018. Fakenewsnet: A data repository with news content, social context and dynamic information for studying fake news on social media. *arXiv preprint arXiv:1809.01286*.

Chenhao Tan, Vlad Niculae, Cristian Danescu-Niculescu-Mizil, and Lillian Lee. 2016. Winning arguments: Interaction dynamics and persuasion strategies in good-faith online discussions. In *Proceedings of the 25th international conference on world wide web*, pages 613–624.

Enrica Troiano, Carlo Strapparava, Gözde Özbal, and Serra Sinem Tekiroğlu. 2018. A computational exploration of exaggeration. In *Proceedings of the 2018 Conference on Empirical Methods in Natural Language Processing*, pages 3296–3304, Brussels, Belgium. Association for Computational Linguistics.

Bibek Upadhayay and Vahid Behzadan. 2020. Sentimental liar: Extended corpus and deep learning models for fake claim classification. In *2020 IEEE International Conference on Intelligence and Security Informatics (ISI)*, pages 1–6. IEEE.

Vorakit Vorakitphan, Elena Cabrio, and Serena Villata. 2021. " don't discuss": Investigating semantic and argumentative features for supervised propagandist message detection and classification. In *Recent Advances in Natural Language Processing (RANLP 2021)*.

Henning Wachsmuth, Nona Naderi, Yufang Hou, Yonatan Bilu, Vinodkumar Prabhakaran, Tim Alberdingk Thijm, Graeme Hirst, and Benno Stein. 2017. Computational argumentation quality assessment in natural language. In *Proceedings of the 15th Conference of the European Chapter of the Association for Computational Linguistics: Volume 1, Long Papers*, pages 176–187.

William Yang Wang. 2017. " liar, liar pants on fire": A new benchmark dataset for fake news detection. *arXiv preprint arXiv:1705.00648*.

Xuewei Wang, Weiyan Shi, Richard Kim, Yoojung Oh, Sijia Yang, Jingwen Zhang, and Zhou Yu. 2019. Persuasion for good: Towards a personalized persuasive dialogue system for social good. *arXiv preprint arXiv:1906.06725*.

Thomas Wolf, Lysandre Debut, Victor Sanh, Julien Chaumond, Clement Delangue, Anthony Moi, Pierric Cistac, Tim Rault, Rémi Louf, Morgan Funtowicz, Joe Davison, Sam Shleifer, Patrick von Platen, Clara Ma, Yacine Jernite, Julien Plu, Canwen Xu, Teven Le Scao, Sylvain Gugger, Mariama Drame, Quentin Lhoest, and Alexander M. Rush. 2020. Transformers: State-of-the-art natural language processing. In *Proceedings of the 2020 Conference on Empirical Methods in Natural Language Processing: System Demonstrations*, pages 38–45, Online. Association for Computational Linguistics.

Diyi Yang, Jiaao Chen, Zichao Yang, Dan Jurafsky, and Eduard Hovy. 2019. Let's make your request more persuasive: Modeling persuasive strategies via semi-supervised neural nets on crowdfunding platforms. In *Proceedings of the 2019 Conference of the North American Chapter of the Association for Computational Linguistics: Human Language Technologies, Volume 1 (Long and Short Papers)*, pages 3620–3630.

Joel Young, Craig Martell, Pranav Anand, Pedro Ortiz, Henry Tucker Gilbert IV, et al. 2011. A microtext corpus for persuasion detection in dialog. In *Workshops at the Twenty-Fifth AAAI Conference on Artificial Intelligence*.

Justine Zhang, Jonathan Chang, Cristian Danescu-Niculescu-Mizil, Lucas Dixon, Yiqing Hua, Dario Taraborelli, and Nithum Thain. 2018. Conversations gone awry: Detecting early signs of conversational failure. In *Proceedings of the 56th Annual Meeting of the Association for Computational Linguistics (Volume 1: Long Papers)*, pages 1350–1361.

Breaking through Inequality of Information Acquisition among Social Classes: A Modest Effort on Measuring "Fun"

Chenghao Xiao[★] **Baicheng Sun**[♠] **Jindi Wang**[★] **Mingyue Liu**[★] **Jiayi Feng**[♦]
[★] Department of Computer Science, Durham University
[♠] School of Social Science, Tsinghua University
[♦] Beijing Jiaotong University
chenghao.xiao@durham.ac.uk

Abstract

With the identification of the inequality encoded in information acquisition among social classes, we propose to leverage a powerful concept that has never been studied as a linguistic construct, "*fun*", to deconstruct the inequality. Inspired by theories in sociology, we draw connection between social class and information cocoon, through the lens of fun, and hypothesize the measurement of "how fun one's dominating social cocoon is" to be an indicator of the social class of an individual. Following this, we propose an NLP framework to combat the issue by measuring how fun one's information cocoon is, and empower individuals to emancipate from their trapped cocoons. We position our work to be a domain-agnostic framework that can be deployed in a lot of downstream cases, and is one that aims to deconstruct, as opposed to reinforcing, the traditional social structure of beneficiaries (Jin et al., 2021).

1 Introduction

Does a researcher necessarily want to be surrounded by research-related content at any time of a day?

Would under-privileged members in society be aware if they are consuming entertainment content all the time?

This paper starts with posing the above questions on two extreme cases, which indicate a misalignment of a (content, concept) pair that members of different social classes are stuck in, during the process of information acquisition.

While under-privileged social class is identified to be trapped in entertainment content (Xu et al., 2020), which in turn reinforces their social class; higher social class is prone to content that causes anxiety, especially during the periods of a day that members in this class are in urgent need of escaping from their social roles and mental burdens (Wang, 1999; Oh and Pham, 2022), while trapped in highly

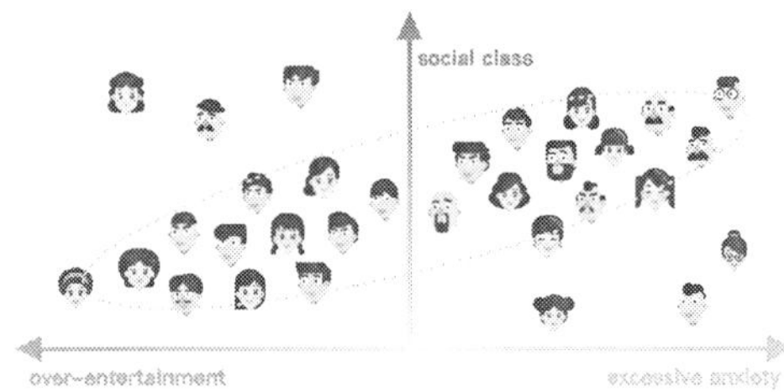

Figure 1: Theoretical Relation between Fun and Social Class Status Depicted in Social Science (Oh and Pham, 2022; Xu et al., 2020; Wang, 1999)

anxious content due to the preference they have shown to the algorithms, attributable to their social roles.

We argue that there exists inequality of information acquisition among social classes, through which a powerful concept we leverage might be able to help interpret: "fun" – a construct that has never been studied by the NLP community, or never studied as a *linguistic* construct at all, and one that we try to distinguish from "humor", with the latter having been heavily investigated in NLP research.

In this work, we draw upon deconstructing the inequality among social classes, in combat with the issue that advancements of NLP techniques are in fact sometimes reinforcing traditional social structure of beneficiaries (Jin et al., 2021) in society - an evaluation heuristic proposed recently by Jin et al. (2021) on aligning NLP with social good.

Moreover, we aim not to only address the inequality posed with social groups that are under-privileged socio-economically. We in turn believe that every social class is under-privileged in different ways, with an example discussed above regarding some social groups that are typically deemed privileged oftentimes do not actually have the privilege to liberate from their social roles (Oh and Pham, 2022). We propose, by understanding a key concept in interpreting social cocoons - ***how fun a social cocoon is*** - we could facilitate and empower

Proceedings of the Second Workshop on NLP for Positive Impact (NLP4PI), pages 101 - 112
December 7, 2022

members of different social classes to emancipate from their cocoons based on their needs.

The paper is structured as follows: We first turn to theories in sociology (Section 2) to draw connection between social class and information cocoon, through the lens of "fun" - an under-studied concept, and introduce our NLP framework as an external regularization to confront the issues involved. Section 3 introduces the first part of our framework by training an intermediate language model to understand the concept of fun at a population level. Following that, Section 4 shows the strong utility of the intermediate model in terms of its transferability in downstream tasks, corroborated respectively in zero-shot and cross-domain user-aware fine-tuning setups. Moreover, in Section 4 we not only propose some real-life cases to deploy our framework, but also conduct user studies to align their perception with our intermediate model. We consider our work to be a framework that mitigates the Matthew effect of inequality in information acquisition in traditional social structure (Jin et al., 2021) and put "NLP for social good" into practice.

2 "Fun" Framework

In this section, we sketch the thinking heuristics of our framework by basing it on the grounds of sociology theories, drawing connection between social class and information cocoon, through the lens of "fun".

We theoretically reason that, the measurement of "how fun a social cocoon is", has been a strong indicator of the social class, or the under-privileged position, that an individual is stuck in, and thus is a metric that shows strong utility toward helping individuals of different social classes to combat the ubiquitous inequality in information acquisition.

Lastly, we introduce the "Fun" framework, enabling members of a specific social group to escape to the other side of this metric with an NLP model.

2.1 Concepts

Information cocoon Do we feel at ease after sporadically spending a whole day online? A positive answer may not be easily drawn, for the existence of algorithms and that big data is increasingly turning itself from servicing to controlling - a process in which stands information cocoon as a major consequence.

People are gradually losing their subjectivity and degrading to complete recipients of information. The perniciousness comes right from this unconscious process of being besieged by a closed information system, making individuals more vulnerable and less adaptable to unfamiliar topics or conflicting views (Sunstein, 2007). Thus, it is likely to incur extremism and political polarization in terms of mass-level behavior (Barberá et al., 2015), which is often provocative and incivility-prone (Gervais, 2015).

Under micro-narratives, information cocoon pertains to one's everyday experience and actual social network. Sociological studies have shown that, even before the invention of the Internet, humans had already been unconsciously restricted by materiality and social relationships in the real world (Fei et al., 1992). People are largely influenced by their primary groups, i.e., kinships, close friends, and neighbors (Cooley, 1955). In extreme circumstances, primary groups set the boundary that one can reach to in their lifetime. Considering the empirical evidence that the stronger the tie connecting two individuals, the more similar they will be (Granovetter, 1973), primary groups have in fact formed a pre-Internet information cocoon, where individuals develop their mindsets and habits in similar ways. However, instead of strong ties, weak ties are more useful in expanding the flow of information (Granovetter, 1973, 2018, e.g., job-seeking, political mobility) . This further indicates the significance of diversity and expansion of relationships when transferring and acquiring information.

Thus, it is only fair to say that the Internet constructs an unprecedentedly personalized yet information-intense space through algorithms, making information cocoon a non-negligible problem. In the past, it was relatively safe for people to be immersed in similar ideas, as they were not likely to build connections beyond their primary groups and accordingly have less risks confronting opposition and information overload. By contrast, the combination of the Internet and recommender systems nowadays forges a dilemma: users are, on the one hand, empowered to jump out of their primary groups, yet on the other hand, **thrown into a digital primary group**, in which information is passively sent, not actively sought.

Retrieved to the earliest definition by Sunstein (2006), the negative effect of information cocoon is mainly the illusionary friendliness and comfort brought by like-minded opinions and homogeneous messages (Sunstein, 2006). We must concede that digital information acquisition nowadays fails to keep its technological promises (Harambam et al., 2018), for accurately identifying users' needs and offering customized information. In other words, a familiar environment, created by the "sorting" mechanism, cannot guarantee the bottom line of being harmless to the Internet users (Gervais, 2015).

Fun: A taken-for-granted yet understudied concept To counterpoise the negative feelings caused by information cocoon and empower individuals to retrieve their subjectivity, we turn to "fun", a taken-for-granted yet understudied concept, for help, especially during a time when we have seen the cognitive reduction of fun led by COVID-19 (Oh and Pham, 2022) and the deterioration of online environment[1]. Fun pertains to almost every aspect of our life, yet never gets serious attention. It soothes everyday tension and seasons bland normalcy. However, even among the very little research that mentioned fun as an independent concept, namely psychological investigation of fun (Oh and Pham, 2022) and physical education studies (MacPhail et al., 2008; Bengoechea et al., 2004; Scanlan and Simons, 1992), fun is related to distraction, reduced to the by-product of other social facts, or used interchangeably with happiness, well-being, enjoyment, sense of achievement, deviance, and humor (Fincham, 2016). The sophisticated crossover amidst these positive affective states makes it hard to theorize fun as an independent phenomenon (Fincham, 2016; Blythe et al., 2004).

Besides, though we all crave for fun, it is not seen as an essential factor as water is to humans. We tend not to exchange things deemed as more secularly important for fun. For instance, few parents would allow their kids to stay at home and have unbridled fun simply because fun is marginalized by regimentations in schools. Besides, fun is too contingent to handle, for having too much fun is sometimes frivolous and frowned upon (Fincham, 2016; Goffman, 1961). Additionally, to theorize fun sounds contradictory to its quotidian nature. Consequently, there is no specific and distinctive branch in sociology that sets its goal to understand fun theoretically until the advent of *The Sociology of Fun* by Ben Fincham in 2016 (Fincham, 2016).

It is worth mentioning that fun is a broader concept compared to humor, in spite of their similarities (Ruch, 2001; Fincham, 2016). Fun is highly contextual and diverse, while humor is simply more about making people laugh (Martin and Ford, 2018). Thus, jokes are important sources for studies aiming to detect humor (Yang et al., 2021; Weller and Seppi, 2019). By contrast, laughter is not necessary to make people feel fun (Fincham, 2016). From a sociological perspective, humor is more hierarchical, while fun requires equality to take place (Podilchak, 1991). The semantic archaeology of fun has shown its intertwining history with **social class, judgement and transgression** (Blythe and Hassenzahl, 2018), revealing its rebellious nature and tendency toward equality. This not only distinguishes itself from other emotion-related concepts, but also add up to the legitimacy of using "fun" as a weapon to combat the inequality caused by information cocoons. Fun is not that simple but digs deeper into human's mental need for participation and freedom. It is common for both a person who has just finished a book and a couple playing badminton to feel fun (Oh and Pham, 2022).

In a word, what really matters is not trying to universalize people's experience of fun, but to uncover the common mechanism of cultivating fun. In order not to be confused by the countless realizations of fun in real life, psychological studies become inspiring, for they try to offer the fundamental pillars of the mechanism to produce fun, among which stands out the definition by Oh and Pham (2022): **an experience of liberating engagement**.

2.2 Tackling Inequality of Information Acquisition through the Lens of "Fun"

To this point, it might have already been clear that we are to leverage the concept of fun as a conceptual weapon to provide individuals with freedom to move along their information cocoons, which to different extent, indicates the social classes, or under-privileged positions that they are in.

By its very nature of geographic space, one can easily associate information cocoon with semantic space from the perspective of natural language processing. However, it is identified that existing endeavors that utilize language models, especially the state-of-the-art contextualized ones such as BERT (Devlin et al., 2019) and their variants like Sentence Transformers (Reimers and Gurevych, 2019) to study information cocoon, mostly concern political polarization (Jiang et al., 2021), news and items recommendation (Shi et al., 2021; Song et al.,

[1]https://www.microsoft.com/en-us/online-safety/digital-civility

2022), and the spread of Covid-19 misinformation (Röchert et al., 2021), while few studied information cocoons in cultural consumption (Xu et al., 2020). Xu et al. (2020) leveraged word embedding models to analyze information cocoon in digital media, with the purpose of studying information cocoon as a cultural space and its relationship with social class, indicating that the disadvantages of vulnerable groups in the process of acquiring knowledge may further widen social inequality.

In the quest for information equality among social classes, we propose that formulating the implicit "geographical space" expressed in the information cocoon as a continuous representation of "fun" is not only capable of addressing the **anxiety issues posed with higher social class** but is also a panacea for helping **under-privileged social class escape from their "knowledge-absent" cocoons**, by adjusting their scale of "fun" to attain/filter knowledgeable recommendations, instead of being stuck in entertainment content (Xu et al., 2020).

We introduce a computational framework for measuring fun in language. This framework can be understood in a two-step setup: a) intermediate pre-training at a population level. b) Individual-level user-aware fine-tuning. We first train an intermediate model to understand fun at a population level, then use it to serve as a better initialized point for downstream user-aware fine-tuning. As we will show, the intermediate model is already good at making zero-shot inference. Further, it makes adapting to each individual's unique perception of fun much more accurate and stabler, in a few-shot fine-tuning setting.

3 Intermediate Task: Can Language Models Understand What Fun is?

Under the current pre-training - fine-tuning paradigm in solving NLP tasks, we expect further an intermediate task (Poth et al., 2021) to bridge a vanilla pre-trained language model to a user with a few labeled data points that indicate their unique perception toward fun. To this end, an intermediate language model that has been fine-tuned to understand what fun generally is at a **population level** is needed. Such of an intermediate model allows faster and stabler adaptation to specific users in downstream applications as we will show in Section 4.

3.1 Dataset Collection

We aim to look for a one-size-fits-all data source that is targeted toward readers in seek of fun, enabling their reactions to be used as a proxy indicator of this concept; while covering as diverse genres as possible, serving as an inclusive cornucopia of human language to learn a generic model for domain-agnostic perception of fun, instead of focusing on a specific domain/topic. Extracting data from one source eliminates cross-dataset annotation inconsistency.

Example Data Source In this work, we realize these above-mentioned heuristics by presenting an effective data source. We highlight that this is an example data source that can demonstrate the utility of our designed mechanism and as proof of concept, yet not an optimal one. Cracked.com is based on the Cracked magazine, which collects interesting content covering topics from movies, TV, video games, music, sports, history, science, sex, tech, news, celebrities, to "weird world". Albeit it claims to be "the America's only humor site", we find that the linguistic connotation of the spirit behind the platform is extremely close to our defined concept of *fun*, as the site covers substantial informative content from a wide range of fields, *instead of the well-perceived definition of humor*, which mostly concerns punchlines and jokes (Mihalcea and Strapparava, 2005; Yang et al., 2015).

3.2 Automatic Scoring Mechanism

We make the intuitive assumption that readers of the data source are a specific group of people seeking for fun content. Thus, simple features like # of comments are intuitively highly correlated with the measurement of **engagement**. Further, it is in a **liberating** fashion due to the nature of the platform studied. Therefore, readers' reactions approximate how fun the content is - how much **liberating engagement** is shown at a population level.

We scraped all the posts from the website, from Jan, 2005 to March, 2022, yielding over 15k articles on diverse topics. In the same vein as Yang et al. (2021) who used naturally available user reactions on twitter posts as a proxy to indicate humor, we novelly define an automatic scoring mechanism to annotate how *fun* the content is as follows:

$$Fun = \tanh\left(\frac{n}{\alpha \cdot \frac{1}{|I_y|}\sum_{i \in I_y} n_i}\right), \qquad (1)$$

where n denotes the number of comments in

an observed article; I_y denotes the set of articles in the specific year that the article falls in, where $I_y \in I$, with I representing the full set of articles from 2005 to 2022. We perform a mean normalization over each year by dividing the number of comments by the sum of all n_i in a given year I_y, since the posts show significantly different average number of comments every year. Generally, newer articles get less comments to date. Intuitively, our defined metric serves as a proxy indicator of the engagement of a post compared to other posts in the same year. We further introduce a coefficient α to denote "non-tolerance toward not fun", which together with $tanh()$, could be used to twist the distribution of fun scores (Figure 2). Mathematically, a higher α (higher non-tolerance toward not fun) makes the score distribution right-skewed, as less posts could receive high fun scores. Notably, α can potentially be parameterized in later user-aware fine-tuning of downstream tasks (giving each user an interpretable non-tolerance score), which is out of scope of this paper.

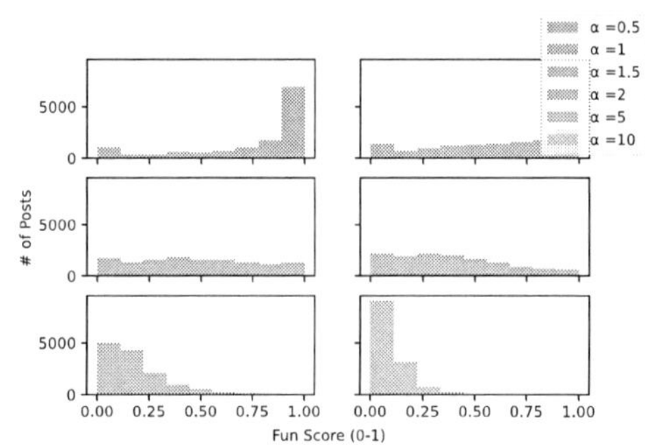

Figure 2: Twisting fun score distribution with α

3.3 In-domain Learning of Fun

To validate the proposed scoring mechanism and the utility of *fun* as a universal metric to understand content in a continuous space, we first conduct an experiment with three language models: BERT-base (Devlin et al., 2019), RoBERTa-base (Liu et al., 2019), and LongFormer-base (Beltagy et al., 2020). 10% of the data is used as the hold-out test set. The models are fine-tuned with over 50 epochs (Zhang et al., 2020) for stabler performance, with a learning rate of $3e-5$, instead of the commonly adopted 3 epochs.

The result is shown in Table 1. We observe that, while early epochs are extremely fluctuating - given the regression nature of the task and the nuanced nature of the concept studied, the models can typically reach to an optima where increased epochs bring diminished fluctuations. In the later epochs of training, RoBERTa can stably converge to a performance close to .50 R-squared and an F1 score over 75% on the test set. To attain an F1 score, we transform the 0-1 scale in the regression task into a binary classification using a decision threshold (0.5 by default). Given how "fun" is less of a universal phenomena compared to "humor", our experiment demonstrates a surprising result - achieving a performance even better than what Weller and Seppi (2019) reported on a similar task using Reddit joke posts and their up-votes, which again in turn proves the utility of our scoring mechanism to be learned against by the LMs.

Model	F1	R-Squared
$\text{BERT}_{\text{base}}$		
+ max seq. 128	0.748	.437
+ max seq. 512	0.751	.460
$\text{RoBERTa}_{\text{base}}$		
+ max seq. 128	0.753	.448
+ max seq. 512	0.758	**.499**
$\text{LongFormer}_{\text{base}}$		
+ max seq. 2048	**0.760**	.497

Table 1: In-domain learning

Length matters for fun A linguistic property of fun we try to validate is the importance of informative content conveyed, which we hypothesize to be supported by the length of the text, distinguishing the concept of ***fun*** from existing studies on ***humor***, with the latter mostly characterized as one-liners (Mihalcea and Strapparava, 2005; Yang et al., 2015) that typically have a maximum sequence length of 10-30 words. We run both BERT and RoBERTa with a maximum sequence length of 128 and 512 tokens. This part of the experiment shows that length does matter in order for textual content to be perceived as "fun", corroborated by the R-squared performance boost by a margin of respetively 5.3% and 11.4% on BERT and RoBERTa brought by taking in a longer text. This is further validated by the on-par performance of Longformer, which can be thought of as a variant of RoBERTa that enables computational complexity to scale linearly with sequence length. For Longformer, we consider a maximum of 2048 tokens. Notably, taking in texts that are too long brings less pronounced advantages, which we hypothesize to be due to:

(1) the limited attention of readers in seek of "fun" distribute to in-depth reading, and (2) there exists a certain length that suffices for readers to engage - 512 tokens suffice in our case.

4 Helping Individual Users to Break through Inequality in Information Acquisition

When deploying in a user-specific setting, we expect the in-domain training in section 3.3 to serve as an intermediate task (Poth et al., 2021). It is thus of interest to study how well the previous intermediate pre-training on the in-domain data source could transfer to users, respectively under (1) zero-shot inference and (2) further fine-tuning settings.

4.1 Zero-shot Inference

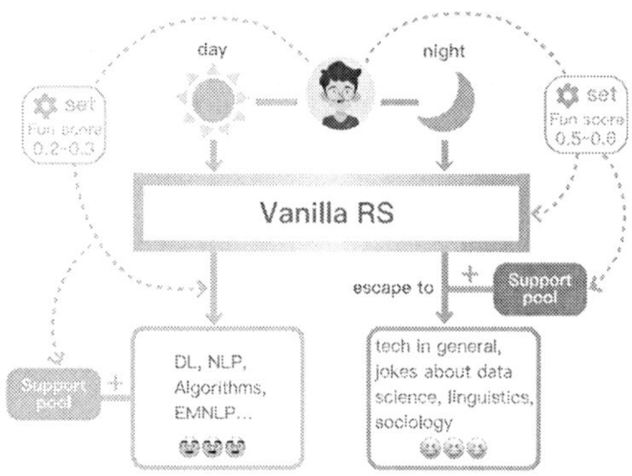

Figure 3: User case: "A day of an NLP researcher", empowered by our 'Fun' framework. While trapped in the cocoons of NLP-related content, one is given the option to turn up the 'Fun' range to receive recommendations from other domains, generated from the vanilla content pool and borrowed from a supporting pool.

Complementing the example that "an NLP researcher might not be keen to read about NLP before they go to bed" (Figure 3), we present an interesting case study.

We consider a binary setting, by taking in two target data sources, Medium[2] and Not Always Right[3]. We first collect 50 posts from Medium, using an account that has been "fine-tuned" by an NLP researcher by using the account for a year. The recommended posts are all about NLP. We then collect the same number of posts from Not Always Right, a website dedicated to high-quality fun stories.

[2] https://medium.com/

[3] https://notalwaysright.com/

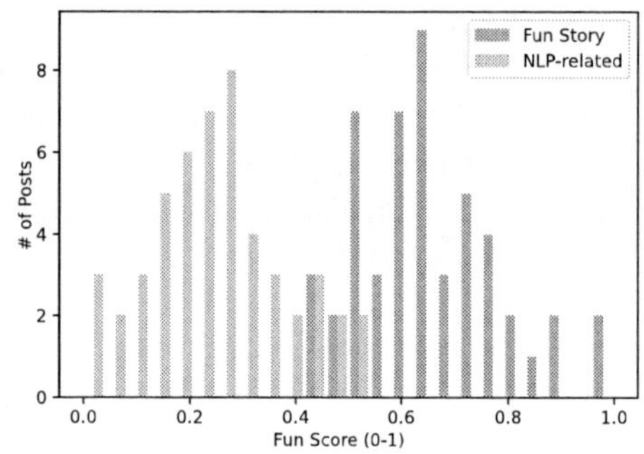

Figure 4: Significant distribution discrepancy in zero-shot cross-domain inference, using RoBERTa checkpoint trained in Section 3.3

We then leverage the model checkpoints trained to understand *fun* in section 3.3 to infer on them. Figure 4 shows the predictions yielded on these two target sources, indicating a significant distributional discrepancy ($p < .001$). This further proves that in an industrial deployed setting, it is possible to help a specific group of people escape to content of other genres and domains, by sampling posts of user-determined fun score from a supporting set. We further propose a possible way to implement this framework in Appendix A, through a plug-in user interface we design.

4.2 Cross-Domain User-aware Fine-tuning

In this section, we study with three human annotators, with the goal of adapting a language model to their unique perception of fun. We ask them to annotate 300 posts each from a generic Medium dataset covering a wide range of genres and topics. With the annotated dataset we aim to find the best strategy to adapt to their exact perception, under this few-shot learning setting (210 posts excluded 30% data as test set). We find that the in-domain training in Section 3.3 serves as a powerful intermediate task that stabilizes the following user-aware further fine-tuning.

4.2.1 User Annotation

Dataset To perform experiments on cross-domain fine-tuning, we leverage a 190k Medium dataset[4]. As opposed to directly collecting Medium posts on an account "fine-tuned" by a user in Section 4.1, this generic Medium dataset comprises of high-quality articles of diverse topics and genres.

[4] https://www.kaggle.com/datasets/fabiochiusano/medium-articles

Fun Spectrum	Description and Scoring Guidance
Most fun.	0.8 < fun score ≤ 1.0: Make you forget surroundings and have inner motives to practice what you see from it.
	0.6 < fun score ≤ 0.8: Feel intrigued and devote a great amount of attention to repeat watching or reading it.
	0.4 < fun score ≤ 0.6: Start to have revealing happiness (e.g., laughter) and is likely to share or imitate the content.
	0.2 < fun score ≤ 0.4: Learn something new or inspiring but require self-supervision to keep concentrated.
	0 < fun score ≤ 0.2: Not very interested and reluctant to pay attention to if needed.
Not fun at all.	0: Feel detested or indifferent, not willing to spend time on.

Table 2: Annotation Instruction for Cross-domain Fine-tuning

We ask 3 annotators to annotate their fun perception on 300 articles each, based on the annotation instruction in the next sub-section. To validate the **non-universality** of fun perception of different individuals, we secretly put a same pool of 100 articles as the last 100 posts they annotate. Other 200 articles for each annotator are randomly sampled from the 190k articles.

Annotation Guidelines Given the cruel fact that creating an unequivocal definition of "fun" is almost impossible, for its discursive and subjective nature, we design a reference instruction (Table 2) for target groups to annotate fun score.

From game designing to physical education and leisure studies, fun has gained increasing attention and revealed some enlightening commonalities: positive emotion and sense of engagement. When exposed to something fun, some may laugh, while others are likely to share. Whatever their actual actions are, these fun moments are engaging and getting people focused. This illustrates the essential characteristics of fun: a broader ideation encompassing not only punchlines, but educational and inspiring content that may have further influences on individuals, distinguishing it from humor and funny.

Thus, knowing "how fun manifests in real life" is what really matters. Correspondingly, based on previous studies, qualitative descriptions are used in the instruction sheet as presentation of fun. We expect respondents to annotate provided content, referring to the sectional instruction (Table 2), and give out their fun perception on a specific post. Scoring could be more granular than the instructed range (e.g., 0.66) to accord with the diffused feature of fun in real life.

Non-universality of Fun Perception We further present the inter-annotator agreement in Table 3, computed on the secret pool of 100 articles shared

Inter-Annotator Agreement	
	Pearson's r
User 1 and 2	0.536
User 1 and 3	0.457
User 2 and 3	**0.652**
	Krippendorff's alpha
All users	0.405

Table 3: Inter-Annotator Agreement

by the three annotators. It is shown that users have unique perception toward fun. For instance, user 1 shares lower Pearson's correlation with the other two annotators. On top of that, the Krippendorff's alpha among the three annotators is not extremely high, again indicating the non-universality of fun perception. However, even for the most sophisticated individual, our method yields better results (Table 4 as described in the 4.2.2) than the baseline methods, showing the performance boost brought by the intermediate pre-training and as well proving the utility of our automatic scoring mechanism to learn against. However, the sophisticated nature of some users' understanding toward fun in turn necessitates more training data from them.

4.2.2 User-aware Fine-tuning Performance

In this section, we leverage the checkpoints in in-domain training to learn further in a user-aware setting.

Table 4 shows the results of different fine-tuning settings, and the superiority of our methods. For simplicity, we only present experiments with RoBERTa (Liu et al., 2019), since it provides the best result (Section 3.3) and is computationally cheaper than Longformer (Beltagy et al., 2020) if the latter takes in a maximum of 2048 tokens.

For the baseline method, we directly take a RoBERTa pre-trained checkpoint, and fine-tune it on the user data. For our methods, we define

Model	Avg. R-squared	Max. R-squared	Min. R-squared	Var.
		User 1		
RoBERTa + ft.	.016	.256	-.624	.019
RoBERTa$_{\text{fun-shallow}}$ (ours) + ft.	.053	.248	-.356	.013
RoBERTa$_{\text{fun-deep}}$ (ours) + ft.	**.093**	**.265**	**-.138**	**.010**
		User 2		
RoBERTa + ft.	.274	.544	-.706	.063
RoBERTa$_{\text{fun-shallow}}$ (ours) + ft.	.412	.626	-.081	.025
RoBERTa$_{\text{fun-deep}}$ (ours) + ft.	**.450**	**.660**	**-.003**	**.021**
		User 3		
RoBERTa + ft.	.085	.519	-1.551	.225
RoBERTa$_{\text{fun-shallow}}$ (ours) + ft.	.208	.519	-2.816	.191
RoBERTa$_{\text{fun-deep}}$ (ours) + ft.	**.407**	**.520**	**-.105**	**.011**

Table 4: Cross-domain fine-tuning performance

a RoBERTa$_{\text{fun-shallow}}$ and a RoBERTa$_{\text{fun-deep}}$. For RoBERTa$_{\text{fun-shallow}}$, we first fine-tune a RoBERTa checkpoint on our in-domain Cracked.com dataset for 3 epochs, then further fine-tune it on the user-annotated data. While for RoBERTa$_{\text{fun-deep}}$, we do the same for 50 epochs, then further fine-tune. The utility of pre-training long enough on our in-domain dataset is proved as shown in Table 4.

We hypothesize that, this amount of user data is not sufficient for a pre-trained language model to understand **what is fun** from scratch. A language model is not able to accurately capture which words and what combinations of them make an article fun through a few hundred of examples of diverse genres. Even though some articles show similar topics and fun scores, it is extremely hard for a RoBERTa to find the salient areas to put attention to through a few examples, if it is allowed to look at the first 512 tokens of an article.

By contrast, our methods mitigate this inefficiency through providing an extra resource of 15k articles to indicate what fun is. Albeit being "cross-domain", words, expressions and language in general that express the concept of ***fun*** could be quite transferable. As shown in the result, training long enough (50 epochs) first on our in-domain dataset enables the models to attain deeper understanding of fun, for later stabler transferring.

For each run, we hold out 30% data (90 articles) as test set for each user. For each setting and user, we repeat each further fine-tuning 3 times with 50 epochs, with different random seeds and data splits, yielding 150 unique stages for each combination, to get a closer look at the training progress (The results in Table 4 are based on these epoch-level computations). We again use R-squared as the evaluation metric which measures how well a regression model explains the observed data.

The baseline method is extremely fluctuating throughout the 50 epochs for each run, occasionally "hitting" a not-bad result on the test set and could drop dramatically in the next epoch, resulting in extremely high variance. By contrast, our methods typically "wander" around at a stabler range of R-squared on the test set throughout the training, with significantly lower intra-epoch variance. In real-life deployment, this stability is extremely important in efficiently adapting to user preferences without drastically fluctuating performances. Notably, the baseline method typically reach and wander around an average training loss of 0.004 in the last few epochs, while our methods lead it to an average training loss of 0.0005, meaning that the pre-training on the in-domain dataset has already put the training to a better optima. Thus, it is evident that giving more user-specific data, the further fine-tuning could be more robust with our in-domain intermediate training.

Also, we give out a description of attaining user-specific data and user-aware fine-tuning in a possible real-life deployment at the end of Appendix A, on top of the vanilla zero-shot intermediate models described in the last section.

5 Conclusion

In this work, we identify a misalignment of a (content, concept) pair existing among social classes - one's information cocoon and the corresponding degree of fun. This passively decided characteristic might reinforce, as opposed to help deconstruct the traditional social structure of beneficiaries, and therefore is originally not a manifestation of the advancement of AI algorithms contributing to social good.

In combat with this prevalent issue, we propose an NLP framework, which is composed of 1) an intermediate language model that could understand/predict the degree of liberating engagement (the degree of fun) of text at a population level. 2) further user-aware fine-tuning method to adapt the intermediate model to each individual's unique perception of fun. Moreover, we propose some possible real-life cases to deploy our framework in a platform-agnostic setup as an external regularization over recommender systems, such as a web-based plug-in that could filter content based on user-defined fun range, without having to explicitly interact with or adjust the algorithms behind the recommender system of a platform.

Limitations

We consider our work to be a framework that mitigates the inequality in the traditional social structure of beneficiaries (Jin et al., 2021), and establish it to be a work promoting "NLP for social good". Nonetheless, we envision more detailed implementations to be studied that regulate its usage in practice. As Jin et al. (2021) put it, stage-4 NLP applications should be most careful about their ethical concerns. Our work can also be posed with extreme use cases. For instance, what if our framework in turn helps under-privileged people to immerse themselves in entertainment content? - if they are given the complete freedom to do so. Therefore, we call for more regulated usage of our proposed framework. However, we position our framework to be one that provides humans with dignity, freedom, and fairness (Zeng et al., 2019), under an era where discriminating AI algorithms are prevalent.

Moreover, we do notice some biases existing in the in-domain *fun* models, brought by domain-specific content in our scraped dataset (Cracked.com). For instance, inferring with these models on a one-word input, "LGBT", gives a score of around 0.87-0.95, showing the extensive interest that American people hold for politically correct-related discussions on controversial issues. With "sequence length is a domain" (Varis and Bojar, 2021) considered, these biases are significant. Thus, we highlight that what we present here is a novel framework, rather than an optimized solution. The dataset we leverage is a demonstration of a feasible way of empowering this framework, rather than an optimal one. We envision more endeavors to be made for more generic annotated data for this concept. Although in this paper we provide what can be formulated as a "distant-supervised approach" (*i.e.* an automatic scoring scheme) for the sake of studying this concept, annotation can still potentially provide less bias toward learning on the concept of *fun* that is loyal and inclusive (Joshi et al., 2020) to the perception of a wider audience from all socio-demographic groups.

Acknowledgements

We thank Haoting Dai from Princeton University, Hanshen Li from Alibaba-Ant Group, Zhongtian Sun, Tom Winterbottom and James Burton from Durham University for their helpful discussion and valuable feedback. We thank three anonymous reviewers for their valuable comments.

References

Pablo Barberá, John T Jost, Jonathan Nagler, Joshua A Tucker, and Richard Bonneau. 2015. Tweeting from left to right: Is online political communication more than an echo chamber? *Psychological science*, 26(10):1531–1542.

Iz Beltagy, Matthew E Peters, and Arman Cohan. 2020. Longformer: The long-document transformer. *arXiv preprint arXiv:2004.05150*.

Enrique García Bengoechea, William B Strean, and DJ Williams. 2004. Understanding and promoting fun in youth sport: coaches' perspectives. *Physical Education & Sport Pedagogy*, 9(2):197–214.

Mark Blythe and Marc Hassenzahl. 2018. The semantics of fun: Differentiating enjoyable experiences. In *Funology 2*, pages 375–387. Springer.

Mark A Blythe, Kees Overbeeke, Andrew F Monk, and Peter C Wright. 2004. *Funology: from usability to enjoyment*. Springer.

Charles H Cooley. 1955. Primary groups. *Small groups*, pages 15–17.

Jacob Devlin, Ming-Wei Chang, Kenton Lee, and Kristina Toutanova. 2019. BERT: Pre-training of deep bidirectional transformers for language understanding. In *Proceedings of the 2019 Conference of the North American Chapter of the Association for Computational Linguistics: Human Language Technologies, Volume 1 (Long and Short Papers)*, pages

4171–4186, Minneapolis, Minnesota. Association for Computational Linguistics.

Hsiao-tung Fei, Xiaotong Fei, Gary G Hamilton, and Wang Zheng. 1992. *From the soil: The foundations of Chinese society*. Univ of California Press.

Ben Fincham. 2016. *The sociology of fun*. Springer.

Bryan T Gervais. 2015. Incivility online: Affective and behavioral reactions to uncivil political posts in a web-based experiment. *Journal of Information Technology & Politics*, 12(2):167–185.

Erving Goffman. 1961. *Encounters: Two studies in the sociology of interaction*. Ravenio Books.

Mark Granovetter. 2018. *Getting a job: A study of contacts and careers*. University of Chicago press.

Mark S Granovetter. 1973. The strength of weak ties. *American journal of sociology*, 78(6):1360–1380.

Jaron Harambam, Natali Helberger, and Joris van Hoboken. 2018. Democratizing algorithmic news recommenders: how to materialize voice in a technologically saturated media ecosystem. *Philosophical Transactions of the Royal Society A: Mathematical, Physical and Engineering Sciences*, 376(2133):20180088.

Julie Jiang, Xiang Ren, Emilio Ferrara, et al. 2021. Social media polarization and echo chambers in the context of covid-19: Case study. *JMIRx med*, 2(3):e29570.

Zhijing Jin, Geeticka Chauhan, Brian Tse, Mrinmaya Sachan, and Rada Mihalcea. 2021. How good is NLP? a sober look at NLP tasks through the lens of social impact. In *Findings of the Association for Computational Linguistics: ACL-IJCNLP 2021*, pages 3099–3113, Online. Association for Computational Linguistics.

Pratik Joshi, Sebastin Santy, Amar Budhiraja, Kalika Bali, and Monojit Choudhury. 2020. The state and fate of linguistic diversity and inclusion in the NLP world. In *Proceedings of the 58th Annual Meeting of the Association for Computational Linguistics*, pages 6282–6293, Online. Association for Computational Linguistics.

Yinhan Liu, Myle Ott, Naman Goyal, Jingfei Du, Mandar Joshi, Danqi Chen, Omer Levy, Mike Lewis, Luke Zettlemoyer, and Veselin Stoyanov. 2019. Roberta: A robustly optimized bert pretraining approach. *arXiv preprint arXiv:1907.11692*.

A MacPhail, T Gorely, D Kirk, and G Kinchin. 2008. Exploring the meaning of fun in physical education through sport education. *Research Quarterly for Exercise and Sport*, 79(13):344–356.

Rod A Martin and Thomas Ford. 2018. *The psychology of humor: An integrative approach*. Academic press.

Rada Mihalcea and Carlo Strapparava. 2005. Making computers laugh: Investigations in automatic humor recognition. In *Proceedings of Human Language Technology Conference and Conference on Empirical Methods in Natural Language Processing*, pages 531–538, Vancouver, British Columbia, Canada. Association for Computational Linguistics.

Travis Tae Oh and Michel Tuan Pham. 2022. A liberating-engagement theory of consumer fun. *Journal of Consumer Research*, 49(1):46–73.

Walter Podilchak. 1991. Distinctions of fun, enjoyment and leisure. *Leisure studies*, 10(2):133–148.

Clifton Poth, Jonas Pfeiffer, Andreas Rücklé, and Iryna Gurevych. 2021. What to pre-train on? Efficient intermediate task selection. In *Proceedings of the 2021 Conference on Empirical Methods in Natural Language Processing*, pages 10585–10605, Online and Punta Cana, Dominican Republic. Association for Computational Linguistics.

Nils Reimers and Iryna Gurevych. 2019. Sentence-BERT: Sentence embeddings using Siamese BERT-networks. In *Proceedings of the 2019 Conference on Empirical Methods in Natural Language Processing and the 9th International Joint Conference on Natural Language Processing (EMNLP-IJCNLP)*, pages 3982–3992, Hong Kong, China. Association for Computational Linguistics.

Daniel Röchert, Gautam Kishore Shahi, German Neubaum, Björn Ross, and Stefan Stieglitz. 2021. The networked context of covid-19 misinformation: Informational homogeneity on youtube at the beginning of the pandemic. *Online Social Networks and Media*, 26:100164.

Willibald Ruch. 2001. The perception of humor. In *Emotions, qualia, and consciousness*, pages 410–425. World Scientific.

Tara K Scanlan and Jeffery P Simons. 1992. The construct of sport enjoyment. *Motivation in sport and exercise*, 199215.

Shaoyun Shi, Weizhi Ma, Zhen Wang, Min Zhang, Kun Fang, Jingfang Xu, Yiqun Liu, and Shaoping Ma. 2021. Wg4rec: Modeling textual content with word graph for news recommendation. In *Proceedings of the 30th ACM International Conference on Information & Knowledge Management*, pages 1651–1660.

Yu Song, Shuai Sun, Jianxun Lian, Hong Huang, Yu Li, Hai Jin, and Xing Xie. 2022. Show me the whole world: Towards entire item space exploration for interactive personalized recommendations. In *Proceedings of the Fifteenth ACM International Conference on Web Search and Data Mining*, pages 947–956.

Cass R Sunstein. 2006. *Infotopia: How many minds produce knowledge*. Oxford University Press.

Cass R. Sunstein. 2007. *Republic.com 2.0*. Princeton University Press.

Dusan Varis and Ondřej Bojar. 2021. Sequence length is a domain: Length-based overfitting in transformer models. In *Proceedings of the 2021 Conference on Empirical Methods in Natural Language Processing*, pages 8246–8257, Online and Punta Cana, Dominican Republic. Association for Computational Linguistics.

Ning Wang. 1999. Rethinking authenticity in tourism experience. *Annals of tourism research*, 26(2):349–370.

Orion Weller and Kevin Seppi. 2019. Humor detection: A transformer gets the last laugh. In *Proceedings of the 2019 Conference on Empirical Methods in Natural Language Processing and the 9th International Joint Conference on Natural Language Processing (EMNLP-IJCNLP)*, pages 3621–3625, Hong Kong, China. Association for Computational Linguistics.

Huimin Xu, Zhicong Chen, Ruiqi Li, and Cheng-Jun Wang. 2020. The geometry of information cocoon: Analyzing the cultural space with word embedding models. *arXiv preprint arXiv:2007.10083*.

Diyi Yang, Alon Lavie, Chris Dyer, and Eduard Hovy. 2015. Humor recognition and humor anchor extraction. In *Proceedings of the 2015 Conference on Empirical Methods in Natural Language Processing*, pages 2367–2376, Lisbon, Portugal. Association for Computational Linguistics.

Zixiaofan Yang, Shayan Hooshmand, and Julia Hirschberg. 2021. CHoRaL: Collecting humor reaction labels from millions of social media users. In *Proceedings of the 2021 Conference on Empirical Methods in Natural Language Processing*, pages 4429–4435, Online and Punta Cana, Dominican Republic. Association for Computational Linguistics.

Yi Zeng, Enmeng Lu, and Cunqing Huangfu. 2019. Linking artificial intelligence principles. In *SafeAI@ AAAI*.

Tianyi Zhang, Felix Wu, Arzoo Katiyar, Kilian Q Weinberger, and Yoav Artzi. 2020. Revisiting few-sample bert fine-tuning. In *International Conference on Learning Representations*.

A Industrial Deployment: A Proposal

We also demo a possible case to deploy our framework in real-life scenarios. We design a Chrome extension (Figure 5) that can filter existing recommended posts based on user-defined fun range. A Chrome extension allows us to retrieve information from the platform pages, as well as injecting HTML tags to them. We propose it to be a simple way to deploy our model as an extension backend to quantitatively score the text data that is captured, and is generalizable across different platforms without having to explicitly interact with their recommender systems.

Figure 6 shows the working process of the Chrome extension we develop for Quora.com. After users install the ***fun*** extension on Chrome and start it, the extension would start to continuously capture posts under the current page and check whether the current posts have been scored according to their IDs in the database. If a post ID has not existed, the text content of that post will be input to our model for scoring, and the score with the corresponding post ID will be stored in the Web SQL Database and display to the bottom of that post on the page.

Figure 5 shows our framework deployed as an plug-in that can be applied to Quora.com. As an example, when the user selects fun scores between 0.6 and 0.8 and clicks the **Search** button, the current page will be filtered based on the selected range and display the first 50 posts within that range.

Moreover, it is possible for users to modify the fun scores inferred by the vanilla zero-shot model. These modified fun scores would be used as ground-true user-specific fun perception to fine-tune a user-aware model, making it possible to understand user's unique perception for better "escape".

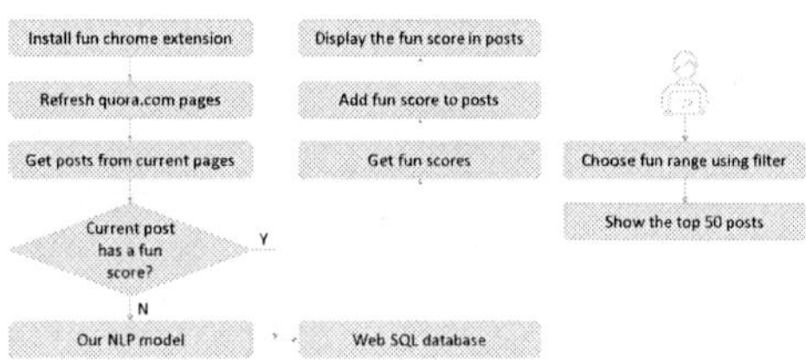

Figure 6: Fun chrome extension workflow

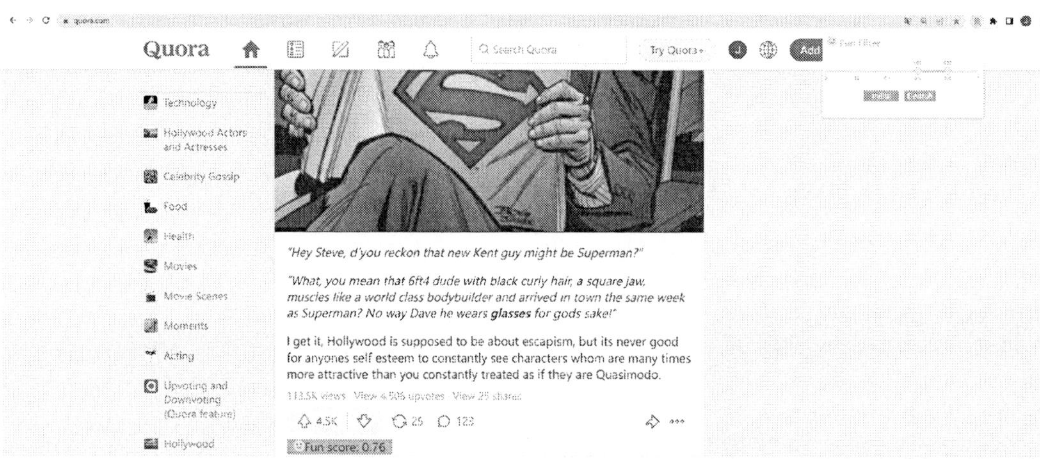

Figure 5: Deployment of fun filter in quora.com

Using NLP to Support English Teaching in Rural Schools

Luis Chiruzzo † luischir@fing.edu.uy
Laura Musto † laura.musto@fic.edu.uy
Santiago Góngora † sgongora@fing.edu.uy

Brian Carpenter ‡ bcarpent@iup.edu
Juan Pablo Filevich † juan.filevich@fing.edu.uy
Aiala Rosá † aialar@fing.edu.uy

† Universidad de la República, Montevideo, Uruguay
‡ Indiana University of Pennsylvania, Indiana, PA, USA

Abstract

We present a web application for creating games and exercises for teaching English as a foreign language with the help of NLP tools. The application contains different kinds of games such as crosswords, word searches, a memory game, and a multiplayer game based on the classic battleship pen and paper game. This application was built with the aim of supporting teachers in rural schools that are teaching English lessons, so they can easily create interactive and engaging activities for their students. We present the context and history of the project, the current state of the web application, and some ideas on how we will expand it in the future.

1 Introduction

This paper presents an ongoing project on developing a web application that uses NLP tools for building exercises for teaching English as a foreign language (EFL). The aim of the platform, called CINACINA[1], is to assist teachers in the creation of activities based on some topic or text they are working in the classroom.

As we are a Spanish speaking country, the universalization of English teaching throughout all primary schools is one of the objectives of the national public education administration in our country. Some of the obstacles for achieving this goal in rural schools are the lack of qualified specialized teachers and the poor Internet connectivity in rural areas, which renders solutions based on videoconferencing impractical for these purposes. Consequently, a program was designed for these schools where classroom teachers, who may not have a good command of English, learn in conjunction with children, with remote support of English teachers. In this context, the application we are building is meant to be an aid to rural school teachers, providing exercises that could be used out of the box, tools for creating new ones, and an interactive platform with exercises and games that helps to motivate the kids learning the language.

The rest of this document is structured as follows: section 2 presents related work and important concepts to understand the context of the project; section 3 introduces the history of the project, how and why we began creating it; section 4 describes the application built so far and its main features; section 5 presents the interactions we have had with the community and how it impacted the project; and finally section 6 shows some conclusions and future work.

2 Background

The interest in educational applications has been present in the NLP area since its beginnings (Litman, 2016), being the automatic correction of students' assignments one of the most explored topics. This interest has been increasing in the Computational Linguistics community, leading to the creation in 2017 of the Association for Computational Linguistics Special Interest Group for building EDUcational applications (SIGEDU)[2], which organizes an annual workshop specialized in this area, BEA: Workshop on Innovative Use of NLP for Building Educational Applications. The BEA workshop had its 17th edition[3] this year, associated with the NAACL annual conference.

Within the area of Educational NLP, particular work has been done on the application of NLP to language teaching, a sub-area that has received the name Intelligent CALL or ICALL (CALL: Computer Assisted Language Learning) (Volodina et al., 2014). There is an annual workshop associated with this area (NLP4CALL), which will have its 11th edition in 2022[4]. Our work, framed in this sub-

[1] http://cinacina.fic.edu.uy/

[2] https://sig-edu.org/

[3] https://sig-edu.org/bea/2022

[4] https://spraakbanken.gu.se/en/research/themes/icall/nlp4call-workshop-series/nlp4call2022

Proceedings of the Second Workshop on NLP for Positive Impact (NLP4PI), pages 113 - 121
December 7, 2022 ©2022 Association for Computational Linguistics

area of NLP for language teaching, focuses on the development of a platform of educational activities to support the teaching of English as a second language. An example of such an application for creating English exercises is Language Muse (Burstein et al., 2013), which allows to select a text from a catalog, or use own texts, and generate from them exercises that evaluate morphological, syntactic or semantic concepts. A similar application but for multiple languages, REVITA, is presented in Katinskaia et al. (2018). In Agirrezabal et al. (2019), the development of activities for vocabulary learning from transformations of children's stories using NLP tools is described. A work that has an approach closely related to ours is Fenogenova and Kuzmenko (2016), which builds English exercises of different types, but mainly focused on learning collocations in English for more advanced students.

2.1 English teaching in our country

For several decades English and other foreign languages have been taught in secondary education. In 2006, the National State Education Administraion (ANEP) set the goal of teaching English to primary school children nationwide[5]. However, the main problem was the lack of qualified teachers.

In 2007, the country adopted the One Laptop per Child (OLPC) program[6], which is developed under the umbrella of Ceibal[7]. In 2012, a new program was developed to teach English via videoconferencing with qualified teachers teaching remotely and students using laptops and Internet-based resources under the guidance of the classroom teacher (Brovetto, 2015).

However, many rural schools could not introduce the teaching of English due to access or connectivity issues in rural areas. Rural schools represent almost half of the schools in the country[8]. Of 1040 rural schools, 60% do not have a stable Internet connection or are accessible for teachers of English to come to teach at the school[9].

Consequently, a new program was designed in 2018 (Romano, 2019), in which the classroom teacher is regarded as a professional trained to facilitate learning. Classroom teachers may not have a good command of English, but the program is designed to allow teachers and students to learn in conjunction. Technology plays a crucial role in this program.

Most importantly, this English teaching program can be adapted to the distinct multigrade and multiserviced pedagogy necessary for teaching in rural schools. Presently, over half of rural schools use it. Also, it is worth pointing out that it is also used in 42 special needs schools. As a result, it is expected that the country will soon be able to reach the goal of teaching English to all primary school children.

2.2 University extension

The concept of university extension, especially in Latin American universities, refers to an activity in which university and non-university actors collaborate to solve problems that affect a community, particularly with a focus on often neglected populations. During an extension project, it is expected that all the actors contribute with their respective knowledge, so that all can share to and learn from the rest in order to create new knowledge (Arocena, 2010). This has points in common with other concepts such as university outreach and engagement, although it is not exactly the same. Notice that the focus on often neglected populations implies that this kind of projects will generally be related to social good, and try to make a positive impact.

In our university in particular, extension is considered one of the three main functions of the university, together with teaching and research. The current trend is to try to create spaces that articulate the three functions, where researchers (often teachers), students, and members of the community interact in order to come up with a solution to a problem. These spaces are called *integral training spaces*. In this project, our target community are the teachers and students at rural schools. Throughout the years tens of undergraduate students have collaborated in this project, interacting with the community in very enriching ways, which complements their training as professionals.

3 History of the project

In 2016 we worked on a prototype system for automatically building crosswords from news text. The system would first extract suitable definitions from the news and then create the crosswords puzzle (Es-

[5]https://www.anep.edu.uy/sites/default/files/images/Archivos/publicaciones-direcciones/Politicas-linguisticas/documentos/comisionpoliticaslinguisticaseducacion%20publica.pdf

[6]https://laptop.org/

[7]https://www.ceibal.edu.uy/es/institucional

[8]https://www.anep.edu.uy/15-d/m-s-17000-ni-y-ni-os-asisten-escuelas-rurales-en-todo-el-pa-s

[9]https://www.anep.edu.uy/15-d-noticias-pol-ticas-ling-sticas/programa-anep-ingl-s-sin-l-mites-se-implementar-en-paraguay

teche et al., 2017). The national public education authorities saw that work and considered it had the potential to be applied in teaching. They were starting a project for trying to universalize English teaching at elementary schools, with special focus on bringing English classes to rural schools that were far away from the urban areas and had connectivity issues. Because of this, one constraint was that the tools we built had to use minimal bandwidth and should ideally run on the OLPC laptops.

Beginning in 2018, we started creating a series of prototypes of different tools and games that could be used in the context of teaching English to schoolchildren. Our aim was to bring NLP tools into the classroom that would help teachers create exercises and activities for their classes. The first attempts included: a prototype for a game application that created crosswords, word search puzzles, and a version of the battleship game adapted to practicing English oral skills (Percovich et al., 2019); and a prototype for a tool that built classic English practice exercises such as multiple choice, fill in the blanks, and joining definitions (González et al., 2021). These prototypes were tested in three rural schools during 2018, obtaining very positive feedback that helped to keep us going. However, we noticed two important things: the prototypes were still too raw to be used in a classroom without assistance, and more importantly the level of English needed to solve the exercises in the system was too high, we needed to simplify them.

In 2020, more researchers with background in linguistics and teaching English as a foreign language joined the team. They started analyzing the tool and the content we had created, trying to adapt it and also to build new content for a more beginner level based on texts provided by the Education Administration. This helped improve the contents of the prototypes, and further visits to rural schools showed that this was very useful. However, we must note that using only manually curated content was not one of the objectives we had in mind when we started working on this: we want to use NLP tools to facilitate the teachers' jobs. So at the same time we continued to explore ways to improve the tools, and create new types of games and exercises. For example some teams worked on generating QA exercises for reading comprehension automatically generated from texts (Morón et al., 2021; Berger et al., 2022), while others focused on automatic correction of texts and automatic simplification.

So far, the prototypes we had been building were all separate tools, which complicated their use in the classroom. In 2021 we were granted funding from our country's National Research and Innovation Agency (Agencia Nacional de Investigación e Innovación - ANII[10]), and we could hire a web developer that would create a unified platform to integrate the different prototypes. The aim was to create a web tool that could integrate the different games and exercises we had built. The platform would let the users quickly fix the errors that the NLP tools introduced, and also would serve as an environment to develop and deploy new tools and exercises.

Furthermore, since 2019 we have created several instances of *extension workshops*, which are small courses in which undergraduate students can get credits for participating in extension related projects. In our case, the students participated in the design and prototyping of new games or exercises, and also had to participate in a visit to a rural school where they could show the work and interact with the teachers and children. These activities are very enriching for the undergraduate students, because they can get out in the field to know other contexts and ways of working that they are not used to, which helps in their training.

4 Description of the application

We developed a web application that can be accessed by teachers and students. So far there are three types of users: students (with limited access), teachers (with more permissions like creating and managing games and exercises), and superusers that could also do administrative tasks.

Our intention is to make the application open source under the CC BY-NC-SA 4.0 license. Since the application is rapidly evolving as we regularly add new features and content, we are waiting to reach a stable version before releasing the code. For now the application is available to use and we are open for any suggestions. In the following sections we will describe only the most relevant content that is currently included.

4.1 Words and Definitions

The platform has a database of words and definitions. These <word, definition> pairs can be added manually on demand, but they can also be extracted using automatic processes, so it is important that

[10]https://www.anii.org.uy/

in the platform all words and definitions can be edited. Each word belongs to one or more categories, which can also be defined and assigned on demand. This base of words and definitions are used throughout the platform for generating the different games, e.g they are used as clues for crosswords, or as words to search in the word search puzzles.

In the first games application prototype (Percovich et al., 2019) we included a simple automatic definition extraction process. That process was rule-based and was very simple, so the number of <word, definition> it could extract from arbitrary text was very limited. The extractor was run over all of Simple English Wikipedia[11] content, obtaining an initial set of definitions, but these had two main problems: Sometimes the definition was too complex (even coming from Simple English Wikipedia); and often the definition obtained was not usable in the context of a crossword intended for children (e.g. obtaining a definition for the surname 'Brown' instead of the color 'brown'). This set of pairs were used as the first word base for the platform, and they were later on manually curated and simplified.

During the development of the first prototype, the Education Administration provided us with a list of English words that should be learned by kids at the beginners level, together with their simple categories such as 'animals', 'colors' and 'family'. This initial list was expanded using word embeddings (Mikolov et al., 2013) based technique: trying to find the closest words to the starting set that still belonged to the original category. Then we manually inspected the resulting words to see if they belonged to the correct category.

4.2 Games and exercises

The current version of the platform includes five games and exercises that can be built automatically. They all use the words and definitions base, and some can also take an input text, such as a story or article a teacher wants to work in class, to generate the exercise.

The crossword game (Fig. 1) can build crosswords using the definitions base for the clues. Teachers or students can create crosswords randomly or by selecting a category of words. As mentioned above, the initial process for extracting definitions was not comprehensive enough, so

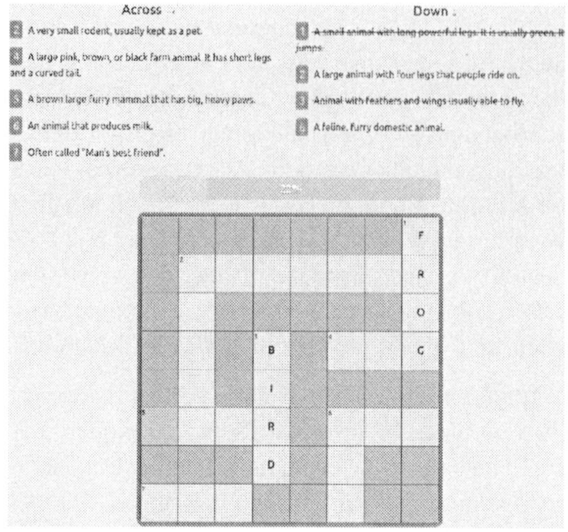

Figure 1: Crosswords game, words are selected from the 'animals' category.

the feature for creating crosswords by extracting clues from free text is currently disabled. We are currently working on the integration of a new definition extractor based both on rules and on a definition generation model that uses the T5 architecture (Raffel et al., 2020), which showed very promising results in our initial tests.

However, a teacher has another functionality for creating a static crossword from the word categories. They can then manually edit its definitions in case there are any errors, and save it. This creates a URL that can be accessed by their students, so all the classroom can solve the same crossword.

The platform can also build word search puzzles with words selected from the categories (Fig. 2). Originally the easy mode showed the textual words as clues, and the hard mode only displayed the

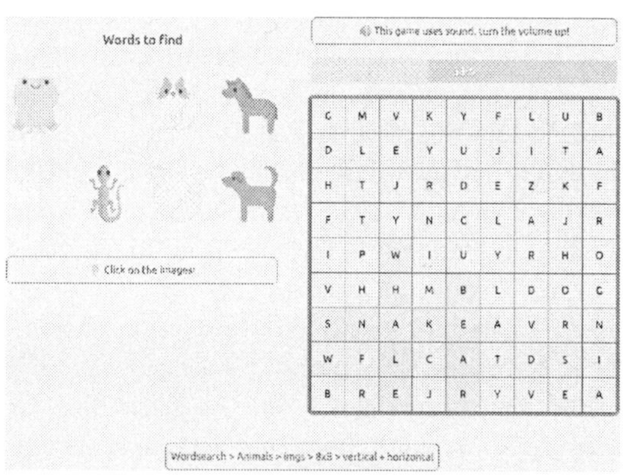

Figure 2: Word search game using the pictures mode, words are selected from the 'animals' category.

[11]https://simple.wikipedia.org/

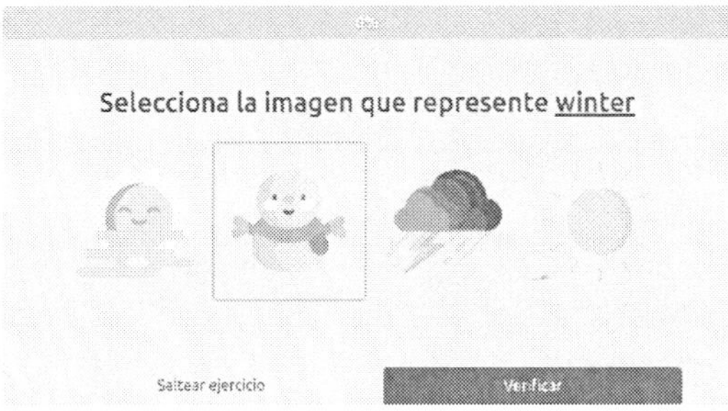

Figure 3: Language practice game in easy mode, the student must select the picture that represents a word.

category. But after some visits to schools, many school teachers requested we added also a game mode that shows pictures of the words to search.

The language practice game (Fig. 3) is a more classical type of exercise, where the students must select the picture that corresponds to a word (easy mode) or the correspondence between definitions and pictures (hard mode).

The story game is a game (Fig. 4) in which the students must first read a short story, and then they are shown a shuffled list of sentences extracted from the story that they must put in the correct order. The process obtains lemmas and named entities from the text, and calculates a score for each term based on how frequent it is and if it is included in the title, as children stories often include prominent entities in the title. Then it selects sentences that are the most salient based on the inclusion of the main terms of the text. It is also possible to create a story game based on a free text input by the teacher.

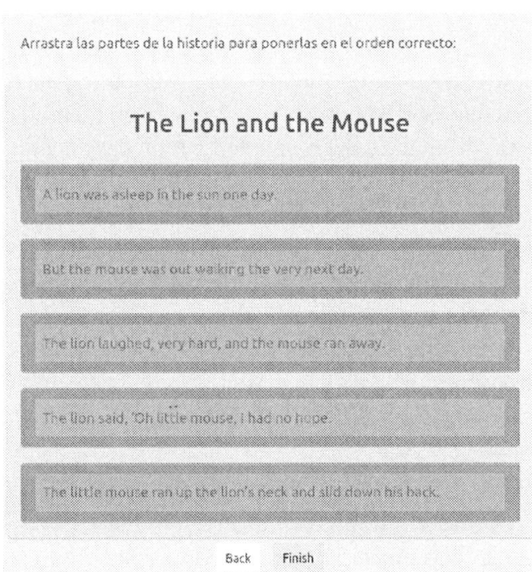

Figure 4: Story game with sentences shuffled, the student must put them in the correct order.

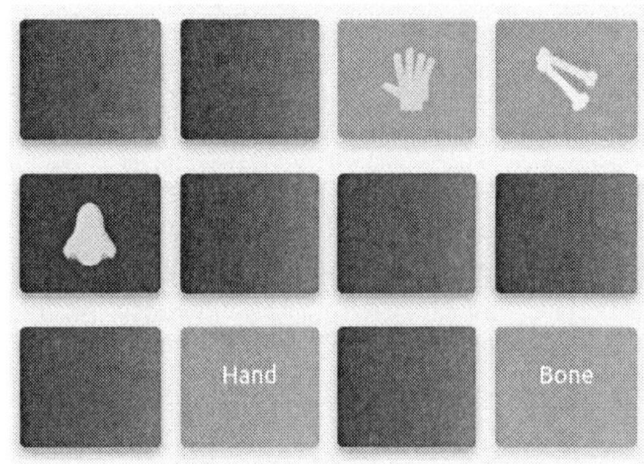

Figure 5: Memory game in easy mode using words selected from the 'body' category.

The memory game (Fig. 5) is a simple game of cards where students must try to match a word to an image (easy mode), or a definition (hard mode). Although this game does not use any advanced NLP tools, it was greatly sought after by the teachers at rural schools.

The Sea Animals (Fig. 6) game is the only multiplayer competitive game in the platform. Probably because of this, it is the game that is enjoyed the most by the kids in the classroom. The game is based on the classical battleship pencil and paper game, adapted to practice oral English skills in the classroom: instead of encoding the coordinates as letters and numbers, the map displays subjects and predicates. One player must read aloud the subject and predicate they want to target, and the other player must understand it in order to correctly play the game, which encourages practicing oral skills. The subjects and predicates are extracted automatically from the parse trees of a collection

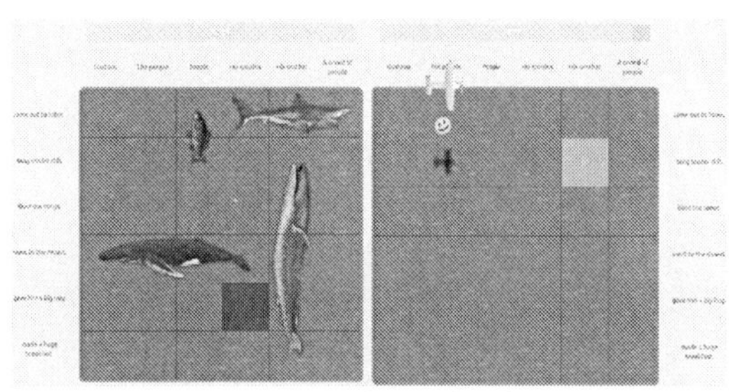

Figure 6: Sea Animals, inspired in the battleship game, the players must read aloud sentences (subject + predicate) to indicate coordinates in the grid.

of texts, and they are categorized so that they form grammatical sentences for the same map.

4.3 Expected use case

We will describe an expected interaction between users for this application. In this example the idea is that the teacher wants to use a custom crossword in their class, based on a text they are already working with.

1. A teacher logs in the application and uses the "Create crossword" functionality.
2. They paste a text they want to work with during class.
3. The application extracts as many clues as it can from the text, and creates a crossword using those clues and completing with preloaded clues.
4. The teacher checks the resulting crossword, fixing any errors that could be introduced by the process.
5. When the crossword is ready, the app returns a URL that the teacher can distribute among their students, so that everyone can work on the same crossword.

5 Contact with the community

As mentioned in section 2.2, an extension project involves many actors, and it must include an interaction, a dialogue between the university and the target community. It is expected that all actors are impacted in some way by the project. Our main ways of interacting with the community in this project have been the visits to rural schools and the training sessions with rural school teachers.

5.1 Visits and impact

Between 2018 and 2022, we have made 18 visits to a total of 14 rural schools from all over the country, each school had between 5 and 30 students. Only one of the visits had to be done remotely using videoconferencing tools, due to the sanitary situation in 2020 caused by the COVID-19 pandemic. Around 50 undergraduate students of the Engineering and Communications careers have participated in the project since its beginning.

There are 1600 rural school teachers, and 800 work in schools where they are the only teacher in charge. 100% of rural schools follow a multigrade pedagogy. This is not only because some have very few students but also because multigrade pedagogy gives room to a particular circulation of knowledge (Santos, 2016). This model does influence the learning of English in the way students interact with one another. Our classroom observations support this, where children of different ages (from 4 to 12 years old) interacted and helped each other to play the games on the platform. We noticed a great level of engagement with the tool, especially with the Sea Animals game but also with the rest of the games.

Survey 2019	Survey 2022
Memory game	Improve difficulty management
Improve difficulty management	Games for speech and listening
Improve texts and definitions	More multiplayer games
More games	Graphical and usability improvements
Offline mode	Accessibility improvements
	Social media features
	Offline mode
	Keep open source and free
	Unique users for teachers

Table 1: Main highlights and requests for improvements to the tool according to a teachers' survey in 2019 and in 2022.

We have offered two training sessions for teachers: one via videoconferencing (30 participants) and one face-to-face (40 participants) in a city far away from the capital city and within easy access to teachers in the region. In these sessions we provided a quick introduction to NLP and the project, and the teachers had the chance to experiment with the platform and provide feedback. Table 1 shows the main requests that the teachers had for the tool. The left side shows the main improvement ideas mentioned in 2019 (an earlier version of the tool) and the right side shows the results for the latest survey in 2022.

We note that some of the topics brought up in 2019 were solved, such as creating the memory game, and others remain. For example, we took steps towards managing the language difficulty in the games. Most of the content has been curated and preloaded since many rural school teachers are not proficient in their knowledge of the English language. However, more language-proficient teachers will be able to edit the tool's results in order to fix issues or to tailor them to their needs. We strive to ensure the project will adapt to the language proficiency of most teachers. Another frequent request is that we add more games to the tool, but upon analyzing the suggested game ideas and other requests, we noticed that the suggestions made this year generally ask for more complex features. This could mean the teachers are starting to understand the potential of the tool and want to push the limits of what it can do.

One interesting point that was mentioned in both surveys is the possibility of "offline mode". As mentioned before, the connectivity in rural areas is not the best. In 2019 the prototype worked in a completely offline mode, and this was highlighted in the surveys as a nice feature. However, as the platform grew, we needed to move much of the heavy processing to a server, while still trying to use as little bandwidth as possible. Thus, in 2022 there is a new request to bring back some offline functionalities, for example solving crosswords or other games offline once they are already created.

In all our school visits and teacher workshops, there was agreement on the need for a web platform for games and activities adapted to the EFL national curricula. Further insights into the nature of NLP, and access to manipulate them to suit teachers' needs, are exceptionally relevant for English language teachers. NLP developments have posed the language teaching field unprecedented challenges.

Further proof of the web application's positive impact is that we have been contacted by material writers and authorities from one of the other two existing English teaching programs, Department of Second Languages (Departamento de Segundas Lenguas[12]), which is a face-to-face program that works with 10% of schools and heavily relies on the use of technology as well. Much of their interest lies in the fact that using this application can free them, to a certain extent, from relying on paid websites. The department has informally agreed to help the project collect data to develop a tool for the automatic correction of texts. This is hugely relevant to the project and a healthy signal of the interest it sparks.

For undergraduate students, the project provided them with an invaluable and unique opportunity to gain insights into education in rural areas.

During the course of the project, our team became more interdisciplinary. The work of engineers, linguists, and specialists in education and in the field of communication studies opened new horizons to the project. Some of them have already been identified and submitted for funding, namely, the need to cater for accessibility and improve the graphic design and user interface.

5.2 Issues

In the first prototypes, we found out during the visits that the English level of the exercises was too high. On top of this, the initial hands on experiences with teachers showed that the performance of the NLP tools, such as the definition extractor, was not good enough or comprehensive enough for the types of texts a school teacher might use. We want to highlight this potential mismatch between what we tried to build and what the teachers and students wanted: We started the project with the idea of bringing NLP tools that would help teachers and students to engage with activities in the classroom, but we found out that in the first iterations they needed something simpler, with less automatic processing and more preloaded content. Because of this, special care had to be taken to curate the content of the platform, so that better suited exercises could be created from scratch in the classroom.

The platform and the activities can be adapted to work with students with different levels of command of the language. We are currently working on expanding the content to cater for this. Now that the platform has a wider content base, and many of the more basic features are covered, the teachers are starting to ask for more complex functionalities, so we can start to develop and introduce new tools that require more use of NLP.

6 Conclusions

We presented an ongoing research and extension project that uses NLP tools for aiding English teaching in rural schools. We described several activities that are integrated in the web application: a tool for building crosswords, one for building word searches, a language practice game, a memory game, and a story game. There is also a multiplayer game inspired in the well-known battleship game, dubbed Sea Animals, which lets students practice

[12]https://www.dgeip.edu.uy/departamentos/lenguas/

oral skills. More activities are still in development or in a prototype phase and are not included in the platform yet.

As future work we plan to incorporate more NLP in the existing activities, as well as create more activities that can exploit this processing better. For example more games that use plain text (such as stories or articles) as an input, because those are typically the most useful for the teachers working on a particular topic.

We will plan our school visits to receive more structured teacher feedback and a more precise analysis of student interaction with the games. In addition, we have outlined a plan to do a three-visit observation of teachers who are proficient speakers of English to see how they manage the tools. We are also planning to provide access as teachers to a group of teachers willing to work closely with the project in order to understand their needs and how they work with the system.

Current state of the art in many NLP tasks allows us to increase the complexity of some games as a way of improving its mechanics, e.g. the story game could try to solve the chronological graph of events and use this order instead of the narrative one. The BookNLP library[13] has interesting features that can enrich the story game in different ways. We also have a generator of QA exercises for reading comprehension which is being integrated in the tool, allowed by recent advances in methods for question generation.

We also look for developing more multiplayer games, since those are the most engaging for the students. This vision was also shared by the teachers that answered our survey. In this line, the story game could be extended as a multiplayer game using mechanics inspired in the *Timeline* board game, where two or more players compete putting events in the correct order to win.

Lastly, we also plan to include a model for automatic correction of texts. This would help teachers to reduce the amount of work required to detect common mistakes of Spanish-speaking English students.

Acknowledgements

We would like to thank all of those that made this work possible: School teachers and students for testing and reporting bugs and suggestions for the platform; *Ceibal* and *Políticas Lingüísticas-ANEP* for the support, guidance and logistics. Part of this work was financially supported by *Fondo Sectorial de Educación: Inclusión Digital* (ANII - Fundación Ceibal - IDRC, 2020).

[13]https://github.com/booknlp/booknlp

References

Manex Agirrezabal, Begoña Altuna, Lara Gil Vallejo, Josu Goikoetxea, and Itziar Gonzalez Dios. 2019. Creating vocabulary exercises through nlp. *Digital Humanities in the Nordic Countries. Proceedings, 2019.*

Rodrigo Arocena. 2010. Curricularización de la extensión: ¿por qué, cuál, cómo? *Integralidad: tensiones y perspectivas*, 9.

Gonzalo Berger, Tatiana Rischewski, Luis Chiruzzo, and Aiala Rosá. 2022. Generation of english question answer exercises from texts using transformers based models. In *2022 IEEE Latin American Conference on Computational Intelligence (LA-CCI)*. IEEE.

Claudia Brovetto. 2015. Ceibal en Inglés. Un caso de integración de pedagogía y tecnología. In *Octavo Foro de Lenguas de ANEP*, pages 13–22. Programa de Políticas lingüísticas, Montevideo, Uruguay.

J. Burstein, J. Sabatini, J. Shore, B. Moulder, and J. Lentini. 2013. A user study: Technology to increase teachers' linguistic awareness to improve instructional language support for english language learners. In *Proceedings of the 2nd Workshop on Natural Language Processing for Improving Textual Accessibility (NLP4ITA)*, Atlanta, Georgia. Association for Computational Linguistics.

Jennifer Esteche, Romina Romero, Luis Chiruzzo, and Aiala Rosa. 2017. Automatic definition extraction and crossword generation from spanish news text. *CLEI Electronic Journal*, 20(2).

Alena Fenogenova and Elizaveta Kuzmenko. 2016. Automatic generation of lexical exercises. In *Proceedings of the Workshop on Computational Linguistics and Language Science*.

Bernabé González, Isabel Ivagnes, Joaquín Lejtreger, Luis Chiruzzo, and Aiala Rosá. 2021. Application of language technologies to assist english teaching. In *2021 40th International Conference of the Chilean Computer Science Society (SCCC)*, pages 1–8. IEEE.

Anisia Katinskaia, Javad Nouri, and Roman Yangarber. 2018. Revita: a language-learning platform at the intersection of its and call. In *Proceedings of the Eleventh International Conference on Language Resources and Evaluation (LREC 2018)*, Miyazaki, Japón. European Language Resources Association (ELRA).

Diane Litman. 2016. Natural language processing for enhancing teaching and learning. In *Thirtieth AAAI conference on artificial intelligence*.

Tomas Mikolov, Kai Chen, Greg Corrado, and Jeffrey Dean. 2013. Efficient estimation of word representations in vector space. *arXiv preprint arXiv:1301.3781*.

Martín Morón, Joaquín Scocozza, Luis Chiruzzo, and Aiala Rosá. 2021. A tool for automatic question generation for teaching english to beginner students. In *2021 40th International Conference of the Chilean Computer Science Society (SCCC)*, pages 1–5. IEEE.

Analía Percovich, Alejandro Tosi, Luis Chiruzzo, and Aiala Rosá. 2019. Ludic applications for language teaching support using natural language processing. In *2019 38th International Conference of the Chilean Computer Science Society (SCCC)*, pages 1–7. IEEE.

Colin Raffel, Noam Shazeer, Adam Roberts, Katherine Lee, Sharan Narang, Michael Matena, Yanqi Zhou, Wei Li, and Peter J. Liu. 2020. Exploring the limits of transfer learning with a unified text-to-text transformer. *Journal of Machine Learning Research*, 21(140):1–67.

Shirley Romano. 2019. Inglés sin Límites: Un proyecto democrático de enseñanza de inglés en Educación Primaria Rural. pages 9–17. ANEP.

Limber Santos. 2016. La Didáctica Multigrado más allá de la escuela rural. *Quehacer Educativo*, 140:91–99.

Elena Volodina, Lars Borin, and Ildikó Pilán, editors. 2014. *Proceedings of the third workshop on NLP for computer-assisted language learning*. LiU Electronic Press, Uppsala, Sweden.

“Am I Answering My Job Interview Questions Right?”: A NLP Approach to Detecting the Degree of Explanation in Job Interview Responses

Raghu D. Verrap
Texas A&M University
raghudv@tamu.edu

Ehsanul Haque Nirjhar
Texas A&M University
nijrhar71@tamu.edu

Ani Nenkova
Adobe Research
nenkova@adobe.com

Theodora Chaspari
Texas A&M University
chaspari@tamu.edu

Abstract

Providing the right amount of explanation in an employment interview can help the interviewee effectively communicate their skills and experience to the interviewer and convince that she/he is the right candidate for the job. This paper examines natural language processing (NLP) approaches, including word-based tokenization, lexicon-based representations, and pre-trained embeddings with deep learning models, for detecting the degree of explanation in a job interview response. These are exemplified in a study of 24 military veterans who are the focal group of this study, since they can experience unique challenges in job interviews due to the unique verbal communication style that is prevalent in the military. Military veterans participated in mock interviews with industry recruiters and data from these interviews were transcribed and analyzed. Results indicate that the feasibility of automated NLP methods for detecting the degree of explanation in an interview response. Features based on tokenizer analysis are the most effective in detecting under-explained responses (i.e., 0.29 F1-score), while lexicon-based methods depict the higher performance in detecting over-explanation (i.e., 0.51 F1-score). Findings from this work lay the foundation for the design of intelligent assistive technologies that can provide personalized learning pathways to job candidates, especially those belonging to sensitive or under-represented populations, and helping them succeed in employment job interviews, ultimately contributing to an inclusive workforce.

1 Introduction

Artificial intelligence (AI) can empower a plethora of assistive tools for enhancing one’s visual, hearing, communication, cognitive, and motor skills (Zdravkova, 2022). By automating natural language processing (NLP) and understanding, AI technologies can enable individuals who belong to sensitive populations, to better express themselves or better understand the world around them. Intelligent interview training is one such technology that can facilitate training in a safe environment on specific verbal and nonverbal behaviors and can help individuals effectively adapt to cognitively demanding and socially challenging interview situations (Hemamou et al., 2019b). This technology can further contribute to an inclusive workforce. Since the employment interview comprises the first step of the job hiring process, intelligent interview training augmented with NLP can detect linguistic and semantic communicative behaviors that might jeopardize candidates’ performance in the interview, suggest the exact modifications needed to effectively communicate their skills, and facilitate access to training material and information in a personalized manner (Marienko et al., 2020).

Military veterans is a group that can particularly benefit from assistive interview training technologies. In many countries around the world, military veterans face major barriers to participating in the civilian workforce after separation from active duty (McAllister et al., 2015; Ahern et al., 2015). The military background and training of most veterans is significantly different compared to the general job candidate population, who usually comprise of relatively younger fresh college graduates. Military veterans often find it challenging to clearly articulate their strengths and “brag" about their achievements in the civilian employment interview setting. Particularly, they can experience unique verbal communication gaps, such as ineffective translation of relevant military experience and technical skills, over-explaining their responses, and excessive use of military jargon, that hamper them from successfully obtaining a job in the civilian workforce (Roy et al., 2020). Intelligent job interview training systems can potentially track these linguistic behaviors of interest and provide military veterans the right feedback at the right time.

We conduct a linguistic analysis of veterans’ responses in civilian interview settings. We focus on the degree of explanation in the response, since

Proceedings of the Second Workshop on NLP for Positive Impact (NLP4PI), pages 122 - 129
December 7, 2022 ©2022 Association for Computational Linguistics

this construct is particularly relevant to the interview success and unexplored by previous work, and particularly we investigate a range of NLP systems to detect over/under-explained, succinct, and comprehensive responses (Hagen et al., 2022). To accomplish this task, we examine NLP systems that rely on text tokenization, lexicon-based analysis, and deep learning methods. These are evaluated on transcripts from mock interviews between 24 military veterans and 5 industry recruiters. A total of 163 responses provided during the interviews were coded by third-party annotators with respect to the degree of explanation. Results indicate the feasibility of automated NLP analysis for detecting the outcome of interest. Particularly, features based on tokenizer analysis are the most effective in detecting under-explained responses (i.e., 0.29 F1-score), while lexicon-based methods depict the higher performance in detecting over-explanation (i.e., 0.51 F1-score). Challenges that were met during data analysis, namely, the small data sample, subjectivity in coding, and uneven class distributions, are described. Discussion of these results further provides ways in which the proposed NLP analysis can contribute to the design of assistive technologies for interview training.

2 Related Work

Prior work in assistive technologies for interview training has focused on helping users demonstrate effective social skills and positive personality cues. The TARDIS project, for example, designed a game simulation platform through which interviewees interacted with a virtual agent in an effort to improve social cues and affective expressions during the interview (Anderson et al., 2013; Gebhard et al., 2018). The system automatically detected and analyzed smiles, head nods, and body movements, which were used by a machine learning algorithm to classify the mental state (e.g., stressed, bored, hesitant) and affective state (e.g., positive/negative mood) of the user. During the virtual interview, the user received credits in the game when depicting behaviors that were deemed as effective for the interview. At the end, users received a series of statistics for each of the focal behaviors, which were also visualized over time. MACH—My Automated Conversation coacH is another automated interview training system that provided feedback to the user regarding their performance based on the analysis of facial expressions, speech, and prosody (Hoque et al., 2013). Similarly, Hartholt *et al.* designed a virtual reality system that simulated various interview settings, including the interviewer's propensity toward the interviewee (i.e., friendly, neutral, unfriendly) and the physical space of the interview (e.g., break room, office) (Hartholt et al., 2019). A user would interact with the training system by starting from easy to more challenging scenarios. No additional feedback was provided to the user.

Another line of work has evaluated interviewees based on multimodal data that were mostly collected in an asynchronous manner. Chen *et al.* estimated applicants' personality traits based on the audiovisual analysis of monologue job interviews (Chen et al., 2017). Linguistic analysis was conducted with a Bag-Of-Words text representation. Hemamou *et al.* designed a hierarchical attention model, called "HireNet" that predicted the hirability of an interviewee based on asynchronous video interviewing. HireNet relied on multimodal information from text, audio, and video (Hemamou et al., 2019a,b). Similarly, Ngugen & Gatricia-Perez and Muralidhar *et al.* analyzed acoustic and visual cues of video resumes and examined their effectiveness in estimating the candidate's hireability and social and communication skills (Nguyen and Gatica-Perez, 2016; Muralidhar et al., 2016). Finally, Naim *et al.* analyzed interviewees' performance in mock job interviews using their facial expressions (e.g., smiles, head gestures, facial tracking points), language (e.g., word counts, topic modeling), and prosodic information (e.g., pitch, intonation, and pauses). Results presented in the MIT Interview Dataset suggest that the use of unique words and personal pronouns, and the degree of speech fluency significantly affect one's interview performance (Naim et al., 2016).

The contributions of this paper in comparison to prior work are: (1) While previous work focuses on global characteristics of the interviewee (e.g., personality, social/communication skills) and overall descriptors of the interview outcome (e.g., hireability, performance), this paper provides a closer study to turn-level behaviors that can affect the job interview outcome, thus laying out the foundation toward intelligent assistive technologies that can analyze micro-level data and provide users with detailed feedback at the turn-level; (2) In contrast to the majority of prior work, this paper analyzes data from synchronous interactions between an interviewer and an interviewee, which are more dynamic and diverse; and (3) Prior work has mostly focused on college students or fresh college graduates, while this research investigates a unique population that comprises of military veterans facing unique challenges when preparing for a job interview, thus outlining unique design characteristics when it comes to creating assistive technologies for this population.

3 Data

3.1 Data Collection

We use data from an ongoing research study with U.S. military veterans who participated in a mock job interview conducted by experienced interviewers from the industry. Currently, 24 participants completed the study. Data from one participant is excluded from this paper due to technical issues in pre-processing. The average age of participants was 36.4 years (stand. dev. = 10.6 years), and two out of the 24 participants were female. The study was conducted in a hybrid format, where the interviewees (i.e., military veterans) were present in the lab, and the interviewers (i.e., industry experts) were connected via Zoom video conferencing. In order to obtain naturalistic conversational data in the mock job interview, we created customized job postings tailored to each participant's résumé, which were shared with both the interviewees and the interviewers. Interviewees were instructed to think that they applied for the aforementioned job and they were participating in the corresponding job interview. The interviewers were instructed to conduct the interview based on the job posting, and ask questions in a similar fashion as they would normally do as part of their job role. The average length of the interviews was about 18 minutes (stand. dev. = 6.4 minutes). Audio and video of the interviews were recorded, while the transcripts of the interviews were obtained by the automatic speech recognition functionality provided via Zoom. Transcripts were manually checked for errors, such as spelling mistakes, incomprehensible words, disfluencies, and non-verbal vocalizations. Next, interviews were checked manually to mark the start and end timestamps of each question and their corresponding responses. If the interviewer provided any prompts or asked for additional information after a response, these turns were considered as a part of the response to the original question. In total, 163 responses to the interview questions from the participants were recorded and were used for further analysis. This study has been approved by the institutional review board of the authors' university.

Degree of Explanation	No. of Samples
Under-explained	16
Succinct	67
Comprehensive	58
Over-explained	17
Total Samples	158

Table 1: Distribution of classes characterizing the degree of explanation to an interview question.

3.2 Behavioral Annotation

In order to label the degree of explanation in the responses to the interview questions, behavioral annotation was performed by three third-party annotators, who were undergraduate students in psychology and had previous experience in behavioral coding and annotation tasks. Consistently with previous work (Busso et al., 2016; Lefter et al., 2014), annotators were asked to watch the individual questions and the corresponding responses from the interview and rate the degree of explanation in each response into the following four possible categories. **Under-explained (Class 0)**: Short response that does not fully answer the interviewer's question. Such responses might end abruptly; **Succinct (Class 1)**: Concise and to-the-point responses that answer the interviewer's question fully and briefly; **Comprehensive (Class 2)**: Detailed response that answers the fully answers the question; and **Over-explained (Class 3)**: Very long response to the question with excess verbiage and too much detail that potentially affects the coherence of the answer.

The numerical labels are assigned based on the expected increasing order in response length for each of these categories (i.e., succinct responses are expected to be shorter compared to comprehensive ones). The annotation process resulted in a moderate annotator agreement of Fleiss' $\kappa = 0.437$ (Fleiss, 1971; Hallgren, 2012). After the annotation, five responses yielded labels with complete disagreement. These were excluded from the rest of the analysis, which renders the sample size, $N = 158$. The final labels were obtained by aggregating annotations through majority voting. Table 1 shows the distribution of labels obtained from this aggregation. It is to be noted that both "Under-explained" and "Over-explained" classes are minority classes, although they are the classes of interest, since these types of responses tend to contribute most to perceived hireability and job interview performance.

4 Methods

Since the numbers of samples belonging to the classes of interest (i.e., "Under-explained", "Over-explained") is much lower compared to the majority classes, it would be counter-productive to formulate the target problem as a 4-way classification task. To resolve this issue, we examine the association between the response length and the explanation labels. Intuitively, we anticipate that responses belonging to the "Under-Explained" and "Succinct" classes will have significantly shorter length compared to the ones belonging to the "Comprehensive" and "Over-Explained" classes. Response length is measured in terms of word count (i.e., the number of words in the response) and response duration (i.e., the duration of the response in seconds). Both these measures exhibit significantly high Pearson's correlation coefficients with the explanation labels (i.e., $r = 0.68, p < 0.01$ for word count, $r = 0.66, p < 0.01$ for response duration). This suggests that the shorter responses tend to fall into "Under-explained" and "Succinct" categories, while the longer responses belong to the "Comprehensive" and "Over-explained" classes. To further confirm this, a binary classification task is conducted to identify whether a response falls into the short (i.e., "Under-explained", "Succinct") or long (i.e., "Comprehensive", "Over-explained") category. For this purpose, a logistic regression model with response length as feature and with leave-one-subject-out cross-validation is used, which resulted in an macro-average F1-score of 0.87. This suggests that we can simply classify the responses into the short (i.e., "Under-explained", "Succinct") or long (i.e., "Comprehensive", "Over-explained") category before estimating the original classes. Therefore, to estimate the degree of explanation, in the following analysis, we formulate two binary classification problems (i.e., "Under-explained" vs. "Succinct", "Comprehensive" vs. "Over-explained") instead of a 4-class problem.

We pursue three different approaches for these binary classification tasks. The first approach employs a tokenizer that breaks text into word tokens, followed by a decision tree that conducts the binary classification task. The second approach utilizes a lexicon-based model of psycholinguistic speech attributes, followed by a decision tree. The third approach leverages a transformer-based model pre-trained on a large corpus of English text in self-supervised manner. Since the classes of each of the binary classification tasks are unbalanced, the F1-score is used as evaluation metric for the following systems. F1-score is reported for each class using a leave-one-subject-out cross-validation. According to this, the responses from one interviewee are included in the test set and the responses from the remaining interviewees are included in the train set, with this procedure repeating until all interviewees are part of the test set.

4.1 Tokenizer

We extract the linguistic information from the participants' responses to the interview questions using NLTK tokenizer (Bird et al., 2009). The NLTK tokenizer breaks each response into chunks at the word-level that can be considered as discrete elements. Tokens are generated from the response text without any truncation and padding. A total of 510 tokens with frequency more than three are selected as features for conventional machine learning models. The frequency of the corresponding tokens serves as the feature vector of length 510 to a decision tree model that conducts the binary classification tasks.

4.2 Lexicon-based method

In order to identify the psycholinguistic content of the participants' responses to the interview questions, we employ the Linguistic Inquiry and Word Count (LIWC) toolbox (Pennebaker et al., 2015). This tool measures the count (or percentage) of words from several constructs, known as LIWC categories. The LIWC categories include general descriptors (e.g., word count, words per sentence), summary variables (e.g., analytical thinking, clout), standard linguistic dimensions (e.g., pronouns, verbs), psychological constructs (e.g., affect, cognition), personal concern constructs (e.g., work, leisure), informal language marker (e.g., filler words, assents), and punctuation (e.g., periods, commas). Overall, we obtain 93 LIWC features from each sample, that comprise the input features of a binary decision tree.

4.3 Deep learning method

We further explore the use of deep learning models for the considered binary classification tasks. We use the RoBERTa-base (Liu et al., 2019) as the backbone network, a popular transformer-based model (Vaswani et al., 2017) pre-trained on a large corpus of English text in self-supervised manner. The input of this model comprises of the segments resulting from the Tokenizer (Section 4.1), namely, the first 510 tokens. The input is connected to two fully connected layers with 768 nodes each, ReLU activation, and dropout, following by the final output layer. As the dataset is highly unbalanced, we perform undersampling on the majority class and oversampling on the minority class. In addition, we freeze the initial 75% layers of the RoBERTa base pre-trained model. The model is trained for 20 epochs with a learning rate of 10^{-5}.

5 Experiments

Results obtained by the different NLP systems are summarized in Table 2. The F1-score for the "Succinct" and "Comprehensive" classes is significantly higher than the other two, since these are the majority classes. The deep learning method that relies on the RoBERTa model further achieves higher score than the Tokenizer and Lexicon-based methods for the "Succinct" and "Comprehensive" classes. This is anticipated as these two classes have a relatively high number of samples, thus the deep learning model can effectively learn their linguistic representation. Meanwhile, the lexicon-based features achieve the highest performance for the "Over-explained" class, which might be due to the fact that these two types of responses can be effectively differentiated via psycholinguistic dimensions. Statistical analysis via t-tests between the two classes of interest indicates that comprehensive responses depict significantly more positive emotional tone compared to over-explained responses ($\mu_3 = 56.83\%$, $\mu_4 = 44.47\%$, $p < 0.05$), where μ_3 and μ_4 are the mean values of the comprehensive and over-explained responses, respectively. This might be attributed to the fact that over-explained responses merely report content without depicting one's affective view. Comprehensive responses also include a significantly larger percentage of long words (i.e., words greater than six letters) compared to over-explained responses ($\mu_3 = 17.14\%$, $\mu_4 = 13.67\%$, $p < 0.01$) and significantly more work-relevant words ($\mu_3 = 4.88\%$, $\mu_4 = 3.39\%$, $p < 0.05$). This indicates that comprehensive responses are characterized by more complex expression (Smith-Keiling and Hyun, 2019) and communicate one's work-related experiences. On the contrary, over-explained responses have a significantly larger number of male references compared to comprehensive ones ($\mu_3 = 27.24\%$, $\mu_4 = 67.55\%$, $p < 0.05$) and include more past tense verbs ($\mu_3 = 3.87\%$, $\mu_4 = 5.39\%$, $p < 0.05$), potentially because over-explained responses are overly focused on one's immersion to past military experiences which are typically associated with male references. Finally, the Tokenizer method achieves the highest F1-score for the "Under-explained" class, potentially because these types of responses depict distinctive patterns with respect to the frequency of tokens compared to the "Succinct" class.

6 Discussion

The increasingly complex and demanding employment market and future workforce requires mature handling of content and emotions by the job candidates, therefore failing to explain one's skills or over-sharing information can be detrimental to succeeding in the employment interview (Cismas, 2021). Results from this study indicate that various types of NLP techniques can be effective in automatically identifying the degree of explanation in job interview responses, which can be particularly valuable when designing training technologies to prepare candidates for future employment. While previous work has focused on behavioral impressions that can affect the overall outcome of the interview (Anderson et al., 2013; Gebhard et al., 2018; Hoque et al., 2013; Hartholt et al., 2019), this paper focuses on linguistic behaviors at the turn-level, which can serve as the foundation for providing tangible low-level feedback to the interviewee. Training technologies that rely on automated NLP systems, such as the ones examined in this paper, can help pinpoint exact turns in the dialog that effectively serve the job interview outcome (i.e., succinct, comprehensive responses), as well as turns that might hurt the interview outcome (i.e., under-explaining, over-explaining). Intelligent cognitive enhancement technologies can potentially assist job candidates in helping them effectively communicate their skills to the interviewers. Such technologies need to rely on robust NLP approaches, that are adequately generalizable to unseen users and new contexts and depict reliable performance, especially for the detection of classes of interest, such as the under-explaining and over-explaining classes in our case. In addition, NLP technologies need to be effectively meshed with human-computer interaction (HCI) interfaces, in order to provide feedback in the right form (e.g., visual, tactile) and the right time (e.g., during practice, post-practice). In addition to detecting points of improvement, explaining their role in interview performance and suggesting appropriate changes to those responses would pave the way for personalized learning pathways. It is also essential to consider the degree of expla-

Methods	F1-score			
	Under-explained	Succinct	Comprehensive	Over-explained
Tokenizer	0.29	0.81	0.74	0.26
Lexicon-based method	0.22	0.78	0.83	0.51
Deep learning method	0.27	0.89	0.84	0.39

Table 2: F1-score for each class of interest obtained by the considered methods.

nation in the context of other linguistic behaviors (e.g., excessive use of military jargon, ineffective translation of military experience to the civilian job context), gestures (e.g., rigidity in posture), and vocal expressions (e.g., voice loudness), which will allow us to design technologies that can assist veteran interviewees in a holistic manner. User studies are needed to be conducted so that we can better understand the effectiveness of these technologies in the overarching goal of assisting military veterans to succeed in civilian job interviews.

7 Conclusion

We examined linguistic behaviors of military veterans that are indicative of the degree of explanation in job interview responses. We investigated different types of linguistic descriptors, ranging from word-based tokenization and lexicon-based representations, to pre-trained embeddings with deep learning models. Our results indicate that pre-trained embeddings are effective in detecting succinct and comprehensive responses, which contain the majority of samples. Lexicon-based features can reliably detect over-explained responses, potentially because of their unique psycholinguistic characteristics related to affect, work experience, and complex expression. Finally, under-explained answers are best recognized via the token-based approach, which might be due to the fact that these are characterized by significantly different frequency of tokens compared to the succinct responses. Results from this study lay the foundation toward intelligent interview training technologies that provide personalized learning by detecting verbal behaviors important for the job interview, explaining their role to the user, and suggesting appropriate changes that can effectively help users secure their desired job.

Limitations

The results of this work should be considered in the light of the following limitations. First, while it is difficult to obtain large-scale corpora from real-life interpersonal interactions, the relatively small size of the dataset prevents results of this study from adequately generalizing to other individuals and populations. In addition, due to the demographics of the region from which the data was sampled, the current dataset is highly skewed toward White male participants. As part of our future work, we will be verifying those findings with additional data that will include more diverse participants, which will allow us to make these technologies truly inclusive to all people. Second, the moderate agreement level (i.e., $\kappa = 0.437$) will be addressed via adjudication meetings. Third, this work takes into account the interviewee's response in isolation without considering the content of the question. Future work will incorporate the interview context, turn-taking between interviewer and interviewee, and acoustic information from speech, which is expected to yield improved performance.

Ethics Statement

The authors of this paper strove to maintain highest standards of professional conduct and ethical practice when conducting this work via respecting and maintaining the privacy of the participants of this study and security of the data and disclosing all pertinent system capabilities and limitations. This work is guided by the values of equality, inclusiveness, and respect for others, since it aims to render assistive interview technologies accessible to populations such as military veterans who have traditionally faced challenges in entering the workforce and have not actively been the focus of prior studies in computing that have examined the automated processing of interview data.

Acknowledgements

The authors would like to acknowledge the National Science Foundation (NSF) for funding this work (NSF #1956021, NSF #1955721, the Don & Ellie Knauss Veteran Resource and Support Center (VRSC) at Texas A&M University for their partnership in this research, and undergraduate students, Luis Garcia, Li Wen Jan, Albin Kyle Myscich, and Felicity Woodson for their contribution in data transcription, annotation, and pre-processing.

References

Jennifer Ahern, Miranda Worthen, Jackson Masters, Sheri A Lippman, Emily J Ozer, and Rudolf Moos. 2015. The challenges of afghanistan and iraq veterans' transition from military to civilian life and approaches to reconnection. *PloS one*, 10(7):e0128599.

Keith Anderson, Elisabeth André, Tobias Baur, Sara Bernardini, Mathieu Chollet, Evi Chryssafidou, Ionut Damian, Cathy Ennis, Arjan Egges, Patrick Gebhard, et al. 2013. The tardis framework: intelligent virtual agents for social coaching in job interviews. In *International Conference on Advances in Computer Entertainment Technology*, pages 476–491. Springer.

Steven Bird, Ewan Klein, and Edward Loper. 2009. *Natural language processing with Python: analyzing text with the natural language toolkit.* " O'Reilly Media, Inc.".

Carlos Busso, Srinivas Parthasarathy, Alec Burmania, Mohammed AbdelWahab, Najmeh Sadoughi, and Emily Mower Provost. 2016. Msp-improv: An acted corpus of dyadic interactions to study emotion perception. *IEEE Transactions on Affective Computing*, 8(1):67–80.

Lei Chen, Ru Zhao, Chee Wee Leong, Blair Lehman, Gary Feng, and Mohammed Ehsan Hoque. 2017. Automated video interview judgment on a large-sized corpus collected online. In *2017 Seventh International Conference on Affective Computing and Intelligent Interaction (ACII)*, pages 504–509. IEEE.

Suzana Carmen Cismas. 2021. Strategies to enhance students' employability and job interview abilities by didactic role-plays. *Reading Multiculturalism. Human and Social Perspectives*, page 23.

Joseph L Fleiss. 1971. Measuring nominal scale agreement among many raters. *Psychological bulletin*, 76(5):378.

Patrick Gebhard, Tanja Schneeberger, Elisabeth André, Tobias Baur, Ionut Damian, Gregor Mehlmann, Cornelius König, and Markus Langer. 2018. Serious games for training social skills in job interviews. *IEEE Transactions on Games*, 11(4):340–351.

Ellen Hagen, Md Nazmus Sakib, Neha Rani, Ehsanul Haque Nirjhar, Ani Nenkova, Theodora Chaspari, Sharon Lynn Chu, Amir Behzadan, and Winfred Arthur, Jr. 2022. Interviewer perceptions of veterans in civilian employment interviews and suggested interventions. International Military Testing Association.

Kevin A Hallgren. 2012. Computing inter-rater reliability for observational data: an overview and tutorial. *Tutorials in quantitative methods for psychology*, 8(1):23.

Arno Hartholt, Sharon Mozgai, and Albert" Skip" Rizzo. 2019. Virtual job interviewing practice for high-anxiety populations. In *Proceedings of the 19th ACM International Conference on Intelligent Virtual Agents*, pages 238–240.

Léo Hemamou, Ghazi Felhi, Jean-Claude Martin, and Chloé Clavel. 2019a. Slices of attention in asynchronous video job interviews. In *2019 8th International Conference on Affective Computing and Intelligent Interaction (ACII)*, pages 1–7. IEEE.

Léo Hemamou, Ghazi Felhi, Vincent Vandenbussche, Jean-Claude Martin, and Chloé Clavel. 2019b. Hirenet: A hierarchical attention model for the automatic analysis of asynchronous video job interviews. In *Proceedings of the AAAI conference on artificial intelligence*, volume 33, pages 573–581.

Mohammed Hoque, Matthieu Courgeon, Jean-Claude Martin, Bilge Mutlu, and Rosalind W Picard. 2013. Mach: My automated conversation coach. In *Proceedings of the 2013 ACM international joint conference on Pervasive and ubiquitous computing*, pages 697–706.

Iulia Lefter, Gertjan J Burghouts, and Leon JM Rothkrantz. 2014. An audio-visual dataset of human–human interactions in stressful situations. *Journal on Multimodal User Interfaces*, 8(1):29–41.

Yinhan Liu, Myle Ott, Naman Goyal, Jingfei Du, Mandar Joshi, Danqi Chen, Omer Levy, Mike Lewis, Luke Zettlemoyer, and Veselin Stoyanov. 2019. Roberta: A robustly optimized bert pretraining approach. *arXiv preprint arXiv:1907.11692*.

Maiia Marienko, Yulia Nosenko, and Mariya Shyshkina. 2020. Personalization of learning using adaptive technologies and augmented reality. *arXiv preprint arXiv:2011.05802*.

Charn P McAllister, Jeremy D Mackey, Kaylee J Hackney, and Pamela L Perrewé. 2015. From combat to khakis: An exploratory examination of job stress with veterans. *Military Psychology*, 27(2):93–107.

Skanda Muralidhar, Laurent Son Nguyen, Denise Frauendorfer, Jean-Marc Odobez, Marianne Schmid Mast, and Daniel Gatica-Perez. 2016. Training on the job: Behavioral analysis of job interviews in hospitality. In *Proceedings of the 18th acm international conference on multimodal interaction*, pages 84–91.

Iftekhar Naim, Md Iftekhar Tanveer, Daniel Gildea, and Mohammed Ehsan Hoque. 2016. Automated analysis and prediction of job interview performance. *IEEE Transactions on Affective Computing*, 9(2):191–204.

Laurent Son Nguyen and Daniel Gatica-Perez. 2016. Hirability in the wild: Analysis of online conversational video resumes. *IEEE Transactions on Multimedia*, 18(7):1422–1437.

James W Pennebaker, Ryan L Boyd, Kayla Jordan, and Kate Blackburn. 2015. The development and psychometric properties of liwc2015. Technical report.

Deborah Roy, Jana Ross, and Cherie Armour. 2020. Making the transition: How finding a good job is a risky business for military veterans in northern ireland. *Military Psychology*, 32(5):428–441.

Beverly L Smith-Keiling and Hye In F Hyun. 2019. Applying a computer-assisted tool for semantic analysis of writing: Uses for stem and ell. *Journal of microbiology & biology education*, 20(1):70.

Ashish Vaswani, Noam Shazeer, Niki Parmar, Jakob Uszkoreit, Llion Jones, Aidan N Gomez, Łukasz Kaiser, and Illia Polosukhin. 2017. Attention is all you need. *Advances in neural information processing systems*, 30.

Katerina Zdravkova. 2022. The potential of artificial intelligence for assistive technology in education. In *Handbook on Intelligent Techniques in the Educational Process*, pages 61–85. Springer.

Identifying Condescending Language: A Tale of Two Distinct Phenomena?

Carla Perez-Almendros and Steven Schockaert
School of Computer Science & Informatics, Cardiff University, UK
{perezalmendrosc, schockaerts1}@cardiff.ac.uk

Abstract

Patronizing and condescending language is characterized, among others, by its subtle nature. It thus seems reasonable to assume that detecting condescending language in text would be harder than detecting more explicitly harmful language, such as hate speech. However, the results of a SemEval-2022 Task devoted to this topic paint a different picture, with the top-performing systems achieving remarkably strong results. In this paper, we analyse the surprising effectiveness of standard text classification methods in more detail. In particular, we highlight the presence of two rather different types of condescending language in the dataset from the SemEval task. Some inputs are condescending because of the way they talk about a particular subject, i.e. condescending language in this case is a linguistic phenomenon, which can, in principle, be learned from training examples. However, other inputs are condescending because of the nature of what is said, rather than the way in which it is expressed, e.g. by emphasizing stereotypes about a given community. In such cases, our ability to detect condescending language, with current methods, largely depends on the presence of similar examples in the training data.

1 Introduction

Patronizing and Condescending Language (PCL) has been a topic of interest across a wide range of disciplines, including Politics, Journalism and Medicine (Huckin, 2002a; Chouliaraki, 2006; Draper, 2005; Oldenburg et al., 2015). The use of PCL implies a position of superiority of the author regarding the person or community they are referring to, suggesting an imbalance in terms of power or privilege (Foucault, 1980). Especially when directed towards vulnerable communities, PCL fuels discrimination and perpetuates inequalities (Ng, 2007; Mendelsohn et al., 2020), feeds stereotypes and misinformation (Fiske, 1993), and makes it more difficult for underrepresented groups to overcome social difficulties (Nolan and Mikami, 2013).

The NLP community has recently also turned its attention to the study of PCL, focusing on the task of detecting and categorizing this kind of harmful discourse. For instance, Wang and Potts (2019) introduced the *Talk Down* dataset, which is focused on condescending language in social media, while Perez-Almendros et al. (2020) introduced the *Don't Patronize Me!* (DPM) dataset, which is focused on the way in which vulnerable communities are described in news stories. From the NLP point of view, the study of PCL is interesting because it is more subtle, and therefore presumably harder to detect, than other forms of harmful language, such as hate speech (Basile et al., 2019) and offensive language (Zampieri et al., 2019, 2020). Moreover, identifying PCL often seems to require a deep commonsense understanding of human values (Pérez-Almendros et al., 2022). Consider the following example from the DPM dataset:

> "People across Australia ordered pizzas to be delivered on Saturday night, with the ample leftovers donated to local homeless shelters."

We can understand that, although donating food can be socially valuable, the impact of this particular action is painted in an excessively positive light (e.g. as evident in the phrase *ample leftovers*). Moreover, this seems to refer to a campaign to increase the consumption of pizzas with the excuse to help homeless people, which as humans we might also find condescending. However, an NLP model might struggle to infer such connotations.

Based on the premise that PCL detection would present unique challenges, SemEval-2022 featured a task devoted to PCL detection and categorization (Perez-Almendros et al., 2022). The top-ranked submissions for this task achieved a remarkably strong performance, which seems to somewhat

Proceedings of the Second Workshop on NLP for Positive Impact (NLP4PI), pages 130 - 141
December 7, 2022 ©2022 Association for Computational Linguistics

undermine the assumption that the subtle nature of PCL would make its detection inherently hard. Moreover, even the best systems (Deng et al., 2022; Wang et al., 2022; Hu et al., 2022), relied on a judicious use of more or less generic text classification techniques, improving on the RoBERTa (Liu et al., 2019) baseline by addressing the class imbalance, adding a contrastive learning loss, using ensembles of language models, etc. In particular, there was little evidence of the presumed need to focus on commonsense understanding of human values.

In this paper, we present an analysis of the SemEval-2022 PCL detection dataset, in light of the aforementioned observations. Our central argument is that the dataset contains examples of two rather distinct types of condescending language, and that the difference between the two is fundamental to understanding why the task, as it has been formulated, might be significantly easier than the task of detecting condescending language in general. We argue that a deeper understanding of these two phenomena might lead to a better performance on PCL detection, which in turn can mitigate the discourse of condescension towards vulnerable communities. We will refer to these two types as *Linguistic PCL* and *Thematic PCL*.

Linguistic PCL Some instances of PCL are related to the way in which a given claim is expressed. Consider the following example:

> "...we must rally together as humans, understanding that we have a responsibility to help the world's most vulnerable to survive and rebuild their lives [...]"

In this sentence, we can see two common aspects of PCL. First, expressions such as *we must* or *we have a responsibility*, indicate an authority voice and attitude (Simpson, 2003). Second, the sentence evokes the idea of a *saviour* and a *victim*. Note how the condescending tone of the sentence is related to linguistic aspects that are relatively easy to identify (e.g. the presence of modal verbs such as *must*) and largely independent of the community being referred to. We will refer to such cases as *linguistic PCL*. Our hypothesis is that detecting linguistic PCL is relatively straightforward for language models, as this is ultimately about learning to detect a particular writing style (Iyer and Vosoughi, 2020).

Thematic PCL There are also examples of PCL where the message itself is condescending, irrespective of how it is formulated. We will refer to such cases as *Thematic PCL*. Consider the following example:

> "The problem of what to do about the Dreamers, as the immigrants are known[...]"

Calling young immigrants *Dreamers* has condescending connotations, as it implies that the author is in a privileged position which the immigrants aspire to reach. To recognize this, we need a deeper understanding about the nature of condescending language, and we need access to particular world knowledge. For instance, we need to know that the author refers to the DREAM Act[1] and that this tries to protect young immigrants brought to the US as children and fulfill their aspiration to live in America as a *dreamed life*. Our hypothesis is that detecting themed PCL often requires a level of understanding about human values, and the world in general, that goes above what we can expect to be captured by standard language models. However, the training and test data from the SemEval task is focused on a small number of vulnerable communities, with the same communities being covered in the training and test data. As such, the model may detect instances of PCL by identifying that they express a similar argument as some training example, rather than by developing an understanding of the underlying reasons why a given example is condescending. In this case, we can expect the model to fail to detect PCL towards communities that are not seen in the training set. Similarly, the model may struggle to adapt when the themes appearing in PCL towards previously seen communities change.

Overview In this paper, we present an analysis of the SemEval-2022 dataset, aimed at testing the aforementioned hypotheses about linguistic and themed PCL. First, we carry out two experiments in which models are trained such that they are prevented, to some extent, from learning about condescending themes associated with individual communities. Our experiments show that there are some communities for which this leads to a dramatic drop in performance, while for other communities there was no negative impact at all. This suggests that there is indeed considerable overlap in the kinds of themed PCL that can be found in the training and test sets of the SemEval dataset, but only for some communities. We then complement

[1]www.americanimmigrationcouncil.org/research/dream-act-overview

these results with a qualitative analysis based on ideas from critical Discourse Analysis (CDA), a technique which emerged from Critical Linguistics in the 1970s (Fowler et al., 2018; Fairclough and Chouliaraki, 1999; Fairclough, 2013; Wodak, 2004; Van Dijk, 2015; Huckin et al., 2012). CDA looks at the relation between power and language, and how discourse expresses social hierarchy and inequalities. This qualitative analysis provides further suppors for the idea that (i) PCL detection models can identify Linguistic PCL even if they have not seen similar cases during training while (ii) their ability to detect instances of themed PCL is much more dependent on the training examples.

2 Related Work

The Study of PCL The discourse of condescension has been widely studied in disciplines such as Sociolinguistics, Politics, Psychology, Medicine, Cultural Studies, Public Relations, Journalism and International Cooperation (Huckin, 2002a,b; Giles et al., 1993; Margić, 2017; Chouliaraki, 2006, 2010). Within the NLP community, the study of PCL is more recent, although there is a longer tradition of looking at harmful language more generally (Basile et al., 2019; Zampieri et al., 2020; Conroy et al., 2015; Da San Martino et al., 2020; Feng et al., 2021; Farha et al., 2022). As already mentioned in the introduction, Wang and Potts (2019) and Perez-Almendros et al. (2020) addressed condescension in different types of discourse, while other recent works addressed some closely related aspects, such as how language conceals power relations (Sap et al., 2020), expresses authoritarian voices as empathy (Zhou and Jurgens, 2020) or dehumanizes minorities (Mendelsohn et al., 2020).

PCL towards vulnerable communities is a subtle and subjective kind of language, often unconscious and well intended (Wilson and Gutierrez, 1985; Merskin, 2011). An author might use PCL while trying to help a community or individual, raise their voice for them or move the audience to action. However, PCL can be very harmful, as it routinizes discrimination (Ng, 2007), creates stereotypes (Fiske, 1993) and reinforces inequalities (Nolan and Mikami, 2013; Chouliaraki, 2006, 2010), feeding the dichotomy of a *saviour* (Bell, 2013; Straubhaar, 2015) and a *helpless victim*. PCL contributes to the "distorted and stereotyped representation" (Caspi and Elias, 2011) that vulnerable communities or underrepresented groups frequently receive in the media.

The Coverage of Minorities in the Media Our emphasis on the distinction between *thematic* and *linguistic* PCL draws from previous analysis of the relation between discourse and power, and how language can reinforce inequalities and exclusion. Such studies are mainly based on Critical Discourse Analysis (CDA), which is concerned with the analysis of unbalanced power relations and privilege in public discourse and the construction of identities in the media. It also draws our attention to the influence (voluntary or not) that the author of a public discourse has over the construction of an image in the mind of the audience by, for instance, their selection of words, use of linguistic structures and omissions when depicting a specific community or situation (Huckin, 2002a). Huckin (2002a) suggests that, in the critical study of a discourse, an analyst should look for certain linguistic or stylistic features in a text, such as the use of modal verbs (modality) or the identity of the subject and the object of an action (transitivity), to find expressions of power imbalance and inequality. He also suggests to look at recurrent themes and stereotypes in the media coverage of minorities. Along this direction, the same author studied the treatment of homelessness in the US in 1999 (Huckin, 2002b). He collected a corpus of 163 newspapers articles and editorials which mentioned the keyword *homeless* and analyzed, among others, the more recurrent themes and stereotypes related to this community. For instance, he shows that the analyzed data includes "desire of independence" or "lack of life skills" as common themes when referring to causes of homelessness. Also, the theme "bad grooming" is highlighted as one effect of homelessness. "Religious support", "food donation" and "donated clothes" are common themes in the discussion of public responses, which represent shallow and ephemeral solutions for a structural, deep-rooted problem, and thus again reinforce the charitable, *saviour-victim* treatment of a community. Using a similar approach, Díaz-Rico (2012) analyzed 93 articles about Mexican immigrants from the Los Angeles Times, published in 2010. She claims that the selection of topics and themes is the most important aspect of Journalism and that newspapers use the drama of a story to gain attention from their audience. Although the language and topics she analyses in this work are often openly discriminatory and offensive, she also finds expres-

	Neg.Inst.	Pos.Inst.	%Pos.Inst.
Migrant	1052	36	3.3
Immigrant	1031	30	2.8
Refugee	981	86	8.1
In need	906	176	16.3
Poor fam.	759	150	16.5
Vulnerable	1000	80	7.4
Women	1018	52	4.9
Disabled	947	81	7.9
Homeless	899	178	16.5
Hopeless	881	124	12.3
All data	9474	993	9.5

Table 1: Number of negative and positive training examples per community. We also report the percentage of positive instances.

	Neg.Inst.	Pos.Inst.	%Pos.Inst.
Migrant	359	12	3.2
Immigrant	383	17	4.3
Refugee	390	26	6.3
In need	357	42	10.5
Poor fam.	267	56	17.3
Vulnerable	382	18	4.5
Women	390	22	5.3
Disabled	308	24	7.2
Homeless	337	57	14.5
Hopeless	342	43	11.2
All data	3515	317	8.3

Table 2: Number of negative and positive test examples per community. We also report the percentage of positive instances.

sions that, through rhetorical figures, connotation and semantic selection, reinforce power relations and inequalities (e.g."help new arrivals get on their feet", or "ballot crusade").

3 Methodology

In Sections 4 and 5, we describe experiments in which PCL classifiers are trained in a way that (partially) prevents them from learning about community-specific thematic PCL. This will allow us to better characterise the abilities of fine-tuned language models, as the overlap between the themes covered by the training and test sets is reduced. In this section, we first describe the basic experimental setup that we rely on throughout the paper (Section 3.1). Subsequently, we describe a simple strategy for characterizing topics or themes that are strongly associated with particular vulnerable communities or groups (Section 3.2).

3.1 Experimental Setup

Dataset We use the dataset that was provided for the Patronizing and Condescending Language Detection Task at SemEval-2022 (Perez-Almendros et al., 2022). This dataset consists of 14,299 annotated paragraphs (10,467 for training and 3,832 for testing). The paragraphs were extracted from English news stories and cover traditionally vulnerable communities and underrepresented groups. In particular, each paragraph mentions at least one of the following vulnerability-related keywords: *immigrants*, *migrants*, *refugees*, *poor families*, *in need*, *hopeless*, *homeless*, *disabled*, *women* and *vulnerable*. We only use the binary labels from the dataset, i.e. whether a paragraph is considered to contain PCL or not[2]. We show the number of positive and negative instances for each community for the training data in Table 1 and for the test data in Table 2.

Training Details For our experiments, we fine-tune RoBERTa-base (Liu et al., 2019) on different versions of the training set. While better results have been reported for RoBERTa-large and DeBERTa (Hu et al., 2022; Deng et al., 2022; Wang et al., 2022), we found the results with RoBERTa-base to be more stable across different runs, which is more important than the absolute level of performance for the analysis in this paper. We train our models for 5 epochs, using the Transformers library (Wolf et al., 2020). We use AdamW with a learning rate of 1e-5 and a batch size of 4. All the reported results have been averaged over 5 runs. As can be seen in Tables 1 and 2, the SemEval dataset is highly imbalanced, with 9,474 negative and 993 positive cases of PCL. For this reason, when training the language model, we down-sample the negative cases to 5,000 and over-sample the positive cases five times.

3.2 Community-Related Terms

We associate each of the vulnerable communities from the SemEval dataset with a set of terms, which essentially describe the topics or themes that are specific to, or at least strongly related to, that community. To associate terms with a given community, we compare the set of paragraphs, from the SemEval dataset, in which the keyword associated

[2]The dataset also includes a categorisation of positive examples according to the taxonomy from Perez-Almendros et al. (2020), as well as labels which indicate the level of inter-annotator agreement for a given example.

Community	Associated terms
Immigrants	First-generation, resentment, cultures, foreign-born, undocumented, sentiment, spouses, applicant
Migrants	Hatred, incoming, dreamers, coast, trafficking, racism, protections, deported, gangs, rescued
Refugees	Repatriation, offshore, queer, seekers, resettlement, camps, fled, abuses, mercy, forget
In need	Donor, desperately, Christ, drought, kindness, foster, budgets, compassionate, humanitarian, blankets
Poor families	Diapers, nutritious, scholarship, rice, poverty, expenses, savings, malnutrition, babies, orphans
Vulnerable	Droughts, prey, strategies, hub, resilience, crop, proactive, exploitation, fragile, hazards
Women	Feminist, maternity, abortions, husbands, beauty, fertility, unsafe, empowering, motivated, honour
Disabled	Assistive, pension, impaired, heroes, integrating, consideration, allowance, disadvantaged, begging
Homeless	Downpour, jobless, addicts, evicted, shelters, hungry, streets, rough, roofs, soup

Table 3: Selection of terms found for the different communities, with $k = 100$.

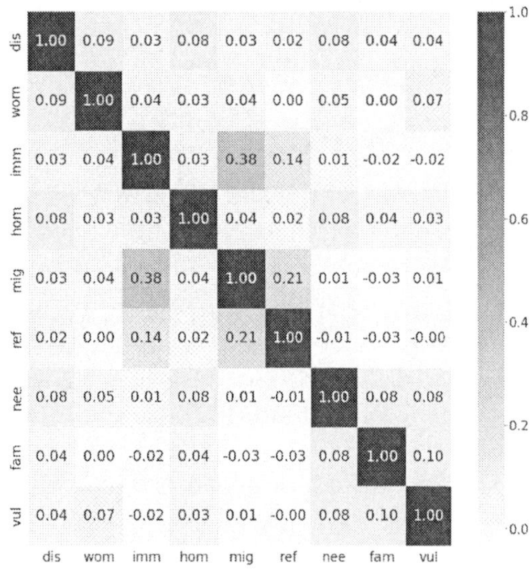

Figure 1: Similarity between the different communities from the SemEval dataset. The communities are identified by the following keywords: disabled (dis), women (wom), immigrants (imm), homeless (hom), migrants (mig), refugees (ref), in need (nee), poor families (fam) and vulnerable (vul).

with that community is mentioned (e.g. *homeless*) with the remaining paragraphs. We first select those terms that are mentioned in at least five paragraphs for the considered community. Then we rank these terms according to Pointwise Mutual Information (PMI), i.e. by comparing how strongly the presence of a given term (e.g. *addicts*) is associated with the presence of the community keyword (e.g. *homeless*). Finally, we select the top-k highest ranked terms for each community, where we have considered $k = 100$ and $k = 500$ in our experiments. Note that the selected terms are not necessarily indicative of PCL. However, even for $k = 100$ we observed that many of the selected terms reflect stereotypes and condescending attitudes. Table 3 shows a selection of terms that were found for $k = 100$.

Finally, we analyse to what extent the ten keywords from the SemEval dataset refer to distinct communities. To this end, we represent each keyword/community as a PMI-weighted bag-of-words vector. Figure 1 displays the cosine similarities between the vectors we obtained for the different communities. As can be seen, and somewhat unsurprisingly, there is a high degree of overlap between *migrants* and *immigrants*. For this reason, these two communities/keywords will be merged for the analyses in this paper. We can furthermore see that *migrants* and *refugees* are also somewhat similar in the dataset, but since the similarity between *immigrants* and *refugees* is much lower, we keep *refugees* as a separate community. Note that we omitted the keyword *hopeless* in Figure 1, as we found this keyword to be too generic to be viewed as describing a particular community. For this reason, we will not consider this keyword in our community-specific experiments and analysis.

4 Omitting Community-Specific Training Data

Our main hypothesis, as outlined in the introduction, is that the SemEval PCL detection task is easier than one might expect because it involves a combination of linguistic PCL, which is easier to detect, and thematic PCL. While we believe that thematic PCL can be hard to detect in general, our hypothesis is that it is simplified, in the context of the SemEval dataset, because of the overlap between the themes covered in the training and test data. If a language model is truly able to recognize PCL, then it should be capable of identifying (thematic) PCL about communities it has not seen during training. In this section, we report the results of an experiment where we test the performance of the model per community in two settings. First, we consider the standard setting, where the model has had access to the entire training set. Second, we consider the setting where all examples about the community being tested were removed from the training set. Note that for the latter case, we need to train a separate model for every community, each time omitting the corresponding training examples.

	Full Training	Comm. Omitted
Migr. + Imm.	**43.6**$_{\pm 7.89}$	25.3$_{\pm 3.27}$
Refugees	50.4$_{\pm 8.36}$	**54.0**$_{\pm 5.12}$
In need	**55.3**$_{\pm 3.12}$	51.2$_{\pm 1.04}$
Poor families	52.7$_{\pm 6.34}$	**53.7**$_{\pm 7.18}$
Vulnerable	**54.7**$_{\pm 3.75}$	51.6$_{\pm 3.29}$
Women	31.5$_{\pm 8.79}$	**41.7**$_{\pm 7.53}$
Disabled	**54.6**$_{\pm 5.52}$	52.4$_{\pm 3.85}$
Homeless	**60.2**$_{\pm 1.85}$	54.4$_{\pm 2.49}$
All communities	53.2$_{\pm 2.54}$	-

Table 4: Performance of RoBERTa-base models fine-tuned with (Full Training) and without (Comm. Omitted) training examples about the test community. Result are reported in terms of F1-score % and are averaged over 5 runs. We also report the standard deviation.

The results are summarized in Table 4. We can make a number of clear observations. First, the performance of the model that was trained on the full training set varies substantially across the different communities. For instance, the F1 score for *homeless* is almost twice as high as that for *women*. Second, excluding training examples about the test community has a substantial impact on the results for some communities, but not for others. For *migrants + immigrants*, we can see a particularly large drop in performance, which suggests that PCL towards this community is more likely to be thematic than for the other communities. For some of the other communities, we also see drops, although these are much smaller. Surprisingly, for some communities, the performance improves when omitting training examples from that community, which is most pronounced for *women*. This suggests that PCL towards women is more likely to be linguistic (and thus community-independent), while the model may have learned incorrect associations from the themes that are present in the training examples about women. This will be further explored in the qualitative analysis.

5 Masking Community-Specific Terms

We now present a variant of the experiment from the previous section, where no training examples are removed, but we instead mask (some) occurrences of community-related terms, as identified in Section 3.2, in the training data. Note that we mask occurrences of such terms regardless of the community a training example is about (e.g. a term that was identified for *refugees* would still be masked in examples about *immigrants*). This setup has the advantage that the number of training examples remains constant. Moreover, the model may now also be prevented from learning thematic PCL by training on related communities. For instance, in the setting from Section 4, the model may be able to learn condescending themes about the *homeless* community from training examples mentioning the *vulnerable* keyword.

The results are reported in Table 5, where the masking probability for mentions of community-related terms is varied from 0% to 100%. The main findings from Section 4 are confirmed by this experiment. In particular, for *migrants + immigrants*, we find that masking community-related terms leads to a substantial drop in performance (especially when 100% of the mentions are masked). This again suggests that the classifier, in the standard setting, heavily relies on the fact that condescending themes from the test set are also present in the training set. For *women*, we can see that masking can improve the results, which again suggests that the type of PCL for this community is mostly linguistic. In fact, for all but two communities, the best overall results are obtained with some degree of masking. This suggests that linguistic PCL is prevalent across the dataset, and that the fine-tuned RoBERTa-base model is susceptible to lean incorrect associations between thematic terms and the presence of PCL.

6 Qualitative Analysis

The experiments in Sections 4 and 5 have revealed stark differences in the robustness of PCL detection models across different communities, when the model is (partially) prevented from learning community-specific themes during training. In particular, our results suggest that PCL examples for *migrants + immigrants* are often thematic in nature, with the same themes recurring in both the training and test sets. Conversely, the results for *women* suggest that PCL towards that community is more likely to be linguistic in nature. In this section, we supplement our findings with a qualitative analysis, where we focus on these two communities.

	Top-100 community-based terms					Top-500 community-based terms					Baseline
	100%	80%	60%	40%	20%	100%	80%	60%	40%	20%	0%
Migr. + Imm.	27.7	38.0	31.6	35.7	40.0	25.2	34.3	42.3	36.0	34.9	**43.6**
Refugees	49.9	50.1	47.1	**52.2**	**53.0**	49.6	49.5	48.1	48.5	**53.5**	50.4
In need	**55.6**	55.2	**55.8**	**56.5**	**58.6**	**56.9**	54.7	**58.6**	**57.1**	55.1	55.3
Poor families	**55.9**	**57.5**	52.0	47.8	52.7	51.7	52.2	52.1	50.2	46.6	52.7
Vulnerable	54.3	**56.8**	52.7	**57.5**	**55.8**	48.4	47.5	**56.3**	54.1	52.3	54.7
Women	31.0	**37.6**	**39.3**	**41.0**	**39.7**	**38.2**	**39.8**	**39.9**	**39.5**	**35.9**	31.5
Disabled	51.8	49.3	52.4	48.7	48.0	45.8	46.3	54.4	52.1	53.0	**54.6**
Homeless	58.5	58.4	57.8	57.7	**62.1**	54.6	54.9	**61.3**	60.0	57.9	60.2
All communities	52.3	**53.4**	51.6	52.5	**53.9**	51.2	50.7	**54.6**	52.9	52.3	53.2

Table 5: Performance of RoBERTa-base models fine-tuned on variants of the training set in which community-related terms are masked. Results are shown with the $k = 100$ and the $k = 500$ top terms from each community, and with varying masking probabilities. Configurations which outperform the baseline (i.e. the setting where the original training set is used) are shown in bold, while the best overall result for each community is underlined. Result are reported in terms of F1-score % and are averaged over 5 runs. The standard deviation is reported in Appendix A

Migrants + Immigrants In Table 6, we can see examples of PCL which were consistently[3] classified correctly when including the community in the training set, but where the model was unable to recognise the PCL when trained without examples from the test community. Therefore, these are paragraphs where we would expect to see community-related themes that make the message condescending. Note that the word *Dreamer* is present in all the examples from this table. It thus seems safe to infer that the model has learned that this term is highly predictive of the presence of PCL, when such examples are included in the training data. The use of other terms such as *deportation*, *undocumented* or *citizenship* are also strongly related to the community and might help the model to identify the presence of PCL.

In contrast, the examples of PCL in Table 7 were consistently identified correctly, whether the training examples for *migrant + immigrant* were included or not. As expected, we can indeed think of these examples as being primarily *linguistic PCL*, in the sense that what makes them condescending is *how* the message is expressed, more than *what* is being expressed. For instance, in the first example we can see an excess of flowery wording and adjectives to express a message, the use of metaphors and an almost poetic style to describe a vulnerable situation, which are common features of PCL (Perez-Almendros et al., 2020). The second and third examples also show clear differences in power and privilege, for instance, through the use of expressions such as *we have a moral responsibility*, *show them solidarity* or *permitting them to work and study without fear*. The last example conveys a distance between the author and the community (*breaking through the barrier of migrant communities*) and expresses presuppositions and an authority voice based on the idea of a *saviour-victim* relation (*I grapple with this, I'm trying to help, to make things better, but many women find comfort in the norms and the way things are*). These examples of *linguistic PCL* are independent of the community they are addressing, which is why the model still recognises them even when no training examples for the *migrants + immigrants* community are provided.

Women Table 8 shows examples of PCL that were missed when using the full training set, but consistently classified correctly when omitting *women* examples. In the first paragraph, the phrase *their shame continues*, a community-independent value judgement, makes the text condescending. The second and third example express a *saviour-victim* relation, where the differences between power and vulnerability, as well as an admiration towards the *saviour*, are explicitly stated. As these examples are clearly linguistic, we can expect that a model which has not seen *women* examples should be able to classify them correctly. Surprisingly, all three paragraphs were missed by the model that was trained on the full training data. To understand why this is the case, note that 95% of the training examples for *women* are negative. As a result, several of the terms that are associated

[3]We focus on cases where the classification is consistent across different runs of our experiments, i.e. with different random seeds, to reduce the influence of instances that were classified correctly or incorrectly by chance.

Classified correctly only with full training set
On the campaign trail, **Trump** promised to **deport** all **undocumented** migrants. Since taking office, he appeared to soften on **dreamers**, a relatively well-educated and industrious group who he described as "incredible kids"
But without resolution, the centrists warn they will have enough petition signatures by Tuesday to force House votes later this month, including on their preferred bill which provides young **"Dreamer"** immigrants **protection** from **deportation** and a chance to apply for **citizenship**.
Passage of the measure came over the opposition of Democratic leaders who demanded the promise of a vote to protect **"Dreamer"** immigrants brought to the country illegally as children. A band of tea party Republicans was also against the legislation over what it sees as spiralling spending levels.
The New York senator said he was hopeful about talks on so-called **Dreamers**, more than 700,000 young immigrants brought to the US as children who were **protected** under the Obama-era Deferred Action for Childhood Arrivals **(Daca)** programme.

Table 6: Examples of PCL for *migrants + immigrants*, which are consistently classified correctly when the model is trained on the full training set, but consistently misclassified when training examples about this community are excluded from the training set. In bold, we highlight some community-specific themes that are common in examples of PCL, which the model is unable to learn when not presented with similar examples during training.

Classified correctly even without community-specific training examples
The Irish famine led to a massive influx of Irish immigrants to New York during the late 1840s and 1850s. As the **downtrodden** Irish escaped the famine in their home country, however, **they came to a place where life was just as tough**. Disembarking from **coffin ships**, Irish newcomers were **greeted with a new life of hardship, slums and tough, endless labor**.
Vatican City: As record numbers of people flee conflict, persecution and poverty, governments, citizens and the Church **have a moral obligation** to safeguard migrants and **show solidarity** with them, the Pope has said.
Barack Obama implemented the DACA program five years ago to **help bring** the children of undocumented immigrants **out of the shadows** of illegality, **permitting them** to study and work **without fear**.
It's been hard **breaking through the barrier of migrant communities**. Many women from my own community do not take my work seriously and do not support it, and **I grapple with this. I'm trying to help, to make things better, but many women find comfort in the norms and the way things are**.

Table 7: Examples of PCL for *migrants + immigrants*, which are consistently classified correctly both when including or excluding the community from the training set. in bold, we highlight the presence of some common linguistic features of PCL.

Classified correctly only without community-specific training examples
Many of these women now lie in unmarked graves, a situation that is slowly being rectified by the work of the voluntary Justice for Magdalenes Group. **Their shame continues**.
However, "when **a major male rock star who could do anything at all with his life decides to focus on the rights of women and girls worldwide** - well, all **that's worth celebrating**. We're proud to name that rock star, Bono, our first Man of the Year," it said.
A Cosmopolitan spokesperson says with a focus on empowerment, **the magazine is "proud of all that the brand has achieved for women around the world"**.

Table 8: Examples of PCL for *women*, which are classified correctly only when excluding the community from the training set. In bold, we highlight the presence of some common linguistic features of PCL.

with women (almost) exclusively appear in negative training examples. This can lead the model to believe that these words are indicative of a lack of PCL. By masking community-related terms, or omitting training examples from this community entirely, we can prevent the model from learning such coincidental associations.

7 Conclusions

We have studied the challenge of detecting Patronizing and Condescending Language (PCL), with the aim of improving our understanding of its na-

Classified correctly only with partial masking
"Eleven months into his administration, the country is showing signs of progress in most sectors of the economy. With the implementation of the free senior high school programme, most students, **especially those from poor families, who hitherto would not have progressed to the senior high school, have the opportunity now to receive** secondary education **to make them better and more functional in society**", Dr Nyarko said.
Today, Brooklyn is home to people of all races, most struggling to make ends meet. Council flats continue to degrade as the population swells – **unemployment and homelessness sees people of different races** lining up side-by-side **for a plate of free food**. It's a representation of **the rainbow nation in trauma, with its colours dulled and blended together by suffering**.
Helping refugee children fit in a bonus for Juventus football camp.
Swimming superstar Adam Peaty is set to unveil **a new motorbike for charity** in memory of schoolgirl Imogen Evans, who used the service. The Shropshire and Staffordshire Blood Bikes is a charity which **saves lives** by delivering vital blood supplies to those in need.
RADIO Veritas, the leading faith-based AM station in Mega Manila, continues **its commitment to charity and public service** through an initiative dubbed as "**Good Samaritan**". Since it was launched last June 2017 (airing every Monday to Friday from 1-2 p.m.), Radio Veritas has listed 182 cases of pleads and requests that have been fulfilled through this program. It serves as a platform **for those in need to make on-air appeals** for legal, spiritual, medical, material and financial assistance, and **link them to "Good Samaritans" who are willing to share**.

Table 9: Examples of PCL for different communities which are consistently classified correctly when partially masking community-related terms, but that are missed when training either on all data or removing all the community-specific training examples.

ture. We highlighted the distinction between two types of PCL. On the one hand, linguistic PCL is concerned with how the message is expressed and is largely community-independent. On the other hand, thematic PCL is more concerned with the message itself, and often relates to aspects that are highly community-specific. Our analysis suggests that for some communities, instances of PCL are mostly linguistic, while for other communities, thematic PCL is more prevalent. Moreover, detecting thematic PCL remains highly challenging in settings where the training data does not include examples covering similar themes. A better understanding of these phenomena can help future work to improve the detection of PCL and, eventually, contribute to more responsible and inclusive communication. As a first step, we envisage that a more fine-grained annotation of PCL detection datasets will be needed, distinguishing between (sub-categories of) linguistic and thematic PCL, to help us train better models and allow for a more insightful evaluation.

8 Ethical and societal implications

With our study of Patronizing and Condescending Language towards vulnerable communities we aim at contributing to more ethical communication. PCL is more subtle and subjective than other kinds of harmful language, such as hate speech or offensive language, but equally damaging, especially when spread by the media. Crucially, the use of PCL is often unintentional, hence developing tools that flag instances of PCL, which could work similarly to spelling and grammar checkers, can bring about meaningful change. This makes PCL detection an important social challenge that should be addressed by the NLP community. Although recent works have shown that fine-tuned language models can identify PCL to some extent, this paper tries to deepen our understanding of the nature of this kind of language,and of the fundamental challenges that still remain to be solved in this area. Among the limitations of this work, we include the small size of the analyzed dataset, as well as the limited number of communities that are covered.

References

Valerio Basile, Cristina Bosco, Elisabetta Fersini, Debora Nozza, Viviana Patti, Francisco Manuel Rangel Pardo, Paolo Rosso, and Manuela Sanguinetti. 2019. Semeval-2019 task 5: Multilingual detection of hate speech against immigrants and women in twitter. In *Proceedings of the 13th International Workshop on Semantic Evaluation*, pages 54–63.

Katherine M Bell. 2013. Raising Africa?: Celebrity and the rhetoric of the white saviour. *PORTAL Journal of Multidisciplinary International Studies*, 10(1).

Dan Caspi and Nelly Elias. 2011. Don't patronize me: media-by and media-for minorities. *Ethnic and Racial Studies*, 34(1):62–82.

Lilie Chouliaraki. 2006. *The spectatorship of suffering*. Sage.

Lilie Chouliaraki. 2010. Post-humanitarianism : Humanitarian communication beyond a politics of pity. *International Journal of Cultural Studies*.

Niall J Conroy, Victoria L Rubin, and Yimin Chen. 2015. Automatic deception detection: Methods for finding fake news. *Proceedings of the Association for Information Science and Technology*, 52(1):1–4.

Giovanni Da San Martino, Alberto Barrón-Cedeno, Henning Wachsmuth, Rostislav Petrov, and Preslav Nakov. 2020. Semeval-2020 task 11: Detection of propaganda techniques in news articles. In *Proceedings of the Fourteenth Workshop on Semantic Evaluation*, pages 1377–1414.

Yong Deng, Chenxiao Dou, Liangyu Chen, Deqiang Miao, Xianghui Sun, Baochang Ma, and Xiangang Li. 2022. Beike nlp at semeval-2022 task 4: Prompt-based paragraph classification for patronizing and condescending language detection. *arXiv preprint arXiv:2208.01312*.

Lynne Díaz-Rico. 2012. *Tools for Discourse Analysis*, pages 149–159. SensePublishers, Rotterdam.

Peter Draper. 2005. Patronizing speech to older patients: A literature review. *Reviews in Clinical Gerontology*, 15(3-4):273–279.

Norman Fairclough. 2013. *Language and power*. Routledge.

Norman Fairclough and Lilie Chouliaraki. 1999. Discourse in late modernity.

Ibrahim Abu Farha, Silviu Vlad Oprea, Steven Wilson, and Walid Magdy. 2022. Semeval-2022 task 6: isarcasmeval, intended sarcasm detection in english and arabic. In *Proceedings of the 16th International Workshop on Semantic Evaluation (SemEval-2022)*, pages 802–814.

Zhida Feng, Jiji Tang, Jiaxiang Liu, Weichong Yin, Shikun Feng, Yu Sun, and Li Chen. 2021. Alpha at semeval-2021 task 6: Transformer based propaganda classification. In *Proceedings of the 15th International Workshop on Semantic Evaluation (SemEval-2021)*, pages 99–104.

Susan T Fiske. 1993. Controlling other people: The impact of power on stereotyping. *American psychologist*, 48(6):621.

Michel Foucault. 1980. *Power/knowledge: Selected interviews and other writings, 1972-1977*. Vintage.

Roger Fowler, Bob Hodge, Gunther Kress, and Tony Trew. 2018. *Language and control*. Routledge.

Howard Giles, Susan Fox, and Elisa Smith. 1993. Patronizing the elderly: Intergenerational evaluations. *Research on Language and Social Interaction*, 26(2):129–149.

Dou Hu, Zhou Mengyuan, Xiyang Du, Mengfei Yuan, Jin Zhi, Lianxin Jiang, Mo Yang, and Xiaofeng Shi. 2022. PALI-NLP at SemEval-2022 task 4: Discriminative fine-tuning of transformers for patronizing and condescending language detection. In *Proceedings of the 16th International Workshop on Semantic Evaluation (SemEval-2022)*, pages 335–343, Seattle, United States. Association for Computational Linguistics.

Thomas Huckin. 2002a. Critical discourse analysis and the discourse of condescension. *Discourse studies in composition*, 155:176.

Thomas Huckin. 2002b. Textual silence and the discourse of homelessness. *Discourse & Society*, 13(3):347–372.

Thomas Huckin, Jennifer Andrus, and Jennifer Clary-Lemon. 2012. Critical discourse analysis and rhetoric and composition. *College composition and communication*, pages 107–129.

Aarish Iyer and Soroush Vosoughi. 2020. Style change detection using bert. In *CLEF (Working Notes)*.

Yinhan Liu, Myle Ott, Naman Goyal, Jingfei Du, Mandar Joshi, Danqi Chen, Omer Levy, Mike Lewis, Luke Zettlemoyer, and Veselin Stoyanov. 2019. RoBERTa: A robustly optimized BERT pretraining approach. *arXiv preprint arXiv:1907.11692*.

Branka Drljača Margić. 2017. Communication courtesy or condescension? linguistic accommodation of native to non-native speakers of english. *Journal of English as a lingua franca*, 6(1):29–55.

Julia Mendelsohn, Yulia Tsvetkov, and Dan Jurafsky. 2020. A framework for the computational linguistic analysis of dehumanization.

Debra L Merskin. 2011. *Media, minorities, and meaning: A critical introduction*. Peter Lang.

Sik Hung Ng. 2007. Language-based discrimination: Blatant and subtle forms. *Journal of Language and Social Psychology*, 26(2):106–122.

David Nolan and Akina Mikami. 2013. 'the things that we have to do': Ethics and instrumentality in humanitarian communication. *Global Media and Communication*, 9(1):53–70.

Jan Oldenburg, Jorge Aparicio, Jörg Beyer, Gabriella Cohn-Cedermark, M Cullen, T Gilligan, U De Giorgi, Maria De Santis, Ronald de Wit, SD Fosså, et al. 2015. Personalizing, not patronizing: the case for patient autonomy by unbiased presentation of management options in stage i testicular cancer. *Annals of Oncology*, 26(5):833–838.

Carla Perez-Almendros, Luis Espinosa-Anke, and Steven Schockaert. 2020. Don't patronize me! an annotated dataset with patronizing and condescending language towards vulnerable communities. In *Proceedings of the 28th International Conference on Computational Linguistics*, pages 5891–5902.

Carla Pérez-Almendros, Luis Espinosa-Anke, and Steven Schockaert. 2022. Pre-training language models for identifying patronizing and condescending language: An analysis. *LREC*.

Carla Perez-Almendros, Luis Espinosa-Anke, and Steven Schockaert. 2022. SemEval-2022 task 4: Patronizing and condescending language detection. In *Proceedings of the 16th International Workshop on Semantic Evaluation (SemEval-2022)*, pages 298–307, Seattle, United States. Association for Computational Linguistics.

Maarten Sap, Saadia Gabriel, Lianhui Qin, Dan Jurafsky, Noah A Smith, and Yejin Choi. 2020. Social bias frames: Reasoning about social and power implications of language. In *Association for Computational Linguistics*.

Paul Simpson. 2003. *Language, ideology and point of view*. Routledge.

Rolf Straubhaar. 2015. The stark reality of the 'white saviour'complex and the need for critical consciousness: A document analysis of the early journals of a freirean educator. *Compare: A Journal of Comparative and International Education*, 45(3):381–400.

Teun A Van Dijk. 2015. Critical discourse analysis. *The handbook of discourse analysis*, pages 466–485.

Ye Wang, Yanmeng Wang, Baishun Ling, Zexiang Liao, Shaojun Wang, and Jing Xiao. 2022. PINGAN ominisinitic at SemEval-2022 task 4: Multi-prompt training for patronizing and condescending language detection. In *Proceedings of the 16th International Workshop on Semantic Evaluation (SemEval-2022)*, pages 313–318, Seattle, United States. Association for Computational Linguistics.

Zijian Wang and Christopher Potts. 2019. Talkdown: A corpus for condescension detection in context. In *Proceedings of the 2019 Conference on Empirical Methods in Natural Language Processing and the 9th International Joint Conference on Natural Language Processing*.

Clint C Wilson and Felix Gutierrez. 1985. Minorities and the media. *Beverly Hills, CA, London: Sage*.

Ruth Wodak. 2004. Critical discourse analysis. *Qualitative research practice*, 185:185–204.

Thomas Wolf, Julien Chaumond, Lysandre Debut, Victor Sanh, Clement Delangue, Anthony Moi, Pierric Cistac, Morgan Funtowicz, Joe Davison, Sam Shleifer, et al. 2020. Transformers: State-of-the-art natural language processing. In *Proceedings of the 2020 Conference on Empirical Methods in Natural Language Processing: System Demonstrations*, pages 38–45.

Marcos Zampieri, Shervin Malmasi, Preslav Nakov, Sara Rosenthal, Noura Farra, and Ritesh Kumar. 2019. Semeval-2019 task 6: Identifying and categorizing offensive language in social media (offenseval). In *Proceedings of the 13th International Workshop on Semantic Evaluation*, pages 75–86.

Marcos Zampieri, Preslav Nakov, Sara Rosenthal, Pepa Atanasova, Georgi Karadzhov, Hamdy Mubarak, Leon Derczynski, Zeses Pitenis, and Çağrı Çöltekin. 2020. Semeval-2020 task 12: Multilingual offensive language identification in social media (offenseval 2020). *arXiv preprint arXiv:2006.07235*.

Naitian Zhou and David Jurgens. 2020. Condolences and empathy in online communities. In *Proceedings of the 2020 Conference on Empirical Methods in Natural Language Processing (EMNLP)*, pages 609–626.

A Appendix: Standard deviation for Table 3.

	Top-100 community-based terms					Top-500 community-based terms					Baseline
	100%	80%	60%	40%	20%	100%	80%	60%	40%	20%	0%
Migr. + Imm.	±4.76	±8.78	±8.56	±6.83	±3.02	±6.82	±6.89	±6.47	±7.24	±6.77	±7.89
Refugees	±3.17	±6.11	±2.81	±3.76	±3.61	±7,72	±1,60	±2,56	±5,30	±4,85	±8.36
In need	±1.19	±1.21	±1.87	±1.45	±3.77	±1.10	±1.65	±2.44	±2.80	±3.46	±3.12
Poor families	±3.31	±03.05	±6.93	±6.24	±4.89	±3.90	±5.92	±5.60	±4.44	±2.62	±6.34
Vulnerable	±6.28	±4.80	±7.90	±3.70	±6.27	±3.33	±2.26	±6.12	±5.35	±2.47	±3.75
Women	±9.92	±5.44	±4.91	±2.74	±3.97	±2.60	±06.05	±8.62	±4.76	±7.10	±8.79
Disabled	±2.81	±5.59	±5.23	±2.42	±4.52	±3.15	±02.06	±4.43	±6.51	±4.54	±5.52
Homeless	±0.79	±2.94	±2.64	±5.22	±1.95	±1.86	±2.63	±03.01	±1.84	±5.74	±1.85
All communities	±1.49	±2.15	±1.70	±1.39	±0.87	±3.59	±1.15	±2.59	±2.59	±1.97	±2.54

Table 10: Standard deviation for Table5 over 5 runs.

BELA: Bot for English Language Acquisition

Muskan Mahajan
Sri Venkateshwar International School
Sector 18, Dwarka
New Delhi
muskanmahajan2004@gmail

Abstract

In this paper, we introduce a conversational agent (chatbot) for Hindi-speaking youth called BELA—Bot for English Language Acquisition. Developed for the young underprivileged students at an Indian non-profit[1], the agent supports both Hindi and Hinglish (code-switched Hindi and English, written primarily with English orthography) utterances. BELA has two interaction modes: a question-answering mode for classic English language learning tasks like word meanings, translations, reading passage comprehensions, etc., and an open-domain dialogue system mode to allow users to practice their language skills.

We present a high-level overview of the design of BELA, including the implementation details and the preliminary results of our early prototype. We also report the challenges in creating an English-language learning chatbot for a largely Hindi-speaking population.

1 Introduction

Our paper introduces 'BELA', Bot for English Language Acquisition, an application of conversational agents (chatbots) in the domain of English language learning. BELA is developed for young underprivileged students at an Indian non-profit called Udayan Care. We were motivated to develop BELA for the students at Udayan Care because we observed a lack of volunteer support by the non-profit's English language mentors, leading to a halt in the mentees' second-language acquisition. Therefore, BELA is intended to emulate an English language mentor for the Udayan Care students, and support the non-profit's volunteers by reducing their workload.

Our conversational agent has two interaction modes: a retrieval mode to facilitate question-answering on classic English tasks like word meanings, translations, reading passage comprehensions, etc. (called the Tutor Bot), and a generative mode to facilitate open-domain chit-chat on general topics like the movies, songs, food, and environment (called the Buddy Bot).

Three tenets have governed the design of BELA:

1. **Support for Hindi utterances**: BELA is developed for a learner population which communicates largely in Hindi and Hinglish language (Hafiz, 2021). BELA's natural language understanding pipeline uses a language identifier, an Indic-language transliterator and a translator to support Hindi and Hinglish utterances.

2. **Reliability of answers to learners' queries**: BELA's responses to thesaurus/meaning-related queries are generated using tested translation and thesaurus APIs.[2]

3. **Graceful failure**: BELA's dialogue management system routes user utterances unrelated to language learning to the generative Buddy Bot.

Some challenges to developing BELA were the lack of data for intent classification and dialogue management, and a lack of a database of reading passages and English videos levelled by learner-proficiency level. Our paper discusses how we overcame these challenges.

Organization: The rest of the paper is organized as follows: We begin with a high-level overview of the Tutor Bot and the Buddy Bot, the two interaction modes of our conversational agent (Section 2); We next discuss the natural language understanding and dialogue management strategy of our conversational agent (Section 3); Further, we discuss in detail the first prototype implementation of the agent (Section 4); We next present related

[1] https://udayancare.org/

[2] https://developer.oxforddictionaries.com/

Proceedings of the Second Workshop on NLP for Positive Impact (NLP4PI), pages 142 - 148
December 7, 2022 ©2022 Association for Computational Linguistics

work (Section 5), and close with concluding remarks (Section 6)

2 Interaction Modes

Our conversational agent has two interaction modes: an English language question-answering mode called the Tutor Bot, and a general chit-chat mode called the Buddy Bot.

2.1 Tutor Bot

Tutor Bot is a retrieval-based response generator that provides answers classic English language learning queries. Some of these tasks as identified by us after a detailed survey with the Udayan Care mentees were: getting reading recommendations, word meanings, word antonyms/synonyms, 'word of the day,' English video recommendations, phrase pronunciations, writing prompts, phrase translations, grammatical/spelling corrections, and advice on the four core English skills (reading, writing, speaking, listening).

Every user utterance routed to the Tutor Bot is classified into one of these ten tasks, termed user intents, by the intent classifier. Further, the utterance is routed to a helper function corresponding to the identified intent. The helper function generates the required response. The design of these helper functions is described in Section 4.

2.2 Buddy Bot

Buddy Bot is a neural response generator that performs chit-chat on the following topics: movies, music, food, and environment. This interaction mode aims to help language learners learn new phrases, prepare the learners for conversations in real-life settings, and also help improve user adherence to the bot.

Buddy Bot uses the text completion endpoint of OpenAI's GPT-3 to generate a response based on the current user utterance and past conversations. The prompt design for the GPT-3 text completion model is discussed in great detail in Section 4.

3 Natural Language Understanding & Dialogue Management

The natural language understanding and dialogue management system of our agent is simple and intuitive.

3.1 Natural Language Understanding

The user utterance is first routed to a language identifier; BELA uses the XLM-RoBERTa Transformer model[3] from HuggingFace for language detection. If the detected language is Hindi, it is run through a Python API for transliteration[4]. The transliterated text, which is in the Devnagari script, is passed through a Transformer-based Machine Translator from Salesken.ai[5].

The final output is an English query that is routed to the dialogue management system, discussed below.

3.2 Dialogue Management

Firstly, the user utterance is routed to the mode classifier of the dialogue management system to classify the query as being related to English learning (for eg: asking for the translation of a sentence) or not (for eg: asking for an opinion on a movie actor).

If the query is unrelated to English learning, it is routed to Buddy Bot. If the query is related to English learning, it is routed to the Tutor Bot. Here, the query is classified into one of ten intents discussed in Section 2. The following section discusses the mode classifier and intent classifier in greater detail.

3.2.1 Mode classifier

The mode classifier is a binary classifier to predict whether a user utterance is related to English learning. To classify the user utterance, we use the output from a BERT encoder as the input to a linear classification layer trained with a crossentropy loss function.

The classifier dataset consists of utterances that are related to English-language learning (positive examples), and general utterances (negative examples). The positive examples were taken from the dataset created for the English-query intent classifier. The general utterances are sampled from user discussions on the following subreddits[6]: r/Food, r/Movies, r/MovieDetails, r/MusicSuggestions, r/AskReddit, r/AskScience, r/Politics, r/AskSocialScience, and r/AskGames.

The training data information is shown in Table 1. And the evaluation results are shown in Table 2.

[3] https://huggingface.co/papluca/xlm-roberta-base-language-detection

[4] https://pypi.org/project/google-transliteration-api/

[5] https://huggingface.co/salesken/translation-hi-en

[6] a subreddit is a forum dedicated to a specific topic on the website Reddit.

3.2.2 English query intent classifier

The query intent classifier is a multi-class classifier to predict the nature of the user's English learning query. The user utterance is classified into one of the following ten intents: *getReadRecommendations, getWordMeaning, getSynonymAntonym, getWordOfTheDay, getPrononciation, getVideoRecommendations, getTranslation, getWritingPrompts, getCorrection*, and *getAdvice*. This classifier uses the output from a BERT encoder as the input to a linear classification layer trained with a crossentropy loss function.

To train our classifier, we created a dataset of utterances and the corresponding intent/query label. Since the training data size is of utmost importance for text classification tasks, we have used text augmentation techniques like back translation, and paraphrase generation using Parrot Paraphraser (Damodaran, 2021). We have also included utterances with spelling mistakes in our dataset to make the classifier robust to the common spelling mistakes made by the language learner.

The training data information is shown in Table 3. And the evaluation results are shown in Table 4.

4 BELA Prototype Implementation

4.1 Tutor Bot Implementation

In the previous section, we discussed that the user utterance/query classified by the mode classifier as related to English learning is routed to the Tutor Bot. Here, the query is classified into one of ten intents by the intent classifier. In the following section, we discuss the helper function related to each user intent of the Tutor Bot, and the datasets used to create them.

4.1.1 Helper-function Datasets

1. **CEFR level predictor dataset**

   This is a dataset[7] provided by Adam Montgomerie to predict the Common European Framework of Reference for Languages (CEFR) level of a blob of text, a measure of English text complexity for an English as Second Language (ESL) learner. The dataset contains 1500 example texts split over the 6 CEFR levels. The texts are a mixture of dialogues, stories, articles, and other formats. (Montgomerie, 2021)

[7]https://github.com/AMontgomerie/CEFR-English-Level-Predictor/tree/main/data

Train	3040
Validation	380
Test	380

Table 1: Mode Classifier Data

Train accuracy	0.998
Test accuracy	0.987

Table 2: Mode Classifier Evaluation Results

   We used these passages for training a TFIDF-based CEFR level predictor which achieves 27.6% more accuracy than the baseline described by Montgomerie (Table 5).

2. **CEFR levelled reading passages**

   We scraped reading passages from an ESL website[8] with free reading exercises and saved them to a file called passages.csv. Subsequently, we passed these passages through the CEFR-predictor trained by us; and stored the passage-CEFR label pairs in a file called cefr-levelled-passages.csv.

   We use these passages for the 'Reading recommendation' helper function discussed in Section 4.1.2.

3. **CEFR levelled word list** We created a list of words and their corresponding CEFR label and stored it in cefr-levelled-words.csv. The list was scraped from English Vocabulary profile[9], a website with information about words and phrases used by learners at each CEFR level.

   We use this list of words for the 'Word of the day' helper function discussed in Section 4.1.2.

4. **CEFR levelled videos**

   We used the TED – Ultimate Dataset[10] from Kaggle to retrieve a set of educational English-language videos, their titles, URLs, descriptions and transcripts. Then, we found the CEFR level of each video using the CEFR level predictor on the video transcripts. The

[8]https://www.myenglishpages.com/english/
[9]https://www.englishprofile.org/wordlists
[10]https://www.kaggle.com/datasets/miguelcorraljr/ted-ultimate-dataset

Train	1520
Validation	190
Test	190

Table 3: Intent Classifier Data

Train accuracy	0.997
Test accuracy	0.995

Table 4: Intent Classifier Evaluation Results

video links, descriptions and their CEFR labels are stored in cefr-levelled-tedtalks.csv.

We use these videos for the 'Video recommendation' helper function discussed in Section 4.1.2.

4.1.2 Helper functions

1. **Reading Recommendation helper function**

   This function prompts the user with four questions[11] to assess their CEFR level, i.e. their English proficiency level. The CEFR level is stored in the chatbot state for other helper functions.

   After determining the CEFR level, the function retrieves a reading passage of the same CEFR level from cefr-levelled-passages.csv. This passage is also accompanied by three multiple-choice questions (MCQs) on the passage to facilitate top and bottom-up processing of the text. (British Council, 2001) The MCQs are generated by OpenAI's GPT-3 fed with a prompt shown in Figure 4.

2. **Word Meaning helper function**

   This function performs the role of identifying the word whose meaning is to be found using regex extraction techniques and providing its definition and examples using the Oxford Thesaurus API.

3. **Synonym-Antonym helper function**

   This function performs the role of identifying the word whose synonym/antonym is to be found using regex extraction techniques and providing it using the Oxford API.

4. **Word of the Day helper function**

   The function provides the user with a new word daily accompanied by its definition and usage to help augment the user's vocabulary. The new word given is in line with the user's CEFR level. The CEFR level is either inferred from the chatbot state or assessed using the four question-survey discussed earlier. The words are retrieved from cefr-levelled-words.csv

5. **Video Recommendation helper function**

   The function provides the user with a TedTalk link, accompanied by its description. The video is in line with the user's CEFR level and provides the learner with an opportunity for language immersion. The video and the description are retrieved from cefr-levelled-tedtalks.csv

6. **Pronunciation helper function**

   This function uses Google Translate's Text-to-Speech API[12] with the language parameter set to 'English' and tld (top-level domain) parameter set to "co.in" to provide pronunciations of English words/phrases in an Indian accent.

7. **Writing prompts helper function**

   This function provides the user with a letter, essay or miscellaneous writing prompt based on their request, to help them improve their writing skills. The prompts are retrieved from writingPrompts.csv.

8. **Grammar/Spelling helper function**

   This function performs the two-pronged role of identifying the phrase/word to be corrected using regex extraction techniques and correcting it using 'Gramformer'. Gramformer[13] is a framework that uses Transformers to detect and correct grammatical errors in natural language text.

9. **Translator helper function**

Baseline Accuracy	41.8%
Train Accuracy	72.2%
Test Accuracy	69.4%

Table 5: CEFR Predictor Evaluation Results

[11] Based on https://bit.ly/CEFR_Self_assessment

[12] https://pypi.org/project/gTTS/

[13] https://github.com/PrithivirajDamodaran/Gramformer

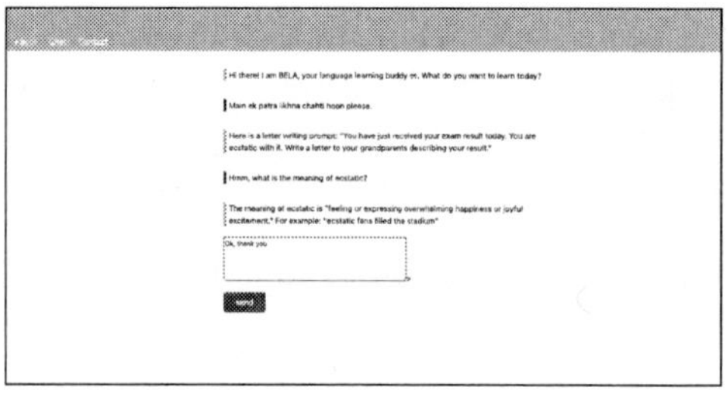

Figure 1: An interaction between the user and the Tutor Bot. Here, the user makes a query in the Hinglish language which translates to "I want to write a letter today."

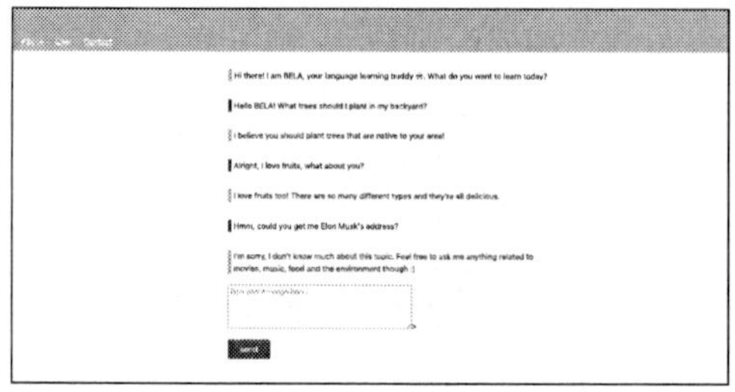

Figure 2: An interaction between the user and the Buddy Bot. Here, the agent politely nudges the user to a relevant topic if they discuss anything beyond movies, music, food and environment.

This function identifies the word/phrase whose translation is to be found from the user utterances using regex extraction techniques; identifies the language of the phrase; and returns a translation. The function uses the XLM-RoBERTa[14] transformer model from HuggingFace for language detection and a Transformer-based Machine Translator from Salesken.ai[15] for Hindi-English translation.

10. **Advice helper function**

    This function provides the user with two pieces of advice for improving each of these English language skills: Listening, Speaking, Reading, and Writing (LSRW). These pieces are taken from credible research focused on LSRW skill acquisition for ESL learners. (Gomathi, 2014)

4.2 Buddy Bot Implementation

Buddy Bot is a neural response generator that performs chit-chat on the following topics: movies, music, food and environment. This interaction mode aims to help language learners learn new phrases, prepare the learners for conversations in real-life settings, and also help improve user adherence to the bot.

Buddy Bot uses the text-completion endpoint of OpenAI's GPT-3 to generate a response based on the current user utterance and past conversation. The text completion model is 'programmed' using a prompt (Figure 3) that provides instruction on how the BuddyBot should function. The prompt gives the text completion model an identity: a "chit-chat bot that talks to users on the topics of movies, music, food and the environment." Before responding to the user, the bot also performs a topic-relevance check- is the user utterance related to one of the four topics? This behaviour was injected into the model by providing two examples to the GPT-3 prompt. If the user-utterance is not related to one of the four topics, the Buddy Bot politely nudges the user to it.

We limited the scope of conversations of the Buddy Bot to just four topics to prevent the extraction of sensitive data, including personally identifiable information (PII) — names, phone numbers, addresses, etc., through training data extraction attacks. (Carlini et al., 2020)

5 Related Work

5.1 Hindi and Hinglish Conversational Agents

Indian telecom companies like Haptik (Haptik.AI, 2021b) and AmplifyReach have developed multilingual chatbots that support Hindi and Hinglish languages. However, these bots are dedicated to the domain of customer service and use proprietary software (Haptik.AI, 2021a) for multilingual natural language understanding.

5.2 Using Dialogue Systems for Learning

Li et al. (2022) developed an online language learning tool to provide learners with conversational experience by using dialog systems as conversation practice partners. The conversational agent simulated a human resource professional interviewing users as potential job candidates; the researchers also explored making the system more adaptive to user profile information by using reinforcement learning algorithms.

In another work, Ruan et al. (2021) created 'EnglishBot', which used Automatic Speech Recognition to converse with students interactively on

[14]https://huggingface.co/papluca/xlm-roberta-base-language-detection

[15]https://huggingface.co/salesken/translation-hi-en

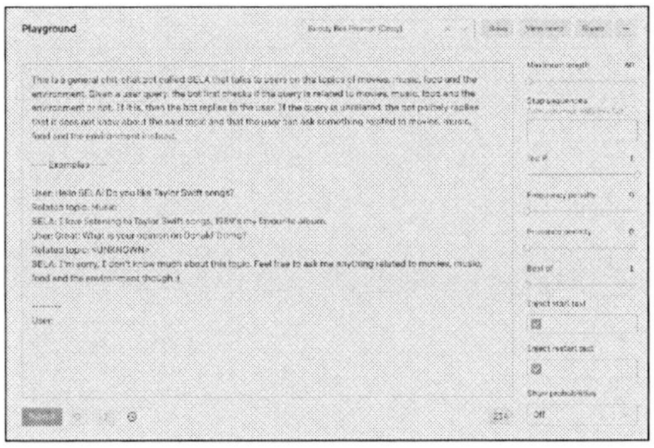

Figure 3: GPT-3 prompt for the Buddy Bot

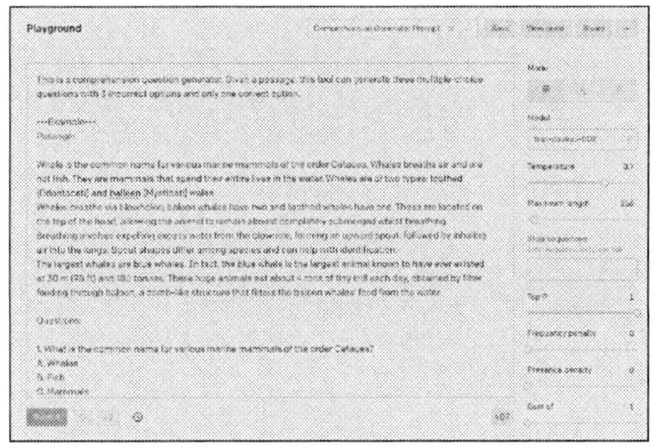

Figure 4: GPT-3 prompt to generate multiple-choice questions (MCQs) of the reading passages.

college-related topics and provided adaptive feedback.

6 Conclusion

BELA is our first step toward making personalised second-language acquisition more accessible to Hindi-speaking learners. Our future work would focus on increasing the range of English learning tasks that BELA can assist with, improving the Hinglish language understanding pipeline and making the dialogue management system more robust to failure.

Limitations

BELA's Tutor Bot can only cater to limited English language learning tasks. Therefore, our future work will focus on adding more skills to the Tutor Bot, including the ability to paraphrase passages, make edits to passages, provide exercises based on grammar topics, etc.

BELA's natural language understanding pipeline tends to translate the named entities in the Hinglish queries. For example, here is a query in the Hinglish language: "Translate *mujhe jio ka sim chahiye* to English." This query literally means "Translate *I want a Jio sim*," where Jio is the name of a telecom company. However, the NLU Pipeline infers Jio as the hindi verb meaning life and outputs the response "I want a live sim."

India also has regional variations of the Hinglish language. As we get more people to use BELA, we aim to use the user messages to improve BELA's natural language understanding pipeline.

Finally, while GPT-3 used in the Buddy Bot provides detailed and context-aware responses to general chit-chat queries, the presence of a pay-wall to the GPT-3 API limits the scalability of the Buddy Bot.

Ethics Statement

In today's globalised economy, English fluency has become important to facilitate communication and improve a person's job prospects. BELA is our first step toward making personalised English-language acquisition more accessible for the young students at Udayan Care. However there are a few ethical challenges to deploying BELA, especially the Buddy Bot interaction mode:

1. **GPT-3 and Toxicity**: The Buddy Bot, which is based on GPT-3, a large-language model, can have the tendency to generate offensive text. Therefore, we have to anticipate and plan for text-generation mishaps either by adding more safeguards to the text generation prompts, or by fine-tuning the Buddy Bot on more examples to make it robust to adversarial user input.

2. **Fine-tuning GPT-3 on Indic-language data**: We need to fine tune the Buddy Bot on Indic-language dialog datasets to allow it to support languages like Hindi and Hinglish. This is a challenge because dialog generation data for low-resource languages is scarce.

References

The British Council. 2001. Top down.

Nicholas Carlini, Florian Tramèr, Eric Wallace, Matthew Jagielski, Ariel Herbert-Voss, Katherine Lee, Adam Roberts, Tom B. Brown, Dawn Song, Úlfar Erlingsson, Alina Oprea, and Colin Raffel. 2020. Extracting training data from large language models. *CoRR*, abs/2012.07805.

Prithiviraj Damodaran. 2021. Parrot: Paraphrase generation for nlu.

B.S. Gomathi. 2014. Enriching the skills of rural students with effective methods of teaching english language using lsrw skills. In *International Journal of Education and Information Studies*, pages 65–69.

Jasmin Hafiz. 2021. https://www.milestoneloc.com/guide-to-hinglish-language/.

Haptik.AI. 2021a. Linguist pro - building multilingual chatbots for business.

Haptik.AI. 2021b. The next big thing for multilingual chatbots: Hinglish.

Yu Li, Chun-Yen Chen, Dian Yu, Sam Davidson, Ryan Hou, Xun Yuan, Yinghua Tan, Derek Pham, and Zhou Yu. 2022. Using chatbots to teach languages. In *Proceedings of the Ninth ACM Conference on Learning @ Scale*, L@S '22, page 451–455, New York, NY, USA. Association for Computing Machinery.

Adam Montgomerie. 2021. Attempting to predict the cefr level of english texts.

Sherry Ruan, Liwei Jiang, Qianyao Xu, Zhiyuan Liu, Glenn M Davis, Emma Brunskill, and James A. Landay. 2021. Englishbot: An ai-powered conversational system for second language learning. In *26th International Conference on Intelligent User Interfaces*, IUI '21, page 434–444, New York, NY, USA. Association for Computing Machinery.

A Appendix

A.1 Helper function datasets

cefr-levelled-passages.csv	Link
cefr-levelled-words.csv	Link
cefr-levelled-tedtalks.csv	Link
writingPrompts.csv	Link

Table 6: Helper function datasets

A.2 Dialogue Management classifier datasets

Mode Classifier Dataset	Link
Intent Classifier Dataset	Link

Table 7: Dialogue Management classifier datasets

A.3 GPT-3 Prompts

Reading Comprehension MCQ	Link
BuddyBot	Link

Table 8: GPT-3 Prompts

Applicability of Pretrained Language Models: Automatic Screening for Children's Language Development Level

Byoung-Doo Oh[1], **Yoon-Kyoung Lee**[2], **and Yu-Seop Kim**[1]
[1]Department of Convergence Software, Hallym University, Republic of Korea
[2]Division of Speech Pathology and Audiology, Hallym University, Republic of Korea
iambd822@gmail.com, {ylee, yskim01}@hallym.ac.kr

Abstract

The various potential of children can be limited by language delay or language impairments. However, there are many instances where parents are unaware of the child's condition and do not obtain appropriate treatment as a result. Additionally, experts collecting children's utterance to establish norms of language tests and evaluating children's language development level takes a significant amount of time and work. To address these issues, dependable automated screening tools are required. In this paper, we used pretrained LM to assist experts in quickly and objectively screening the language development level of children. Here, evaluating the language development level is to ensure that the child has the appropriate language abilities for his or her age, which is the same as the child's age. To do this, we analyzed the utterances of children according to age. Based on these findings, we use the standard deviations of the pretrained LM's probability as a score for children to screen their language development level. The experiment results showed very strong correlations between our proposed method and the Korean language test REVT (REVT-R, REVT-E), with Pearson correlation coefficient of 0.9888 and 0.9892, respectively.

1 Introduction

Language development is directly related to cognitive and intellectual development and is impacted by environmental factors including social interactions such as conversation with parents, etc (Sirbu, 2015). Language delay is the inability of a child to understand or use spoken language appropriately for their age, and it can result in language impairments. Language impairments are disorders of language that has a negative impact on all facets of life, including academic performance and social interaction, and restricts a child's wide range of potential (Bird et al., 1995; Conti-Ramsden and Botting, 2004; Hulme et al., 2020). In this situation, Tomblin et al. (1997) reported that many children with language impairment were not receiving appropriate treatment because their parents were unaware of the child's condition. In addition, many studies anticipate that following the COVID-19 pandemic, quarantine measures including social distancing and mask wearing will include a negative impact on children's language development (Charney et al., 2021; Deoni et al., 2021; Viola and Nunes, 2022).

To address this issue, experts have developed language tests that may be used prior to make diagnosing language impairments. Standardized formal test analyzes linguistic abilities to screening a child's language development level. For example, PPVT-IV (Peaboby Picture Vocabulary Test-IV) (Dunn and Dunn, 2006) and EVT-2 (Expressive Vocabulary Test-II) (Kathleen T. Williams, 2008) evaluate receptive vocabulary and expressive vocabulary, respectively. Language sample analysis (LSA) analyzes linguistic abilities like grammar, pragmatics, and semantics as a measure (Schober-Peterson and Johnson, 1993; Robert E. Owen Jr, 2013). These methods evaluate a child's language development level compared with standardized norms from the same age group's children who have normally developed. In other words, it evaluates if a child has linguistic abilities that are age-appropriate. If a child's scores on these methods are lower than the norm for the same age group, tests to diagnose language impairment are performed. However, moving forward with the standardized formal test and LSA process requires

Proceedings of the Second Workshop on NLP for Positive Impact (NLP4PI), pages 149 - 156
December 7, 2022 ©2022 Association for Computational Linguistics

Topic	Family			
Turn	**Number**	**Person**		**Utterances**
		Interviewer	KR	어제 형이랑 뭐하고 놀았어?
			EN	What did you play with brother yesterday?
1	1	Child	KR	(장난감) 장난감 가지고 놀고 청소도 했어요.
			EN	We played with (toys) toys and cleaned.
	2	Child	KR	그리고 (음) 형이 자꾸 나만 시켜요.
			EN	And (um) my brother keeps making me do it.
		Interviewer	KR	아 그랬구나.
			EN	Oh, I see.
	...			...

Table 1: Example of the data collected by the Hallym Conversation & Pragmatic Assessment Protocol.

a lot of time and work, and the same is true for establishing reliable standardized norm.

Consequently, recent studies tried to an automated screening test that used the acoustic features of children's speech (Maier et al., 2009; Gong et al., 2016). They classified children with speech and language impairments from those with typical development using machine learning which is support vector machine and linear regression. They made it easier to collect data and made it possible to develop a system that could automatically screen for children's speech and language impairments. However, it still has to depend on data to train machine learning models, and cannot be used in another languages. At the same time, they only classified normal and impaired, and it is difficult to distinct the language development level like the existing language tests. In particular, although acoustic features are suitable for discriminating speech impairments due to problems such as speech organs, it is not suitable for discriminating language impairments because it has no linguistic characteristics.

The pretrained language model (pretrained LM), such as GPT2 (Radford et al., 2019) and GPT3 (Brwon et al., 2020), is being developed for a variety of languages and has achieved good performance in a variety of downstream tasks of natural language processing. In the grammatical error correction (GEC) task, studies using only pretrained LM have been performed (Bryant and Briscoe, 2018; Yasunaga et al., 2021). To identify grammatical errors in sentences, Bryant and Briscoe (2018) and Yansunaga et al. (2021) used normalized log probability and probability score, respectively, based on the pretrained LM. The basis for these studies was the observation that grammatical sentences (s_{good}) had a higher probability score of the pretrained LM than non-grammatical sentences (s_{bad}).

$$p(s_{bad}) < p(s_{good}) \quad (1)$$

Based on these characteristics, we focused on a pretrained LM's applicability like unsupervised learning that do not depending on training data for a specific task. In this paper, we used pretrained LM to assist experts in quickly and objectively screening the language development level of children. First, the pretrained LM calculates the probability of a word sequence for each utterance (i.e. sentence) of the child. Following that, a screening score for children's language development level is calculated using the standard deviation of these scores. The advantages of this method are as follows:

- Since it doesn't need procedures like fine-tuning carried out in supervised learning, it doesn't depend on data. As a result, it is relatively free of the cost and time required for data collection.
- It can screen not only children whose language development is slow, but also children whose language development is fast.
- It can be applied in various languages differently from another automated screening methods because pretrained LMs are being developed for various languages.

The format of this paper is as follows. The data we used are described in Section 2. Section 3 describes how to screen children's language development level using pretrained LMs. The

Age	Children	No. of Sentences (Avg)	No. of Tokens
2-year-old	16	69.13	3K
3-year-old	17	104.44	6K
4-year-old	43	89.34	21K
5-year-old	40	83.93	21K
6-year-old	27	102.85	20K
Total	143	89.94	71K

Table 2: Details on our age-specific data.

Type	Details
Maze words	Repetitions
	Revisions
Silence pauses	More than 3 seconds
Inaccurate pronunciation	-

Table 3: Removed word types.

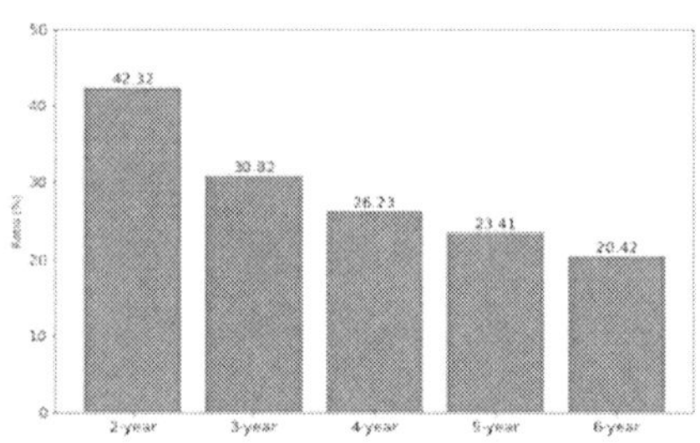

Figure 1: Ratio of age-specific single-word utterances.

experimental settings and results are discussed in Section 4, and our findings and conclusions are compiled in Section 5. Finally, we discuss the ethical considerations and limitations of our proposed method in Section 6.

2 Transcription Data

In the field of speech therapy, a rule called conversation protocol is used to ensure reliability of norms and analysis when collecting children's data (i.e. utterances). Conversation protocols allow only specific topics in the interview, and experts encourage children to speak on their own. As a result, we used the Hallym Conversation & Pragmatic Assessment Protocol (Lee and Choi, 2017) that the Division of Speech Pathology and Audiology at Hallym university created to collect data. Standardized formal test and LSA examine the age-related differences in scores in children who have developed normally in order to verify their norms. So, children between the ages of 2 and 6 who the experts assessed to have developed normally were the subjects of data. The data we used were collected by experts after approved the Institutional Review Board of Hallym University[1]. It is a total of 143 children, and each child includes an average of 89 utterances. Table 1 shows the collected data, while Table 2 shows age-specific details of the data.

The words that are used by people of all ages and make it interrupt to analyze a language development level are indicated with special characters (i.e. symbols) in LSA and then excluded from the analysis. As a result, after analyzing them, we removed these words. These word types are shown in the following Table 3.

Single-word utterances, such as "yes" or "no" and utterances using only proper nouns for people or things, are frequently appeared in children. Because these utterances frequently appear in children of all ages, they interfered with the classification of children's age for language development levels in previous studies based on supervised learning (Oh et al., 2021; Oh et al., 2022). As children grow older, these utterances tend to become less frequent and utterances with complete sentence become more. We believe that this tendency is a useful linguistic characteristic for screening to children's language development level based on pretrained LM. The ratio of these utterances in age-specific children's overall utterances is shown in Figure 1.

[1] The study was conducted according to the guidelines of the Declaration of Helsinki and is approved by the Institutional Review Board of Hallym University (HIRB-2019-036, HIRB-2021-093).

LM	Params	Ratio of $p(s_{bad}) < p(s_{good})$
KoGPT2-SKT	125M	72.7 %
KoGPT3-Kakao	6B	83.2 %

Table 4: Correlation with grammar assessment for Korean pretrained LM's probability.

3 Automatic Screening based on Pretrained LMs

Children's language systems, including their grasp of grammar, steadily improve as they grow older. In this situation, the basis of our proposed method can evaluate the sentence's grammaticality using several values (e.g., probability, normalized log probability, etc) that can be calculated from a pretrained LM (Bryant and Briscoe, 2018; Yasunaga et al., 2021). These characteristics demonstrate the feasibility of using a pretrained LM to screen children's language development level. To screen the child's language development level, we only use the pretrained LM's probability as a score for the child's utterance and calculate the standard deviation of these scores. The rest of this section details more into pretrained LMs which is used in this paper and the scoring method we used to screen for children's language development level.

3.1 Pretrained LMs for Korean

Yasunaga et al. (2021) verified that the pretrained LM's probability may be used to assess the grammaticality of English sentences. Based on GPT2, grammatical sentences (s_{good}) were evaluated highly scores in around 94% of all the data which is consist of (s_{good}, s_{bad}) pairs. So, we verified if the Korean pretrained LM provided the same observations as these experiments.

In this paper, we used KoGPT2[2] (KoGPT2-SKT) released by SK Telecom Co., Ltd and KoGPT3[3] (KoGPT3-Kakao) released by Kakao Corp. as Korean pretrained LMs. Additionally, we used the Korean grammaticality assessment corpus (National Institute of Korean Language) to validate the Korean pretrained LMs. The Korean grammaticality assessment corpus consists of (s_{good} , s_{bad}) pairs. Korean pretrained LMs likewise had the same tendency as the observations of Yasunaga et al. (2021), as shown in Table 4.

3.2 Scoring for language development level

We evaluate the language development level with all utterances the child makes in conversations with experts. Consequently, the score for the utterance was calculated by the probability of a word sequence in the pretrained LM.

$$p(s_i) = P(w_1, w_2, w_3, \dots, w_n) \quad (2)$$

$$p(child) = [p(s_1), p(s_2), \dots, p(s_i)] \quad (3)$$

, where s_i is the i-th utterance and w_n is the n-th word that makes up s_i, $p(s)$ is a score for one utterance, and $p(child)$ is score set calculated for child's all utterances.

However, these scores can be verified as in Equation (1) only by comparing s_{good} and s_{bad} having the same meaning. And the data we used was collected by having a conversation about a specified topic, however these topics have a wide meaning such as family and friend. We may organize these issues into the following three intuitions:

Intuition (1). Relativity of probability distributions for sentences. A grammatical sentence gets a high score based on the pretrained LM's probability. It can evaluate grammaticality in sentences that have the same meaning. As a result, even though they are grammatical sentences, sentences with different meanings have different probability distributions.

Intuition (2). A conversational topic having a wide meaning. Each child might have a different story to tell even about the same topic because the topic is so broad. For example, while talking friends, child-A can talk a story he played with friend, hereas child-B can talk a story about a conflict with friend. In other words, the utterances' contents differ from one another.

Intuition (3). Age-related variations in the frequency of single-word utterances. As shown in Section 2, children use basic positive and negative words like "yes" and "no" less frequently as they grow older. That is, people of all ages use these words.

These intuitions can be summed up as follows: children's utterances have different probability

[2] https://github.com/SKT-AI/KoGPT2

[3] https://github.com/kakaobrain/kogpt

Methods	Age group				
	2-year-old	**3-year-old**	**4-year-old**	**5-year-old**	**6-year-old**
REVT-R	18.04	30.35	44.39	58.18	70.92
REVT-E	20.16	37.06	52.38	64.81	75.06
Ratio of single-word utterances	29.25	19.65	23.43	18.73	21.0
KoGPT2-SKT	12.97	18.43	30.50	34.11	41.55
KoGPT3-Kakao	12.02	16.06	26.84	30.09	36.26

Correlation Coefficient (r)	Ratio of single-word utterances	REVT-R	-0.6451
		REVT-E	-0.6946
	KoGPT2-SKT	**REVT-R**	**0.9888**
		REVT-E	**0.9892**
	KoGPT3-Kakao	REVT-R	0.9876
		REVT-E	0.9868

Table 6: Experiment results of the correlation analysis for our proposed method and REVT.

Age	Average	Max	Min
2-year-old	3.14	18	1
3-year-old	3.88	38	1
4-year-old	5.49	108	1
5-year-old	6.43	72	1
6-year-old	7.27	85	1

Table 5: Details on token length in age-specific sentence.

distributions. For instance, single-word utterances will get a lower score. Additionally, even when speaking on the same topic in complete sentences, the distribution of scores may differ. To utilize pretrained LM's probability correctly, we must get around these limits. We believed that characteristics of linguistic which is universal and changes with age-specific, it may be a key in overcoming these limits. We concluded that the solution is a departure from the single-word utterances that always emerges inside different probability distributions, which can be summarized as follows: (1) The deviation of probability is little since single-word utterance occurs more frequently as the child becomes younger. (2) As children grow older, the deviation of probability is bigger since single-word utterances and utterances with complete sentence appearing appropriately. Consequently, to screen the children's language development levels, we calculated the standard deviation of the $p(child)$.

$$score(child_N) = \sqrt{\frac{(p(s_1)-\mu)^2 + \dots + (p(s_i)-\mu)^2}{i}} \quad (2)$$

, where μ is the average of the pretrained LM's probability for the child's utterances and i is the number of utterances.

4 Results and Discussion

To ensure consistency and reliability of the analysis, LSA chooses 30 to 50 of the utterances made by children and analyzes them as a certain number of utterances (Harris et al., 1986; Ingram, 2002; Trudeau and Sutton, 2011; Andonova, 2015). By omitting this procedure, we aim to provide an automated screening that experts can use easily and quickly. As a result, we evaluated by the child's all utterances. This data, which is detailed in Table 5, includes utterances of various lengths.

REVT (Hong et al., 2009) is a standardized formal test in the Korean language that measures both receptive (REVT-R) and expressive (REVT-E) vocabulary in individuals between the ages of 2 and 16. The norms of REVT-R and REVT-E were constructed by the Seoul Community Rehabilitation Center for the disabled to children who have normally developed of 5,119 and 5,145 individuals, respectively, and provided for use. Consequently, to evaluate the reliability of our proposed method, we evaluated the correlation with the norms of the REVT. The results as shown in Table 6.

Table 6 shows the standardized norms or calculated scores for which each method by age. First, we confirmed whether a simple method, ratio of single-word utterances, could be used as the age-specific score for children's language development level. This is because we confirmed that there was a significant difference by age in Figure 1. But it showed a very low correlation with REVT. Our investigation revealed that the reason was that some children their age used single-word utterance more frequently. Next, we confirmed the possibility of our proposed method. It was able to confirm a strong correlation with REVT. KoGPT2-SKT in particular shown extremely strong correlation with REVT-R and REVT-E, with Pearson correlation coefficients of 0.9888 and 0.9892, respectively. Despite being little less than this, KoGPT3-Kakao also showed a respectable correlation. In actuality, KoGPT3-Kakao is a latest model, and as shown by Table 4, it performs better in grammar assessment. We believe that the somewhat different model structures in the two pretrained LM—as well as the different training dataset—are what caused the difference in the correlation coefficients. These findings demonstrated the potential for using a pretrained LM to address the limitations of language tests, which are expensive, time-consuming, and difficult to utilize across a variety of languages.

5 Conclusion

In this paper, we used pretrained LMs for automated screening and tried to address limitations in the existing language tests, such as the number of data and the diversity of languages. At this time, we preprocessed the utterance by analyzing age-specific linguistic patterns of children to use the pretrained LM efficiently. Additionally, the correlation with REVT, a standardized formal test for Korean language, was evaluated to demonstrate the reliability of our proposed method. The experimental results revealed a strong correlation between our proposed method, which is based on KoGPT2-SKT, and the norms for REVT-R and REVT-E, with Pearson correlation coefficients of 0.9888 and 0.9892, respectively. These observations demonstrate the potential for the pretrained LM to automatically screen children's language development levels and are expected to address several issues with the limitations of language tests such as standardized formal tests and LSA.

Furthermore, we believe that the pretrained LM demonstrated the potential for applicability in various issues needing skills in natural language processing. Future work will focus on make up for automatic screening based on pretrained LMs and investigating automatic transcription methods for collecting children's utterance data using automatic speech recognition.

6 Ethical Considerations and Limitations

If our proposed method is successful, it is possible to screen a child's language development level quickly and objectively prior to having an expert perform a language test. And if a problem is identified at this time, the child can get early diagnostic tests and treatment. Additionally, because expert direct analysis is not included, the language test's cost may be reduced, increasing its accessibility to parents. As the language test gets easier, though, it's possible that unneeded diagnoses and treatments may be provided.

Next, the issues that could occur if our proposed method operates improperly were then taken into consideration as follows: The first is the failure to screening for children who has abnormally developed (recall failure). Recall failure has a problem of missing the treatment time because it cannot properly diagnose and treat a child who has abnormally developed. Second, it involves screening children who has normally developed (precision failure). To children who has normally developed, precision failure can lead in unneeded diagnosis and treatment. We also take into consideration the following potential misuses of this method: Future issues with discrimination might arise if this method is expanded to evaluate children's intellectual development level. In other words, it is possible to discriminate and educate children with high and low developmental levels, which undermining the fundamental purpose of education. Consequently, this method should be performed under strictly managed by a group of experts in relevant fields, such as language pathology or speech therapists.

Technically, the method we propose relies solely on a pretrained LMs; no extra learning, such as fine-tuning, is involved. Consequently, this method is relatively free to the bias issue that training data in supervised learning might bring. The bias of the corpus that was used to develop the pretrained LM at this time may cause some concern. However, the appropriacy and factuality of a sentence's content are not factors we believe should be taken into consideration when evaluating a child's language development level. And, since this technique does not need for extra training, it does not consider the data collection from users. Although we cannot collect it directly right now since speech recognition technique is not being employed, but this will change as technique advances. Consequently, these applications must adhere to research ethics regulations such as the IRB for data collection.

Finally, the test results of our proposed method, including the language test, may vary depending on the level of participation like the child's sociable or active nature. Consequently, we have to take these into consideration as well.

Acknowledgments

This work was supported by the National Research Foundation of Korea (NRF) grant funded by the Korea government (MSIT) (No. 2022R1A5A8019303), Institute of Information & communications Technology Planning & Evaluation (IITP) grant funded by the Korea government (MIST) [No.2021-0-02068, Artificial Intelligence Innovation Hub (Artificial Intelligence Institute, Seoul National University)], and ′R&D Program for Forest Science Technology (Project No. 2021390A00-2123-0105)′ provided by Korea Forest Service (Korea Forestry Promotion Institute).

References

Elena Andonova. 2015. Parental report evidence for toddlers' grammar and vocabulary in Bulgarian. *First Language*, 35(2):126-136.

Judith Bird, Dorothy VM. Bishop, Norman H. Freeman. 1995. Phonological awareness and literacy development in children with expressive phonological impairments. *Journal of Speech, Language, and Hearing Research*, 38(2):446-462.

Tom B. Brown, Benjamin Mann, Nick Ryder, Melanie Subbiah, Jared Kaplan, Prafulla Dhariwal, Arvind Neelakantan, Pranav Shyam, Girish Sastry, Amanda Askell, Sandhini Agarwal, Ariel Herbert-Voss, Gretchen Krueger, Tom Henighan, Rewon Child, Aditya Ramesh, Daniel M. Ziegler, Jeffrey Wu, Clemens Winter, Christopher Hesse, Mark Chen, Eric Sigler, Mateusz Litwin, Scott Gray, Benjamin Chess, Jack Clark, Christopher Berner, Sam McCandlish, Alec Radford, Ilya Sutskever, and Dario Amodei. 2020. Language Models are Few-Shot Learners. *Advances in neural information processing systems*, 33, pages 1877-1901.

Christopher Bryant and Ted Briscoe. 2018. Language model based grammatical error correction without annotated training data. In *Proceedings of 13th workshop on innovative use of NLP for building educational applications*, pages 247-253, New Orleans, Louisiana. Association for Computational Linguistics.

Sara A. Charney, Stephen M. Camarata, Alexander Chem. 2021. Potential impact of the COVID-19 pandemic on communication and language skills in children. *Otolaryngology–Head and Neck Surgery*, 165(1):1-2.

Gina Conti-Ramsden and Nicola Botting. 2004. Social difficulties and victimization in children with SLI at 11 years of age. *Journal of Speech, Language, and Hearing Research*, 47(1):145-161.

Sean CL. Deoni, Jennifer Beauchemin, Alexandra Volpe, Viren D'Sa, Resonance Consortium. 2021. Impact of the COVID-19 pandemic on early child cognitive development: initial findings in a longitudinal observational study of child health. MedRxiv:2021.08.10.21261846. Version 2.

Lloyd M. Dunn and Duglas M. Dunn. 2007. *Peabody Picture Vocabulary Test Fourth Edition.* Bloomington, MN: NCS Pearson Inc.

Jen J. Gong, Maryann Gong, Dina Levy-Lambert, Jordan R. Green, Tiffany P. Hogan, John V. Guttag. 2016. Towards an Automated Screening Tool for Developmental Speech and Language Impairments. In *Proceedings of 17th Annual Conference of the International Speech Communication Association*, pages 112-116.

Margaret Harris, David Jones, Susan Brookes, Julia Grant. 1986. Relations between the non-verbal context of maternal speech and rate of language development. *British journal of developmental psychology*, 4(3):261-268.

Gyung-Hun Hong, Young-Tae Kim, Kyung-Hee Kim. 2009. Content and Reliability Analyses of the Receptive and Expressive Vocabulary Test (REVT). *Korean Journal of Communication Disorders*, 14(1):34-45. [in Korean].

Charles Hulme, Margaret J. Snowling, Gillian West, Arne Lervåg, Monica Melby-Lervåg. 2020. Children's language skills can be improved: Lessons from psychological science for educational policy. *Current Directions in Psychological Science*, 29(4):372-377.

David Ingram. 2002. The measurement of whole-word productions. *Journal of Child Language*, 29(4):713-733.

Yoon-Kyoung Lee and Ji-Eun Choi. 2017. *Hallym conversation and pragmatic assessment protocol*. Manuscript in preparation.

Andreas M. Maier, Tino Haderlein, U Eysholdt, Frank Rosanowski, Anton Batliner, Maria E. Schuster, Elmar Nöth. 2009. PEAKS–A system for the automatic evaluation of voice and speech disorders. *Speech Communication*, 51(5):425-437.

National Institute of Korean Language. 2021. *National Institute of the Korean Language Grammaticality Assessment Corpus*, Version 1.1. [in Korean].

Byoung-Doo Oh, Yoon-Kyoung Lee, Hye-Jeong Song, Jong-Dae Kim, Chan-Young Park, Yu-Seop Kim. 2021. Age group classification to identify the progress of language development based on convolutional neural networks. *Journal of Intelligent & Fuzzy Systems*, 40(4):7745-7754.

Byoung-Doo Oh, Yoon-Kyoung Lee, Jong-Dae Kim, Chan-Young Park, Yu-Seop Kim. 2022. Deep Learning-Based End-to-End Language Development Screening for Children using Linguistic Knowledge. *Applied Sciences*, 12(9):4651-4664.

Robert E. Owen Jr. 2013. *Language disorders: A functional approach to assessment and intervention 6th Ed.* Allyn and Bacon, Boston, MA.

Debra Schober-Peterson and Cynthia J. Johnson. 1993. The performance of eight-to ten-year-olds on measures of conversational skilfulness. *First Language*, 13(38):249-269.

Alec Radford, Jeffrey Wu, Rewon Child, David Luan, Dario Amodei, Ilya Sutskever. 2019. Language Models are Unsupervised Multitask Learners. *OpenAI blog*, 1(8):9.

Anca Sirbu. 2015. The significance of language as a tool of communication. *Scientific Bulletin" Mircea cel Batran" Naval Academy*, 18(2):405.

Bruce J. Tomblin, Nancy L. Records, Paula Buckwalter, Xuyang Zhang, Elaine Smith, Marlea O'Brien. 1997. Prevalence of specific language impairment in kindergarten children. *Journal of speech, language, and hearing*, 40(6):1245-1260.

Natacha Trudeau and Ann Sutton. 2011. Expressive vocabulary and early grammar of 16- to 30-month-old children acquiring Quebec French. First Language, 31:480-507.

Thiago Wendt Viola and Magda Lahorgue Nunes. 2022. Social and environmental effects of the COVID-19 pandemic on children. *Jornal de pediatria*, 98:4-12.

Kathleen T. Williams. 2007. *Expressive Vocabulary Test Second Edition*. Circle Pines, MN: AGS Publishing.

Michihiro Yasunaga, Jure Leskovec, Percy Liang. 2021. LM-Critic: Language Models for Unsupervised Grammatical Error Correction. In *Proceedings of 2021 Conference on Empirical Methods in Natural Language Processing*, pages 7752-7763, Online and Punta, Dominican Republic. Association for Computational Linguistics.

Transformers-Based Approach for a Sustainability Term-Based Sentiment Analysis (STBSA)

Blaise W. Sandwidi
CEG Department
International Finance Corporation (IFC)
2121 Pennsylvania Avenue N.W.,
Washington, DC 20433 U.S.A
bsandwidi@ifc.org

Suneer P. Mukkolakal
ITS Department
The World Bank
1818 H Street, N.W.,
Washington, DC 20433 U.S.A
spallitharammalm@worldbankgroup.org

Abstract

Traditional sentiment analysis is a sentence-level or document-level task. However, a sentence or paragraph may contain multiple target terms with different sentiments, making sentiment prediction more challenging. Although pre-trained language models like BERT have been successful, incorporating dynamic semantic changes into aspect-based sentiment models remains difficult, especially for domain-specific sentiment analysis. To this end, in this paper, we propose a Term-Based Sentiment Analysis (TBSA), a novel method designed to learn **Environmental, Social, and Governance (ESG)** contexts based on a sustainability taxonomy for ESG aspect-oriented sentiment analysis. Notably, we introduce a technique enhancing the ESG term's attention, inspired by the success of attention-based neural networks in machine translation (Bahdanau et al., 2015) and Computer Vision (Bello et al., 2019). It enables the proposed model to focus on a small region of the sentences at each step and to reweigh the crucial terms for a better understanding of the ESG aspect-aware sentiment. Beyond the novelty in the model design, we propose a new dataset of 125,000+ ESG analyst-annotated data points for sustainability term-based sentiment classification, which derives from historical sustainability corpus data and expertise acquired by development finance institutions. Our extensive experiments combining the new method and the new dataset demonstrate the effectiveness of the Sustainability TBSA model with an accuracy of 91.30% (90% F1-score). Both internal and external business applications of our model show an evident potential for a significant positive impact toward furthering sustainable development goals (SDGs).

1 Introduction

In 2015, the United Nations (UN) adopted the 2030 Agenda and its 17 Sustainable Development Goals (SDGs; Nations (2015)), addressing global challenges including poverty, inequality, climate change, environmental degradation, peace, and justice. The Secretary General's Roadmap for financing this collective and transnational effort invites all stakeholders to consider environmental, social, and governance (ESG) issues. ESG matters have assumed relevance for investors, regulators, and industry participants, while ESG criteria are increasingly used to measure the impact of investment activities on sustainable development. However, ESG-integrated investing remains challenging, even for world-class asset managers, institutional investors, and pension funds, because of data gaps in coverage of emerging markets and a lack of analytical capacity. Further, these markets present the greatest opportunities for investors to achieve impacts through the SDGs because their development needs are the most significant.

At the same time, there is growing recognition of the fundamental role played by data, primarily structured data, in achieving the objectives set out in the SDGs (Griggs et al., 2013; Nilsson et al., 2016; Conforti et al., 2020; Vinuesa et al., 2020). Structured data and SDG metrics are essential to ensure the successful design of local projects but are often absent when required for insights into beneficiaries' needs and values (Conforti et al., 2020). Unstructured data can provide such insights. Natural language processing (NLP) techniques can process such qualitative data to provide relevant facts and figures to project developers. Expected benefits are time and cost reductions, higher operations efficiencies, due diligence improvements, and better sustainability impact assessments (Conforti et al., 2020; Sokolov et al., 2021; Ulibarri et al., 2019). Recent progress in masked language modeling such as Google BERT (bidirectional encoder representations from transformers, (Devlin et al., 2019), RoBERTa (robustly optimized BERT approach (Liu et al., 2019)), and DeBERTa (decoding-enhanced BERT, (He et al., 2021))—combined

Proceedings of the Second Workshop on NLP for Positive Impact (NLP4PI), pages 157 - 170
December 7, 2022

with cloud computing, is unlocking the potential for creating analytical capacity to assess unstructured data at scale and is facilitating SDG-aligned financing for emerging markets to address the $4.2 trillion USD annual shortfall in investments needed to meet the SDGs (OECD, 2020).

Despite these advances, NLP research and applications that contribute to sustainable development are absent (Conforti et al., 2020). This gap is attributed to the lack of high-quality sustainability data and the scarcity of relevant labeled data to train sustainability-domain language models. Our work proposes a sustainability-domain adaptation of transformer-based models to perform various NLP tasks, such as ESG term extraction and sentiment analysis. Such a sustainability domain-specific language model is a significant advance; pre-trained models and commercial sentiment analysis solutions perform poorly at predicting ESG sentiments because of differences in domain-specific vocabulary (these models are trained using datasets such as restaurant or movie reviews or tweets that are not relevant to sustainability analysis). Domain-specific models are also necessary to process sustainability reporting documents which are typically lengthy, complex, and use terms that do not carry emotional connotations, unlike movie or restaurant reviews. Hence the need to create a specific taxonomy for context-based ESG sentiment analysis (Ulibarri et al., 2019).

Development finance institutions have decades of archival sustainability data created from project due diligence and monitoring. We use examples of such data to create a unique ESG taxonomy and human-annotated dataset. Namely, we equip two pre-trained language models (RoBERTa and DeBERTa) to understand ESG context by fine-tuning and modifying the models into a sustainability term-based sentiment analysis (STBSA) model, thereby creating a new approach based on an ESG taxonomy of more than 1,200 terms. We then train the models with human-annotated data to predict the context of ESG terms in sentences and classify words by positive, negative, or neutral ESG sentiment. Significantly, our experiments find that the STBSA model (based on RoBERTa) performs with 91.30% accuracy (90% F1-score) and outperforms the current state-of-the-art baseline models for sentiment analysis tasks.

2 Related Work

Aspect-based Sentiment Analysis. In the beginning, work on sentiment analysis mainly focused on identifying the overall sentiment of a unit of text. The amount of text varied from an entire document (Pang et al., 2002; Turney, 2002) to merely paragraphs or sentences (Hu and Liu, 2004). However, only considering the overall sentiment fails to capture the sentiments over the aspects on which an entity can be reviewed or sentiment expressed toward different entities. To remedy this, two new tasks have been introduced: aspect-based sentiment analysis (ABSA) and targeted sentiment analysis. Aspect-based sentiment analysis assumes a single entity per unit of analysis and tries to identify sentiments towards different aspects of the entity (Lu et al., 2011; Lakkaraju et al., 2014; Alghunaim, 2015; Bagheri et al., 2013; Brody and Elhadad, 2010). However, it considers only one single entity in the given text.

Target-based or target sentiment analysis is another task that identifies polarity towards a target entity, as opposed to over an entire volume of text (Saeidi et al., 2016; Mitchell et al., 2013; Jiang et al., 2011; Dong et al., 2014; Vo and Zhang, 2015). Jiang et al. (2011) were the first to propose targeted sentiment analysis on Twitter. They demonstrated the importance of targets by showing that 40% of sentiment errors are due to not considering them in classification. However, this task only identifies the overall sentiment, and the existing corpora consist only of text with one single entity per unit of analysis. This task caters to more generic text by making fewer assumptions while extracting fine-grained information.

ESG-domain transformers-based models. In recent years, transformer-based models have become the default solution for NLP tasks such as search, machine translation, or sentiment analysis (Tunstall et al., 2022). Only a few studies apply language models to the sustainability area. ClimateBERT, proposed by Bingler et al. (2021), analyzes companies' climate risk using the Task Force on Climate-Related Financial Disclosures framework. Another application, developed by Ulibarri et al. (2019), is an artificial neural network classifier for modeling environmental impact statement documents from the US Environmental Protection Agency. Finally, Nugent et al. (2020) demonstrate that fine-tuning BERT using large amounts of business and financial news data from the Reuters News

Archive led to better results with classification tasks such as detecting ESG controversies.

Terms-based sentiment analysis. Term-based sentiment analysis is particularly valuable in domain-specific text, which very much resembles how a human domain expert comprehends this text content. Domain-specific text such as sustainability reporting documents are very complex, often ambiguous, and may have multiple target terms in a single sentence. Moreover, the same terms may have different meanings or polarity depending on the context in which they appear (Ulibarri et al., 2019), demanding a different approach. Zhang et al. (2022) show that previous methods for aspect-based sentiment models are unable to achieve the same performance as human-level sentiment understanding. Additionally, Bahdanau et al. (2015) argue that basic encoder-decoder architecture with a fixed-length vector is a bottleneck in improving those models' performance. Inspired by the above research, both aspect-based sentiment and transformers-based architectures, we proposed a novel architecture that addresses the issue of long and complex sentences by expending the ABSA to emphasize parts of a source sentence that are relevant to predicting ESG sentiment.

3 Methodology

Most aspect-based sentiment analysis methodologies comprise multi-grained NLP tasks and consist of two major subtasks: target term extraction and sentiment classification (Yang et al., 2021). Accordingly, this section introduces our approach for ESG terms selection and extraction and presents the model design for conducting ESG sentiment classification.

3.1 ESG Taxonomy Development and Extraction

ESG taxonomy. This work uses an ESG risk taxonomy or collection of ESG terms based on the International Finance Corporation's (IFC) Environmental and Social Performance Standards and Corporate Governance Methodology.[1] The eight Environmental and Social Performance Standards and the six Corporate Governance Methodology parameters provide the highest level of aggregation of the taxonomy. The lowest level comprises 1,200 unique ESG risk terms (with more than 4,750 variations, including acronyms, abbreviations, and spelling variants). This taxonomy organizes information by IFC performance Standards, ESG subthemes, and topics and is compatible with sustainability disclosure standards such as the UN SDGs, the Global Reporting Initiative (GRI), and the Sustainability Accounting Standards Board (SASB) framework. Details on the whole structure of the taxonomy can be viewed in Appendix A.

ESG terms selection. Three rules govern the creation of the ESG term taxonomy. First, the relevance of the term within the text to ESG context, such as "endangered species," "child labor," "water pollution," "climate change," "biodiversity impacts," or "gender-based violence." Second, avoidance of broader concepts and stop words. For example, rather than use words like "water," we use specific composites such as "potable water," "water pollution," and "drinking water." Third, the use of nouns rather than adjectives as adjectives may qualify a wide variety of nouns, are often unspecific, and can increase instances of false positives. In addition to these rules, we use unsupervised machine learning techniques to add new risk terms and incorporate emerging ESG topics.

3.2 Sustainability-Domain Model Architecture

Problem statement and ESG sentiment definition. A **positive** ESG sentiment is a statement that expresses the perception of a company's or project's positive impact(s) on society or the absence of ESG risk. For instance, a statement such as "The company managed to significantly limit the risk of child labor in the supply chain" is considered positive in line with IFC's ESG standards. In contrast, a negative ESG sentiment is a statement that indicates a lack of compliance with IFC's ESG standards or the occurrence of an ESG risk event. For instance: "Evidence has surfaced of a

[1]IFC's Performance Standards on Environmental and Social Sustainability are a global benchmark for sustainability practices. To date, 130 financial institutions in 38 countries have adopted the Equator Principles, based on these standards. Leading development institutions—including the European Bank for Reconstruction and Development and the Asian Development Bank—adopted practices rooted in these standards. Between 2006 and 2016, an estimated US$4.5 trillion in investments across emerging markets adhered to IFC's standards or to principles inspired by them (Corporation, 2016). In 2011, IFC was the first development financial institution (DFI) to require corporate governance analysis for every investment transaction as part of its due diligence process. IFC's Corporate Governance Methodology evaluates the corporate governance risks and opportunities of client companies. It was distilled into the Corporate Governance Development Framework used by 34 DFIs in their investment processes

widespread use of child labor in the cocoa sector in emerging markets". **Neutral** ESG sentiments are factual statements that either refer to an ESG context but do not express positive or negative sentiments or are irrelevant in the ESG context. ESG terms used for labeling purposes do not per se imply positive or negative sentiments, even if a word may be considered positive (e.g., training) or negative (e.g., penalties and fines). Only the context in which these terms are used matters. Therefore, while the term "child labor" may be linked with a negative sentiment, stating **the absence of child labor** expresses a positive ESG sentiment. Finally, the sentence's structure can be complex, with multiple target terms. For instance: "The world's largest chocolate manufacturers provided support in addressing large-scale deforestation in the cocoa sector, but there is still evidence of child labor in the supply chain." When considering "deforestation" and "child labor", a traditional sentiment classification will fail to identify the correct sentiments. Hence the need to develop an approach which can handle the complexity and potential ambiguity of words and sentences expressing ESG sentiments.

The new approach. To meet this challenge, we propose to extend previous aspect-based sentiment works (Tang et al., 2016; Zhang et al., 2022) by enabling the transformer-based model to automatically and explicitly emphasize parts of a source sentence that are relevant to predicting a target word polarity. We call this novel architecture **ESG terms attention augmentation**. It is inspired by the success of attention-based neural networks in machine translation (Bahdanau et al., 2015) and Computer Vision (Bello et al., 2019). Its design and functioning are described in detail below.

A sentence-aspect pair (S, A_t) is given. The sentence is represented as $S = \{w_1^s, w_2^s, w_3^s, ..., w_n^s\}$ which consists of series of n words. The ESG aspect, also called a risk term is denoted as $A_t = \{w_1^a, w_2^a, w_3^a, .., w_t^a\}$ which is a part of S. A sentence S may consist of one or more ESG risk terms. STBSA aims to build a sentiment classifier that can precisely predict the ESG sentiment of sentence S for a specific ESG risk term, including multiple target terms with different sentiments. The overall architecture of the STBSA model, adapted from Zhang et al. (2022), is illustrated in Figure 1.

ESG terms attention augmentation. Because a sentence may contain multiple target terms that describe different sentiments that are difficult to predict using BERT or RoBERTa, we propose an innovative approach to achieve STBSA via transformer-based models. (Sun et al., 2019) and (Zhang et al., 2022) show improvements to the attention mechanic for sentiment analysis tasks based on transformer models by constructing an auxiliary sentence in addition to the original sentence. Similarly, we annotate and copy target words from sentences during pre-processing and create two copies of such terms in the sentence—one at the beginning and one in its original position. This modification of the sentence structure has two advantages: First, since the text input is changed, the outputs of the transformer-based model differ. Second, since an additional target term appears at the beginning of the sentence, its frequency increases and gains more attention in the model.

Human expert annotations. We designed a rigorous process to prepare a human-annotated training dataset with the labeling rules described in annotator guidelines. Three criteria are used to select the ESG documents to annotate: Relevance, Reliability, and Vintage. Content relevance is determined by the potential of text to support decisions, such as company sustainability reports and ESG-related news reports. Reliability refers to a qualified source of data and analysis prepared or reviewed by ESG experts. Data vintage is ascertained by using current sources, with a preference for the most recent data. The training dataset comprises three ESG sentiment types – positive, negative, and neutral – which are manually assigned to each sentence based on the targeted term.

Model fine-tuning procedure. We embrace a data-centric artificial intelligence (AI) strategy by proposing a sustainability-domain algorithm based on high-quality labeled data provided by human experts. Our model uses a transfer learning technique, used with success in computer vision, to train a convolutional neural network on one task and then adapt it to a new task (Tunstall et al., 2022). The fine-tuned model comprises the model body (initially trained for masked word predictions) and the custom classification head. During transfer learning, the body weights from general-purpose language models (the RoBERTa and DeBERTa corpus) are used for initialization, a starting point to create the sustainability domain-specific model based on the custom ESG taxonomy and human-annotated ESG data.

Hyperparameter settings. Meta AI and Mi-

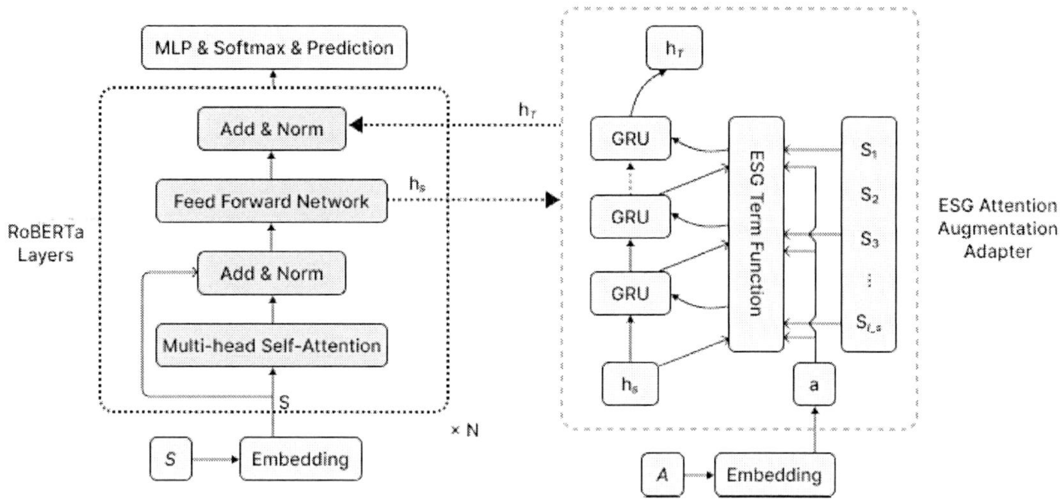

Figure 1: shows the STBSA framework adapted from Zhang et al. (2022). The blue blocks are the pre-trained RoBERTa model, which is frozen during the fine-tuning steps. The right green blocks represent the "ESG term attention augmentation" modifications performed during the fine-tuning, on top of the RoBERTa layers and with ESG-expert annotated data.

crosoft released the pre-trained RoBERTa and DeBERTa models on Hugging Face. [2] Our best performing fine-tuned RoBERTa is composed of the pre-trained RoBERTa layers and a custom classification head, consisting of two hidden layers (of 786 and 56 dimensions) and a softmax output layer (of 3 dimensions). The best and most stable model was found with 8 epochs, 0.1 dropout rate, 32 as batch size, 5e-6 as learning rate, 42 seed values, and 800 of the model's warm-up steps. We used the warm-up optimization strategy (He et al., 2016) by training the model with a varying learning rate along with all the training steps. A linear scheduler initialized the learning rate with a value near zero. After 800 training steps, the learning rate reached a preset peak value (5e-6) and slowly decreased.

3.3 Machine Learning Operations and Bias Management Process

Experiment context. As NLP models have shown a good level of accuracy in classifying general English language sentiments, we were challenged by the black-box nature of the neural models and inherent bias that training data poses. This motivated us to start developing a Proof of Concept (POC), led by the World Bank Group Technology and Innovation Lab, which successfully validated the use of LIME (Ribeiro et al., 2016), SHAP (Lundberg and Lee, 2017), and Fairlearn (Bird et al., 2020) in understanding the model behavior and fine-tuning the model to avoid bad bias.

Machine learning operations (MLOps). Training models to achieve acceptable accuracy and F1-scores requires robust processes to monitor data drift and retrain models to perform consistently on new input data. Such methods must include approaches to understand model biases and explain performance. Our research advances the use of Explainable AI frameworks and techniques to improve understanding of model performance. A mature MLOps and data management process is the cornerstone of training a trustworthy and fair model (Schwartz et al., 2022). Our experiments applied the MLOps process described in Figure 2. This approach has four domains: Domain Data, Data Science, Trust Analysis, and Consumption. All four parts maintain feedback loops to each other to achieve the overall objective of increasing the quality of ML inferences.

Figure 2 describes the process, which starts with domain data experts collecting, cleaning, and analyzing input data. Labeled data is quality assured by evaluating inter-annotator agreements. This approach prevents individual labeler bias from impacting the model. Next, the data science stage focuses on training and testing the model with labeled data. Section 4.2 describes model selection and performance metrics. Following this, the Trust Analysis step centers on model evaluation. This step

[2]RoBERTa base: `https://huggingface.co/roberta-base`; DeBERTa base: `https://huggingface.co/microsoft/deberta-base`.

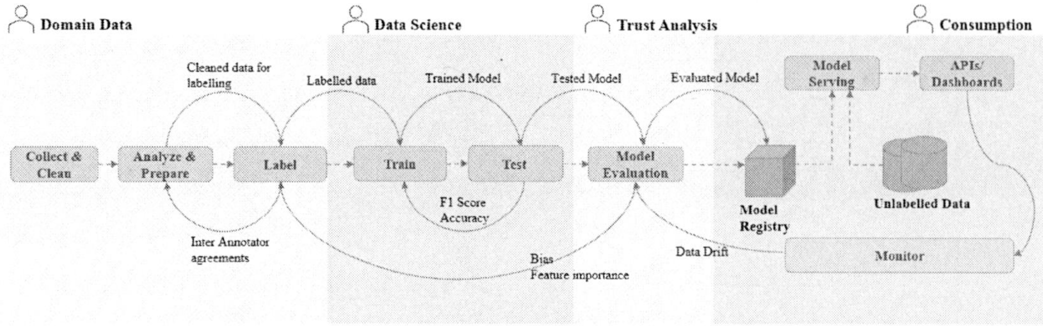

Figure 2: Phases of MLOps

determines if the model has any unforeseen biases that may skew the results. We experimented with LIME (local interpretable model-agnostic explanations, Ribeiro et al. (2016)) and SHAP (Shapley additive explanations, (Lundberg and Lee, 2017)) to understand how the model makes predictions. Model sensitivity analysis and feedback are provided to domain experts and data scientists to adjust the labeled data and model architecture.

Lastly, models are published in the model registry for the final step, Consumption. The model serving component uses the most recent version of the model from the model registry and predicts outcomes on API or Batch requests. Subsequently, model monitoring provides feedback at the model evaluation stage to assess data drift. The key theme of this proposal is that any production-grade AI/ML system must be a multi-stakeholder and interdisciplinary undertaking. An MLOps model brings forth these experts systematically and collectively works to make the model's prediction more relevant to the business problem that the model is trying to address.

4 Experiment

4.1 Experiment Settings

Proposed Dataset. Using rules outlined in ESG sentiment annotation guidelines, six ESG analysts worked over 1.5 years to refine the ESG taxonomy and produce labeled data for model training. The final training dataset comprised 126,480 sentences taken from ESG news, IFC internal project documentation, project evaluations by the World Bank Group Independent Evaluation Group, IFC Compliance Advisor Ombudsman project assessment reports, and publicly available information, including IFC ESG project disclosures and public disclosures by listed companies including annual and sustainability reports. The labeled dataset is presented in Table 1.

Quality assurance of labeled data. ESG sentiment annotation guidelines and inter-annotator agreement metrics ensure the creation of high-quality training data. Only sentences with consensus from at least two labelers are eligible as training data to mitigate the risk of conflicting labels. Consistency of labeling among annotators or inter-annotator agreement is tracked using Cohen's kappa coefficient, which measures the reliability of agreement between two labelers, considering the possibility that agreements could occur by chance (Cohen, 1960). In addition to Cohen's kappa, the percentage of inter-annotator agreement is used as a secondary quality indicator. These annotator agreement metrics improve the consistency of training data and manage inevitable differences between annotators (Pustejovsky and Stubbs, 2012; Bobicev and Sokolova, 2017). The average Cohen's kappa value was 0.75, indicating substantial agreement among labelers.

Train, validation, and test datasets. The final labeled set of 126,480 sentences comprised 37,054 (29%) positive, 27,579 (22%) negative, and 61,847 (49%) neutral labels. We randomly split this set into 107,540 sentences (85%) designated for model training and validation and 18,940 sentences (15%) for model evaluation. The subsets' class distribution is similar to the final set labeled above.

4.2 Experiment Results

Pre-trained model performance. Table 2 shows accuracy and F1-scores for the pre-trained RoBERTa-base and DeBERTa-base models on the test set. As expected, pre-trained models poorly predict ESG sentiments without domain-specific

ESG document type	Sentence count	Positive labels	Negative labels	Neutral labels
ESG news report	35,560	33.38%	26.34%	40.26%
IFC internal project documents	29,796	34.80%	18.36%	46.83%
Public company disclosures	19,213	26.96%	10.44%	62.60%
Public DFI project disclosures	31,900	29.35%	15.86%	54.79%
Independent project evaluations	10,011	2.70%	56.65%	40.64%
Total	**126,480 (100%)**	**37,054 (29%)**	**27,579 (22%)**	**61,847 (49%)**

Table 1: ESG sentiment labeled dataset

training. Most predictions are neutral. Pre-trained models can assess context information in ESG text but are less successful at predicting positive and negative ESG sentiments as these models are not trained on these types of labels.

Baseline model performance. For a further baseline comparison, we used the Fin-BERT model (Araci, 2019) as a benchmark to compare the performance of our model. Three arguments justify this choice: the domain proximity of financial and sustainability reporting (Nugent et al., 2020; IIRC, 2011); the FinBERT model's availability and usage metrics on open-source platforms, notably on Hugging Face; and, most importantly, its use of similar sentiment classes (positive, negative, neutral). FinBERT shows 69 % accuracy and 54% F1-score on the test data. Compared with the pre-trained RoBERTa-base and DeBERTa-base models, Fin-BERT demonstrates better performance, particularly for negative and positive sentiment predictions.

ESG fine-tuned model performance. The four last lines of Table 2 show the accuracy and F1-score of fine-tuned models. Compared to the FinBERT baseline, we observe a significant increase in accuracy from 69% to 88% and F1-score from 54% to 84% for the RoBERTa-base model fine-tuned for ESG. The fine-tuned DeBERTa and FinBERT models show similar levels of accuracy and F1-score. These results demonstrate that after ESG-domain training, the models demonstrate improved performance. After additional modifications to input data to emphasize ESG terms (attention augmentation), we reached 91.30% accuracy and 90.2% F1-score with RoBERTa. Detailed metrics, including Precision and Recall of the STBSA model, are presented in Appendix C.

Adjusting for imbalanced training data. ESG sentiment classes are not distributed equally. This data structure is expected in the ESG domain because most ESG terms occur in neutral contexts. To address this imbalanced classification issue (Hovy and Prabhumoye, 2021), we under-sampled the neutral class to obtain a new data structure with 37,054 positive labels (36%), 27,579 negative labels (27%), and 37,000 neutral labels (36%). The experiment based on this data structure shows both accuracy and F1-score of 91%. These adjustments do not lead to a substantial performance gain and result in a significant loss of labeled data (20%). As a result, we decided to continue experimenting with the complete labeled data set.

4.3 Real-world deployment of the STBSA by IFC (World Bank Group)

Our STBSA model has been deployed in an IFC internal machine-learning platform called MALENA or Machine Learning ESG Analyst. The platform's primary use is support for ESG due diligence and impact assessment of IFC projects. As of September 2022, the model successfully analyzed more than 112,000 ESG-related text documents, including documents proprietary to IFC and public records disclosed through the IFC Project Information and Data Portal. The model identified more than 14 million ESG risk terms, with 3,318,476 detected in a positive context, 1,141,755 in a negative context, and 10,359,769 in a neutral context. ESG sentiment profiles for close to 8,533 companies in 175 countries, seven regions, and 33 investment sectors are derived from model inferences. An active learning mechanism allows expert IFC users to provide feedback on model predictions, leading to improvements in model performance.

5 Positive impact

5.1 Strengthen ESG due diligence and Impact Assessment

The MALENA platform offers a unique solution to sustainability-domain stakeholders (investors, regulators, project proponents, etc.) to better conduct ESG due diligence. It enables the use of NLP to

Models	Accuracy(%)	F1-score (%)
Pertained models		
RoBERTa-base (Liu et al., 2019)	68.00	27.00
DeBERTa-base (He et al., 2021)	17.00	10.00
Baseline model		
FinBERT (Araci, 2019)	69.23	54.07
ESG-fine-tune models		
RoBERTa-base + ESG-fine-tuning	88.00	84.00
DeBERTa-base + ESG-fine-tuning	87.00	82.00
FinBERT + ESG-fine-tuning	87.44	87.31
RoBERTa-base + ESG-fine-tuning+ **Attention Augmentation** =**proposed-STBSA**	91.30 %	90.20 %

Table 2: Experiment results. Table 2 shows the model's accuracy and F1-score for pretrained RoBERTa and DeBERTa, for the baseline model (FinBERT), and for our ESG fine-tuned models. Accuracy and F1-score are calculated based on the randomly selected 18,940 sentences, including 5,572 positive, 4,121 negative, and 9,247 neutral labels. The STBSA model Error analysis is presented in Appendix D - Table 4.

identify and manage ESG risks during project appraisal, to support early-stage Environmental and Social Impact Assessment (ESIA) review, and to monitor the evolution of climate coverage in the media in order to dynamically hedge climate change risk. For instance, a recent experiment conducted by Curmally et al. (2022) on a sample of 530 IFC projects demonstrated that project sentiment scores (derived from our STBSA on projects' early-stage assessment documents, namely ESIAs) perform efficiently as proxies for project risk assessments and to predict E&S performances. Such information is crucial for allocating resources and technical expertise, determining legal requirements, and creating extensive and thorough environmental and social action and remediation plans. Additionally, our model offers a new comprehensive framework and an efficient tool to measure with increased accuracy the positive impact of investments in sustainable activities, both in emerging and developed markets. As we approach 2030, an accurate sentiment profile can be used as a proxy to assess how and to what extent projects or investment benefit local communities and indigenous people, respect the natural environment and contribute to the SDGs.

5.2 Redirect financing to green investments

Investors can play an essential role in redirecting finance to emerging markets by aligning investment strategies with the SDGs. However, gaps in sustainability data and analytical capacity are significant blockers (IFC and Amundi, 2021). Research finds that unstructured data (news articles, annual, integrated, impact and sustainability reports,etc.) is underused in analyzing investment performance (Varco, 2016). Our model has a significant implication in helping investors evaluate to what extent their activities are aligning with and contributing to the SDGs. The proposed ESG taxonomy can be leveraged as a framework to detect investment opportunities in corporate disclosures, and check project, or portfolio SDG-alignment. Facilitating SDG-aligned financing for emerging markets has the potential to address the \$4.2 trillion USD annual shortfall in investments needed to meet the SDGs (OECD, 2020). Further, our STBSA model allows rapid assessments of Task Force on Climate-Related Financial Disclosures (TCFD) documents and other corporate disclosures. Analysis of such texts can help align portfolios with the Paris Agreement on Climate Change(Kölbel et al., 2022) and redirect financing to green and climate-fostering investment (Rolnick et al., 2019). IFC intends to make our STBSA model, as well as MALENA's insights and analytical capabilities, available to institutional investors and asset managers to identify ESG risks better and construct SDG-aligned investment portfolios.

5.3 Offer a Climate Analytics Solution as a global public good

AI-based platforms like MALENA can play a transformative role in addressing the gaps in sustainability data and limited analytical capacity. By reviewing public unstructured text disclosures, they can also address gaps in emerging-market coverage. Our model handles capacity constraints associated with reviewing large amounts of text by conducting this first level of analysis at scale Stede and Patz (2021). Further, by structuring the review of these disclosures using IFC's longstanding, market-tested ESG taxonomy (based on IFC's

ESG standards and aligned with the SDGs), IFC offers its ESG expertise at a level only accessible with. Widespread use of the public good version of MALENA will democratize access to ESG capacity globally, given the significant overlap with IFC's target markets. The demonstration effect of creating bespoke AI solutions to address development problems is already contributing to a vibrant AI for SDGs ecosystem in the development finance community as several risk guarantee agencies, development banks, and export credit agencies are interested in learning from IFC's experience using AI.

6 Discussion and Conclusion

In this paper, we proposed a novel approach to realize a term-based sentiment analysis built on a unique ESG taxonomy to address the limitations of the aspect-based sentiment analysis models and off-the-shelf sentiment analyzers for sustainability-domain applications. Furthermore, using historical sustainability corpus data and expertise from a development finance institution (IFC), we produced an unprecedented human-annotated dataset of 125,000+ sentences for ESG sentiment classification. The subsequent experiments demonstrated the effectiveness of this model with an accuracy of 91.3% and a 90% F1-score, outperforming the current state-of-the-art baseline models by over 20 points (Araci, 2019). Our STBSA model addresses three challenges. First, it offers a new model design with capabilities to handle multiple target terms and different sentiments by leveraging an ESG domain-specific taxonomy with more than 1,200 ESG risk terms. Recent studies underscored the difficulties of developing sustainability domain-specific taxonomies (Nugent et al., 2020; Ulibarri et al., 2019; Lennox et al., 2019), which are blockers to building more efficient and better-performing models. Second, it proposes an unprecedented sustainability domain NLP model, which yields a far higher performance (91.3% accuracy, 90% F1-score) than baseline models such as FinBERT (Araci, 2019) or similar studies such as the ones presented by (Ulibarri et al., 2019) or (Bingler et al., 2021) with 70% and 75% accuracy respectively. Our model fills a critical research gap in the NLP literature. Third, for investors in emerging markets, it offers the potential to enhance ESG due diligence and impact assessments resulting in a positive impact for green investments and contributing to achieving the UN SDGs.

These findings, while promising, have limitations and create opportunities for future research. First, the model can only understand and predict ESG sentiment in English (about 75% of the corpus). There are obvious benefits to expanding its understanding to additional languages such as French, Mandarin, Portuguese and Spanish. Second, as our STBSA model is derived from "black box" systems, the explainability and transparency framework proposed in this paper needs to be fully implemented to enable users to understand its design, operation, and biases, and to trust its predictions. This paper emphasizes data-driven AI and keeping humans in the loop and proposes a new multi-stakeholder framework for operationalizing AI systems. It is essential to ensure that complex and computationally heavy models, such as illustrated in this paper, do not penalize developing countries with limited data, leading to model biases (Conforti et al., 2020). This awareness may help mitigate underlying word embeddings biases of pre-trained language models associated with specific demographics such as gender, ethnic minorities, and local communities (Hovy and Prabhumoye, 2021). This paper provides a first but decisive step toward further research at the intersection of NLP and ESG. We intend to partially release the model and ESG-annotated data as a public good to enable a strong baseline for sustainability domain research, given its major value for the research community either to replicate our approach or to stimulate further research. We hope the results and dataset inspire the NLP and sustainability research communities to actively explore how advanced language modeling can be applied to ESG and impact data to support creating solutions furthering the SDGs.

Acknowledgements

We appreciate the feedback from ESG Specialists and Data Scientists. The views and conclusions of this paper are those of the authors and do not reflect the official policy or position of IFC.

References

Abdulaziz Alghunaim. 2015. *A vector space approach for aspect-based sentiment analysis*. PhD dissertation, Massachusetts Institute of Technology.

Dogu Araci. 2019. Finbert: Financial sentiment analysis with pre-trained language models. *ArXiv*, abs/1908.10063.

Ayoub Bagheri, Mohammad Hossein Saraee, and Franciska de Jong. 2013. Care more about customers: Unsupervised domain-independent aspect detection for sentiment analysis of customer reviews. *Knowl. Based Syst.*, 52:201–213.

Dzmitry Bahdanau, Kyunghyun Cho, and Yoshua Bengio. 2015. Neural machine translation by jointly learning to align and translate. *CoRR*, abs/1409.0473.

Irwan Bello, Barret Zoph, Ashish Vaswani, Jonathon Shlens, and Quoc V. Le. 2019. Attention augmented convolutional networks. *2019 IEEE/CVF International Conference on Computer Vision (ICCV)*, pages 3285–3294.

Julia Anna Bingler, Mathias Kraus, Markus Leippold, and Nicolas Webersinke. 2021. Cheap talk and cherry-picking: What climatebert has to say on corporate climate risk disclosures. *Corporate Finance: Governance*.

Sarah Bird, Miro Dudík, Richard Edgar, Brandon Horn, Roman Lutz, Vanessa Milan, Mehrnoosh Sameki, Hanna Wallach, and Kathleen Walker. 2020. Fairlearn: A toolkit for assessing and improving fairness in ai. *Microsoft, Tech. Rep. MSR-TR-2020-32*.

Victoria Bobicev and Marina Sokolova. 2017. Inter-annotator agreement in sentiment analysis: Machine learning perspective. In *Proceedings of the International Conference Recent Advances in Natural Language Processing, RANLP 2017*, pages 97–102, Varna, Bulgaria. INCOMA Ltd.

Samuel Brody and Noemie Elhadad. 2010. An unsupervised aspect-sentiment model for online reviews. In *Human Language Technologies: The 2010 Annual Conference of the North American Chapter of the Association for Computational Linguistics*, pages 804–812, Los Angeles, California. Association for Computational Linguistics.

Jacob Cohen. 1960. A coefficient of agreement for nominal scales. *Educational and Psychological Measurement*, 20:37 – 46.

Costanza Conforti, Stephanie Hirmer, Dai Morgan, Marco Basaldella, and Yau Ben Or. 2020. Natural language processing for achieving sustainable development: the case of neural labelling to enhance community profiling. In *Proceedings of the 2020 Conference on Empirical Methods in Natural Language Processing (EMNLP)*, pages 8427–8444, Online. Association for Computational Linguistics.

International Finance Corporation. 2016. Sustainability is opportunity: How ifc has changed finance.

Atiyah Curmally, Blaise W. Sandwidi, and Aditi Jagtiani. 2022. *Chapter 9: Artificial intelligence solutions for environmental and social impact assessments*, pages 163 – 177. Edward Elgar Publishing, Cheltenham, UK.

Jacob Devlin, Ming-Wei Chang, Kenton Lee, and Kristina Toutanova. 2019. BERT: Pre-training of deep bidirectional transformers for language understanding. In *Proceedings of the 2019 Conference of the North American Chapter of the Association for Computational Linguistics: Human Language Technologies, Volume 1 (Long and Short Papers)*, pages 4171–4186, Minneapolis, Minnesota. Association for Computational Linguistics.

Li Dong, Furu Wei, Chuanqi Tan, Duyu Tang, Ming Zhou, and Ke Xu. 2014. Adaptive recursive neural network for target-dependent Twitter sentiment classification. In *Proceedings of the 52nd Annual Meeting of the Association for Computational Linguistics (Volume 2: Short Papers)*, pages 49–54, Baltimore, Maryland. Association for Computational Linguistics.

David John Griggs, Mark Stafford-Smith, Owen Gaffney, Johan Rockström, Marcus C. Öhman, Priya Shyamsundar, Will Steffen, Gisbert Glaser, Norichika Kanie, and Ian R. Noble. 2013. Policy: Sustainable development goals for people and planet. *Nature*, 495:305–307.

Kaiming He, X. Zhang, Shaoqing Ren, and Jian Sun. 2016. Deep residual learning for image recognition. *2016 IEEE Conference on Computer Vision and Pattern Recognition (CVPR)*, pages 770–778.

Pengcheng He, Xiaodong Liu, Jianfeng Gao, and Weizhu Chen. 2021. Deberta: Decoding-enhanced bert with disentangled attention. *ArXiv*, abs/2006.03654.

Eduard H. Hovy and Shrimai Prabhumoye. 2021. Five sources of bias in natural language processing. *Language and Linguistics Compass*, 15.

Minqing Hu and Bing Liu. 2004. Mining and summarizing customer reviews. *Proceedings of the tenth ACM SIGKDD international conference on Knowledge discovery and data mining*.

IFC and Amundi. 2021. Artificial intelligence solutions to support environmental, social, and governance integration in emerging markets.

IIRC. 2011. Towards integrated reporting: Communicating value in the 21st century. *International Integrated Reporting Council*.

Long Jiang, Mo Yu, Ming Zhou, Xiaohua Liu, and Tiejun Zhao. 2011. Target-dependent Twitter sentiment classification. In *Proceedings of the 49th Annual Meeting of the Association for Computational*

Linguistics: Human Language Technologies, pages 151–160, Portland, Oregon, USA. Association for Computational Linguistics.

Julian F Kölbel, Markus Leippold, Jordy Rillaerts, and Qian Wang. 2022. Ask BERT: How Regulatory Disclosure of Transition and Physical Climate Risks Affects the CDS Term Structure. *Journal of Financial Econometrics*. Nbac027.

Himabindu Lakkaraju, Richard Socher, and Chris Manning. 2014. Aspect specific sentiment analysis using hierarchical deep learning. In *Annual Conference on Neural Information Processing Systems (NIPS), Workshop on Deep Learning and Representation Learning, 2014*, pages 1–9, Montreal, Canada.

Robert J. Lennox, Diogo Veríssimo, William M. Twardek, Colin R. Davis, and Ivan Jarić. 2019. Sentiment analysis as a measure of conservation culture in scientific literature. *Conservation Biology*, 34.

Yinhan Liu, Myle Ott, Naman Goyal, Jingfei Du, Mandar Joshi, Danqi Chen, Omer Levy, Mike Lewis, Luke Zettlemoyer, and Veselin Stoyanov. 2019. Roberta: A robustly optimized BERT pretraining approach. *CoRR*, abs/1907.11692.

Bin Lu, Myle Ott, Claire Cardie, and Benjamin Ka-Yin T'sou. 2011. Multi-aspect sentiment analysis with topic models. *2011 IEEE 11th International Conference on Data Mining Workshops*, pages 81–88.

Scott M. Lundberg and Su-In Lee. 2017. A unified approach to interpreting model predictions. *ArXiv*, abs/1705.07874.

Margaret Mitchell, Jacqui Aguilar, Theresa Wilson, and Benjamin Van Durme. 2013. Open domain targeted sentiment. In *Proceedings of the 2013 Conference on Empirical Methods in Natural Language Processing*, pages 1643–1654, Seattle, Washington, USA. Association for Computational Linguistics.

United Nations. 2015. Transforming our world: The 2030 agenda for sustainable development.

Måns Nilsson, David John Griggs, and Martin Visbeck. 2016. Policy: Map the interactions between sustainable development goals. *Nature*, 534 7607:320–2.

Timothy Nugent, Nicole Stelea, and Jochen L. Leidner. 2020. Detecting esg topics using domain-specific language models and data augmentation approaches. *ArXiv*, abs/2010.08319.

OECD. 2020. *Global Outlook on Financing for Sustainable Development 2021*. Organisation for Economic Co-operation and Development (OECD), Paris.

Bo Pang, Lillian Lee, and Shivakumar Vaithyanathan. 2002. Thumbs up? sentiment classification using machine learning techniques. In *Proceedings of the 2002 Conference on Empirical Methods in Natural Language Processing (EMNLP 2002)*, pages 79–86. Association for Computational Linguistics.

James Pustejovsky and Amber Stubbs. 2012. *Natural Language Annotation for Machine Learning - a Guide to Corpus-Building for Applications*. O'Reilly.

Marco Ribeiro, Sameer Singh, and Carlos Guestrin. 2016. "why should I trust you?": Explaining the predictions of any classifier. In *Proceedings of the 2016 Conference of the North American Chapter of the Association for Computational Linguistics: Demonstrations*, pages 97–101, San Diego, California. Association for Computational Linguistics.

David Rolnick, Priya L. Donti, Lynn H. Kaack, Kelly Kochanski, Alexandre Lacoste, Kris Sankaran, Andrew Slavin Ross, Nikola Milojevic-Dupont, Natasha Jaques, Anna Waldman-Brown, Alexandra Sasha Luccioni, Tegan Maharaj, Evan D. Sherwin, Surya Karthik Mukkavilli, Konrad Paul Kording, Carla P. Gomes, Andrew Y. Ng, Demis Hassabis, John C. Platt, Felix Creutzig, Jennifer T. Chayes, and Yoshua Bengio. 2019. Tackling climate change with machine learning. *ACM Computing Surveys (CSUR)*, 55:1 – 96.

Marzieh Saeidi, Guillaume Bouchard, Maria Liakata, and Sebastian Riedel. 2016. Sentihood: Targeted aspect based sentiment analysis dataset for urban neighbourhoods. In *COLING*.

Reva Schwartz, Apostol Vassilev, Kristen Greene, Lori Perine, Andrew Burt, and Patrick Hall. 2022. Towards a standard for identifying and managing bias in artificial intelligence.

Alik Sokolov, Jonathan Mostovoy, Jack Ding, and Luis Seco. 2021. Building machine learning systems for automated esg scoring. *The Journal of Impact and ESG Investing*.

Manfred Stede and Ronny Patz. 2021. The climate change debate and natural language processing. In *Proceedings of the 1st Workshop on NLP for Positive Impact*, pages 8–18, Online. Association for Computational Linguistics.

Chi Sun, Luyao Huang, and Xipeng Qiu. 2019. Utilizing bert for aspect-based sentiment analysis via constructing auxiliary sentence. In *NAACL*.

Duyu Tang, Bing Qin, Xiaocheng Feng, and Ting Liu. 2016. Effective LSTMs for target-dependent sentiment classification. In *Proceedings of COLING 2016, the 26th International Conference on Computational Linguistics: Technical Papers*, pages 3298–3307, Osaka, Japan. The COLING 2016 Organizing Committee.

Lewis Tunstall, Leandro von Werra, and Thomas Wolf. 2022. *Natural Language Processing with Transformers: Building Language Applications with Hugging Face*. O'Reilly Media, Incorporated.

Peter Turney. 2002. Thumbs up or thumbs down? semantic orientation applied to unsupervised classification of reviews. In *Proceedings of the 40th Annual*

Meeting of the Association for Computational Linguistics, pages 417–424, Philadelphia, Pennsylvania, USA. Association for Computational Linguistics.

Nicola Ulibarri, Tyler A. Scott, and Omar Perez-Figueroa. 2019. How does stakeholder involvement affect environmental impact assessment? *Environmental Impact Assessment Review*, 79:106309.

Chris Varco. 2016. The value of esg data: Early evidence for emerging markets equities.

Ricardo Vinuesa, Hossein Azizpour, Iolanda Leite, Madeline Balaam, Virginia Dignum, Sami Domisch, Anna Felländer, Simone Daniela Langhans, Max Tegmark, and Francesco Fuso Nerini. 2020. The role of artificial intelligence in achieving the sustainable development goals. *Nature Communications*, 11.

Duy-Tin Vo and Yue Zhang. 2015. Target-dependent twitter sentiment classification with rich automatic features. In *IJCAI*.

Heng Yang, Biqing Zeng, Jianhao Yang, Youwei Song, and Ruyang Xu. 2021. A multi-task learning model for chinese-oriented aspect polarity classification and aspect term extraction. *Neurocomputing*, 419:344–356.

Kai Zhang, Kun Zhang, Mengdi Zhang, Hongke Zhao, Qi Liu, Wei Wu, and Enhong Chen. 2022. Incorporating dynamic semantics into pre-trained language model for aspect-based sentiment analysis. In *Findings of the Association for Computational Linguistics: ACL 2022*, pages 3599–3610, Dublin, Ireland. Association for Computational Linguistics.

Appendix

A Structure of the ESG taxonomy

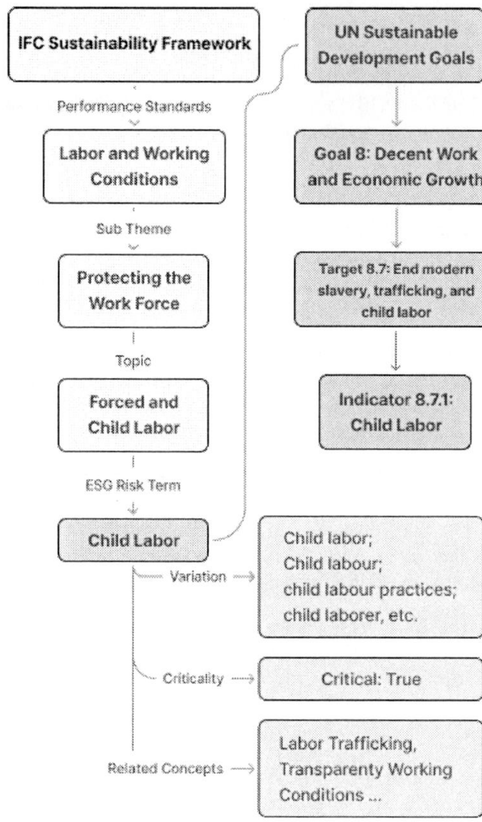

Figure 3: This figure shows the different levels of the ESG taxonomy used to train our STBSA for one ESG risk term, here "Child Labor". This structure includes the IFC Sustainability Framework (top level), the IFC Performance Standards and Corporate Governance Methodology, a Subtheme, a Topic, a target ESG Risk Term (here "Child Labor"), and its variations and related terms. This figure also provided indications on how the target ESG term "Child Labor" is mapped to the United Nations Sustainable Development Goals (SDGs), notably to SDG 8 (Decent Work and Economic Growth), to the Target 8.7 (End modern slavery, trafficking, and child labor) and to the indicator 8.7.1 (Child Labor).

B Ethical and Societal Implications

AI Models that are trained to achieve higher levels of statistical accuracy. While that is important, this research's focus on MLOps, the Trust Analysis framework acknowledges the existence of bad bias in the data and strives to reduce Ethical and societal impact. Without a strong MLOps and Trust analysis framework, machine learning models have the potential to yield statistically high performance but are ethically poor. This paper presents humans in the loop to ensure trained models do not exhibit bad bias. The proposed framework is explained in section 3.3.

C Detailed Metrics for the Sustainability Term-Based Sentiment Analysis (STBSA) Model

Appendix C presents the model Precision and Recall for each sentiment class: Positive, Neutral, and Negative (see Table 3 - Panel A). Additionally, the appendix shows the STBAS model performance over three different aspects, namely Environmental and Social, Corporate Governance, and Climate Change. This subdivision intends to identify any underperformance of the model and determine if there are systemic biases related to a particular aspect of the three pillars composing the Environmental, Social, and Governance domains (see Table 3 - Panel B).

D The Sustainability Term-Based Sentiment Analysis (STBSA) Model Error Analysis

Appendix D Table 4 displays three review examples and their prediction results by the RoBERTa-base model, FinBERT, and our STBSA. As we can see from the "RoBERTa-base" column when there are multiple target terms, the vanilla RoBERTa makes the wrong classification; this model is not trained to classify sustainability term-based sentiment analysis. Fin-BERT, to some extent, is able to predict certain ESG sentiments correctly but fails the sentence with multiple ESG terms with different sentiments.

Panel A: Sentiment Class	Samples	Precision	Recall	F1-Score	Accuracy
Positive	5,572	87.20	92.70	89.80	
Neutral	9,247	92.60	88.30	90.40	
Negative	4,121	89.40	91.00	90.20	
Micro-Avg	18,940	90.20	90.20	90.20	
Macro-Avg	18,940	89.70	90.70	90.10	
					91.30

Panel B: Label Type	Samples	Accuracy	F1-Score
Environmental and Social	14,413	90.50	90.5
Corporate Governance	1,165	89.00	88.4
Climate Change	3,362	89.10	88.50

Table 3: The panel A of this table presents the model Precision and Recall for each class sentiment class (Positive, Neutral, and Negative) Accuracy and F1-score are calculated based on the randomly selected 18,940 sentences, including 5,572 positive, 4,121 negative, and 9,247 neutral labels. The panel B shows the detailed metrics for the Sustainability Term-Based Sentiment Analysis (STBSA) Model. The model Accuracy and F1-score are calculated based on the randomly selected 18,940 sentences, including 14,413 environmental and social labels, 1,165 corporate governance labels, and 3,362 climate change-related labels

Case Examples: The label in brackets represents the ground truth provided by ESG analysts	RoBERTa-base	FinBERT	STBSA
ESG terms: "communities" (Pos), "displacement" (Neg), "armed conflict" (Neg) **Sentence**: We intend to maintain our support for extending the benefits and services of the state to **communities** that have been historically marginalized and communities that have been significantly impacted by the **displacement** and the violence of the **armed conflict**.	**Pos/ Neg/ Neg** ✗ ✗ ✗	**Pos/ Neg/ Neg** ✓ ✗ ✗	**Pos/ Neg/ Neg** ✓ ✓ ✓
ESG terms: "deforestation" (Pos), "child labor" (Neg) **Sentence**: World's largest chocolate manufacturers provided support in addressing large-scale **deforestation** in the cocoa sector, but there is still evidence use of **child labor** in the supply chain.	**Pos/ Neg** ✗ ✗	**Pos/ Neg** ✓ ✗	**Pos/ Neg** ✓ ✓
ESG terms: "Sustainability" (Neu), "climate change" (Neg) **Sentence**: The Head of the Communication and **Sustainability** Office agreed, saying that the **climate change** is one of the greatest threats to life on earth with alarming and long-term effects.	**Neu/ Neg** ✓ ✗	**Neu/ Neg** ✓ ✗	**Neu/ Neg** ✓ ✓

Table 4: Error analysis of three sentences with multiple target ESG terms. The colored words in parentheses represent the ground truth provided by IFC's ESG analysts. The symbol ✓ means the predicted sentiment is correct, and the symbol ✗ means the predicted sentiment is wrong

Hate-CLIPper: Multimodal Hateful Meme Classification based on Cross-modal Interaction of CLIP Features

Gokul Karthik Kumar **Karthik Nandakumar**
Mohamed Bin Zayed University of Artificial Intelligence (MBZUAI)
Abu Dhabi, UAE
{gokul.kumar, karthik.nandakumar}@mbzuai.ac.ae

Abstract

Hateful memes are a growing menace on social media. While the image and its corresponding text in a meme are related, they do not necessarily convey the same meaning when viewed individually. Hence, detecting hateful memes requires careful consideration of both visual and textual information. Multimodal pre-training can be beneficial for this task because it effectively captures the relationship between the image and the text by representing them in a similar feature space. Furthermore, it is essential to model the interactions between the image and text features through intermediate fusion. Most existing methods either employ multimodal pre-training or intermediate fusion, but not both. In this work, we propose the Hate-CLIPper architecture, which explicitly models the cross-modal interactions between the image and text representations obtained using Contrastive Language-Image Pre-training (CLIP) encoders via a *feature interaction matrix* (FIM). A simple classifier based on the FIM representation is able to achieve state-of-the-art performance on the Hateful Memes Challenge (HMC) dataset with an AUROC of 85.8, which even surpasses the human performance of 82.65. Experiments on other meme datasets such as Propaganda Memes and TamilMemes also demonstrate the generalizability of the proposed approach. Finally, we analyze the interpretability of the FIM representation and show that cross-modal interactions can indeed facilitate the learning of meaningful concepts. The code for this work is available at https://github.com/gokulkarthik/hateclipper.

1 Introduction

Multimodal memes, which can be narrowly defined as images overlaid with text that spread from person to person, are a popular form of communication on social media (Kiela et al., 2020). While most Internet memes are harmless (and often humorous), some of them can represent hate speech.

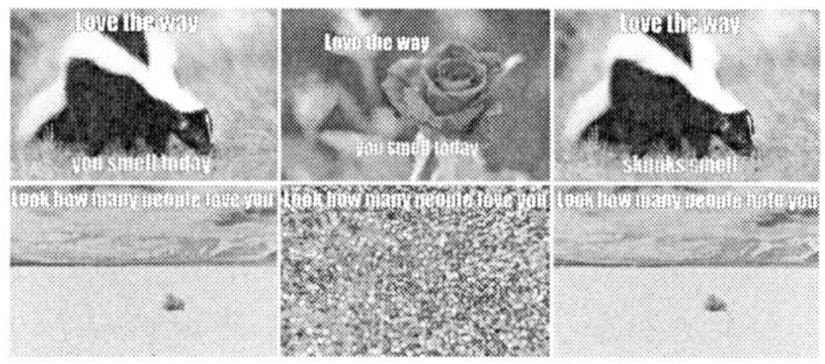

Figure 1: Illustrative (not real) examples of multimodal hateful memes from Kiela et al. (2020). While the memes on the left column are hateful, the ones in the middle are non-hateful image confounders, and those on the right are non-hateful text confounders.

Given the scale of the Internet, it is impossible to manually detect such hateful memes and stop their spread. However, automated hateful meme detection is also challenging due to the multimodal nature of the problem.

Research on automated hateful meme detection has been recently spurred by the Hateful Memes Challenge competition (Kiela et al., 2020) held at NeurIPS 2020 with a focus on identifying multimodal hateful memes. The memes in this challenge were curated in such a way that only a combination of visual and textual information could succeed. This was achieved by creating non-hateful "confounder" memes by changing only the image or text in the hateful memes, as shown in Figure 1. In these examples, an image/text can be harmless or hateful depending on subtle contextual information contained in the other modality. Thus, multimodal (image and text) machine learning (ML) models are a prerequisite to achieve robust and accurate detection of such hateful memes.

In a multimodal system, the fusion of different modalities can occur at various levels. In early fusion schemes (Kiela et al., 2019; Lu et al., 2019; Li et al., 2019), the raw inputs (e.g., image and text) are combined and a joint representation of both modalities is learned. In contrast, late fusion approaches (Kiela et al., 2020), learn end-to-end

Proceedings of the Second Workshop on NLP for Positive Impact (NLP4PI), pages 171 - 183
December 7, 2022

models for each modality and combine their outputs. However, both these approaches are not appropriate for hateful memes because the text in a meme does not play the role of an image caption. Early fusion schemes are designed for tasks such as captioning and visual question answering, where there is a strong underlying assumption that the associated text describes the contents of the image. Hateful memes violate this assumption because the text and image may imply different things. We believe that this phenomenon makes the early fusion schemes non-optimal for hateful meme classification. In the example shown in the first row of Figure 1, the left meme is hateful because of the interaction between the image feature "skunk" and the text feature "you" in the context of the text feature "smell". On the other hand, the middle meme is non-hateful as "skunk" got replaced by "rose" and the right meme is also non-hateful because "you" got replaced by "skunk". Thus, the image and text features are related via common attribute(s). Since modeling such relationships is easier in the feature space, an intermediate fusion of image and text features is more suitable for hateful meme classification.

The ability to model relationships in the feature space also depends on the nature of the extracted image and text features. Existing intermediate fusion methods such as ConcatBERT (Kiela et al., 2020) pretrain the image and text encoders independently in a unimodal fashion. This could result in the divergent image and text feature spaces, making it difficult to learn any relationship between them. Thus, there is a need to "align" the image and text features through multimodal pretraining. Moreover, hateful meme detection requires faithful characterization of interactions between fine-grained image and text attributes. Towards achieving this goal, we make the following contributions in this paper:

- We propose an architecture called Hate-CLIPper for multimodal hateful meme classification, which relies on an intermediate fusion of aligned image and text representations obtained using the multimodally pretrained Contrastive Language-Image Pretraining (CLIP) encoders (Radford et al., 2021).

- We utilize bilinear pooling (outer product) for the intermediate fusion of the image and text features in Hate-CLIPper. We refer to this representation as feature interaction matrix (FIM) which explicitly models the correlations between the dimensions of the image and text feature spaces. Due to the expressiveness of the FIM representation from the robust CLIP encoders, we show that a simple classifier with few training epochs is sufficient to achieve state-of-the-art performance for hateful meme classification on three benchmark datasets without any additional input features like object bounding boxes, face detection and text attributes.

- We demonstrate the interpretability of FIM by identifying salient locations in the FIM that trigger the classification decision and clustering the resulting trigger vectors. Results indicate that FIM indeed facilitates the learning of meaningful concepts.

2 Related Work

The Hateful Memes Challenge (HMC) competition (Kiela et al., 2020) established a benchmark dataset for hateful meme detection and evaluated the performance of humans as well as unimodal and multimodal ML models. The unimodal models in the HMC competition include: **Image-Grid**, based on ResNet-152 (He et al., 2016) features; **Image-Region**, based on Faster RCNN (Ren et al., 2017) features; and **Text-BERT**, based on the original BERT (Devlin et al., 2018) features. The multimodal models include: **Concat BERT**, which uses a multilayer perceptron classifier based on the concatenated ResNet-152 (image) and the original BERT (text) features; **MMBT** (Kiela et al., 2019) models, with Image-Grid and Image-Region features; **ViLBERT** (Lu et al., 2019); and **Visual BERT** (Li et al., 2019). A late fusion approach based on the mean of Image-Region and Text-BERT output scores was also considered. All the above models were benchmarked on the "test seen" split based on the area under the receiver operating characteristic curve (AUROC) (Bradley, 1997) metric. The results indicate a large performance gap between humans (AUROC of 82.65 [1]) and the best baseline using Visual BERT (AUROC of 75.44).

The challenge report (Kiela et al., 2021), which was released after the end of the competition, showed that all the top five submissions (Zhu, 2020; Muennighoff, 2020; Velioglu and Rose, 2020;

[1] https://ai.facebook.com/blog/hateful-memes-challenge-and-data-set/

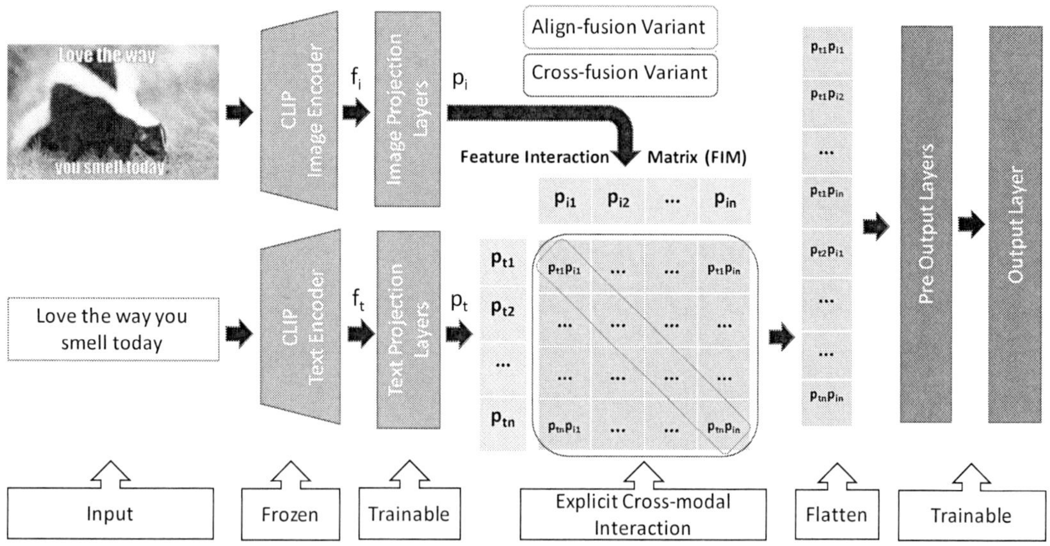

Figure 2: Proposed architecture of Hate-CLIPper for Multimodal Hateful Meme Classification.

Lippe et al., 2020; Sandulescu, 2020) achieve better AUROC than the baseline methods. This improvement was achieved primarily through the use of ensemble models and/or external data and additional input features. For example, Zhu (2020) used a diverse ensemble of VL-BERT (Su et al., 2019), UNITER-ITM (Chen et al., 2019), VILLA-ITM (Gan et al., 2020) and ERNIE-Vil (Yu et al., 2020) with additional information about entity, race, and gender extracted using Cloud APIs and other models. This method achieved the best AUROC of 84.50 on the "test unseen" split.

Mathias et al. (2021) extended the HMC dataset with fine-grained labels for protected category and attack type. Protected category labels include race, disability, religion, nationality, sex, and empty protected category. Attack types were labeled as contempt, mocking, inferiority, slur, exclusion, dehumanizing, inciting violence, and empty attack. Zia et al. (2021) used CLIP (Radford et al., 2021) encoders to obtain image and text features, which were simply concatenated and passed to a logistic regression classifier. Separate classification models were learned for the two multilabel classification tasks - protected categories and attack types. MOMENTA (Pramanick et al., 2021) also uses representations generated from CLIP encoders, but augments them with the additional feature representations of objects and faces using VGG-19 (Simonyan and Zisserman, 2014) and text attributes using DistilBERT (Sanh et al., 2019). Furthermore, MOMENTA uses cross-modality attention fusion (CMAF), which concatenates text and image features (weighted by their respective attention scores) and learns a cross-modal weight matrix to further modulate the concatenated features. MOMENTA reports performance only on the HarMeme dataset (Sandulescu, 2020).

Although bilinear pooling (Tenenbaum and Freeman, 2000) (outer product) of different feature spaces has shown improvements for different multimodal tasks (Fukui et al., 2016; Arevalo et al., 2017; Kiela et al., 2018), it is not well experimented with multimodally pretrained (aligned feature space) encoders like CLIP or for the Hateful Meme Classification task.

3 Methodology

Our objective is to develop a simple end-to-end model for hateful meme classification that avoids the need for sophisticated ensemble approaches and any external data or labels. We hypothesize that there is sufficiently rich information available in the CLIP visual and text representations and the missing link is the failure to model the interactions between these feature spaces adequately. Hence, we propose the Hate-CLIPper architecture as shown in Figure 2. In the proposed Hate-CLIPper architecture, the image i and text t are passed through pretrained CLIP image and text encoders (whose weights are frozen after pretraining) to obtain unimodal features f_i and f_t, respectively. We use

# proj. layers	# p.o. layers	Fusion	Model	Dev seen	Test seen	# t.params.
1	1	Concat	Baseline	76.72	79.87	3.9M
1	3	Concat	Baseline	79.02	83.73	6M
1	5	Concat	Baseline	78.6	83.8	8.1M
1	7	Concat	Baseline	78.63	83.29	10.2M
1	1	CMAF	MOMENTA	77.36	80.15	4.5M
1	3	CMAF	MOMENTA	76.85	82	6.6M
1	5	CMAF	MOMENTA	79.51	83.35	8.7M
1	7	CMAF	MOMENTA	78.88	82.4	10.8M
1	1	Cross	HateCLIPper	**82.62**	85.12	1.1B
1	3	Cross	HateCLIPper	82.19	82.66	1.1B
1	1	Align	HateCLIPper	81.18	85.46	2.9M
1	3	Align	HateCLIPper	81.55	**85.8**	5M
1	5	Align	HateCLIPper	80.88	85.46	7.1M
1	7	Align	HateCLIPper	81.09	84.88	9.2M

Table 1: AUROC of Hate-CLIPper variants and other fusion approaches on HMC dataset. Expansions: proj. -> projection; p.o. -> pre-output; t.params. -> trainable parameters; M -> million; B -> Billion.

# proj. layers	# p.o. layers	Fusion	Model	Dev	Test	# t.params.
1	1	Concat	Baseline	89.9	88.93	4M
1	3	Concat	Baseline	89.9	88.82	6.1M
1	5	Concat	Baseline	89.18	88.55	8.2M
1	7	Concat	Baseline	89.83	88.82	10.3M
1	1	CMAF	MOMENTA	89.11	88.34	4.5M
1	3	CMAF	MOMENTA	89.75	88.73	6.6M
1	5	CMAF	MOMENTA	89.11	88.34	8.7M
1	7	CMAF	MOMENTA	89.61	88.66	10.8M
1	1	Cross	HateCLIPper	**90.98**	**90.41**	1.1B
1	3	Cross	HateCLIPper	**90.98**	89.95	1.1B
1	1	Align	HateCLIPper	89.11	88.34	2.9M
1	3	Align	HateCLIPper	89.11	88.34	5M
1	5	Align	HateCLIPper	89.68	88.66	7.1M
1	7	Align	HateCLIPper	89.68	88.66	9.2M

Table 2: Micro F1 scores of Hate-CLIPper variants and other fusion approaches on Propaganda Memes dataset. Expansions: proj. -> projection; p.o. -> pre-output; t.params. -> trainable parameters; M -> million; B -> Billion.

pre-trained CLIP encoders from the original work (Radford et al., 2021), where the model is trained on Image-Text matching with 400 million <image, text> pairs collected from the Internet.

Trainable Projection Layers: Note that CLIP is pre-trained using contrastive learning on 400 million image–text pairs from the Internet. This multimodal pretraining encourages similarity between the feature spaces of the image and its corresponding text caption. However, in the dataset used for pretraining, the image and text pairs usually convey the same meaning, which is not always the case in hateful memes. Therefore, to better model the semantic relationship between the image and text feature spaces of memes, we further add trainable projection layers at the output of the CLIP image and text encoders. The main purpose of projection layers is not to ensure same dimensionality for both text and image embeddings, but to achieve better alignment between the text and image spaces. While CLIP is already trained to align the two spaces at a high-level, this needs to be further finetuned for the specific task/dataset at hand. Instead of finetuning the entire CLIP model using small datasets, it is more prudent to add projection layers and only learn these projection layers based on the given datasets. These projection layers map the unimodal image and text features f_i

and f_t to the corresponding image projection p_i and text projection p_t, respectively. The projection layers are designed such that both p_i and p_t have the same dimensionality n. The use of customized trainable projection layers after the CLIP encoders is one of the key differences between the proposed architecture and the one used in (Zia et al., 2021).

Modeling Full Cross-modal Interactions: The important component of the Hate-CLIPper architecture is the explicit modeling of interactions between the projected image and text feature spaces using a *feature interaction matrix* (FIM). The FIM representation $R \in \mathbb{R}^{n \times n}$ is obtained by computing the outer product of p_i and p_t, i.e., $R = p_i \otimes p_t$. The FIM can be flattened to get a vector r of length n^2 and passed through a learnable neural network classifier to obtain the final classification decision. This approach is different from the traditional concatenation (Concat) technique employed in the literature (Zia et al., 2021; Pramanick et al., 2021), which simply concatenates the two representations to obtain a vector of length $2n$. Since the FIM representation directly models the correlations between the dimensions of the image and feature spaces, it is better than the Concat approach, where the task of learning these relationships from limited data samples falls on the subsequent classification module. We refer to the fusion of text and image features using the FIM as *cross-fusion*.

Modeling Reduced Cross-modal Interactions: One of the limitations of the cross-fusion approach is the high dimensionality of the resulting representation, which in turn requires a classifier with a larger number of parameters. The diagonal elements of the FIM R represent the element-wise product between p_i and p_t and has a dimension of only n. Note that the sum of these diagonal elements is nothing but the dot product between p_i and p_t, which intuitively measures the alignment (angle) between the two vectors. Therefore, a vector representing the diagonal elements of R indicates the alignment between the individual dimensions of p_i and p_t, which can still be useful for classification as the encoders that we use are pretrained with the alignment task. Hence, we refer to the fusion of text and image features using only the diagonal elements of FIM as *align-fusion*.

Classification Module: The output of the intermediate fusion module is a vector r of dimension d (where $d = 2n$ for the baseline Concat technique, $d = n^2$ for the cross-fusion approach, and $d = n$ for the align-fusion method). We apply a shallow neural network on this feature vector r to obtain the final output o. The shallow neural network consists of a few fully-connected layers (referred to as pre-output layers) and a softmax output layer to produce the final output value o. The first layer of this classifier network maps an input r with d dimensions to a common pre-output dimension m and the rest of the pre-output layers have the same number of hidden nodes m. Each fully-connected layer is followed by ReLU activation and trained with dropout. For binary classification (hateful vs. non-hateful memes), we optimize the trainable (projection and pre-output) layers by minimizing the binary cross-entropy loss between the output o and the true label l. For fine-grained classification (protected category, attack type), we simply add auxiliary output layers and train the model using the total loss for all the classification tasks.

4 Experimental Results

4.1 Datasets

The primary dataset used in our evaluation is the HMC dataset (Kiela et al., 2020), which contains 8500 memes in the training set, 500 memes in the development seen split, 540 memes in the development unseen split, 1000 memes in the test seen split, and 2000 memes in the test unseen split. We also evaluate the proposed approach on the Propaganda Memes dataset Sharma et al. (2022), which is a multi-label multimodal dataset with 22 propaganda classes. Finally, to evaluate the multilingual generalizability, we test the performance on TamilMemes (Suryawanshi et al., 2020), which is a dataset for troll/non-troll classification of memes in the Tamil language. Similar to the HMC dataset, the TamilMemes dataset has meme images and corresponding meme texts that are transliterated from Tamil to English. However, unlike the HMC dataset, the TamilMemes dataset is not compiled with the motive of making only multimodal information useful for target classification.

4.2 Setup

We train Hate-CLIPper and other baselines (concat fusion and attention-based CMAF) based on the train split and evaluate them on the dev-seen and test-seen splits of the HMC dataset using AU-ROC as the evaluation metric. For the Propaganda Memes and the Tamil Memes dataset, the micro F1 score is used as the evaluation metric to ensure a fair comparison with results reported in the literature. We use TorchMetrics library[2] to compute all the evaluation metrics. For multi-label classification in Propaganda Memes dataset, we set 'mdmc_average' to 'global' in computing the micro-F1 score, which does the global average for multi-dimensional multi-class inputs. We use Pytorch on NVIDIA Tesla A100 GPU with 40 GB dedicated memory and CUDA-11.1 installed. The hyper-parameter values for all models are shown in Table 3, which are chosen based on the manual tuning with respect to the target evaluation metric of the validation set. We use ViT-Large-Patch14 based CLIP model consistently for all the experiments in Tables 1 & 2. The models experimented in Table 1 took around 30 minutes (median is 30 minutes and longest is 32 minutes) for the combined training and evaluation. To do a fair evaluation, we use the same evaluation metric as in the previous works for the corresponding datasets.

Hyperparameter	Value
Image size	224
Pretrained CLIP model	ViT-Large-Patch14
Projection dimension (n)	1024
Pre-output dimension (m)	1024
Optimizer	AdamW
Maximum epochs	20
Batch size	64
Learning rate	0.0001
Weight decay	0.0001
Gradient clip value	0.1

Table 3: Hyperparameter configuration for HateCLIPer and other baselines.

4.3 Key Findings

When we interpret Tables 1 & 2 in conjunction with Tables 4 & 5 respectively, we can clearly see that the performance of intermediate fusion with the CLIP encoders is better that that of several early fusion approaches such as MMBT, ViLBERT, and VisualBERT as well as late fusion methods. For instance, on the HMC dataset, the best early fusion approach (Visual BERT) had an AUROC of 75.44 and late fusion method had an AUROC of 69.3 on the test set. These AUROC values are significantly lower than AUROC of the proposed align (intermediate) fusion scheme, which is 85.8. In fact, all

[2]https://torchmetrics.readthedocs.io

Model	Dev Seen	Test Seen
Human	-	82.65
Image-Grid	52.33	53.71
Image-Region	57.24	57.74
Text-BERT	65.05	69
Late Fusion	65.07	69.3
Concat BERT	65.88	67.77
MMBT-GRID	66.73	69.49
MMBET-Region	72.62	73.82
ViLBERT CC	73.02	74.52
Visual BERT COCO	74.14	75.44
CLIP-ViT-L/14-336px	77.3	-
SEER-RG-10B	73.4	-
FLAVA w/o init	77.45	-

Table 4: AUROC of different models on the HMC dataset, compiled from Kiela et al. (2020); Goyal et al. (2022); Singh et al. (2021).

Model	Test
Random	7.06
Majority Class	29.04
ResNet-152	29.92
FastText	33.56
BERT	37.71
FastText + ResNet-152	36.12
BERT + ResNet-152	38.12
MMBT	44.23
ViLBERT CC	46.76
VisualBERT COCO	48.34
RoBERTa	48
RoBERTa + embeddings	58
Ensemble of BERT models	59

Table 5: Micro F1 scores of different models in Propaganda Memes dataset, compiled from Sharma et al. (2022); Dimitrov et al. (2021)

the intermediate fusion methods considered in Table 1 clearly outperform the early and late fusion methods reported in Table 4. These results strongly support the claim that intermediate fusion is more suitable for hate classification.

From Tables 1 & 4, it is clear that cross-fusion and align-fusion variants of Hate-CLIPper achieve the best AUROC for both the evaluation sets of HMC dataset, which is also better than the reported human performance. This trend is also consistent when we replaced ViT-Large-Patch14 with ViT-Base-Patch32. Despite having only n multimodal features, align-fusion performs significantly better than concat-fusion with $2n$ multimodal features and is closer to cross-fusion with n^2 multimodal features. This signifies the importance of pre-aligned image and text representations of CLIP. Hence, for low computational resource conditions, it would be appropriate to replace cross-fusion with align-fusion in the Hate-CLIPper framework.

Our results also show that a single projection layer for each modality and a shallow neural network (1 or 3 layers) for the classifier is sufficient to achieve good performance. This shows that the discriminative power of Hate-CLIPper is mainly a consequence of modeling the interactions between text and image features from CLIP encoders using cross and align fusion. The results on the Propaganda Memes dataset also confirm the same findings. Although the differences between the various configurations shown in Table 2 are marginal, the performance of the proposed approach is a significant leap compared to those reported in the literature (see Table 5).

As noted in Section 2, methods proposed in (Zia et al., 2021) and (Pramanick et al., 2021) are the closest to the proposed approach since both of them use CLIP encoders. Results in Table 1 show that under the same experimental setup, the proposed approach is better than the cross-modal attention fusion (CMAF) scheme used in MOMENTA (Pramanick et al., 2021), when no additional information is utilized. If additional information is available, our proposed approach can also leverage them in the same way (using intra-modal fusion) as MOMENTA. The work in (Zia et al., 2021) claims that train and development seen splits were used for training and development unseen split was used for evaluation. However, a careful analysis of the published code for (Zia et al., 2021) indicates that 400 out of 540 memes in development unseen split (74%) are also included in the development seen split. Since a fair comparison is not possible under these circumstances, we ignore all the results of Zia et al. (2021).

Our ablation experiments (i) with unfrozen CLIP encoders (AUROC of <63), and (ii) Non-CLIP encoders (mBERT (Devlin et al., 2018), VIT (Dosovitskiy et al., 2021)) (AUROC of <59) resulted significantly poor scores in the HMC dataset.

4.4 Multilinguality

The baseline evaluations on TamilMemes dataset (Suryawanshi et al., 2020) used only image based classifiers such as ResNet (He et al., 2016) and MobileNet (Howard et al., 2017) and their test set (300 memes) is different from the released test set (667 memes). Hence, they are not directly comparable to the proposed approach. (Hegde et al., 2021) proposed a multimodal approach for TamilMemes classification. They used pretrained ViT (Dosovitskiy et al., 2021) and BERT (Devlin et al., 2018) as encoders to get the image and text features, respectively. These features were concatenated and used for classification. This model achieved a micro F1 score of 47 on the test set. It is critical to note that the Hate-CLIPper also uses the same encoders of ViT and BERT but they are multimodally pretrained with the CLIP loss. Thus, the Hate-CLIPper achieves state-of-the-art performance with a micro F1 score of 59 on the test set.

For the TamilMemes dataset, both cross and align fusion had the same performance as concat fusion. This could be due to the fact that the pre-aligned text space of CLIP has never encountered Tamil-to-English transliterated text data. Consequently, the resulting text and image feature spaces are not well-aligned, making it difficult to model the relationship between the two feature spaces. Replacing the CLIP text encoder with multilingual BERT (Devlin et al., 2018) also did not lead to any further performance improvement, which can again be attributed to the feature space misalignment caused by the lack of multimodal pretraining using the image and corresponding Tamil text pairs.

5 Interpretability

To determine the interpretability of the feature interaction matrix (FIM), we employ the following simple approach. First, we compute a n^2-dimensional binary trigger vector for each hateful meme, where a value of 1 indicates that the specific element in the FIM R is salient for determining if the given input belongs to the hateful class. These trigger vectors are then clustered into groups using a K-means clustering algorithm. We manually examine these clusters to determine if most samples within a cluster have a common underlying pattern.

To compute the trigger vector, we first reset the feature interaction matrix R to zero values and evaluate the gradient of the loss function for the non-hateful class with respect to R. Let $D \in \mathbb{R}^{n \times n}$ denote the model-specific gradient matrix. Each element in the D matrix represents the direction (positive/negative) of the corresponding element in R matrix towards the hateful class. We then bi-

Figure 3: Hateful memes clustered by K-means clustering algorithm (number of clusters = 15) based on the trigger vector of Hate-CLIPper with cross-fusion. Featuring hateful examples with all the original text in this place would be distasteful; hence the meme text is masked with the exception of few words that are required for discussion. However, the reader can choose to look at the non-censored memes in the appendix

narize the D matrix by setting all elements in the top-20 and bottom 20 percentiles (based on magnitude) to value 1 and assigning 0 values to all the other elements. Then, for each hateful meme (i, t) in the training set, we perform one forward pass through the Hate-CLIPper and compute the meme-specific FIM R. Again we binarize the R matrix by setting all elements in the top-10 and bottom-10 percentiles (based on magnitude) to value 1 and assigning 0 values to all the other elements. Finally, the trigger matrix T is computed for each meme as the element-wise (Hadamard) product of binarized D and R matrices, i.e., $T = D \odot R$. This trigger matrix is then flattened to obtain the trigger vector corresponding to a meme. We apply K-means clustering algorithm available in Scikit-Learn (Pedregosa et al., 2011) on the trigger vectors to group the hateful memes. Samples from the resulting groups of memes are shown in Figure 4.

From Figure 4, we observe that clusters 5, 7, and 11 contain memes related to the same concept. It is interesting to note that Hate-CLIPper is able to produce similar features for the same concept expressed in different modalities. For example in cluster 5, which is characterized by the concept 'death', we can see some memes representing 'death' only in images (b) and other memes representing the same concept only in text (a, d, e). Furthermore, note that the memes (f) and (g), under the same cluster, do not directly relate to death, but the meme texts could hint toward death related events (blow -> blast; popcorn sounds -> bullet sounds) in different contexts. With the clustered memes, we can also identify the positions in FIM R, which get activated for the matching concepts. However, some of the clusters are ambiguous. For example, cluster 13 has memes from different concepts. Also, when the clusters have less than 3 memes or greater than 10 memes, they exhibit greater diversity in terms of the underlying concepts and are not useful for the explanation.

6 Conclusion

In this work, we emphasized the need for intermediate fusion and multimodal pretraining for hateful meme classification. We proposed a simple end-to-end architecture called Hate-CLIPper using explicit cross-modal CLIP representations, which achieves the state-of-the-art performance quickly in 14 epochs with just 4 trainable layers (1 image projection, 1 text projection, 1 pre-output, and 1 output) in the Hateful Memes Challenge dataset, Moreover, our model does not require any additional input features like object bounding boxes, face detection, text attributes, etc. We also demonstrated similar performance in multi-label classification based on the Propaganda Memes dataset. Finally, we performed preliminary studies to evaluate the interpretability of cross-modal interactions.

7 Limitations

From an ethical perspective, the concept of hate speech itself is quite subjective and it is often difficult to draw a clear line between what is hateful and non-hateful. On the technical front, the accuracy of hateful meme classifiers is still far from satisfactory even on carefully curated benchmark datasets, which impedes real-world deployment. Apart from these general limitations, the proposed Hate-CLIPper framework for hateful meme classification also has several specific limitations. Firstly, handling the high dimensionality of the feature interaction matrix is a computational challenge. For $n = 1024$ and $m = 1024$, this requires a model with a billion parameters ($O(n^2m)$). Fortunately, the align-fusion approach performs quite close to the cross-fusion method and requires only $O(nm)$ parameters. The CLIP encoders used in Hate-CLIPper are well-trained on a massive dataset in English. Such models are rarely available for low-resource languages, limiting their direct applicability for such languages. While the multilingual experiment highlights the issues arising from misaligned text and image feature spaces, more thorough ablation studies are required to understand the ability of learnable projection layer(s) to overcome this misalignment. Furthermore, the proposed approach to judge interpretability is simple and ad-hoc and a more systematic evaluation of explainability is needed. The fine-grained labels Mathias et al. (2021) have not been utilized for FIM interpretation.

References

John Arevalo, Thamar Solorio, Manuel Montes-y Gómez, and Fabio A González. 2017. Gated multimodal units for information fusion. *arXiv preprint arXiv:1702.01992*.

Andrew P. Bradley. 1997. The use of the area under the roc curve in the evaluation of machine learning algorithms. *Pattern Recognition*, 30(7):1145–1159.

Yen-Chun Chen, Linjie Li, Licheng Yu, Ahmed El Kholy, Faisal Ahmed, Zhe Gan, Yu Cheng, and Jingjing Liu. 2019. Uniter: Universal image-text representation learning.

Jacob Devlin, Ming-Wei Chang, Kenton Lee, and Kristina Toutanova. 2018. Bert: Pre-training of deep bidirectional transformers for language understanding. *arXiv preprint arXiv:1810.04805*.

Dimitar Dimitrov, Bishr Bin Ali, Shaden Shaar, Firoj Alam, Fabrizio Silvestri, Hamed Firooz, Preslav Nakov, and Giovanni Da San Martino. 2021. Detecting propaganda techniques in memes. *arXiv preprint arXiv:2109.08013*.

Alexey Dosovitskiy, Lucas Beyer, Alexander Kolesnikov, Dirk Weissenborn, Xiaohua Zhai, Thomas Unterthiner, Mostafa Dehghani, Matthias Minderer, Georg Heigold, Sylvain Gelly, Jakob Uszkoreit, and Neil Houlsby. 2021. An image is worth 16x16 words: Transformers for image recognition at scale. In *International Conference on Learning Representations*.

Akira Fukui, Dong Huk Park, Daylen Yang, Anna Rohrbach, Trevor Darrell, and Marcus Rohrbach. 2016. Multimodal compact bilinear pooling for visual question answering and visual grounding. *arXiv preprint arXiv:1606.01847*.

Zhe Gan, Yen-Chun Chen, Linjie Li, Chen Zhu, Yu Cheng, and Jingjing Liu. 2020. Large-scale adversarial training for vision-and-language representation learning.

Priya Goyal, Quentin Duval, Isaac Seessel, Mathilde Caron, Mannat Singh, Ishan Misra, Levent Sagun, Armand Joulin, and Piotr Bojanowski. 2022. Vision models are more robust and fair when pretrained on uncurated images without supervision. *arXiv preprint arXiv:2202.08360*.

Kaiming He, Xiangyu Zhang, Shaoqing Ren, and Jian Sun. 2016. Deep residual learning for image recognition. *2016 IEEE Conference on Computer Vision and Pattern Recognition (CVPR)*.

Siddhanth U Hegde, Adeep Hande, Ruba Priyadharshini, Sajeetha Thavareesan, and Bharathi Raja Chakravarthi. 2021. Uvce-iiitt@dravidianlangtech-eacl2021: Tamil troll meme classification: You need to pay more attention. *ArXiv*, abs/2104.09081.

Andrew G. Howard, Menglong Zhu, Bo Chen, Dmitry Kalenichenko, Weijun Wang, Tobias Weyand, Marco Andreetto, and Hartwig Adam. 2017. Mobilenets: Efficient convolutional neural networks for mobile vision applications. *ArXiv*, abs/1704.04861.

Douwe Kiela, Suvrat Bhooshan, Hamed Firooz, Ethan Perez, and Davide Testuggine. 2019. Supervised multimodal bitransformers for classifying images and text. *arXiv preprint arXiv:1909.02950*.

Douwe Kiela, Hamed Firooz, Aravind Mohan, Vedanuj Goswami, Amanpreet Singh, Casey A. Fitzpatrick, Peter Bull, Greg Lipstein, Tony Nelli, Ron Zhu, Niklas Muennighoff, Riza Velioglu, Jewgeni Rose, Phillip Lippe, Nithin Holla, Shantanu Chandra, Santhosh Rajamanickam, Georgios Antoniou, Ekaterina Shutova, Helen Yannakoudakis, Vlad Sandulescu, Umut Ozertem, Patrick Pantel, Lucia Specia, and Devi Parikh. 2021. The hateful memes challenge: Competition report. In *Proceedings of the NeurIPS 2020 Competition and Demonstration Track*, volume 133 of *Proceedings of Machine Learning Research*, pages 344–360. PMLR.

Douwe Kiela, Hamed Firooz, Aravind Mohan, Vedanuj Goswami, Amanpreet Singh, Pratik Ringshia, and Davide Testuggine. 2020. The hateful memes challenge: Detecting hate speech in multimodal memes.

Douwe Kiela, Edouard Grave, Armand Joulin, and Tomas Mikolov. 2018. Efficient large-scale multimodal classification. In *Proceedings of the AAAI Conference on Artificial Intelligence*, volume 32.

Liunian Harold Li, Mark Yatskar, Da Yin, Cho-Jui Hsieh, and Kai-Wei Chang. 2019. Visualbert: A simple and performant baseline for vision and language. *arXiv preprint arXiv:1908.03557*.

Phillip Lippe, Nithin Holla, Shantanu Chandra, Santhosh Rajamanickam, Georgios Antoniou, Ekaterina Shutova, and Helen Yannakoudakis. 2020. A multimodal framework for the detection of hateful memes.

Jiasen Lu, Dhruv Batra, Devi Parikh, and Stefan Lee. 2019. Vilbert: Pretraining task-agnostic visiolinguistic representations for vision-and-language tasks. *Advances in neural information processing systems*, 32.

Mengmeng Ma, Jian Ren, Long Zhao, Davide Testuggine, and Xi Peng. 2022. Are multimodal transformers robust to missing modality? *ArXiv*, abs/2204.05454.

Lambert Mathias, Shaoliang Nie, Aida Mostafazadeh Davani, Douwe Kiela, Vinodkumar Prabhakaran, Bertie Vidgen, and Zeerak Waseem. 2021. Findings of the WOAH 5 shared task on fine grained hateful memes detection. In *Proceedings of the 5th Workshop on Online Abuse and Harms (WOAH 2021)*, pages 201–206, Online. Association for Computational Linguistics.

Niklas Muennighoff. 2020. Vilio: State-of-the-art visio-linguistic models applied to hateful memes.

F. Pedregosa, G. Varoquaux, A. Gramfort, V. Michel, B. Thirion, O. Grisel, M. Blondel, P. Prettenhofer, R. Weiss, V. Dubourg, J. Vanderplas, A. Passos, D. Cournapeau, M. Brucher, M. Perrot, and E. Duchesnay. 2011. Scikit-learn: Machine learning in Python. *Journal of Machine Learning Research*, 12:2825–2830.

Shraman Pramanick, Shivam Sharma, Dimitar Dimitrov, Md Shad Akhtar, Preslav Nakov, and Tanmoy Chakraborty. 2021. Momenta: A multimodal framework for detecting harmful memes and their targets. *arXiv preprint arXiv:2109.05184*.

Alec Radford, Jong Wook Kim, Chris Hallacy, Aditya Ramesh, Gabriel Goh, Sandhini Agarwal, Girish Sastry, Amanda Askell, Pamela Mishkin, Jack Clark, et al. 2021. Learning transferable visual models from natural language supervision. In *International Conference on Machine Learning*, pages 8748–8763. PMLR.

Shaoqing Ren, Kaiming He, Ross Girshick, and Jian Sun. 2017. Faster r-cnn: Towards real-time object detection with region proposal networks. *IEEE Transactions on Pattern Analysis and Machine Intelligence*, 39(6):1137–1149.

Vlad Sandulescu. 2020. Detecting hateful memes using a multimodal deep ensemble.

Victor Sanh, Lysandre Debut, Julien Chaumond, and Thomas Wolf. 2019. Distilbert, a distilled version of bert: smaller, faster, cheaper and lighter. *arXiv preprint arXiv:1910.01108*.

Shivam Sharma, Firoj Alam, Md Akhtar, Dimitar Dimitrov, Giovanni Da San Martino, Hamed Firooz, Alon Halevy, Fabrizio Silvestri, Preslav Nakov, Tanmoy Chakraborty, et al. 2022. Detecting and understanding harmful memes: A survey. *arXiv preprint arXiv:2205.04274*.

Karen Simonyan and Andrew Zisserman. 2014. Very deep convolutional networks for large-scale image recognition. *arXiv preprint arXiv:1409.1556*.

Amanpreet Singh, Ronghang Hu, Vedanuj Goswami, Guillaume Couairon, Wojciech Galuba, Marcus Rohrbach, and Douwe Kiela. 2021. Flava: A foundational language and vision alignment model. *arXiv preprint arXiv:2112.04482*.

Weijie Su, Xizhou Zhu, Yue Cao, Bin Li, Lewei Lu, Furu Wei, and Jifeng Dai. 2019. Vl-bert: Pre-training of generic visual-linguistic representations.

Shardul Suryawanshi, Bharathi Raja Chakravarthi, Pranav Verma, Mihael Arcan, John Philip McCrae, and Paul Buitelaar. 2020. A dataset for troll classification of TamilMemes. In *Proceedings of the WILDRE5– 5th Workshop on Indian Language Data: Resources and Evaluation*, pages 7–13, Marseille, France. European Language Resources Association (ELRA).

Joshua B Tenenbaum and William T Freeman. 2000. Separating style and content with bilinear models. *Neural computation*, 12(6):1247–1283.

Riza Velioglu and Jewgeni Rose. 2020. Detecting hate speech in memes using multimodal deep learning approaches: Prize-winning solution to hateful memes challenge.

Peng Wang, An Yang, Rui Men, Junyang Lin, Shuai Bai, Zhikang Li, Jianxin Ma, Chang Zhou, Jingren Zhou, and Hongxia Yang. 2022. Unifying architectures, tasks, and modalities through a simple sequence-to-sequence learning framework. *ArXiv*, abs/2202.03052.

Fei Yu, Jiji Tang, Weichong Yin, Yu Sun, Hao Tian, Hua Wu, and Haifeng Wang. 2020. Ernie-vil: Knowledge enhanced vision-language representations through scene graph.

Xinyu Zhou, Cong Yao, He Wen, Yuzhi Wang, Shuchang Zhou, Weiran He, and Jiajun Liang. 2017. East: An efficient and accurate scene text detector. *2017 IEEE Conference on Computer Vision and Pattern Recognition (CVPR)*, pages 2642–2651.

Ron Zhu. 2020. Enhance multimodal transformer with external label and in-domain pretrain: Hateful meme challenge winning solution.

Haris Bin Zia, Ignacio Castro, and Gareth Tyson. 2021. Racist or sexist meme? classifying memes beyond hateful. In *Proceedings of the 5th Workshop on Online Abuse and Harms (WOAH 2021)*, pages 215–219, Online. Association for Computational Linguistics.

A Appendix

A.1 Variations of HateCLIPper

We experimented with several training/architectural modifications to the core Hate-CLIPper framework proposed in the main paper:

1. **Pretraining with captions:** We generated captions that describe each image in the Hateful Memes Challenge dataset with the state-of-the-art transformer based image captioning model, OFA (Wang et al., 2022). Then, we pretrained the image and text encoders of Hate-CLIPper using contrastive loss between the meme images and the generated captions like Radford et al. (2021). Then, finetuning on the target dataset using meme images and meme texts is done as usual.

2. **Finetuning with captions:** We incorporated the generated captions during finetuning of Hate-CLIPper in different ways: (1) replacing image with generated captions and image encoder with the same text encoder, (2) concatenating generated caption with the meme text (3) concatenating features from "meme image + meme text" flow and "meme image+ generated caption" flow.

3. **Unimodal losses:** Linear output layers, for hateful meme classification, are added on top of the image and text projection layers of Hate-CLIPper and the corresponding unimodal losses are jointly optimized with the original multimodal loss as recommended by Ma et al. (2022).

4. **Fine-grained losses:** Linear output layers, for fine-grained hateful meme classification, are added in parallel to the output layer of Hate-CLIPper, and the corresponding fine-grained losses are jointly optimized with the original loss. This is done using fine-grained labels provided by Mathias et al. (2021).

5. **Data augmentation:** We identify the text bounding box regions in the meme images using EAST (Zhou et al., 2017) and replace them with either average pixel value masks or inpainting using Navier-Stokes[3] based method and finetune the Hate-CLIPper as usual.

Although, the above mentioned variations are backed by some reasoning, they either produced the same results or slightly degraded the performance.

[3]https://docs.opencv.org/4.x/d7/d8b/group__photo__inpaint.html

Figure 4: Hateful memes clustered by K-means clustering algorithm (number of clusters = 15) based on the trigger vector of Hate-CLIPper with cross-fusion. This non-censored version is just for more understading and the reader can choose to skip this figure as it features distasteful content.

Author Index